NEW HORIZONS IN LINGUISTICS

John Lyons was born in 1932 and educated at St Bede's College, Manchester, and Christ's College, Cambridge. He took his first degree in classics in 1953 and the Diploma in Education in 1954. After two years' national service in the Navy, he returned to Cambridge as a Ph.D. student in 1956, and the following year he was appointed to a lectureship at the School of Oriental and African Studies, University of London. In 1961 he took up a lectureship in Cambridge. From 1964 to 1976 he held the post of Professor of Linguistics in the University of Edinburgh. Since 1976 he has been Professor of Linguistics in the University of Sussex. He has also held appointments at Indiana University, the University of California, the University of Texas, and the University of Illinois.

He was the first editor of the *Journal of Linguistics* (1965–9); and his publications include *Structural Semantics* (1963), *Introduction to Theoretical Linguistics* (1968) and *Chomsky* (1970). John Lyons is married and has two daughters.

NEW HORIZONS IN LINGUISTICS

Edited by John Lyons

Edinburgh Dec 1979

Penguin Books

Penguin Books Ltd, Harmondsworth, Middlesex, England
Penguin Books, 625 Madison Avenue, New York, New York 10022, U.S.A.
Penguin Books Australia Ltd, Ringwood, Victoria, Australia
Penguin Books Canada Ltd, 2801 John Street, Markham, Ontario, Canada L3R 1B4
Penguin Books (N.Z.) Ltd, 182–190 Wairau Road, Auckland 10, New Zealand

—

First published 1970
Reprinted 1971, 1972, 1973, 1975, 1977

—

Copyright © John Lyons, 1970

—

Made and printed in Great Britain by
Hazell Watson & Viney Ltd, Aylesbury, Bucks
Set in Monotype Times

CONTENTS

Contents

1. INTRODUCTION

John Lyons

What is Linguistics?

LINGUISTICS may be defined as the scientific study of language. This definition, unexceptionable as far as it goes, is one that will be found in a large number of textbooks and popular introductions to the subject. The term 'linguistics' was first used in the middle of the nineteenth century; and there are many scholars currently engaged in research or teaching in the field of linguistics who would say that the subject itself is not much older than the term 'linguistics'. They would claim that earlier linguistic research (in Europe at least) was amateurish and unscientific. Now it is a matter of legitimate dispute just how far back one should go in tracing the history of what we would today recognize as 'linguistics'. We shall not go into this question here. But one point should be appreciated. The investigation of language, like the investigation of many other phenomena (including those that fall within the scope of what are commonly called the 'physical' sciences), has been subject to various changes in the interpretation of the words 'science' and 'scientific', not only in the remoter past, but also more recently.

A recent introduction to linguistics includes in its discussion of 'the characteristics which we would nowadays associate with a science' the following sentence (Crystal, 1968:28): 'Observation of events prior to the setting-up of a hypothesis, which is then systematically investigated via experimentation and a theory developed – this is standard procedure in Linguistics as in other sciences.' In his account of the application of a 'scientific method' to the study of language, the author implies that linguistic theory, insofar as it is scientific, must be developed on the basis of inductive generalization from the events that have first been observed and systematically described; and that the construction of a theory is subsequent to and determined by a description of linguistic data. For convenience of reference, we will call this view of the 'scientific method' the 'inductive' view.

7

Against it, one may argue that certain theoretical assumptions, however inchoate and inexplicit, must of necessity accompany the selection and description of the events held under observation; and that there is no reason why these assumptions and expectations should not be given full theoretical recognition from the outset and used in the construction of a theory, certain of whose empirical consequences can then be deduced according to general logical principles and verified by observation. We may refer to this alternative view of the nature of scientific theory and its role in empirical research as the 'deductive' (or 'hypothetico-deductive') view. Although the inductive approach is still advocated in many standard textbooks of linguistics, the deductive approach has been gaining ground in the last few years, especially in connexion with the development of generative grammar (which we shall be discussing later in this chapter). What should be stressed is that both approaches, in principle at least, recognize the need for carefully controlled and empirically verifiable observations in the study of language; and this we may take to be the most important of the implications of the term 'scientific'.

One topic that commonly finds a place in discussions of the status of linguistics as a science is its 'autonomy', or independence of other disciplines. Linguists have tended to be somewhat insistent on the need for autonomy, because they have felt that, in the past, the study of language was usually subservient to and distorted by the standards of other studies such as logic, philosophy and literary criticism. For this reason the editors of Saussure's posthumous *Cours de linguistique générale* (the publication of which is often taken to mark the beginning of 'modern linguistics') added to the text of the master its programmatic concluding sentence, to the effect that linguistics should study language 'for its own sake' or 'as an end in itself' (Saussure, 1916).

Whatever might be the precise meaning of the phrase 'language as an end in itself', the principle of 'autonomy', as it has been applied in linguistics over the last fifty years, has led to a more *general* conception of the nature and function of language than was possible in the earlier periods of linguistic scholarship. An equally, if not more, important consequence of the principle of 'autonomy' is that it promoted the study of language as a *formal* system. What is meant by a 'formal' system will be explained in later sections of this chapter and, in somewhat greater detail, by other contributors (see especially the chapter by Janet Dean Fodor, pp. 198–214).

Now that linguistics has established its credentials as a mature academic discipline with its own methodology and criteria of relevance (and one can reasonably claim that this is the case), there is no longer the same need to insist upon the principle of 'autonomy'. The last few years have seen an increased interest amongst philosophers, psychologists, anthropologists, literary critics and representatives of other disciplines in linguistic theory and methodology. Some scholars consider that the time may now be ripe for the incorporation of the theory of language into a more embracing synthesis of science and philosophy. It is fitting that these recent developments should be represented (as many of them are) in a volume which bears the title *New Horizons in Linguistics*.

The Origin and Nature of Language

The origin of human language is a problem that has exercised the mind and imagination of man from time immemorial; and various 'solutions' to the problem (similar to the one recorded in *Genesis*) are enshrined in the myths and religious doctrines of many different cultures (cf. Crystal, 1965: 13). The problem was extensively debated in 'naturalistic', as distinct from religious or supernatural, terms by the Greek philosophers, and was of considerable importance in the development of traditional linguistic theory (cf. Lyons, 1968: 4). It has been discussed at various times by philosophers since then, notably in the eighteenth century (cf. Robins, 1967: 149ff.). Since the nineteenth century, however, scholars professionally concerned with the description of language from what we may call a strictly linguistic point of view have (with one or two notable exceptions, e.g. Jespersen, 1922) tended to dismiss the whole question as unworthy of serious discussion. In the course of the nineteenth century, most linguists became convinced that, however far back one traced the history of particular languages in the texts that have come down to us, it was impossible to discern any signs of evolution from a simpler, or more 'primitive' to a more complex, or more 'advanced', stage of development. This conclusion, that all human languages of which we have any direct evidence are of roughly equal complexity, was reinforced by the detailed study of languages spoken by so-called 'primitive' tribes throughout the world. All the evidence so far accumulated by linguists confirms the view that, despite the many reports brought back by earlier travellers from remote and 'backward' parts, there is no group of human beings, in existence at present or known to have existed in the past, which does not possess a 'fully developed' language.

A constantly recurring theme in the various proposals that have been made to account for the origin of language is the attempt to draw parallels between features of human language and the various systems of communication used by other animal species. Whether there is any way of bridging the gap in terms of current psychological theory between human language, as we know it, and animal communication is the subject of the chapter by John Marshall (cf. pp. 229–41).

So far we have interpreted the phrase 'the origin of language' in what may be called the *phylogenetic* sense; that is to say, with respect to some point in the remote and inaccessible past of man's evolutionary development. The phrase can also be given an *ontogenetic* interpretation – with respect to the acquisition of language by children. Various interesting questions arise in this connexion: are children genetically predisposed to acquire one language rather than another? is the process of acquiring one's first language as a child essentially the same as that of learning other languages later in life (it will be observed that, in order not to prejudge the question, I have deliberately distinguished here between the 'acquisition' of one's 'native' language and the 'learning' of other languages subsequently)? can children acquire language independently of contact with other human beings and in isolation from the normal circumstances in which language is used? is there any correlation between the intelligence of a child and the rate at which he acquires his native language? A brief answer to the first of these questions may be given immediately.

Introduction

There is no intrinsic connexion between 'race' and language. Any normal child, regardless of his genetic, or 'racial', characteristics, will acquire the language of the community in which he is brought up. (If this assertion seems to run counter to the evident fact that the children of immigrants sometimes fail to achieve a 'native' command of the language of the country in which they have lived since birth, the explanation is to be sought in sociological, rather than genetic, terms: they have not been fully integrated in the community.) Other aspects of the acquisition of language by children are discussed below (in the chapter by Robin Campbell and Roger Wales, pp. 242–60).

In everything that has been said so far in this chapter, there has been latent a fundamental assumption, which should now be brought to light and discussed. This is the assumption that particular languages (English, Chinese, Swahili, Malay, Eskimo, Amharic, Quechua, etc.) are specific instances of something more general that we may appropriately refer to in the singular as 'language'; in other words, that all human languages have something in common, not shared by anything else, other than the fact that we have learned to apply to each of them the word *language* (or its equivalent in other languages). Put like this, the assumption might seem to be hardly worth discussing. It becomes more interesting if we deliberately introduce into the discussion a few expressions in which the word 'language' appears to be applied in a related, but different, sense. Consider such phrases as 'sign language', 'the language of mathematics', 'the language of bees', 'the language of flowers'. It is easy to see what relates each of these senses of the word 'language' to the sense in which it is employed when we describe English or Chinese as 'languages'. Let us grant that, in its most general sense, the term 'language' may be defined as 'a system of communication'. We might then go on to say that, in the narrower sense in which the linguist uses the term, languages (*natural languages*, to make use of the convenient and suggestive expression which is commonly employed to distinguish such systems of communication as English or Chinese from the so-called *artificial languages* constructed by mathematicians, logicians and computer scientists) are the principal systems of communication used by particular groups of human beings within the particular society ('linguistic community') of which they are members; and that English, Chinese, etc., are languages in this sense. We may have begged one or two questions here: in a fuller discussion we would certainly need to dwell a little longer upon the notion of 'communication' (not to mention the term 'principal'). However, the points involved here are not central to the present theme.

The question which was introduced in the previous paragraph can now be reformulated as follows: is it the case that all natural languages have certain features in common over and above what can be accounted for by virtue of their being systems of communication? There are in fact several such properties that linguists have identified as characteristic of human languages. Two of them only will be mentioned here. The first is *duality of structure*; and the second, *productivity*.

By 'duality of structure' (or 'double articulation') linguists refer to the fact that in all languages so far investigated one finds two *levels* of 'structure', or 'patterning'. There is a 'primary' level, composed of meaningful units: for simplicity, let us call them *words*. And there is a 'secondary' level, the units of which themselves have no meaning (let us grant that this is in general true), but which enter into the formation of the primary units. The secondary units of spoken languages are *sounds*; and of written languages, *letters* (if the languages in question make use of an alphabetic writing system). This distinction of a 'primary' and a 'secondary' level of structure might not be drawn in quite the same terms by all linguists, and it requires some further development and qualification. But it will do for the present.

By the 'productivity' of human language (another term is 'creativity': cf. Chomsky, 1968) is meant the ability that we all have to construct and understand an indefinitely large number of sentences in our native language, including sentences that we have never heard before, and to do this, for the most part, 'naturally' and unreflectingly, without the conscious application of grammatical rules. It is generally agreed that 'To explain how this is possible is the root-problem of linguistic analysis' (Haas, 1966: 117). We shall see later that this problem has been particularly important in the development of generative grammar. It should be emphasized in this section that most theories of the origin of language (whether mythical, philosophical or psychological) and many accounts of the way in which children acquire their native language have failed to give due recognition to this 'creative' aspect of language. Their attempts to solve the problem have been limited to an explanation (more or less satisfactory as the case may be) of the way in which 'names' are attached to 'things'; or, to put it in more general terms, of the way in which the meaning of particular words and utterances is associated with them. Although this problem is by no means trivial, it is of secondary importance when compared with the problem of accounting for the 'productivity' of human language. We might well be able to build a robot capable of identifying all the objects in its environment and applying to each of them its correct and distinctive 'name'. However, unless it were able to produce and 'understand' (that is, respond to in some appropriate manner) an indefinitely large number of new sentences in the way that human beings can, we should not wish to say that it 'knew' the language it had been taught.

These two important properties are *universal*, in the following sense at least: they have been found in all human languages so far investigated. Further questions arise at this point. Are these properties (and various others that have not been mentioned here) *universal* properties of human language in some deeper sense also? Or is it conceivable that there might exist, as yet undiscovered, a community or group of creatures which on all other grounds we should wish to describe as 'human', but whose principal system of communication did not have these properties? Questions of this kind have generally been left to philosophers. But there has recently been a certain amount of discussion from the standpoint of linguistics (cf. Householder, 1970, for a critical summary).

Attempts have also been made to bring biological evidence to bear on the problem (cf. Lenneberg, 1967). Whatever one may think of the more general aspects of the question, it is worth noticing that linguists today are much more interested in determining the universal features of human language than they were only a few years ago, when, as one author has put it, the most daring generalization about language to which many linguists would be prepared to commit themselves might be that 'Some members of some human communities have been observed to interact by means of vocal noises' (Fillmore, 1968: 1).

Some Key Concepts of Modern Linguistics

We have already mentioned the *Cours de linguistique générale* of Ferdinand de Saussure and its importance in the development of modern linguistics. Among the many notions that he introduced into the subject, there are several that are still part of the linguist's stock in trade. We shall take these first.

(1) SYNCHRONIC AND DIACHRONIC. Throughout the nineteenth century linguistic research was very strongly historical in character. One of the principal aims of the subject was to group languages into 'families' (of which the Indo-European family is the best known) on the basis of their independent development from a common source. The description of particular languages was made subsidiary to this general aim; and there was little interest in the study of the language of a given community without reference to historical considerations. Saussure's distinction between the diachronic and the synchronic investigation of language is a distinction between these two opposing viewpoints. Diachronic (or historical) linguistics studies the development of languages through time: for example, the way in which French and Italian have 'evolved' from Latin. Synchronic linguistics (sometimes referred to rather inappropriately as 'descriptive' linguistics) investigates the way people speak in a given speech community at a given point in time. It is now generally agreed that (due attention having been given to the definition of 'speech community') the history of a language is in principle irrelevant to its synchronic description: but this fact was not generally appreciated by earlier linguists. (There is a chapter by Paul Kiparsky on historical linguistics later in the book, pp. 302–15.)

(2) LANGUE AND PAROLE. What is meant by the distinction of *langue* and *parole* (for which there are no generally accepted

equivalents in English) may be explained by taking Saussure's own analogy of a musical performance. Every performance of a particular piece of music is unique, in the sense that it differs from every other performance in innumerable ways. And yet we say that they are all performances of the same work. What they have in common (and it is in terms of this that we identify them) is a certain *structure*, which is itself independent of the physical medium in which it is realized when the work is performed. In much the same way, we can say that there is a common structure 'underlying' the utterances which we produce when we speak a particular language. Utterances are instances of *parole*. The underlying structure in terms of which we produce them as speakers and understand them as hearers is the *langue* in question (English, Chinese, etc.). Like the structure of a piece of music, it is independent of the physical medium (or *substance*) in which it is realized. There are, of course, some obvious and important differences between speaking a language and performing a piece of music, the structure of which has been fully specified in advance by the composer. The analogy must not be pressed too far. It is by no means clear that the language spoken by all the members of a given speech community is as uniform, and structurally deter- minate, as Saussure assumed (see the chapter on sociolinguistics by John Pride, pp. 287–301). There can be little doubt, however, that some kind of distinction between *langue* and *parole* must be drawn, with or without these more particular assumptions. Chomsky (1965: 4) has made a similar distinction in terms of *competence* (langue) and *performance* (parole).

(3) STRUCTURALISM. We have just seen that the language spoken by a particular speech community has a certain structure (or, to use Saussure's own term, a certain *form*), which can be considered and described independently of the *substance* in which it is realized. This rather abstract conception of the nature of language is summed up in the term 'structuralism' (in one sense, at least, of this rather fashionable word).

As developed by Saussure and his more direct followers, the 'structural' approach to the analysis of language involves the segmentation of utterances into elements in terms of two basic, and complementary, relations: *syntagmatic* and *paradigmatic* (Saussure's own term was 'associative'). What is meant by these terms may be made clear by means of a simple example. Why do we say that the phrase *my new car* in English consists of three elements (three words) rather than, say, of four or two? The answer, according to Saussure, rests upon the notion of substitutability. We can substitute *the, his, that,* etc., for *my* in the first position; *old, beautiful,* etc., for *new* in the second position; and *picture, book,* etc., for *car* in the third position. There are three, and only three, places where the operation of substitution can be carried out (at this level of analysis). Sets of elements which can be substituted one for another in a given context are said to be in *paradigmatic* relationship; elements which combine to form a larger unit are said to be in *syntagmatic* relationship.

Now, the substitution of one element for another in the same context may do either of two things. It may change the larger unit into a different unit (of the same class): in which case, we say that the substitutable elements are in *opposition*. Or it may have no positive effect upon the larger unit: in which case, the substitutable elements are said to be in *free variation*. For example, *my* and *his*, or *new* and *old*, are in opposition, in the contexts ... *new car* and *my* ... *car* respectively; whereas *not* and *n't* are in free variation in such contexts as *we did* ... *go*, since *we did not go* and *we didn't go* are, in some relevant sense, equivalent.

At first sight this may seem rather trivial. But the further development of these basic notions has had a profound effect upon twentieth-century linguistic theory. This will be clear from their more detailed application in later chapters. Here one should note the following general points. Segmentation in terms of syntagmatic and paradigmatic relations is relevant at all levels of analysis. The notion of contrast (or opposition) presupposes some prior notion of identity or equivalence; so that the same elements might be in contrast with respect to one kind of equivalence (e.g. their meaning), but in free variation with respect to a different kind of equivalence (e.g., what we may refer to loosely here as their grammatical function).

Finally, under the general rubric of 'structuralism', it might be helpful to introduce the notion of *marked* and *unmarked* terms, since the concept of marking, or markedness, first developed by linguists of the Prague School (Trubetzkoy, Jakobson and others) in the 1930s, has recently been taken up more widely (cf., e.g. Greenberg, 1966; Chomsky & Halle, 1968), and is invoked in a number of the chapters in the present volume. What is meant by this notion may be explained by means of one or two examples. The past tense of regular English verbs is 'marked' by the suffix *-ed* (*loved*, *jumped*, etc.). By contrast, the so-called 'present' tense (except in the third person singular) is 'unmarked' (*love, jump*, etc.). In other words, the presence of *-ed* contrasts with its absence to determine the form as 'past' or 'present'. In a situation of this kind, the unmarked form is usually more general in sense or occurs in a wider range of contexts than the marked form. And, since this is so, it is now customary to employ the terms 'marked' and 'unmarked' in a rather more abstract sense. 'For instance, from the semantic point of view the words *dog* and *bitch* are unmarked and marked for the contrast of sex. The word *dog* is semantically unmarked (or neutral), since it can be applied to either males or females (*That's a lovely dog you've got there: is it a he or a she?*). But *bitch* is marked (or positive), since it is restricted to females and may be used in contrast with the unmarked term to determine the sense of the latter as negative, rather than neutral (*Is it a dog or a bitch?*). That is to say, the unmarked term has a more general sense, neutral with respect to a certain contrast; its more specific negative sense is derivative and secondary, being a consequence of its contextual opposition with the positive non-neutral term' (Lyons, 1968: 79). The past tense form *loved* is marked in this second, more 'abstract', sense of the term 'marking' also, since the unmarked form *love* occurs in a wider range of contexts (and might be called 'non-past' rather than 'present'). Generally speaking, the two notions of 'marking', when they are both relevant, coincide. But they are, in principle, independent of one another. Although it is usually assumed that, in English, the plural is marked by contrast to the singular, as it clearly is in the less 'abstract' sense (*boy-s* v. *boy*. etc.), it is by no means so clear that the same is true from the more 'abstract' point of view.

(4) LANGUAGE AND MEDIUM. One of the principles with which linguists have challenged more traditional conceptions of language has recently been expressed as follows (and similar statements can be found in most of the standard textbooks and more popular introductions to the subject): 'Language is speech and the linguistic competence underlying speech. Writing is no more than a secondary, graphic representation of language ...' (Langacker, 1968: 58; cf. Bloomfield, 1935: 21). This puts the principle in an unnecessarily extreme form (cf. Lyons, 1968: 38ff.). However, with due qualification, the principle is undoubtedly valid: sound (and more particularly the range of sound that can be produced by the human 'speech organs') is the 'natural', or primary, *medium* in which language is manifest, and written language derives from the transference of speech to a secondary, visual medium (cf. Abercrombie, 1966: 17).

Every known language exists, or has existed, as a spoken language, whether or not it also exists in a written form; and thousands of languages have never, or only very recently, been committed to writing. Furthermore, children acquire a command of the spoken language before they start to learn to read and write, and they do so 'naturally', without any training; reading and writing are special skills in which children are generally given formal instruction based upon their prior knowledge of the spoken language.

This, then, is another feature that we might wish to add to our definition of language: the fact that it is primarily a system of *vocal* communication. It is for this reason that phonetics (the study of speech sounds – their production, transmission and reception, and their acoustic properties: see the chapters by Dennis Fry and John Laver, pp. 29–52 and pp. 53–75) is considered to be an integral and important part of linguistics.

(5) LANGUAGE, DIALECT AND IDIOLECT. It is customary, in everyday usage, to draw a distinction between 'languages' and 'dialects' of a language. We might say for example that English is a language and that it has many different dialects, spoken in different countries or different parts of the same country. Although the linguist makes use of the same terminological distinc-

tion in his more technical discussion of language, he does not necessarily accept the implications commonly associated with the word 'dialect' in everyday speech. In particular, he does not accept that a regional dialect (or the dialect of a particular social class) is no more than an inferior version of the standard language. In origin at least a standard language is simply a dialect which, for historical and linguistically 'accidental' reasons, has acquired political and cultural importance in a particular community.

As commonly applied, the distinction between languages and dialects is based very largely upon cultural or political considerations. Many of the so-called 'dialects' of Chinese, for example, are more distinct from one another than, say, Danish and Norwegian, or, even more strikingly, Dutch and Flemish, which are frequently described as different 'languages'.

A further point that should be made is that no very sharp distinction can be drawn between the dialect of one region and that of another neighbouring region. However narrowly we define the speech community, by geographical and social criteria, we shall always find a certain degree of systematic variation in the speech of its members. In the last resort, we should have to admit that every member of every speech community speaks a slightly different dialect: he has his own *idiolect*.

(6) LANGUAGE AND STYLE. It would be a mistake to assume that, once we have set up the scale language-dialect-idiolect, we have allowed for all the synchronically relevant variation found in language. Language is used for a multiplicity of purposes; and what is said, and the way it is said, may depend upon the situation in which an utterance is made, the relations between the participants, and a number of other factors. The word *style* is quite widely employed to refer to one kind of variation in the use of language – such terms as 'colloquial', 'highly formal' or 'friendly' being suggestive of the distinctions that are intended. Another kind of variation has to do with the medium in which the language is realized (cf. spoken v. written English); here there is no generally accepted term, but *mode* has been employed in this sense (cf. Halliday, McIntosh & Strevens, 1964: 91; Gregory,

1967). The two kinds of non-dialectal variation mentioned here are merely illustrative. The question of 'sociolinguistic' variation is discussed in some detail by John Pride in a later chapter (see pp. 287–301).

Both within and outside linguistics the term 'style' has a rather different sense, in addition to the one referred to in the previous paragraph. Style, under this second interpretation, has to do with those components or features of the form of a literary composition which give to it its individual stamp, marking it as the work of a particular author and producing a certain effect upon the reader. The analysis of *style* in this sense is commonly called *stylistics* (see the chapter by James Thorne pp. 185–97).

Levels of Analysis

We have already met the term *level* in connexion with the distinction between words and sounds, which were referred to as units of the 'primary' and 'secondary' level, respectively (see p. 12). But 'sound' and 'word' are highly ambiguous terms and must be qualified, or replaced with other more technical terms, before they will serve for a more precise description of language.

We must distinguish between a *phonetic* and a *phonological* interpretation of 'sound'. Consider what is meant by saying that a given word is composed of a certain number of 'sounds'. Let us grant, for the moment, that the English word *big* is composed of three 'sounds' (as the orthography in this case suggests). From the *phonological* point of view, this statement might be interpreted in terms of the relevant paradigmatic and syntagmatic relations (see p. 16): there are three places at which the substitution of one 'sound' for another could have the effect of changing one word into another. The set of 'sounds' which results from the analysis of a language at the phonological level may be described as the *phonemes* of the language. It has become conventional to put the phonemic representation of words and utterances between oblique 'slashes', in order to make the level of analysis immediately clear in the notation. The word *big* can therefore be written phonemically as /big/. Some linguists have held that the phoneme (which is defined somewhat differently in various systems) is the minimal unit of phonological analysis. Others have taken a different view. Further discussion of this question will be found in the chapter by Erik Fudge (see pp. 76–95). For our purpose, the phoneme will stand as an illustration of one kind of phonological unit.

By contrast, a *phone* (or 'speech sound') is a unit of *phonetic* analysis; and the notational convention for phonetic representation is to enclose the transcription in square brackets. We might want to say, for example, that the word *big* is pronounced, or realized phonetically, as [big]. Phonetics differs from phonology (in so far as we can draw a distinction between the two) in that it considers speech sounds independently of their paradigmatic oppositions and syntagmatic combinations in particular languages. What is involved in the segmentation of continuous speech from the phonetic point of view is discussed in the chapter by Dennis Fry (see pp. 29–52). We have begged a number of questions in saying that there are three phones [b], [i] and [g] in the pronunciation of *big*. The truth is that there are indefinitely many. Just how many will be recognized by the phonetician depends upon the purpose for which he is carrying out the analysis and the criteria he applies. It is by no means true, as our simple illustration might tend to imply, that the same phonological unit is always realized as the same phonetic unit (see below, pp. 76–8).

Phonology, then, is the level at which the linguist describes the *sound system* of a particular language. The level at which he accounts for the way words (the 'primary' units) are put together to form sentences is *syntax*. This is the traditional term (which, in origin, was simply the ordinary Greek word for 'putting together'); and it is still used in essentially the same sense by linguists.

As we remarked above, the term *word* has more than one sense. One ambiguity becomes clear if we compare the following two statements: (1) '*Wrote* and *written* are two forms of the word WRITE'; (2) '*Wrote* and *written* are two different words'. In (1) the term 'word' refers to what is commonly called a *lexical item* (or *lexeme*): that is to say, to a unit which is manifest in one 'form' or another in sentences, but which is itself distinct from all its forms. We have deliberately distinguished between the forms of a lexical item and the lexical item itself by citing the latter in small capitals and the former in italics. This enables us to avoid the confusion that might otherwise arise in making such statements as '*Write* is one of the forms of WRITE', where, following traditional practice, we have used one of the forms of a lexeme to denote the lexeme itself. This is what is done normally when words are listed in a dictionary.

Yet another ambiguity in the term 'word' is revealed if we compare *I wrote* and *I have written* with *I loved* and *I have loved*. From the point of view of their orthographic and phonological representation, the *loved* of *I loved* and the *loved* of *I have loved* (unlike *wrote* and *written*) are identical. Let us say that they constitute two instances of the same *phonological* (and orthographic) *word*. But there is another point of view, from which we might wish to say that the *loved* of *I loved* is a different word from the *loved* of *I have loved*. This sense of 'word' is brought out by describing the *loved* of *I loved* as 'the simple past tense form of LOVE' and the *loved* of *I have loved* as 'the past participle of LOVE'. Considered from this point of view we will say that the two instances of the phonological (and orthographic) word *loved* (like the two different phonological words *wrote* and *written*) represent two distinct *grammatical words*.

There are therefore at least three senses in which the term *word* is used; and linguists have not always been careful to distinguish them. It must now be pointed out that many linguists recognize (for certain languages at least) a level of structure between the phonological and the syntactic. This is its *morphology*. What is meant by a morphological analysis may be illustrated by saying that the word *untruthful* is composed of four smaller grammatical units *un*, *true*, *th* and *ful*. These units, which are minimal grammatical units in the sense that they cannot be subjected to further analysis (except at the phonological level) are *morphemes*. We shall say no more about morphology here at this point, since the chapter by Peter Matthews is devoted specifically to the subject (see pp. 96–114). Here we should warn the reader that the term 'morpheme' is widely used in linguistics in a variety of related, but potentially confusing, senses. In particular, it should be pointed out that for many linguists, who give a rather wider interpretation to the term 'syntax' than is traditional and do not recognize a distinct morphological level, the morpheme is the minimal unit of syntactic analysis.

We come finally to *semantics* – the study of meaning. Not long ago many linguists held the view that semantics was not a branch of their science; that linguistics should be restricted to the investigation of 'form' in language. The historical reasons for this attitude do not concern us here. The last few years have seen a very noticeable renewal of interest in semantic theory; and one approach to the semantic analysis of language is exemplified in the chapter by Manfred Bierwisch (pp. 166–84).

In this section, we have distinguished four 'levels' in the analysis of language – phonology, morphology, syntax, semantics. Linguists agree fairly well among themselves about the application of these four terms (except that many of them will not use the term 'morphology' at all and will apportion its subject matter between phonology and syntax). They will not necessarily use the term 'level'. There is unfortunately a good deal of terminological inconsistency in contemporary linguistics. The term 'level' is given one technical sense in some theories, a different technical sense in others, and is used more loosely (as I have been using it) in others. It is difficult to find a satisfactory alternative term.

The same inconsistency applies with respect to the term *grammar*. Its traditional sense (indeed the sense in which one talks of 'traditional grammar') was relatively wide. In recent years it has tended to be more restricted: (1) to include morphology and syntax, but to exclude phonology and semantics; or (2) to include phonology, with morphology and syntax, but to exclude semantics. Even more recently the term 'grammar' has come to be used once again in the wider sense which includes semantics also. There is little we can do in this situation except to warn the reader to pay particular attention to the way an author defines or exemplifies his use of terminology.

Generative Grammar

One of the most important developments in recent linguistic theory has been the emergence of what is called *generative grammar*. (In this context the term 'grammar' is best taken in its widest sense, to include all levels of analysis.) As it is usually interpreted, 'generative' here combines two different senses. It is important to distinguish these, since there are occasions when one or the other is dominant.

The first sense of the term 'generative' refers to what we mentioned earlier as the 'productive' or 'creative' aspect of language (see p. 12). Any set of rules or statements in terms of which it is possible to describe the structure of an indefinitely large set of sentences may be called a 'generative' grammar. In this sense of the term, it should be noted, there is nothing particularly novel or revolutionary about generative grammar: traditional grammar (though not all more recent linguistic theory) was generative.

In the second sense of the term, 'generative' is held to imply 'formalized' or 'explicit'. From this point of view, a generative grammar may be defined as a system of rules which specifies precisely what combinations of the basic elements (phonemes, morphemes, lexemes, etc.) are permissible, or well-formed. The grammar is said to *generate* (and thereby define as 'grammatical') all the sentences of the languages and to fail to generate (thereby defining as 'ungrammatical') all the non-sentences, or 'ill-formed' combinations of basic elements. The particular way in which generative grammars have been formalized in current linguistic theory has been very strongly influenced by the construction and investigation of artificial languages in logic and mathematics, and in particular by what is called recursive function theory.

Here we should clarify one misunderstanding that has arisen, namely, the claim that a generative grammar 'generates all and only the grammatical sentences' of a language. From one point of view, this statement is no more than a definition of what is meant by the term 'generative' (in the sense of 'explicit'), and is therefore not open to dispute: the language *is* the set of sentences generated by the grammar. The task that the linguist undertakes when he sets out to describe the language of a given speech community is to get the best fit that is possible between the sentences of the language generated by the grammar and the utterances that might be produced and understood, and accepted as normal, by the members of the speech community. One *may* take the additional step of postulating close parallelism between the generative grammar constructed by the linguist and the *langue* (or competence) underlying the *parole* (or performance) of the speakers. But it must be clearly understood that this is an additional step, and one that involves psychological assumptions, which only some linguists (e.g. Chomsky, 1965, 1968), would be prepared to make.

Generative grammars fall into several types, of which one is of particular importance and should be given special mention here. This is the type known as *transformational*. (Strictly speaking, one should call this class the class of 'transformational-generative' grammars, since 'generative', taken in either of the two senses we have distinguished, is independent of 'transformational', and conversely. But 'transformational' is generally used, without qualification, in the sense of 'transformational and generative'.) Transformational grammar has been developed in somewhat different directions, mainly by Harris, Chomsky and their associates, in the course of the last fifteen years.

Within the totality of sentences that we should wish to generate and thus define as grammatical for a particular language (let us say, English), Harris (1957) distinguished two classes: a relatively small class of *kernel sentences* (the set of kernel sentences being described as the *kernel* of the language) and a proportionately larger (and indeed indefinitely large) set of non-kernel sentences. The difference between these two classes of sentences lies in the fact that non-kernel sentences are derived from kernel sentences by means of *transformational* rules. For example, *John ate the apple* is a kernel sentence, which may be transformed into such non-kernel sentences as *The apple was eaten by John* or *Did John eat the apple?*, and each of these may be described as a *transform* of the kernel sentence from which it is derived. Another transform of *John ate the apple* might be *John's eating of the apple*, which is not itself a sentence, but a phrase which can occur within another sentence. There are of course far more complex examples.

Chomsky (1957) took a somewhat different view. In his system no sentences are derived from other sentences; and no sentences are generated without the operation of at least a small number of transformational rules. For Chomsky the difference between kernel and non-kernel sentences depends upon the distinction he draws between optional and obligatory transformations. A kernel sentence is one that is derived (from a *kernel string*) without the application of any optional transformational rules. In Chomsky's subsequent development (1965) of his system the distinction between optional and obligatory transformational rules has disappeared, and with it the difference between kernel and non-kernel sentences. But this question, as well as the more technical points which define, and distinguish, the notion of 'transformation', is best left for the chapter on syntax (see pp. 121–4).

One of the advantages of a transformational grammar is that it enables us to relate superficially distinct sentences and distinguish superficially identical sentences. What is meant by 'superficially distinct' can be explained looking again at one of the examples given above. *John ate the apple* and *The apple was eaten by John* differ syntactically in that the former is 'active', having *John* as its subject and *the apple* as its object, whereas the latter is 'passive', having *the apple* as its subject with *by John* as an adverbial modifier of some kind. (I have deliberately made use of familiar, traditional terminology at this point.) These two sentences differ then in their *surface structure*. But their derivation (one from the other in Harris's system or each from the same underlying kernel string in Chomsky's system) can be interpreted to mean that they are syntactically related, if not identical, at some less 'superficial' level of analysis which we may call their *deep structure*. This is an example of superficially distinct, but 'deeply' related, structures. A phrase like *the love of three colonels* illustrates the converse situation. This phrase has at least two interpretations, which might be rendered as 'the love felt by three colonels' and 'the love felt for three colonels'. Traditional grammar would have said that, according to the first interpretation, the adjectival modifier *of three colonels* is 'subjective' and according to the second interpretation, 'objective'. These terms are revealing in that they suggest that *the love of three colonels* is relatable, in deep structure, to either of two sentences: to *Three colonels love* (*someone*), in which three colonels is the subject, or to (*Someone*) *loves three colonels*, in which *three colonels* is the object.

The terms 'surface structure' and 'deep structure' come from

Hockett (1958: 246) and were not used in the earlier accounts of transformational grammar. It is perhaps futile to argue whether the distinction between the two levels of syntactic structure was implicit from the start of transformational grammar (as I have suggested). Chomsky would maintain that it was; and the statement by Harris (1957: 290) to the effect that 'some major element of meaning appears to be held constant under transformation' can also be interpreted in this light. For it is one of the assumptions made by all linguists who accept the validity of some kind of distinction between deep and surface structure, that the deeper analysis is more relevant for semantic analysis. As we shall see later, some transformational grammarians have recently claimed that the 'deepest' analysis of a sentence *is* its semantic interpretation, or meaning, from which its surface structure is derived by the successive operation of transformational rules (cf. also Chafe, 1967). Whether or not this more extreme claim can be substantiated, it is undeniable that the development of transformational grammar has been a major factor in the current renewal of interest in semantics.

It is also true to say that generative grammar, and more particularly transformational grammar, has aroused more general interest than any other development in linguistics in recent years. This is not to say that the principles of generative grammar, still less the details of any particular system, have been universally accepted. But even those linguists who reject the principles of generative grammar would probably acknowledge their theoretical importance. The generative approach to the analysis of language is strongly represented in the following chapters.

One further point should be made in connexion with generative grammar, and it will serve as a conclusion to this introductory chapter. According to Chomsky (1965: 3): 'Linguistic theory is concerned with an ideal speaker-listener, in a completely homogeneous speech community, who knows its language perfectly and is unaffected by such grammatically irrelevant conditions as memory limitations, distractions, shifts of attention and interest, and errors (random or characteristic) in applying his knowledge of the language in actual performance.' In passages like this, Chomsky groups together, and describes as 'grammatically irrelevant', a number of distinct factors, some of which at least might be held to fall within the scope of what is commonly meant by 'knowing a language'. Most linguists would probably agree that some distinction must be drawn between competence and performance (between *langue* and *parole*: cf. p. 14), and that this will involve a certain degree of 'idealization'. They would not necessarily agree, however, with the way in which Chomsky himself defines linguistic competence; and Chomsky's notion of linguistic competence is in fact criticized in a number of the chapters that follow (notably by Halliday, pp. 140–65 and by Campbell & Wales, pp. 242–60. In view of these criticisms (see also Matthews, 1967*b*: 119–23), it should be emphasized that generative grammar, and more particularly the model of transformational grammar outlined in Chomksy (1965), is not limited in principle to the description of the competence of the 'ideal speaker-listener' as this is defined in the quotation above.

2. SPEECH RECEPTION AND PERCEPTION

D. B. Fry

The main point made by Fry, in the chapter which follows, is that speech perception cannot be accounted for solely in terms of acoustic analysis. It is a form of 'pattern recognition', in which the acoustic input provides 'cues' for the identification of sounds and words, but is not of itself sufficient for their recognition. 'Our perception of speech is influenced by the phonological system and hence is the fruit of the language-learning process. People who have different native languages learn different phonological systems and develop different patterns of sensitivity to acoustic features of one kind or another.'

The distinction between phonetics and phonology has been explained above, as also has the notational difference between square brackets and oblique 'slashes' (p. 20). Technical terms whose sense is not clear from the context are defined in the Glossary.

Fry makes a number of simplifying assumptions in his account of the 'decoding' process. For instance, it will be clear from the previous chapter that 'words' are not necessarily stored in the brain in the form in which they occur in speech and that they cannot always be analysed as strings of 'morphemes': this will be made even clearer in the chapter by Matthews. These facts do not of course invalidate Fry's conclusions, but reinforce them. The process of speech perception is a particularly complex form of 'pattern recognition'. So far we know relatively little about the way linguistic information is 'stored' in the brain and 'indexed' for 'retrieval' in the perception (or production) of speech; although, as Fry explains, something can be inferred from the evidence of error correction.

In view of the definition of the term 'generate' given in the previous chapter, the reader should note that Fry uses it throughout in the sense in which it is commonly used by communications engineers: i.e. in the sense of 'initiate' or 'produce'.

THE cardinal fact which emerges from any discussion of language is that every language is a system, a system which operates on several different levels and with units of differing magnitude – phonemes, morphemes, words, sentences. This is made explicit very frequently in the chapters of this book, as it is elsewhere. What is less often stressed is that knowledge of the system for a particular language is indispensable to every language user, although a little reflection shows that this must indeed be the case. Individuals who talk to each other in English are able to do so because of their knowledge of the English language system; a speaker of English who does not know the system of, say, Mandarin or Turkish will make nothing of messages conveyed to him in either of these languages; if he has learned in some degree the system of French or German, his success in dealing with messages in these languages will be directly determined by the completeness of his knowledge of their system.

Knowledge of the system is equally important whether it is a case of generating speech or receiving it, since every operation with language is based upon this knowledge. Every speaker or listener carries in his cortex a vast store of information about any language he uses. This includes the complete inventory of phonemes and words, the rules for forming morphemes from phonemes and sentences from words, and in addition a great deal of statistical information about the sequences of units which may occur in the language at the various levels. This knowledge is at the disposal of the language user all the time and is employed during both speaking and listening, though there are some parts of the store which are used much more for one purpose than the other. An individual's store of words, for example, contains a far greater number of items which he will recognize when he hears them than of items which he is likely to use spontaneously in his own speech.

Whether we are giving out speech or taking it in, there is continuous activity in the brain, concerned on the one hand with programming the speech output and on the other with processing the speech input. Increasing realization of the importance of these forms of brain action constitutes one of the major developments in our thinking about language and speech of the last twenty-five years and has done much to point the way in which progress is likely to be made in the immediate future. When speech is coming in, the processing of the information plays a vital role at a very early stage and one of the reasons for heading this chapter Reception and Perception is the need to underline this important fact. When we take in a spoken message, it is necessary for our ears to receive sound-waves originating with the speaker; this is far from being sufficient to ensure our decoding of the message, however. As has already been pointed out, if the message is in a language we do not know, we can go no further in the process of decoding, although our ears are exposed to the same sound-waves as those of a listener who does know the language. These sound-waves and the information that the brain is able to extract from them form no more than a rough guide to the sense of the message, a kind of scaffolding upon which the listener constructs or reconstructs the sentences originating in the speaker's brain. He is able to perform this feat of reconstruction because of the store of *a priori* knowledge about the language with which his brain is stocked. This knowledge is made use of at the very earliest stage of decoding, that is in dealing with the acoustic information supplied by the sound-waves, and it plays a vital role at this and every subsequent stage.

It is not simply a knowledge of the language system, in all its details, that enables a listener to decode a spoken message. He has also at his disposal a very wide range of statistical information about the language. In this area, the development of information theory has had a profound influence on linguistics, as on other branches of science (cf. Shannon & Weaver, 1949). Its effect has been to bring sharply into focus the fact that using a language involves knowing a great deal about what is likely to follow at any point in a spoken message, that is a knowledge of sequential probabilities on all levels of the language. When a message is being generated, the speaker is not free at any point to continue in any way whatsoever, for he is constrained by what immediately precedes. Wiener once expressed this fact by saying that 'the most important thing we can know about a message is that it makes sense'. This 'making sense' constrains the speaker at every moment and is invoked by the listener in receiving the message.

The latter does not depend solely upon the sounds he hears in speech, he uses his knowledge of sequential probabilities to predict the continuation of the message and so his decoding is essentially a process of determining 'what the message must have been'. This factor is so powerful that whenever there is a conflict between what the listener thinks is likely and what actually reaches his ear, it is most frequently the first of these that wins the day. This side of speech reception will be discussed more fully later in this chapter but its importance has to be kept clearly in mind throughout any discussion of speech reception.

The decoding of a spoken message is then a twofold process in which the listener receives acoustic information and combines it with linguistic (including statistical) information. The relative weight that is assigned to these two factors depends partly on the conditions in which the message is received. In direct communication between a speaker and a listener in sight of each other in quiet surroundings, linguistic information already has very considerable weight. As the conditions worsen, because the speaker is out of sight of the listener or because of masking noise or distortion in the channel of communication, linguistic information is given more and more weight in the final decision to compensate for the progressive reduction in the available acoustic information; in other words, the harder it is to hear, the more you have to guess.

This chapter will now deal first with the processing of the acoustic information in speech and then with the processing of the linguistic information, in each case reviewing briefly the evidence that has accumulated as a result of research in recent years.

ACOUSTIC PROCESSING IN SPEECH

The first step in the reception of speech is the listener's recognition of sounds which he hears. Recognition is a very common, if not a very well-understood, operation on the part of the brain. The word is generally used to refer to a situation in which a man perceives something and is able at once to place that 'something' in a category already established in his memory on the basis of previous sensory experience. In this sense, recognition is involved in practically all our apprehension of the world external to ourselves. Recognizing the sounds in a spoken message requires that the listener should perceive sounds and place each item in one of a number of categories which correspond in this case, to the phonemes or phonological units of the language system (cf. the chapter by Fudge, pp. 96–114). Sounds in an English message, therefore, would be recognized as belonging each to one of the categories which constitute the English phonological system. One difference, however, between the recognition of speech sounds and the more general case of recognition is that the phonological categories are interdependent; the existence of one category presupposes the existence of all the other categories in the system. This is clearly not the case in most kinds of recognition. To recognize an object as a chair does not in itself presuppose the existence of other categories such as sofa, table, door, window and so on, whereas recognizing the first sound in *kitten* as belonging to the class /k/ presupposes the existence of all the other phonemic classes in the English system.

Just as a very wide variety of sense impressions may cause us to class an object as, say, a chair, so widely different sounds may all be classed in the /k/ phoneme. We might say roughly that having a seat, back and legs are enough to characterize a chair; when these features are visible to us, we tend to place the object in a category 'chair'. In a similar way there are acoustic features which tend to characterize speech sounds belonging to different phonemes in a system. But here again there is an important difference between the two operations of recognition, the non-linguistic and the linguistic. We might very easily assemble a hundred objects, all different, which we would place in the class 'chair'; at the same time we should be well aware of the visible differences between them. In the linguistic case, however, our very perceptions are modified by the language-learning process. We learn to discriminate readily between speech sounds which must be placed in different phonemic categories, but we are much less capable, without special training, of distinguishing between different sounds which the language requires shall be assigned to the same category. The particular varieties of sound which have to be processed in these two ways, that is assigned to a single class or to different classes, depend upon the system of the given language. In English, for example, there are at least four or five varieties of [t] sound which have marked acoustic differences, but the ordinary English listener is not aware of these differences. On the other hand in some Indian languages, there are six classes of [t] sound which must be kept separate if the phonological system is to function properly, and some of the acoustic differences to which the English listener is insensitive are the features which the Indian speaker uses to sort the [t] sounds into their right classes. By contrast, no English listener would be likely to confuse the two English words *red* and *raid*, and yet the vowel sounds in these words are indistinguishable to many Indian speakers. The listener's processing of acoustic information in speech is therefore carried out according to the patterns established by language learning.

Just as visual recognition depends on the perception of visible features, so recognition of speech sounds depends on the perception of audible features of one kind or another. The acoustic cues which give rise to these perceptions have been studied by experimental methods during the past fifteen to twenty years and as a result we now have some well-founded notions as to how they operate in speech.

Acoustic Cues in the Perception of Speech

It is somewhat difficult for the ordinary language user to realize just how wide a variety of sounds he puts into a single phonemic class. If we imagine one English syllable, 'no', as said to us by speakers from different parts of the world, southern English, northern English, Cockney, Scots, Welsh, Irish, American, Australian, and we then imagine these varieties of sound multiplied by the differences for example between a man, woman or child speaker and again by the immeasurably greater number of individual speakers, it becomes clear that the class formed by the various vowel sounds used in this one word is very large. Any single sample of these sounds will show detectable and measurable acoustic differences from any other sample. When the listener puts them all into one class he is therefore disregarding these acoustic differences, either because he is insensitive to them or because he has learned that they are irrelevant from the phonological point of view.

Recognition of speech sounds thus requires the selecting of certain kinds of acoustic information; it is in effect a matter of 'pattern recognition' in which each pattern is an arrangement of acoustic cues. There is a limited number of acoustic dimensions in which such cues are to be found and these can readily be listed, at least to cover the information used in most known languages. The most comprehensive of these dimensions is the distribution of acoustic energy over the sound spectrum. During the whole of an utterance the amount of energy in various parts of the speech frequency range is continually changing. The position and number of energy peaks and the time changes in these all afford important cues for the recognition of speech sounds. (The peaks are due to the normal modes of vibration in the vocal tract. The frequency at each mode is referred to as a formant, and formants are numbered serially from the lowest frequency upwards.) For example, the recognition of vowels and the discrimination of one vowel from another depends very largely on the cues supplied by the first two energy peaks in the spectrum, on formants 1 and 2. Spectrum information is also used in much more complex ways which will be mentioned later.

Then there is the variation of total sound intensity, as distinct from its distribution with respect to frequency. The absolute level of acoustic energy during an utterance will obviously depend on whether the speaker speaks loudly or softly, but at any given volume there are intensity relations between different sounds which are consistently maintained. The whole class of consonant sounds, for instance, will have less overall energy than the class of vowel sounds, or again, in the class of voiceless fricative sounds, [s] and [ʃ] will be of high intensity compared with [θ] and [f].

Next there is the dimension of periodicity. The ear and brain are quick to seize upon the difference between periodic and aperiodic sounds, between tones and noises, and can detect within very close limits the moment at which periodicity begins. In normal speech, all vowel sounds, semi-vowels, liquids and nasals are periodic sounds, while voiceless consonants are aperiodic. Between these two classes, there are the voiced fricatives in which the ear recognizes an underlying periodicity, even though it is accompanied by aperiodic friction noise. In distinguishing between voiced and voiceless plosives, the exact moment at which periodicity begins is among the cues used by the listener.

Finally there is the time dimension itself which provides a great many of the cues in the recognition of speech sounds. Its use is implicit in all the cues so far mentioned, since it is variation with time of any one factor that constitutes the cue, but in addition to this, the relative duration of different acoustic features continually serves as a cue in recognition. The distinction between continuous and interrupted sounds, for example between voiceless plosives and fricatives, depends upon this dimension. In English the [t] sound is most commonly characterized by a short interruption of the flow of sound, followed by noise of short duration, while [s] is a similar noise lasting considerably longer and without the interruption. Again in English, the distinction between post-vocalic voiced and voiceless sounds is carried very largely by the relative duration of the vocalic and the consonantal parts of the syllable; in /biːt/ (*beat*) the vocalic part is relatively short and the interruption caused by the consonant is long, while in /biːd/ (*bead*) the reverse is the case.

Acoustic Cues as a Set of Relations

The sounds of speech are perfectly amenable to measurement with respect to all the dimensions just listed. It is true that acoustic measurements are not by their nature particularly easy to make, but, with some reservations, the acoustic specification of speech sounds is within the capacity of modern methods of study. This does not mean, however, that simply by making acoustic measurements, no matter how many we make or how widely we sample speech sounds in a given language, we can discover how acoustic processing is carried out in speech communication.

There are two major reasons for this. The first is that any cue used in speech will depend upon relative and not on absolute values. This is implicit in the fact that speech decoding is based on pattern recognition, for a pattern, in this sense, is essentially a pattern of relations which can be detected in a variety of stimuli, despite marked differences on an absolute scale in the relevant dimensions. That this must be so in speech follows from the example given above of the factors which produce variability in speech sounds. If we take a sample of the 'same' word uttered by a man, a woman and a child, and make acoustic measurements on each of these, we shall not obtain absolute measurements that are identical or even particularly close to each other. There will be marked differences in overall intensity, spectral distribution of energy, fundamental frequency and duration. The fact that any listener will recognize the same word in all three cases is due to his reliance upon acoustic cues based on relative values, relations within each utterance, relations between the three utterances, and, most important of all, relations between this particular utterance and others which might come from the same speaker, for there is good evidence that the listener is able, on the basis of a very short sample, to infer a whole frame of reference for dealing with any individual's speech.

Plurality of Acoustic Cues in Speech

A straightforward acoustic analysis of speech signals will not therefore yield the cues which listeners use in identifying sounds. We have to examine the relations of acoustic values and the relations of these relations, to make an intensive and extensive study of the interdependence of acoustic values in speech before we can begin to have any idea of exactly what information forms the basis for classifying incoming speech sounds in their phonemic categories.

There is however a second reason why analysis alone cannot tell us how the acoustic processing of speech is done by the listener. By measuring a very large number of samples of a given sound, say [k] in English speech, we may discover quite a number of features which tend to be present in the samples. There will regularly be a brief interruption in the flow of acoustic energy from the mouth, a short silence; the duration of this silence compared with that of a periodic sound which precedes or follows it will tend to fall within a certain range. The silence will in a proportion of samples, but certainly not all, be followed by a short burst of noise, with a spectral peak somewhere in the region of

1000–2000 c.p.s. (cycles per second) and a total intensity some 10–15 decibels below that of a neighbouring periodic sound. If a vowel immediately follows or precedes the [k], the spectral distribution of energy during the periodic sound will show certain features, including a rather rapid change in the frequency of the second formant at the point nearest to the [k] and the moment at which periodicity begins or ends will bear a certain time relation to the burst of noise, if there is one.

These observations do not justify us in saying that we have here the acoustic cues which a listener employs when he classifies an incoming sound as [k]. At the very most we have an indication of *possible* acoustic cues and we are left with the task of demonstrating that a listener operates with any or all of them in given conditions of communication.

The need for such a demonstration has given rise to the development of a number of experimental methods. One which has been widely used for many years is that of subtracting information from the acoustic signal, by filtering or by adding masking noise, and measuring the effect of this on the recognition of the various speech sounds. Much of the pioneering work of the Bell Telephone Laboratories on speech recognition was carried out by means of bandpass filters, and their experiments laid the foundations for much of our present knowledge of the subject (Fletcher, 1953). More recent experiments on similar lines are those of Miller and Nicely (1955) in which masking noise and frequency distortion were both used in an attempt to abstract the dimensions which form the basis for the recognition of sounds.

Subtracting information from the speech signal tells us more about the process of recognition than straightforward acoustic analysis, but it is still not enough to isolate the acoustic cues because what is left in the signal is still a complex which is likely to contain more than one cue for a given recognition. This was in fact one of the conclusions of the Miller and Nicely experiments, that none of the filtering or masking conditions served to isolate a cue dimension. The only way in which this can be done effectively is by the use of speech synthesis, that is by creating artificially speech-like sounds in which only one cue for a given recognition is represented and is systematically varied.

The most important work in this field has been done by workers at the Haskins Laboratories in New York who developed a technique for generating the necessary stimuli and carried out a number of what proved to be classic experiments. There are various ways in which speech-like sounds can be synthesized, but a common feature of most of them is the use of electronic circuits to generate acoustic outputs of which all the dimensions are experimentally controllable. In the original Haskins experiments this control was exercised through the medium of a visible pattern resembling a speech spectrogram. As this method makes the principle particularly clear it will be referred to here for purposes of illustration.

The sound spectrogram shown on the left of Figure 1 represents a very common method of displaying information about the acoustic character of speech sounds. Time is represented on the horizontal scale, frequency on the vertical scale and the darkness of the trace denotes the level of acoustic energy at different moments and frequencies. All the features referred to above as tending to occur in an utterance containing the English sound [k] are displayed here. When we provide a listener with a sample of this utterance in natural speech, he receives the whole complex of acoustic information which this represents. He will certainly decide that initial [k] has occurred, but we shall not know how far this decision has been influenced by the noise burst, the second formant transition, the onset of voicing and other time relations.

The pattern on the right of Figure 1 is the kind of pattern used to control a speech synthesizer, and this one gives an acoustic output which any English listener would recognize as the word *keg*. It is evident that the pattern is a simplification of the spectral pattern on the left. Much of the frequency-intensity information of the spectrogram is not represented in the simplified pattern but the basic shape is reproduced. The importance of the method is that the experimenter is in a position to decide just what acoustic information shall be embodied in the resulting sound. For example, the short burst of noise which very often appears in the spectrogram when there is a voiceless plosive in the utterance is generated here by the noise patch shown at time 0·1. The burst can be given any one of a range of frequency values by

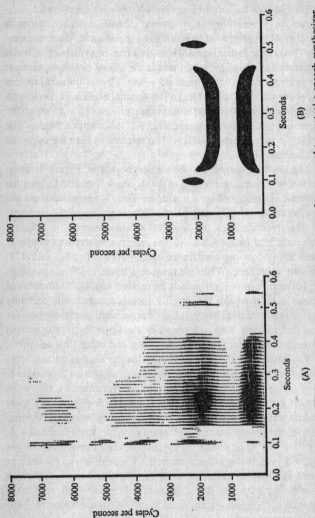

Figure 1. (a) Spectrogram of the word *keg.* (b) Simplified pattern of a type used to control a speech synthesizer.

shifting the position of the noise patch on the vertical scale, whilst keeping all other features of the pattern constant.

One of the earliest Haskins experiments was based on a series of stimuli generated in this way (Liberman *et al.*, 1952). A constant two-formant vowel of the type /e/ was preceded by a short noise burst having some value in the range 360–4320 c.p.s. Groups of listeners received many repetitions of these stimuli in random order and were asked to judge each one as /p/, /t/ or /k/. With this vowel, listeners tended to hear low-frequency bursts (360–1800 c.p.s.) predominantly as /p/, mid-frequency bursts (1800–3000 c.p.s.) as /k/, and high-frequency bursts (3000–4320 c.p.s.) as /t/.

This result was relatively clear-cut when the formant frequencies corresponded to those of a single vowel. When the same range of noise bursts were combined with a range of English vowel colours, the effects were much more complex. Figure 2

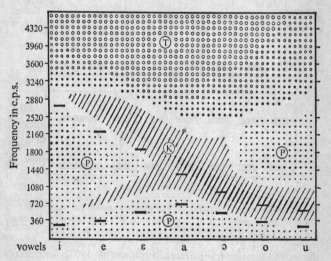

Figure 2. Summary of the results of listening tests with synthesized stimuli in which the frequency of a noise burst was varied over the range shown. The noise was combined with steady state formants whose values are given by the horizontal bars in the figure. The size of the symbol at any place on the map indicates the degree of agreement among subjects. (From *American Journal of Psychology*, 1952, vol. 65, p. 509.)

gives a summary of the results of such experiments: the size of the symbol used at each point in the figure indicates the degree of agreement among the group of subjects who made the judgements. The data show that the frequency of a noise burst is in itself an effective cue for identifying /p/, /t/ and /k/, but they also underline the point made earlier that in seeking acoustic cues we shall generally be concerned with relations, since bursts in the region of 1800 c.p.s., for example, are identified as either /p/ or /k/ depending on vowel-formant frequencies which follow the burst.

Phonemic Categories and Perception

Another example of a series of stimuli used in similar experiments is shown in Figure 3, where the variable is the character of

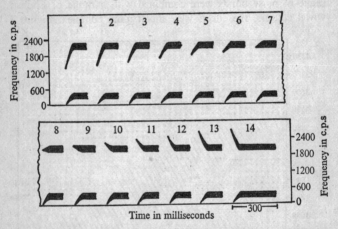

Figure 3. The range of patterns used to produce stimuli for experiments on the effect of second formant transition upon the recognition of /b, d, g/. (From *Journal of Experimental Psychology*, 1957, vol. 54, p. 359).

the second formant transition (Liberman *et al.*, 1957). Recordings of the 14 stimuli, in random order, were played to groups of subjects who were asked to identify each one as /b/, /d/ or /g/. A typical result for an individual subject is given in Figure 4 which illustrates a further important fact about the operations of acoustic cues and about the perception of speech sounds. Every time the subject hears stimuli 1 and 2 he judges that the sound belongs to the class /b/, when he hears 5–8, to the class /d/ and 12–14, to the class /g/. There are three ranges of the stimuli over which he is in no doubt as to what phonemic class the sound

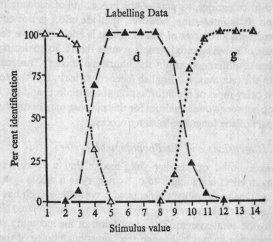

Figure 4. Summary of the results for an individual subject when labelling the stimuli represented in Figure 3. (From *Journal of Experimental Psychology*, 1957, vol. 54, p. 361).

should go into. Between these ranges, there are two areas of uncertainty where the stimuli are not identified consistently. These areas are comparatively narrow, however, and the three categories, /b/, /d/ and /g/ are quite sharply defined. This result led to further experiments designed to discover whether subjects' ability to discriminate remained constant over the whole range of stimuli or whether they were less sensitive to differences between sounds which fell unmistakably within one category. These studies showed that there was indeed a tendency for differential sensitivity to be greater in the boundary regions between the categories than over the range that was well within the categories (see Figure 4). This confirms the view put forward earlier that our perception of speech is influenced by the phonological system and hence is the fruit of the language-learning process. People who have different native languages learn different phonological systems and develop different patterns of sensitivity to acoustic features of one kind or another.

There is a strong tendency, then, for speech sounds to be *perceived* in categories, as part of the processing of acoustic information. It is interesting, however, that the effect is not equally marked with all classes of sound. There is good evidence that in the case of vowel sounds listeners acquire the ability to distinguish degrees of difference within the phonemic classes. This may be due to the fact that, for English listeners at least, it is the vowels which carry most of the information about dialects and discriminating between vowel qualities for this purpose may be an important part of the language-learning process.

Cue Dimensions and the Phonological System

It was pointed out earlier that recognizing a speech sound means in effect assigning it to one category in a whole system of classes. One result of experiments with synthetic speech has been to establish the existence of cue dimensions which relate sub-sets within the total system. The identifying of an incoming sound proceeds not so much through the immediate choice of the one category to which the sound belongs as through the use of acoustic cues to assign the sound to sub-sets. In English, for example, a noise component in the sound places it in a sub-set which includes fricatives, affricates and voiceless plosives; noise continued beyond a certain time in relation to the rest of the utterance puts it in the class of fricative consonants; absence of any underlying periodicity, in certain contexts, makes it a voiceless fricative; high-intensity noise places it in the sub-set /s, ʃ/ as opposed to /f, θ, h/; low-frequency noise components identify it as /ʃ/ and not /s/.

A good illustration of a cue dimension which identifies a sub-set of phonemes is the one referred to above, variation in the second formant transition. The stimuli shown in Figure 3 were used in experiments where subjects had to judge syllables as beginning with /b/, /d/ or /g/. The main function of this cue proves to be, however, to indicate the place of articulation of the sound. A minus transition, that is towards or away from a frequency lower than that of the main second formant, places the sound in the sub-set of sounds with labial articulation, a plus transition in the sub-set of velar sounds, and an intermediate transition in the sub-set of sounds with alveolar or dental articulation. The second formant cue has therefore to be combined with other cues to lead to the identification of a phoneme. A nasal consonant, for example, is recognized by the use of two cues, one indicating nasality and the second the place of articulation. The presence of two marked resonances, one at low frequency and another in the region of 2500 c.p.s., places the sound in the class of nasals, and the second formant transition marks it as bi-labial, alveolar or velar, that is /m/, /n/ or /ŋ/.

Acoustic Decoding of Stress and Tone

This account of acoustic processing has so far referred only to the abstracting of the phoneme string which forms the message. At the same level there takes place the processing of the acoustic information correlated with stress and tone in the linguistic system. The principles which operate here are the same as in phoneme decoding, that is to say the listener uses a variety of acoustic cues in recognizing any rhythm or intonation pattern. While acoustic analysis is a necessary preliminary to determining the cues, it cannot by itself show what the cues are or how they combine when the listener makes his decisions. In order to do this we have to isolate the cue dimensions, to study the effect of variation in a given dimension on listeners' judgements and to combine cues in a controlled and systematic way.

Both intonation and rhythm are clear examples of linguistic features which must depend upon relations among acoustic quantities. One of the principal cue dimensions for intonation is the fundamental frequency of the speech sound-waves and this obviously has different ranges in the speech of men, women and children, in different individuals and within the speech of one individual speaker, since we all change the 'key' of our utterances from moment to moment. It is the direction and extent of variations in fundamental frequency within short time spans which provide the chief cues for the decoding of intonation patterns. Similarly with rhythmic patterns, since speakers speak more quickly or more slowly, more loudly or more softly at different moments, the rate and the intensity of the sound sequence is changing all the time, and yet the listener recognizes the same stress patterns. The cues for these must therefore consist of relations within these dimensions.

There has been a considerable body of experimental work on the acoustic cues for stress and tone and there is not space to review this here. To give one example, it has been possible to show by experiments with synthetic speech that English listeners' stress judgements are cued by the relative duration of parts of the sound sequence, their relative intensity, fundamental frequency and spectrum. These cues interact in a very complex fashion; for example, when there is variation in fundamental frequency in the stimulus, this will cue the recognition of an intonation pattern which has an overriding influence on stress judgements. Of the other dimensions, the listener appears to attach weight to relative duration, relative intensity and spectrum in descending order (Fry, 1958, 1965).

Summary of English Acoustic Cues

The examples given in the preceding sections are intended to give an overall impression of the way in which the acoustic processing of the speech input works. There is a considerable body of information now available about many aspects of the process but there remains also much that is undiscovered. We are far from being able to specify a complete cue system for English sounds in all contexts or indeed for all classes of sounds. To do so would for one thing call for a greater knowledge than we now have of effects of interaction between various cues and the weight any cue will have in influencing the listener's decision.

The following notes summarize, in a very simplified form, some of the conclusions prompted by experiments with synthetic speech about the operation of single cues in the identification of English sounds and may serve to round off this sketch of the present state of knowledge concerning the acoustic processing of speech.

RECOGNITION OF VOWELS

The principal cue for vowel recognition is the frequency and intensity relations of the first two peaks in the spectrum, with some contributions from overall intensity and duration of parts of the utterance.

RECOGNITION OF CONSONANTS

Voiced-voiceless distinction. Presence or absence of periodicity and particularly the moment at which periodicity begins (voice onset time). Relative duration of successive parts of the wave.

Manner of articulation

Plosive: interrupted wave, short noise burst.

Affricate: interrupted wave, longer noise.

Fricative: continuous noise.

Nasal: periodic wave, spectrum peaks in low frequency (below 500 c.p.s.) and mid-frequency bands (2000–2500 c.p.s.).

Lateral: periodic wave, comparatively slow change of second-formant frequency, constant third formant.

Semi-vowels: slow changes of first- and second-formant frequencies.

Place of articulation. Direction and extent of second-formant transition, frequency location of peaks in noise or noise-burst spectrum, width of noise band, overall intensity of noise.

LINGUISTIC PROCESSING IN SPEECH

The end result of the decoding of a spoken message is that the listener's brain arrives at the sentence which was generated in the speaker's brain. The only information which the listener draws from the external world to enable him to do this is that contained in sensory impressions, first and foremost the sound-waves of speech and then the visual and other impressions which constitute the whole context of the message and which all contribute something to the decoding process. The acoustic input is dealt with in the way that has just been sketched out; the rest of the operation is entirely a work of reconstruction by the listener's brain based on the vast store of linguistic information which it carries.

The elaborate and complex operations which go on during the acoustic processing of speech, and they are far more complex than we have been able to indicate in the first section of this chapter, form no more than the prelude to the real work of decoding a spoken message. They yield some decisions as to the phonemic categories in which incoming sounds must be placed, but as we have already said, the redundancy of the language plays an important part even at this stage.

Shannon (1950) suggested a very simple and elegant method of demonstrating a reader's ability to predict the course of printed English which showed that sequential constraints progressively limit the choice of possible letters as one proceeds through a sentence and that the knowledge of the choices is accessible to a reader. Someone who is familiar with printed English is asked to guess in sequence the letters making up a sentence which he has not seen. He suggests letters of the alphabet, one after the other, and is told when he puts forward the correct one for the first position. He then guesses the letter in the second position and so on through the sentence. Suppose that at one point he gets as far as establishing that a particular word begins *ex-*. The range of choices open to him for filling the third position in the word is quite wide, perhaps a dozen letters in all. If later it appears that the sequence is *exch-* the possible choices at the fifth position are reduced to two and should this position be filled by *e*, then there are no alternatives for the next four positions and the subject is compelled to complete the word *exchequer*.

In an exactly similar way the phoneme string which constitutes a spoken message is subject to constraints, and knowledge of these is used by the listener all the time he is decoding speech. Even at the beginning of a message, all the phonemes in the system are not equally probable and this limits the possibilities which have to be scanned in the acoustic processing. The listener at once begins to construct a probable phoneme string determined by acoustic processing, higher-order linguistic constraints and context in its widest sense. It is not necessary for him to identify on an acoustic basis every sound that comes in and he does not in fact do so. There are many points in the sequence where, as in the printed word *exchequer*, the language permits no alternatives so that reconstruction of the message proceeds temporarily on a purely linguistic basis. The function of acoustic processing is in fact twofold: it furnishes the raw material, as it were, upon which the listener bases his predictions of the phoneme string, and it also provides a running confirmation that the predictions have been fulfilled. If at any point the confirmation is not forthcoming, because of an error by the speaker, a previous error in acoustic decoding or the occurrence of a highly unpredictable item in the message, the listener is forced into fresh action, usually in the sense of revising his predictions or perhaps questioning the speaker.

Just as the speaker, in generating his message, is working on a number of different levels at the same time, so the listener in reconstructing it has to work on the same levels and, like the speaker, he works on them all at the same time. This means that, as the message is coming in, the listener is forming the phoneme string, segmenting it into morphemes and forming the morpheme string, reconstructing the word sequence and thus building up the sentence. It might be argued that this postulates an unnecessarily complicated decoding process, and that the same result would be obtained if the listener simply stored up the phoneme string until it reached sentence length, and then made a decision on the whole sentence. Apart from fundamental questions about the nature of a sentence, which such a hypothesis disregards, there is compelling evidence in favour of the theory of multi-level decoding to be found in the correction of errors which goes on in speech (Fry, 1964a, 1969). It is the common experience of every listener that he can and does make corrections at any point in the message where the speaker makes an error. For decoding purposes, he will replace one phoneme, one morpheme, one word by another at the moment when the error occurs; he does not wait until the completion of the sentence and then replace it by a corrected whole sentence. Such corrections are not generally made explicit, but when they occur the listener becomes for the moment aware of the decoding operation. Sometimes they are brought further into the light when the listener makes some such remark as: 'Did you know you said . . . ?' In one form or the other they happen often enough to make it plain that in speech reception the message is built up on phoneme, morpheme, word and sentence level at the same time.

This parallel working of the decoding apparatus requires a great deal of short-term storing of items at each level. The correction of errors, again, demands that the immediate past history of the message at each level should be held in store. All listeners are familiar with the sensation of going back in a message and making a correction at a point well before the one the speaker has actually reached. This too is sometimes made explicit, as when we say: 'I thought you said . . .'. The time between the error and its correction may be quite long, a matter of seconds in some cases, so it would seem that comparatively long sequences are held in the temporary store before it is cleared. A further indication of this is the case of communication made difficult by noise or distance, in which the listener is aware of a considerable time lag 'before the penny drops'.

Higher-Level Linguistic Constraints

So far only sequential dependencies at the phoneme level have been specifically mentioned as playing a part in the decoding, but at the higher levels, too, this factor is all-important. If we try to picture the operation that is taking place, let us say, at the word level, we see that a string of morphemes is being built up which must be identified as a word. This will be done by matching it with some item in the word store. (Words and morphemes will be stored in a form different from that in which they are realized in speech: cf. the chapter on morphology by Matthews, pp. 96–114; see also the chapter on memory and perception by Johnson-Laird, pp. 261–70.) The store contains some tens of thousands of items (since it is here a question of the passive vocabulary) and it is obvious that no decoding operation can possibly depend on the scanning of the whole of this store; only quite restricted sub-sets of the items will be scanned for the purpose. Several factors help to select these sub-sets; syntactic constraints may make it certain that the word is an adjective, or a verb, and so on; semantic constraints may introduce another limitation. In practice, however, the various elements in the context combine to throw up a very small set of words which are highly probable at that point in the word sequence and the scanning operation simply involves looking for a match between what is coming in and the most probable candidates. As fresh information continues to flow in, probabilities are continually re-calculated and hence the number of words that has to be scanned in the word store is always quite small.

This mode of operation fits in well with the view put forward by Broadbent (1967) that there is a 'response bias' in the reception of spoken words. This was based on experiments with dichotic stimulation. There is also a series of experiments by Miller and his co-workers on the influence of context at the syntactic and the lexical level. They were able to show that context had a major effect, both on the decoding and the recall of spoken messages, and that this is so precisely because of the restriction which it imposes upon the number of possible choices open to the listener (Miller, Heise & Lichten, 1951; Miller & Isard, 1963).

SUMMARY OF SPEECH DECODING

In conclusion we shall attempt to summarize briefly the operations involved in speech decoding. We must repeat that there is a vast amount we do not understand about the process; the only thing we can be sure of is that it is immensely more complex than we know. The steps are inevitably set out one after the other but it is important to remember that they represent parallel processes with the very minimum of 'real time' lag between any level and the next immediately below.

1. Incoming acoustic information is processed by the acoustic decoding mechanism which works on a complex of cues appearing in the input.

2. Knowledge of phonological constraints is combined with the results of acoustic processing; only a restricted set of phonemes is possible at any position.

3. The phoneme string is predicted on the basis of the items which are most probable acoustically and linguistically.

4. The phoneme string is segmented into morphemes by reference to knowledge of morpheme-forming rules.

5. Morpheme constraints are applied and morphemes identified by matching with the store of free and bound morphemes, beginning with the most probable item.

6. The morpheme string is formed into words matched with lexical items in the store, the choice being restricted by sequential dependencies.

7. The word sequence is formed which satisfies all syntactic and semantic constraints.

3. THE PRODUCTION OF SPEECH

John Laver

Articulatory phonetics has long been dominated, in practice, if not in theory, by what Laver refers to in this chapter as the 'postural' view of speech production; and the standard phonetic classification of sounds in terms of their 'place' and 'manner' of articulation reflects this. But the postural approach is now giving way to the more dynamic 'parametric' approach, which looks upon 'the physiological system for speech [as] a single, complex system in which the continuous interacting activities of the various linked components are intricately coordinated in time'.

The parametric approach to phonetics leads fairly directly, as Laver explains, to an interest in the neural control systems capable of coordinating the complex movements of the vocal organs during speech production. The study of the functional aspects of the neural control systems used in speech production falls into what Laver calls 'neurolinguistics', and his chapter is primarily concerned with the contribution that the phonetician can make to this important new area of research.

Conclusions about the properties of the neurolinguistic control systems have to be based on observation of the output of the systems; Laver discusses in some detail the conclusions that can be drawn from observation of the characteristics of fluent speech, slips of the tongue and their corrections, and hesitation-signals, about the way that stored linguistic information is selected and arranged into programs for particular utterances, and monitored for successful performance.

IN his Introduction to this book John Lyons suggests that in the past fifty years linguistics has tended to be 'somewhat insistent on the need for autonomy' (p. 8). There is an important sense in which phonetics has not participated in any insistence on autonomy that may have characterized the rest of linguistics in this period. Phonetics, as the study of the medium of spoken language (Abercrombie, 1967:2), has always accepted that, in order to build a theory of how the apparatus of speech works and is used, it must employ a variety of concepts from a wide range of disciplines such as anatomy, physiology, physics and psychology. The boundaries of phonetics as a subject have been set primarily by the object of its study, speech, rather than by considerations of methodology. Phonetics stands at the intersection of all disciplines concerned in any way with the study of speech, and takes parts of its conceptual stock, and parts of its methodology, from each one of them. An essential characteristic of phonetics is thus that it is above all else a synthesizing subject.

That linguistics as a whole should now be less insistent on the principle of autonomy is not an isolated tendency; it is part of a marked trend in all the behavioural sciences, perhaps exemplifying a general process of maturation that these disciplines are undergoing. Where earlier research tended to be somewhat constrained by disciplinary territorial barriers, these barriers now seem to be rapidly weakening, and multidisciplinary approaches to particular problems are increasingly being undertaken (Hymes, 1964; Smith, 1966; Lenneberg, 1967). As a direct result of this trend towards multidisciplinary synthesis there has been a growth of interest in the exploration of topics in the borderlands between the territories of the older disciplines. Examples of such explorations which have a point of departure in linguistics are the fields of psycholinguistics (Saporta, 1961; Lyons & Wales, 1966), and sociolinguistics (Bright, 1966; Fishman, 1968a; Pride, pp. 287–301 below). A similar example, and one which will be the major topic of comment in this chapter, is the field of neurolinguistics.

The movement towards bringing multidisciplinary viewpoints to bear on particular problem areas is very attractive to phonetics, given the inherent synthesizing character of the subject. The next decade or so may well see a number of attempts by phoneticians to locate the theory of speech in broader social, psychological and biological frameworks than have hitherto been used.

This chapter is specifically concerned with the production of speech. The most important new development in the study of this area in recent years, and one with far-reaching implications, is the attempt to use data from direct observation of speech to infer functional properties of the neural control systems in the brain's organization of speech production.

It is difficult to find a satisfactory specific and adequate adjective to characterize such a functional model of the brain's control of speech production. The terms 'neurophysiological', 'neuropsychological' and 'neurolinguistic' each reflect some characteristic of the model. Because the current state of neurological research into language activities restricts us largely to a consideration of functions rather than of detailed mechanisms, perhaps the least satisfactory of the possible labels is 'neurophysiological'. 'Neuropsychological' would be somewhat more acceptable, and would be compatible with a suggestion recently expressed by Chomsky (1968:1) that linguistics is itself a branch of cognitive psychology. However, until this area of research becomes mature enough to acquire a commonly agreed label, the most neutral term 'neurolinguistic', is probably the most satisfactory.

If phoneticians and linguists are to succeed in constructing a neurolinguistic model of the brain's control of speech, thus contributing to the necessarily multidisciplinary study of cerebral functions, they will have to modify their theoretical equipment to accommodate concepts and methods not only from neurophysiology and neuropsychology, but also from other disciplines such as control-systems engineering, computer science and information retrieval.

This expansion of phonetic and linguistic interests into the neurolinguistic processes of speech production may seem a novel departure, but I would like to show that it can be partly explained as a logical development of a trend which has its roots in the history of phonetics in the changing philosophy of articulatory analysis in the early part of this century.

The inherently dynamic nature of the articulation of the speech organs has been recognized for a long time. One of the first writers to comment on this was Hermann Paul (1886), when he wrote that 'A word is not a united compound of a definite number of independent sounds, of which each can be expressed by an alphabetical sign; but it is essentially a continuous series of infinitely numerous sounds, and alphabetical symbols do no more than bring out certain characteristic points of this series in an imperfect way.' Nevertheless, for a long time after Paul wrote this, phonetics continued to find it expedient to describe the articulation of speech as if it consisted of momentarily static postures of the speech organs, linked by glides from one posture to the next (Abercrombie, 1965:121). The phoneticians of the early part of this century acknowledged that these segmental concepts were merely fictions convenient for the purpose of description anp categorization; but however nominal their adherence to this postural view of articulation, it had the unavoidable and prejudicia-effect of focusing their theoretical attention on the static descripl tion of the vocal organs in the particular postures which they thought characterized the material of language. This was especially limiting, for three reasons: it distracted attention from the time-varying, parametric aspects of articulation, it overemphasized the individual independence of a small number of vocal organs, and it tended to perpetuate the attitude towards an alphabetic segmentation of the speech continuum that Paul had criticized.

Dissatisfaction with the unnecessary and inhibiting restraints of the static, postural view grew during the 1920s and 1930s in the teaching, for example, of J. R. Firth and Stephen Jones in London, and of a number of experimental phoneticians in other countries such as Stetson (1928) in America and Menzerath, Lacerda and von Essen in Germany. Gradually speech has been recognized more explicitly as 'a dynamic process involving many coordinated articulatory processes, rather than as a sequence of relatively static postures involving only one or two of the articulatory organs' (Henderson, 1965:16). The dynamic concept of speech production is now one of the foundations of modern articulatory phonetics, though the old-fashioned postural view has not entirely disappeared: it continues to exert an insidiously seductive influence, especially through some of the implications underlying parts of the established descriptive terminology (Henderson, 1965). Descriptive articulatory theory is still therefore far from maximally efficient (Fant, 1968), and the attempt to improve the adequacy and universality of general phonetic descriptive categories has produced a number of recent publications (Peterson & Shoup, 1966; Ladefoged, 1965).

The chief effect of the more dynamic view of speech was that it concentrated analytic attention on the time-varying parameters of articulation. This was particularly encouraged by the invention in the early 1940s of the sound spectrograph (Koenig, Dunn & Lacy, 1946; Potter, Kopp & Green, 1947; Pulgram, 1959). The advent of this instrument was a milestone in the study of speech, as it allowed phoneticians to have, for the first time, easy and relatively cheap access to a wide range of objective, quantifiable information about the acoustics of speech production, and hence to the underlying parameters of articulation.

The sound spectrograph provides graphic records of the spectral and temporal distribution of acoustic energy in any given utterance. The analysis of spectrographic data enabled phoneticians to formulate hypotheses about the nature of the acoustic parameters essential for the minimal specification of intelligible speech. For these hypotheses to be tested, they had to be able to produce synthetic simulations of the minimal acoustic specifications of the sounds of speech, and to use them as experimental stimuli to be presented to human listeners for identification in linguistic terms. People have been trying to produce synthetic speech by means of machines for a very long time, going back at least to von Kempelen in 1769 (Flanagan, 1965:166), and by the time the sound spectrograph appeared, a variety of mechanical and electrical speech synthesizers had been invented which were suitable for testing hypotheses about the intelligibility of synthesized material.

Efforts to synthesize acceptable speech from a minimum amount of acoustic information received an additional impetus during the early 1950s from the requirements of telecommunications. Before the arrival of orbital satellite telecommunication links, there was a growing pressure on the limited capacity of the existing telecommunication channels. Transmitting the totality of the acoustic characteristics of an utterance was becoming increasingly uneconomical, and one way of economizing was to transmit only those acoustic features of a speech message essential for intelligibility. This meant that a way had to be found of breaking down an utterance into its minimal acoustic parameters, and then reconstituting the transmitted parametric information at the other end of the telecommunication link into acceptable speech. There were two distinct problems: the automatic analysis of speech into acoustic parameters, and effective synthesis of the parameters into intelligible speech. Automatic speech analysis proved rather difficult, but a number of very successful electronic speech synthesizers were built, partly with a view to solving the problem of telecommunication economics, during the 1950s (Flanagan, 1965; Fant, 1968). The best synthetic speech is now indistinguishable from normal human speech.

Much of the early testing of hypotheses about the minimal acoustic specification of speech was done by means of programs controlling a synthesizer which were derived directly from phoneticians' interpretations of spectrographic analyses of actual human utterances, in a synthesis-by-analysis procedure. Enough is now known about the acoustic characteristics of typical speech behaviour to allow synthesis-by-rule, where the program controlling the synthesizer is produced by a computer according to sets of rules drawn up by phoneticians and communications engineers (Holmes, Mattingly & Shearme, 1964). The provision of computer speech immediately opens up a wide range of possible technological applications.

The acoustic analysis and synthesis of speech attracted a great deal of research in the 1950s and early 1960s (Lehiste, 1967). However, in this explosive growth of research effort the attention of many workers tended to be monopolized by the study of the acoustic parameters themselves, to the relative disadvantage of the underlying articulatory parameters. This period of acoustic research did achieve remarkably comprehensive and important results, well represented by Fant's (1960) *Acoustic Theory of Speech Production*, but it seems generally agreed that in the last three or four years interest has swung away from the acoustics of speech, back towards the study of articulatory aspects (Lehiste, 1967: vi).

An increasing variety of instrumental analytic techniques are now being applied to the study of articulatory dynamics, and these techniques all provide a continuous record of sequential articulatory events in real time, as they happen. The foremost technique, and one which is arousing wide interest, is electromyography – the registration of the minute electrical voltages produced by muscles as they contract (Fromkin, 1966; Fromkin & Ladefoged, 1966). This technique has been made extremely fruitful by the addition of a computer to process the vast amount of electromyographic data produced in even short utterances (Fromkin & Ladefoged, 1966: 233).

Another promising technique is electrokymography, which records the continuous changes in oral and nasal airflow during speech. This produces detailed information about the timing and type of movements the vocal organs superimpose on the outflowing airstream during articulation. Complementary information about where in the mouth contact is made between tongue and palate can be gained from electropalatography, which uses an artificial palate into which is inserted a number of electrodes for registering the contacts (Kydd & Belt, 1964; Kozhevnikov & Chistovich, 1965).

A fourth technique used for recording the dynamics of articulation is cineradiography (Subtelny & Subtelny, 1962). Modern developments of image intensification, which allows a correspondingly lower dosage of X-ray, should encourage its increasingly wide use.

I suggested above that, throughout the post-war period of research into acoustic phonetics, interest was mainly focused on the parametric approach to the acoustic analysis and synthesis of speech. This emphasis on parameters has been carried over into current articulatory studies (Abercrombie, 1965: 120–24), reinforcing the dynamic view of articulation inherited from the 1930s. A significant area of research which is emerging as the product of this interest in articulatory parameters is the exploration of the possibility of constructing a physiological speech synthesizer (Ladefoged, 1964). A working model of the vocal organs would have exactly the same usefulness for articulatory phonetics as the acoustic synthesizers had for acoustic phonetics: namely, it would enable a phonetician to test the validity of a hypothesis about the articulatory dynamics of an utterance by providing a synthetic simulation whose linguistic intelligibility could be judged by listeners.

An improved knowledge of the acoustic and articulatory

characteristics of speech production has also served to strengthen the attitude that the physiological system for speech is not a set of independent vocal organs, but a single, complex system in which the continuous interacting activities of the various linked components are intricately coordinated in time. In a parametric approach, temporal considerations thus assume a major importance, and modern phonetics increasingly recognizes the need to give an adequate account, in describing the dynamics of articulation, of such temporal features as seriality, duration and rhythm.

Temporal behaviour in articulation can be remarkably delicately controlled: for example, one perceptually important difference between the articulations of the English words *bin* and *pin* is that the onset of vibration of the vocal cords is simultaneous with the moment of opening of the lips for [b], while in the case of *pin*, the onset is delayed for an interval, which can be as short as four-hundredths of a second, after the moment of opening of the lips. The phonetician is led straight into speculation about the nature of the neural systems that can achieve such precise control of the intricately complex musculature of the vocal organs.

Phoneticians are thus being persuaded, by their interest in giving adequate accounts of the dynamics of articulation, to give some thought to the functional properties of the neural section of the neuromuscular speech-chain. I deliberately emphasize the distinction between the two different sections of the neuromuscular speech-chain: namely, between the muscles themselves, as the peripheral terminal of the chain, and the more central neural systems that control the activities of these muscles. The study of speech production could be said to be correspondingly divided into two areas: the study of articulation, concerned with the dynamics of movements of the vocal organs; and the study of the neural functions which construct the neurolinguistic program of motor commands to be carried out by the articulatory muscles. Until very recently, phonetics has largely limited its interest in speech production to the study of articulation; it is now in the process of expanding its theoretical apparatus to include the study of neurolinguistic programming.

It seems quite certain, however, that the development of a

really comprehensive model of neurolinguistic programming is a very long way ahead. A major difficulty is the scarcity of persuasive evidence. To all intents and purposes, the healthy adult brain is not itself accessible to neurolinguistic experiment. There is thus no possibility of directly observing the neural mechanisms involved in constructing a neurolinguistic program. However, it is a widely accepted research strategy that one can infer the properties of an unobservable control system from an examination of the output of that system. Hughlings Jackson, the great neurophysiologist, is reported as once saying 'The study of the causes of things must be preceded by a study of the things caused' (Beveridge, 1961). If we want to know how the brain controls speech, we must first look at speech itself.

There are likely to be two major benefits from any success that phonetics may have in inferring the properties of the neurolinguistic control system. Firstly, it is obviously desirable that we should be able to give a more comprehensive account of language behaviour by adding a neurolinguistic component to linguistic theory. (It is also noteworthy that in neurolinguistics the subdisciplinary boundary between phonetics and linguistics, which has always been of doubtful validity, is largely disappearing.) Secondly, and this is of wider importance, discoveries about the neural control of speech will have general applications to the whole range of cerebral control of voluntary, serial behaviour. Lashley (1951), in a classic article on this topic, supported the view that the study of speech production is a uniquely valuable point of entry into such speculations. He quotes Fournié (1887): 'Speech is the only window through which the physiologist can view the cerebral life', and suggests that 'the problems raised by the organization of language seem ... to be characteristic of almost all other cerebral activity' (Lashley, 1951).

The strategy of inferring properties of control systems from their output can be applied not only to the efficient operation of these systems, but also to their output when malfunctions occur. The evidence from characteristic malfunctions is, if anything, more penetrating than that obtained when the system is operating efficiently. We can distinguish five different conditions of speech to which this strategy can be applied: error-free, continuous speech;

speech containing errors such as slips of the tongue, and their corrections; speech containing discontinuities such as hesitation signals; speech during the language-acquisition period in young children; and speech 'in dissolution', in the gross malfunctions of the speech production process in speech pathology.

It seems very probable that studies of language acquisition and speech pathology will eventually make an important contribution to the development of an adequate neurolinguistic model of the normal, healthy, adult brain, but I shall largely restrict discussion in this chapter to error-free continuous speech, slips of the tongue and their correction, and hesitation signals, which have so far provided the principal evidence.

Before going further, I should emphasize that error-free, continuous speech should not be equated with 'normal speech'. Spontaneous, normal speech is normally far from completely free from errors, and often contains slips of the tongue (Boomer & Laver, 1968); it is also nearly always far from completely continuous, almost invariably containing a variety of hesitation signals, such as pauses, repetitions, and vocalizations such as 'er', 'ah' and 'um' (Boomer, 1965; Goldman-Eisler, 1968).

Using evidence from the speech output, any adequate neurolinguistic model will have to account in detail for the different functions involved in the generation of any speech utterance. The outline which follows below of the neurolinguistic functions is necessarily very simplistic, because of the highly speculative nature of the conclusions which have so far been reached, and because of the severe complexity of the problem.

There seem to be five chief functions: the ideation process, which initiates the approximate semantic content of any verbal message the speaker wishes to communicate; the permanent storage of linguistic information; the planning process, which constructs an appropriate neurolinguistic program for the expression of the idea; the execution of the neurolinguistic program by the articulatory muscle systems; and the monitoring function, which allows the detection and correction of errors. I shall refer to these functions as *ideation, storage, program-planning, articulation* and *monitoring*, respectively.

The least penetrable of the five functions, as far as neurolinguistics is concerned, is that of ideation. The initiation of ideas, of whatever degree of cognitive complexity, constitutes perhaps the most difficult issue raised in considerations of cerebral functions. Neurolinguistics can make two contributions of interest to the cognitive psychology of this area: firstly, it can bring the resources of the linguistic theory of semantics to the description of the semantic structure of the idea expressed; and secondly, it can say something about the relation between the ideation process and the program-planning and monitoring processes, as we shall see below.

In discussing the permanent storage of linguistic information, it is useful to distinguish between *what* is stored, and *how* it is stored. In considering *what* is stored, it is important to recognize that the various neural units used in speech production do not necessarily have any one-to-one correlation with the linguistic elements and the rules governing their combination currently posited by any theory of descriptive linguistics (Peterson, 1968). A starting point is to say simply that storage consists of the neural correlates of potential linguistic behaviour. By itself this is a self-evident statement, but its interest lies in the search it implies for the nature of the relationship between neural units and linguistic elements and rules; a firm hypothesis about the actual relationship is crucial for any adequate neurolinguistic model.

I shall return in a moment to the current search for the characteristics of neural organization of speech, but before I do so, I would like to offer some comments on *how* neurolinguistic information may be stored.

The search for the neural memory trace, or engram, has occupied many neurophysiologists for a long time, without their reaching definitive and compelling results (Lashley, 1950). Two general hypotheses are the possibilities of local storage and non-local storage. Some evidence for local storage in precisely defined areas of the brain comes from speech pathologies correlated with known localized brain damage. It seems unlikely, however, that any extreme theory of local storage is valid for speech. Lenneberg (1967: 60) comments that 'The narrow localization theory, which holds that engrams for words or syntactic rules are stored in certain aggregates of cells, cannot be in accord with the clinical facts.'

An interesting theory of non-local storage has recently appeared, in a model of the memory process based on holography. Holography was originally a concept in the field of optics. The holographic principle is used in photography, using laser-illumination of optical interference patterns themselves originally produced by a laser, to give an apparently three-dimensional optical image. The relevance of holography for memory is that, on the holographic optical record, information about the recorded object is not stored locally, as it would be on a normal photographic film, but uniformly, at every point of the record. Holography thus supplies a model of non-local storage of information which has had an immediate application to the neurophysiology of memory (Longuet-Higgins, 1968; Pribram, 1969).

A major problem in considering the relationship between the storage system and the program-planning function is how the latter can retrieve necessary information from the former. Information retrieval is of course a problem which is not restricted to the field of human memory: in a sense, it is a central problem of our whole technological society, and not surprisingly a new discipline has appeared, devoted to its study. Many of the concepts which it has developed (see the chapter by Bott, pp. 215–28 below) can be applied directly, if cautiously, to the question of how the brain might retrieve neurolinguistic data stored in its memory.

For any retrieval system to work economically, an addressing system is needed for the data in storage. Errors of retrieval can tell us something about the characteristics of such an addressing system. Broadbent (1966: 289) writes 'It is extremely plausible that, in picking out a particular address in storage, one will occasionally go to the wrong address. But the errors which are made will presumably not be random, but rather will be linked to the way in which different possible addresses are organized together.' A clue to one sort of addressing system for lexical storage lies in the tentative hypotheses we explore in trying to recall a forgotten name or word. In these circumstances, we usually seem fairly confident of the rhythmic pattern of the word, and the number and approximate segmental structure of the syllables, though less confident of the identity of all but one or two of the particular segments within the syllables (Brown & McNeill, 1966). On this basis, we can generate a number of words with a similar rhythm and structure to the forgotten word, which can act as associative stimuli leading to its eventual recovery. That is to say, we generally know what area of the lexical store to search for a partially forgotten word, in terms of a phonological rhythm-and-structure addressing system.

It seems extremely likely that the system of storage can have a variety of associative addressing indices. One principal index is almost certainly the semantic index. For example, some slips of the tongue show that lexical addresses can be organized on an associative semantic basis, in such slips as *sleast*, where, in the attempt to retrieve *least*, *slightest* was also activated, and the brain failed to complete its choice between them before the program was articulated. Another associative addressing system is the one based on experiential association that many 'Freudian' slips of the tongue suggest (Freud, 1901).

Finally, on the subject of storage, obviously very long-term memory is involved, and the processes of acquisition, retention and use of the memory-store in speech are subject to the same factors of learning, recall, confusion, and forgetting as any other sort of utilization of memory (cf. the chapter by Johnson-Laird, pp. 261–70 below). The storage system can thus be investigated by using the techniques of experimental psychology. In this connexion, attempts to explore the properties of the lexical storage system by means of word-association tests have resulted in a very large body of literature (cf. the chapter by Clark, pp. 271–86 below). A particularly interesting recent approach is that of Kiss (1967, 1969), who is developing a computer model of lexical selection in which the retrieval operation works as a stochastic process.

I have implied that the retrieval of selected linguistic information from the memory store, with its necessary sub-processes of search and recognition, constitutes part of the program-planning function. The characteristics of the program-planning function make up the central core of any neurolinguistic model of speech production and we have seen that we can infer some properties of the process of retrieving linguistic information from the memory store. However, we have to acknowledge that in general we still know very little about how the brain goes about constructing a neurolinguistic program, at least at the lexical, morphological and syntactic levels. We shall see below that neurolinguistic research has had some small success in reaching conclusions about the neural reality of some phonological units, and about the principles of their neural organization into longer programs, but it would be very premature, at this stage of research, to suggest that the brain actually makes use of neural elements or operations that correspond directly to any of the higher-level structural units or rules laid down in current theories of descriptive linguistics.

A temporizing formulation that avoids such premature commitment would be simply that the planning function organizes a program specifying the neural correlates of the linguistic characteristics of the idea the speaker intends to communicate. This commits us only to the simplistic and convenient position that program planning involves the selection and eventual temporal organization of the neural correlates of lexical items and their morphological and syntactic arrangement, together with their associated phonology – the criterion for each lexical, morphological or syntactic choice being that it should be semantically relevant to the expression of the speaker's initial idea.

This formulation emphasizes that the relation between the idea and the neurolinguistic program is a semantic one. This is a difficult area to conceptualize, precisely because it is only possible to discuss ideas in terms of their expository linguistic programs. Miller, Galanter and Pribram (1960) quote a passage by William James (1890) which I think captures the nature of this difficulty with great clarity:

And has the reader never asked himself what kind of a mental fact is his intention of saying a thing before he has said it? It is an entirely definite intention, distinct from all other intentions, an absolutely distinct state of consciousness, therefore; and yet how much of it consists of definite sensorial images, either of words or of things? Hardly anything! Linger, and the words and things come into the mind; the anticipatory intention, the divination is there no more. But as the words that replace it arrive, it welcomes them successively and calls them right if they agree with it, it rejects them and calls them wrong if they do not. It has therefore a nature of its own of the most positive sort, and yet what can we say about it without using words that belong to the later mental facts that replace it?

This passage implies that the planning function, in retrieving items from the memory store, activates more items than it finally selects for inclusion in the neurolinguistic program to be articulated. This is well supported by those slips of the tongue, mentioned above, where the brain fails to complete its planning choice between competing possible alternatives before the speech-program reaches the articulation stage. A lexical example would be the slip mentioned above: *didn't bother me in the sleast* with competition between *slightest* and *least* (Boomer & Laver, 1968: 10). A syntactic example would be: *He behaved as like a fool* with competition between *like a fool* and either or both of *as if he were a fool* and *as though he were a fool*.

A number of conclusions can be drawn from the suggestion that more items are activated than are selected for inclusion in the final program. Firstly, because the competing alternatives, from amongst which one candidate is finally selected, are presumably all relatively appropriate semantically, the initial activation of a given part of the memory store must be directed on a semantic basis, making use of a semantic addressing system. Secondly, the planning function has to be able to scrutinize the competing candidates, assess their degree of semantic relevance to the expression of the initial idea, and choose the most appropriate item. The semantic structuring of the initial idea thus serves as a predisposition towards both activating particular areas of the memory store, and choosing the most relevant of the individual items that have been activated.

That such a choice between competing candidates seems often to be made is one theoretical justification, following William James, for treating ideation as a separate function from neurolinguistic program planning.

To separate the ideation function from the planning function is not to imply that the latter may not influence the former. It seems intuitively reasonable to assume that the specific restrictions and associations characterizing particular items that are activated by the planning function may allow the brain to reach a revised, and perhaps more precise, formulation of the original idea, which in turn may lead to a revision of parts of the neurolinguistic program.

In trying to infer the characteristics of the neural organization of a speech program from a detailed examination of articulation, one particularly important conclusion has been reached about neural correlates of phonological units: the preparation and articulation of a speech program is not performed on a sound-by-sound, or even on a word-by-word basis. It is much more likely that neural elements corresponding to much longer stretches of speech are assembled in advance, and then allowed to be articulated as a single continuous program.

The concept of a series of skilled movements being prepared as a sequence, in advance of execution, has been recognized for some time. Craik (1947: 61) suggested that complex patterns of muscular movements, as in typewriting, could be prepared and 'triggered off as a whole'. In the field of phonetics, the concept of anticipatory adjustments in articulation is of very long standing; Stetson (1928: 203) aptly called it the 'law of prevision'. More recently, Lashley (1951) wrote that 'There are indications that, prior to the internal or overt enunciation of a sentence, an aggregate of word units is partially activated or readied.'

The linguistic unit in English which seems to be the most promising candidate for the typical preassembled stretch is what has variously been called a 'tone-group' (Halliday, 1967*b*), a 'phonemic clause' (Trager & Smith, 1951), or a 'syntagma' (Kozhevnikov & Chistovich, 1965). For convenience, I shall refer to this unit as the 'tone-group'. The tone-group is a stretch of speech which lasts, on average, for about seven or eight syllables, and which contains only one very prominent syllable, on which a major change of pitch occurs in intonation. This prominent syllable, which I shall refer to as the 'tonic syllable', is usually located at or near the end of the tone-group; as in *Ask them to come into the* gar*den*. The tone-group is also characterized by pauses, which are usually optional but sometimes mandatory, at its boundaries. Here the pauses are not perceived as hesitation signals, unless unduly prolonged; while internal pauses of even very short duration are heard by the listener as hesitations (Boomer & Dittman, 1962). The boundaries of the tone-group often, though not always, coincide with those of the syntactic clause. Lastly, the tone-group is the major unit for carrying intonation patterns, and has a simple correspondence with units of rhythm.

Evidence in error-free, continuous speech that the tone-group is the usual unit of neurolinguistic pre-preparation comes from the fact that intonational and (sometimes) syntactic choices in the early part of the tone-group can depend on choices made in the latter part, and logically therefore have to anticipate the later choices.

Evidence also comes from observation of slips of the tongue. Boomer & Laver (1968) suggest, after Lashley (1951), that tongue-slips are the result of transient malfunctions of the neural organization of a speech program, and show that slips can be plausibly explained as the neural interaction of elements 'simultaneously represented in an interim assembly' (Boomer & Laver, 1968: 9). In an analysis of slips involving segments representing phonemes, they note that the span of interference between an intended segment and the interfering segment usually comes within a single tone-group, and only rarely across a tone-group boundary. They also note that slips nearly always involve the tonic syllable, or the word in which the tonic syllable occurs (the 'tonic word'), usually as the location of the interfering segment. They comment that 'the typical slip involves interference from the tonic word *before* it is uttered' (1968: 8), since the tonic word is usually very late in the tone-group. This is good evidence for believing that 'the tone-group is handled in the central nervous system as a unitary behavioural act, and the neural correlates of the separate elements are assembled . . . before the performance of the utterance begins' (1968: 9).

The conclusion that the tone-group is probably the usual unit of neural pre-preparation was first suggested by Boomer (1965) in a study of hesitation pauses. Using the 'phonemic clause' (tone-group) as his frame of reference, he studied the location of hesitation pauses in the stream of speech, and addressed himself to the question of whether the phonemic clause or the word was the more plausible candidate for the unit of neural encoding in speech. He argued that if it was the word any pauses should occur before points of least certainty on the part of the speaker about his next choice, that is, before words of low probability of occurrence, which carry high information value. The tonic word, typically occurring late in the tone-group (phonemic clause), tends to have the lowest probability of occurrence of all the words in the tone-group: the word-unit model thus predicts that pauses, if they occur, would do so before the tonic word, usually late in the tone group. Boomer found, however, that hesitation pauses tend to occur towards the beginning of phonemic clauses (tone-groups), often after the first word. This evidence, he suggested, 'argues strongly for the phonemic clause rather than the word as the molar encoding unit of speech' (Boomer, 1965: 156).

The suggestion that the preparation of a neural program for the articulation of a tone-group involves the assembly of a number of neural elements, leads us to speculate about the size of the minimal neural unit used in such an assembly process. A small minimal unit seems essential. Ladefoged (1967: 169) points out that 'there must be some stored units: all conceivable utterances cannot be stored as indivisible units in the cortex so that they are available should there be an occasion for their use.' A number of researchers have tried to discover the size of the smallest invariant neural unit in the program of motor commands to the articulatory muscles, by looking closely at the dynamics of connected speech with the help of some of the instrumental techniques mentioned above, electromyography, electrokymography, electropalatography, cineradiography and spectrography. The two favoured candidates are the phoneme and the syllable. In search of the necessary neural invariances, researchers have tried either to demonstrate directly corresponding invariances of muscular activities in articulation, or to find an explanation capable of accounting for discrepancies between the posited neural invariances and observed articulatory variabilities.

Variations in articulation arise from the fact that, in connected speech, neighbouring articulations very often exercise an assimilatory influence on each other, with a tendency for the influence to be largely anticipatory rather than perseverative. The characteristics of an articulation representing a particular phonological element thus often vary according to the context in which the element occurs, especially when the articulation precedes another articulation using substantially the same groups of muscles.

Some researchers have reported findings of articulatory invariances that support the phoneme as the minimal neural unit. Workers at the Haskins Laboratories in New York, investigating adjacent phonemes whose articulations involve different muscle groups, report that they have found invariances in the electromyographic records of the articulations of each phoneme 'regardless of the context in which the phoneme occurs' (Liberman, Cooper, Harris, MacNeilage & Studdert-Kennedy, 1964). Even when adjacent phonemes involve a common muscle group, they report that 'there appears to be a common core of (electromyographic) activity that remains constant' when a phoneme appears in different contexts (Liberman *et al.*, 1967: 84). Similar evidence comes from MacNeilage (1963) : in an electromyographic study he found an invariance in his records for the production of /f/ which was independent of phonetic context.

Fromkin (1968) offers different evidence, which favours the syllable, and which is still based partly on articulatory invariances: in an electromyographic study of /b/ and /p/, she found that there were invariances in the data for each phoneme for its occurrence in either initial or final position in a syllable, but clear differences between the data for the two positions. In this case the brain obviously transmits different neural commands for a phoneme occurring in initial as opposed to final syllable position, and one hypothesis which could explain this is that the syllable constitutes the basic neural unit. She quotes Fry (1964: 219) in support, who writes 'it is at least plausible . . . that syllabification is one feature of the brain's control of motor speech activity, and that the true function of the syllable . . . is to form the unit of neural organization.'

An observation from the field of slips of the tongue also supports the syllable: Boomer and Laver, (1968: 7) found that 'segmental slips obey a structural law with regard to syllable place', in that syllable-initial segments interfere only with other syllable-initial segments, final only with final, and nuclear only with nuclear. This argues that the syllable is more than just a linguistic construct, and has a plausible reality as the smallest unit of neural programming, with segmental phonemes having neural invariance only in terms of their organization within the syllable.

Other work which largely favours the phoneme as the smallest neural unit, but which allows for variability in articulation depending on context, is that of Lindblom (1963), Öhman (1966, 1967), and Öhman, Persson and Leanderson (1967), all from Stockholm. This particularly promising work posits neural invariance of phoneme-sized units, and accounts for variations in articulation which depend on context in terms of different temporal relations between the neural commands for successive articulatory gestures.

One difficulty in trying to account for the variability of articulation is that we do not yet really know enough about the neuromuscular physiology of the vocal organs. We lack, for example, a thorough knowledge of the detailed physiology of the tongue, which is extremely complex. This may be remedied by the growing amount of electromyographic work that is currently being undertaken. Another particularly important area of neuromuscular physiology about which more information is needed is that of the detailed mechanisms of the brain's auditory, tactile and kinesthetic sensory feedback system (Ladefoged, 1967: 163; Fromkin, 1968: 62). The brain clearly uses some sensory feedback information to keep a continuous plot of the movement and position of the vocal organs; it may also use sensory feedback to modify the characteristics of some in-process motor commands, but Lashley (1951) points out that the execution of rapid, accurate movements is often completed in a shorter time than the reaction time for tactile or kinesthetic reports to be made on what happened. Control of continuous articulation thus cannot depend entirely for its accuracy on a chain of sensory-motor reactions. An interesting additional possibility of feedback-control of motor commands is the use of a neural scanning system to report on the motor commands themselves (Fromkin, 1968: 62), thus avoiding the time delay involved in sensory feedback.

While sensory information may not be of prime importance in controlling articulation directly, this information is nevertheless available to the brain for use in the last of the neurolinguistic functions noted in the early part of this chapter – the function of monitoring speech utterances for errors.

Monitoring an utterance for errors such as slips of the tongue is an automatic process which normally operates outside awareness. Not many slips of the tongue remain uncorrected by the speaker, so it seems fair to assume that the monitor system maintains nearly constant surveillance, and is therefore an integral part of the speech-producing process. A speaker also often makes a slip and corrects it without either the speaker or the listener being aware that a slip has occurred. The conscious perception of speech in some sense regularizes and idealizes the actual data of speech (Boomer & Laver, 1968). Conscious awareness is thus not a necessary part of the monitoring process.

The fact that a speaker does correct his slips of the tongue is fundamental evidence of a monitoring function in the speech-producing process. A logical prerequisite of the correction of errors is their detection, and it is useful to distinguish between the system which facilitates detection, and the system which allows correction. In discussing detection, we must be sure about what it is that is being detected. We speak of 'slips of the tongue', which implies literally that the slip is an error of articulation; in fact this is a misconception. Articulation consists of muscular actions, and any and every muscular contraction is the result of a specific neural control program. When errors occur, they are to be attributed to incorrect programs; 'slip of the tongue' is a misnomer : 'slip of the brain', or perhaps 'slip of the mind' would be more accurate.

Monitoring thus serves to detect errors in the neurolinguistic program. It is interesting to consider by what criteria a program can be said to be 'incorrect', or to contain an 'error'. One convenient approach is to say that an incorrect program is one which in some detail distorts the communication of the speaker's idea. It is striking that this leads us straight back into considerations of the relation between an idea and the linguistic program constructed to communicate that idea.

In this formulation, errors which distort accurate communication of the speaker's idea include not only slips of the tongue, but also linguistically orthodox programs which are in some detail semantically inappropriate to the speaker's idea. This gives two general categories of error: those which result in a form not found in the language, such as *didn't bother me in the sleast* (Boomer & Laver, 1968); and those which give linguistically permissible but semantically inappropriate results, such as Lashley's (1951) example of a spoonerism *Our queer old dean* for *Our dear old Queen*, and also such examples of corrections of imprecision as *He was sitting writing at his desk – er – table*. In other words, the revision of a semantically inappropriate choice in a program after its initial utterance is evidence of an error which can be discussed in the same overall framework as other sorts of program errors.

In the category of errors which give linguistically permissible results, it is often only the fact of correction that allows us, as observers, to know that an error has occurred.

The detection system that the monitoring function applies to the two categories of errors has to achieve two results: it has to establish the neurolinguistic characteristics of the program that was articulated, from sensory and neural reports, and it has to evaluate the appropriateness of the performed program for the semantic expression of the speaker's idea. On the basis of the evaluation, and taking into consideration the degree of the accuracy demanded by the situation, the brain can then take any necessary action towards stopping the current program and reprogramming an appropriate correction of the error.

The basic purpose of the monitoring system is to allow the brain to revise inappropriate neurolinguistic programs: it seems reasonable to suggest that the program-planning function may be similarly involved, as part of its normal creative activity, in editorial revision of programs before they reach the articulation stage. If revision is a shared purpose of the planning function and the monitoring function, then the revisionary activities of the two functions can be equated. The successful revisionary activity of the planning function leads to error-free speech, because revisions are carried out before the program is articulated; and the revisionary activity of the monitoring function is reflected in the correction, after articulation, of overt errors. The difference between error-free speech, and speech containing overt errors, in this view, would be a fairly trivial difference of the point in time at which the brain's revisionary resources were applied – before or after articulation of the program. This is substantially the same conclusion as that reached by Hockett, in his distinction between 'covert editing' and 'overt editing', where he writes 'Editing in the internal flow is *covert editing* ... In certain formal circumstances covert editing is thorough, and overt speech is unusually smooth. Much more typically, what is actually said aloud includes various signs of *overt editing*' (Hockett, 1967: 936). I would equate covert editing with revision carried out by the planning function, and overt editing with revision initiated by the monitoring function.

This is really a restatement of the view I put forward early in this chapter, that normal speech is not necessarily error-free speech, and by extension, that errors are part and parcel of the normal process of speech production, and therefore worthy of study.

I have offered some generalities about some aspects of a possible functional model of the brain's neurolinguistic control of speech production. In the present stage of neurolinguistic research these generalities are necessarily more than a little speculative. To conclude, I should emphasize that while models of cerebral functions are usually constrained by criteria of logic, some of these criteria may not be obeyed in the real situation. Donald Boomer wrote to me recently, with a very salutary comment on this topic. He wrote 'Man's brain is an evolutionary outcome, and there is no reason to believe that the evolutionary process is subject to the logical canons of parsimony and elegance. On the contrary in fact.'

4. PHONOLOGY

E. C. Fudge

Most linguists, until recently at least, have looked upon the pho-
neme as one of the basic units of language (p. 20). But they have
not all defined phonemes in the same way (and have frequently
arrived at conflicting analyses of the same data). Some linguists
have described phonemes in purely 'physical' terms; others have
preferred a 'psychological' definition. Some have argued that
grammatical considerations are irrelevant in phonological analysis;
others have maintained that they are essential. These are among the
issues that have divided the various 'schools' of phonology in recent
years, and they are discussed and exemplified by Fudge in his
chapter below. He goes on to explain that phonology, like syntax
and semantics (and indeed almost every branch of linguistics), has
now been strongly influenced by the development of generative
grammar (see p. 23).

I

WHEN the American linguist Edward Sapir (1884–1939) asked a
Southern Paiute speaker to transcribe some words of his language, he was surprised to find that the word pronounced ['paβa]*
was transcribed *papa*: the consonant of the second syllable was
objectively very different from the initial consonant (and any
English speaker, even if phonetically untrained, would have been
able to tell them apart), but for the Southern Paiute speaker they
were obviously felt to be 'the same' (Sapir, 1949: 48–9). Conversely the speaker of Arabic, even if phonetically untrained,
differentiates with ease between the initial consonants of the
English *keel* and *call* (phonetically [kiːl] and [qɔːl] respectively),
whereas the English speaker will not normally notice the difference unless he is phonetically trained. (Notice that the orthographic difference between *k* and *c* is irrelevant in this instance.)

* Forms in square brackets are phonetic transcriptions: for those phonetic
symbols not explained in the text, see Appendix to this chapter (pp. 94–5).

From the point of view of their function in the language we can call [p] and [β] in Southern Paiute *positionally determined variants* of the same linguistic element, or *allophones* of the same *phoneme*; likewise, in English [k] and [q] are allophones of the same phoneme /k/, and *keel* and *call* could be transcribed phonemically as /kiːl/ and /kɔːl/ respectively (cf. p. 20).

This question of 'variants of the same sound element' is in fact even more complex than these facts would indicate. Work using phonetic instruments (see pp. 57–9) has shown that it is extremely difficult for a speaker to produce an utterance, and then give an (objectively) absolutely identical repetition of it. However, it is extremely likely that two such (objectively differing) versions of an utterance will be recognized by another speaker of the language as being 'the same'. To put it another way, a good deal of variation is tolerated within each positionally determined variant: for example, a Turkish speaker will sometimes say [bana gel] for 'come here' (literally 'come to me'), sometimes [bana gæl], and sometimes with a vowel intermediate in quality between [e] and [æ], and other Turkish speakers will hear all the varieties of the utterance as 'the same'.

Yet another dimension of variation is illustrated by the fact that one person's pronunciation of a sound may be phonetically very different from another person's pronunciation of the 'same' sound; the vowels of Southern English [hæt] and Northern English [hat] are phonetically quite distinct, but both are utterances of the same word *hat*. In this case native speakers are aware of the phonetic difference. However, since most words containing an [æ] for the Southerner will have [a] in the corresponding position for the Northerner, on the functional level this difference is ignored and the sounds treated as 'the same'.

Summarizing, then, we have three types of variation:

1. *Variation tolerated from one repetition of an utterance to another*; in other words, variation tolerated within the norm of pronunciation of a given sound in a given position within one variety of speech.

2. *Variation of pronunciation of a sound according to the position in which it occurs*. We may subdivide this type (though it is prob-

77

ably impossible to draw a hard and fast boundary between the sub-types) as follows:

(a) Variation which could be attributed to the phonetic influence of neighbouring sounds; thus the [q] of *call* is articulated further back than the [k] of *keel* because the vowel which follows it is a back vowel (as opposed to the front vowel of *keel*). (Try saying *keel* after you have positioned your mouth to say *call* and you will find difficulty in pronouncing the word.)

(b) Variation which would need to be specified *ad hoc*; when not followed by a vowel, as in *keel*, the pronunciation of Standard English /l/ is usually accompanied by a bunching-up of the back part of the tongue. This gives the sound a so-called 'dark' resonance which is absent when the /l/ is followed by a vowel, as in *leak*. It would hardly be possible to attribute the difference between the [ɫ] of [kiːɫ] and the [l] of [liːk] to any feature of neighbouring sounds.

3. *Variation of pronunciation from speaker to speaker*; here we must exclude variations which involve the use of distinctively different sounds – the stressed vowel of American [təˈmeitou] *tomato* is the same vowel as that of American [pəˈteitou] *potato*, whereas that of British [təˈmɑːtou] is not the same as that of British [pəˈteitou], so the [ei]–[ɑː] variation in *tomato* is to be excluded from this type.

As the discipline of phonetics developed during the second half of the nineteenth century, and the task of phonetic transcription became more and more complex, it was noticed that this task could be greatly simplified by treating variations of types 1 and 2 as automatic and not noting them in the transcription.

To approach the matter from a rather different viewpoint, it is clear that every native speaker of a language has an intuitive knowledge of which (objectively different) sounds are 'the same' for him, and which are not. Such intuitive knowledge of the phonemes of his language forms the basis of the phonological structure of that language, but unfortunately does not lend itself to direct investigation: for this reason various kinds of theoretical framework have been proposed in terms of which the native speaker's knowledge can be made explicit and linked with the observable data. The implications of the term *phoneme* thus vary somewhat depending on the type of framework being used.

Views of the phoneme fall into four main classes:

(i) The 'mentalistic' or 'psychological' view, which regards the phoneme as an ideal sound at which the speaker aims; he deviates from this ideal sound partly because it is difficult to produce an identical repetition of a sound (cf. type 1 variation above) and partly because of the influence exerted by neighbouring sounds (cf. type 2(a) variation). This view originated with the Polish linguist Jan Baudouin de Courtenay (1845–1929), and something rather like it appears to have been adopted by Sapir. Variations of types 1 and 2(a) are handled well, though it is still not an easy matter to devise operational tests for establishing such 'ideal sounds'; for this reason the American linguist Leonard Bloomfield (1887–1949) and his followers rejected the view as untenable, and the English phonetician Daniel Jones, while basically favourable to the view, preferred in practice to take a 'physical' view (class (ii) below – cf. Jones, 1950: 11). However, variations of types 2(b) and 3 cannot be dealt with at all by the 'psychological' view; the fact that Sapir did deal with type 2(b) variation (1949: 53–4) indicates that his view transcended the 'mentalistic' or 'psychological' view (tending, in fact, towards the 'abstract' view – class (iv) below).

(ii) The 'physical' view, which regards the phoneme as a 'family' of sounds satisfying certain conditions, notably:

(a) The various members of the 'family' must show phonetic similarity to one another, in other words be 'related in character' (Jones, 1950: 10).

(b) No member of the 'family' may occur in the same phonetic context as any other; this condition is often referred to as the requirement of *complementary distribution*.

The extreme form of the 'physical' view (as propounded in 1950 by Daniel Jones, 1881–1967) excludes all reference to non-phonetic criteria in the grouping of sounds into phonemes (see below, pp. 89). Furthermore, the fact that members of different phonemes are capable of differentiating meanings (English [p] and [v] as in *pan* v. *van*), whereas members of the same phoneme (English [k] and [q]) are not, is said to be a *corollary* of the definition of the phoneme, and not its *basis* (Jones, 1950: 13–15). And yet it is not easy to see how [e] and [æ] in Turkish could be assigned to the same phoneme on any other grounds than that substitution of one for the other does not give rise to different words and different meaning (for instance, the apparently contrasting [bana gel] and [bana gæl] both mean 'come here', p. 77 above); in fact any cases in which type 1 variation is sufficiently wide will cause trouble unless the differentiating function of phonemes is taken as a basis and not a corollary of the definition.

Phonemic groupings are further subject to the requirement that the phonemic make-up of a word uniquely determines its phonetic form, and vice versa: thus if two words are pronounced alike (e.g. German *Bund* 'federation' and *bunt* 'coloured', which are both [bunt]), they must be phonemically alike (both /bunt/ in this case). This requirement is often called *bi-uniqueness*.

This view, unlike the 'psychological' view (i), handles type 2(b) variations; however, it fails to deal with variations of type 3 (Jones, 1950: 193–205). Jones restricts his phoneme theory to sounds of a single language, where 'a "language" is to be taken to mean the speech of one individual pronouncing in a definite and consistent style' (1950: 9). This is a legitimate restriction to impose on a technical term, but it means that Jones's theory cannot account for the fact that people who speak very differently from each other may yet be said to 'speak the same language' in the generally accepted sense of the term *language*.

(iii) The 'functional' view, which regards the phoneme as the minimal sound unit by which meanings may be differentiated (cf. Bloomfield, 1933: 79, 136) – a kind of converse of the 'physical' view, since meaning differentiation is taken to be a *defining* characteristic of phonemes. Thus [k] and [q] in English do not differentiate meanings, and hence cannot be definitely assigned to different phonemes but both form allophones of the phoneme /k/; they do differentiate meanings in Arabic, and hence must be assigned to different phonemes in Arabic. Moreover, we cannot say that phonemes *are* sounds or families of sounds, since, in every sound, only a certain number of the phonetic features are involved in the differentiation of meanings; it is these so-called *distinctive* features of the sound which make up the phoneme corresponding to it. For example, every segment of the English word [lædə] *ladder* includes the phonetic feature of voicing (vibration of the vocal cords), but this is a *distinctive* feature only in the third segment* – its absence here would give rise to a different word (*latter*), whereas if any other segments are given a voiceless pronunciation (one in which the vocal cords do not vibrate) the result is merely a peculiar version of *ladder*. The distinctiveness of such a feature thus depends on a contrast between it and other possible features belonging to the same set: thus, when distinctive, voicing contrasts with voicelessness. Some approaches have taken these oppositions as the basic elements of phonological structure rather than the phonemes: see in particular the work of N. S. Trubetzkoy (1890–1938) (Trubetzkoy, 1939: 60–75; 1949: 69–87) and R. Jakobson (Jakobson & Halle, 1956).

The 'functional' view avoids the difficulties which beset the 'physical' view as a result of wide variations of type 1; furthermore, since non-distinctive features are excluded from phonemes, variations of type 3 can be conveniently handled provided they are not too great.

(iv) The 'abstract' view, which regards phonemes as essentially independent of the phonetic properties associated with them – this enables *any* type 3 variations to be handled. We discuss this view further in section III.

II

Differences of sound quality of the sort which go to make up vowels and consonants are only one means of making linguistic distinctions – other phonetic differences available for this purpose (see pp. 45–7) include differences of duration (length or quantity), differences of intensity (loudness or stress), and differences of pitch (tone and intonation). Any of these differences may be distinctive alone or in combination with one or more others (Jones,

---

*There is considerable controversy about what phonetic feature is involved in the /t/-/d/ opposition in English. Between vowels (as here) the voicing difference is important, whereas in initial and final positions the pronunciation of /d/ may well be voiceless as well as that of /t/. In initial position, aspiration would be a more important feature, while length of the preceding vowel would constitute the chief difference in final position (the vowel of *bead* is longer than that of *beat*).

1950: 108–92). Stress, tone, and intonation are often grouped under the name of 'prosodic' (Trubetzkoy, 1939: 179–94; 1949: 212–31) or 'suprasegmental' features (Pike, 1947: 63; 1967: 522–4).

If length is distinctive, it is usually simply a matter of short *v.* long, though occasional three-term systems are found, e.g. Estonian (Jones, 1950: 132–3, though see fn. 27).

If stress is distinctive, it is usually phonologically a matter of accented syllables *v.* unaccented syllables: phonetically there may be intermediate degrees of stressing, but these are normally traceable to the effect of compounding or constructions, or to rhythmic considerations (Chomsky & Halle, 1968: 26–43). Stress is usually accompanied by pitch phenomena (perhaps falling pitch, or significantly higher or lower pitch, depending on the language being spoken and the intonation being used), and these are frequently more important as cues to the hearer than are differences of loudness (Fry, 1968: 373). These pitch phenomena may sometimes be of several distinctive types, as in Serbo-Croat (Jones 1950: 150–52, 180–82), in which case we have a language which combines stress distinctions and tone distinctions.

Two types of distinctive pitch difference may be distinguished:

(a) Intonation – here pitch patterns make their distinctive contribution at (roughly) clause or sentence level. Thus in the sentence *I en`joyed ,it,** the pitch pattern operates over the whole sentence, adding the notion that the speaker has reservations (implying a continuation something like *but it could have been a lot better*); from the semantic point of view, we cannot split the pattern into a falling part affecting the meaning of the word *enjoyed* and a rising part affecting the word *it*.

(b) Tone – here pitch patterns make their distinctive contribution at (roughly) word level. Thus the sequence of sounds [sœŋ] in Cantonese can have six entirely distinct meanings depending

---

*Pitch patterns are symbolized by lines of appropriate height and slope standing before the relevant syllables: thus in this case the pitch of the syllable *joyed* starts relatively high and falls to a mid value, while the pitch of *it* starts low and rises to mid.

on the pitch pattern associated with it: [ˈsœŋ] 'hurt', [ˈsœŋ] 'photograph', [ˉsœŋ] 'prime minister', [ˌsœŋ] 'pair of drawers', [ˌsœŋ] 'ascend', [ˌsœŋ] 'above' (Jones 1950: 16). Pitch patterns of this type often lend themselves to groupings analogous to phonemes – such groupings are called *tones* or sometimes *tonemes*. We will use the term 'toneme', as 'tone' is sometimes used for the phonetic pitch pattern (Jones, 1950: 153), and sometimes for the phonemic groupings of pitch patterns; in this chapter 'tone' will be used only as a generic term for pitch phenomena of this type (i.e. in opposition to 'intonation').

As compared with phonemic groupings, it is much more difficult to insist on phonetic similarity as a basic requirement in tonal groupings, and overlapping is frequent; Jones had to content himself with the requirement that members of the same toneme should 'count for linguistic purposes as if they were one and the same' (1950: 153). Two facts may help to explain this difficulty:

(i) There is basically one dimension of variation in pitch phenomena, as opposed to several in the case of sound qualities (place of articulation, voicing, manner of articulation, and such other features as lip-rounding and palatalization).

(ii) Pitch patterns are affected by several systems besides tone (e.g. intonation, and stress of various types).

Because of this difficulty, the 'abstract' approach (cf. section I, part (iv); section III below) is probably the most suitable for handling tonal phenomena.

Distinctive phonetic differences may be considered as characterizing phonological elements of various sizes. Thus sound quality normally characterizes phonemes (single segments), but sometimes longer stretches; for example, the vowels of a Turkish word must be either all front or all back (a phenomenon known as *vowel harmony*), so that the plural affix has the form /lar/ after roots with back vowels (/adamlar/ 'men') and /ler/ after roots with front vowels (/evler/ 'houses'). Length likewise is normally associated with single segments, though sometimes syllables may be involved. Tone is basically syllabic – although differences of voice-pitch are most likely to be restricted to voiced parts of syllables (notably vowels), it usually gives better results to assume that the unit of tone placement is closely related to the syllable, and in many languages identical with the syllable. Stress normally characterizes syllables (being manifested principally by vowels), but there is usually only one main stress per word; in terms of the approach of J. R. Firth (1890–1960) (see below pp. 84–6), this can be expressed by saying that the *domain* of stress is the word, while its *focus* is one particular syllable of the word. In connected speech, main stress may in fact have a longer domain than the word, and the terms *stress-group* (Pike, 1947: 90; 1967: 392–402) or *foot* (Halliday, 1967: 12) may be applied to this. Finally, intonation has a larger domain still (sometimes as long as a whole sentence), called a *tone-group* (Halliday, 1967: 13), a *pause-group* (Pike, 1967: 402–403) or a *phonological phrase* (Chomsky & Halle, 1968: 9–10), as we saw in the example on p. 82.

Thus a whole set of phonologically relevant elements can be defined as the domains of various suprasegmental elements – this set is called the *phonological hierarchy* (Pike, 1967: 409–10). The relations between the various elements of the phonological hierarchy are simple: a sentence consists of a sequence of one or more intonation-groups, each of which consists of a sequence of one or more stress-groups, each of which consists of a sequence of one or more words, each of which consists of a sequence of one or more syllables; the structure of a syllable in terms of segments, however, is more complex, normally consisting of a vowel preceded by one or more consonants and, in some languages, followed by one or more consonants.

The approach of J. R. Firth ('prosodic phonology') extends the principle underlying the phonological hierarchy to permit the handling of certain sound quality and duration elements as features of stretches longer than single segments. For example, the domain of backness or frontness (and to some extent the lip-rounding or absence of rounding) of Turkish vowels is the word (cf. the example given above); the term *prosody* is therefore extended by Firth to include these features. Those distinctive features which are not treated as prosodies (in the case of Turkish vowels, merely openness *v.* closeness) are assigned to what Firth calls *phonematic units*. Only features which are invariant (occurring in all contexts) may be assigned to phonematic units, while all others must be assigned to prosodies of various types: not all prosodic phonologists have followed Firth on this point, however.

Another characteristic of Firth's phonology is that, unlike some others, it gives theoretical recognition to the fact that features of a sound which are distinctive in one position may not be distinctive when that same sound is in another position. For example, the opposition between [m] and [n] in English is distinctive before vowels (*meat* v. *neat*) and in word-final position (*ram* v. *ran*), whereas there is no distinctive opposition between the various nasals before consonants: [limp], [lint], [liŋk] but not [liŋp], [link], etc. Most exceptions to this rule are words involving plural or past tense suffixes, (*hammed* [hæmd] v. *hand* [hænd]), which can be handled by defining 'word-final position' to include position before these suffixes (the propriety of taking grammatical facts into consideration in phonology is discussed in section IV below); there are a few other exceptions, e.g. *James*, *clumsy*. The place of articulation of the nasal is normally identical with that of the following consonant, and we could write the nasal with some more general symbol such as /N/; the sound [ŋ] in 'word-final position' (as defined above) could be regarded as the pronunciation of the phoneme sequence /Ng/.

To handle such cases as these, Firth envisaged the possibility of having a different 'system' (i.e. set of distinctive elements to choose from) for each distinct place in syllable- or word-structure. For example, in English the system associated with the central place in syllable-structure consists exclusively of the vowels, that associated with initial and final places consists exclusively of the consonants, while the post-initial system (accounting for initial consonant clusters like *tr-*, *sn-*, *gl-*) has the members /w/, /l/, /r/, /m/, /n/, and the pre-final system (accounting for final clusters like *-mp*, *-ld*, *-rk*) has the three members /l/, /r/, /N/. This is one aspect of Firth's approach to which the term 'polysystemic' is often applied. By contrast a view like that of Daniel Jones may be called 'monosystemic' – if a feature of a sound is distinctive in one position, it must be treated as distinctive in all positions: 'once a phoneme, always a phoneme'. On this point Firth's approach perhaps suffers from excessive reaction against the 'physical' view (particularly as propounded by Jones): 'polysystemic' too often implies several *entirely distinct* systems, where it would be more appropriate to talk of *partially similar* systems (as, for instance, in the case of the post-initial and pre-final systems just mentioned).

The term *polysystemic* has also been applied to the recognition that there may be significant phonological differences between various divisions of a language: thus Firth held that words of different origins (e.g. Romance and Latin elements in English as opposed to Germanic elements) might need different phonological systems to account for their form and behaviour, while the same might be true for different parts of speech (e.g. initial /ð/ in English is restricted to demonstratives and conjunctions: *the, this, that, they, there, thus, then, though, than*). The monosystemic approach recognizes none of these possibilities.

For more detailed treatments of Firth's approach see Robins (1963), Hill (1966), Palmer (1970), and Fudge (1972).

III

We now return to the question of abstract approaches to phonology. The following non-phonetic criteria can be used in assigning sounds to phonemes, and in setting up classes of phonemes (cf. Sapir, 1949: 42–3):

(a) Involvement in morphological alternations. Thus [ɫ] alternates with [l] in *feel* [fiːɫ] v. *feeling* [fiːliŋ] etc.; since [ɫ] and [l] never contrast we may say this is sufficient ground for assigning both to the same phoneme. (It should be noticed that, although [ɫ] and [l] happen to be phonetically similar, it is not on these grounds that they are assigned to the same phoneme: the 'abstract' approach would make such an assignment even if the two concerned were phonetically very different from each other.) Again, [f] alternates with [v] in *wife–wives*, etc., but this is not an automatic alternation – *graph* has the plural *graphs*, while *caves* has the singular *cave*; [f] and [v] therefore cannot be assigned to the same phoneme. However, we can say that the phonemes /f/ and /v/ have a particularly close relation to one another; this is reinforced by the fact that most /f/–/v/ alternations in final position have morphological significance: *safe* (adjective) v. *save* (verb), etc. The same is true of /θ/ and /ð/, (*breath* v. *breathe*) and to some extent of /s/ and /z/ (*use* (noun) v. *use* (verb)). Thus a voiceless fricative and its voiced counterpart form a closely linked pair in a sense which is not true of a voiceless stop and its voiced counterpart. Again it should be stressed that relationships of this kind may be quite independent of phonetic similarity: the relationships between long and short vowels in English are a case in point – phonetic similarity might give a grouping like that of Table 1, but morphological patterning indicates the arrangement shown in Table 2.

	Front		Back	
	Short	Long	Short	Long
Close	[i] *bit*	[iː] *beat*	[u] *put*	[uː] *boot*
Mid	[e] *bet*	[ei] *bait*	[ʌ] *but*	[ou] *boat*
Open	[æ] *bat*	[ɑː] *part*	[ɔ] *pot*	[ɔː] *bought*

Table 1. English vowels classified on a phonetic basis (with an exemplifying word for each): the remaining diphthongs and the long vowel [əː] of *bird* are not included. The labels represent something like phonetic features, but [ɑː] (labelled 'Front') is phonetically Back, while [ʌ] (labelled 'Back') is phonetically Central.

	F		B	
	S	L	S	L
X	[i]	[ai] *divinity-divine*	[ʌ]	[au] *profundity-profound*
Y	[e]	[iː] *serenity-serene*	[u]	[uː] —
Z	[æ]	[ei] *sanity-sane*	[ɔ]	[ou] *verbosity-verbose*

Table 2. English vowels classified on the basis of morphological alternations, with examples for each alternation. Long vowels [ɑː], [ɔː] and [əː], together with the remaining diphthongs, are excluded from these correspondences. The labels F, B, S, L (Front, Back, Short and Long) correspond fairly straightforwardly to phonetic features, but X, Y, Z do not.

(b) (A criterion for grouping phonemes) Distributional similarity in syllables and words. Thus we can classify the English consonants on the basis of which of /w/, /l/, and /r/ can occur after them initially. We have the following classes:

(i) Before /l/ and /r/ but not before /w/: the phonemes /p/, /b/, and /f/.

(ii) Before /w/ and /r/ but not /l/: /t/, /d/, and /θ/.

(iii) Before all three: /k/, /g/, and /s/.

Classes (i) and (ii) accord well with phonetic similarity, but class (iii) does not – /k/ and /g/ are pronounced as velar stops, while /s/ is pronounced as an alveolar fricative (i.e. phonetically more similar to the pronunciations of /t/ and /d/).

A stronger form of the 'abstract' view is advocated in the approach known as *glossematics*. This was pioneered by the Danish linguist Louis Hjelmslev (1899–1965) and his associates in the Copenhagen Linguistic Circle (notably H. J. Uldall and K. Togeby). For the purposes of this chapter we can state its particular viewpoint as follows: phonetic properties are not involved *at all* in the way phonemes are specified, or in the way they are grouped into classes. In addition to criteria (a) and (b) above, glossematicians have suggested that if two phonemes are pronounced the same in some context, they should be allocated to the same class: however, since pronunciation is involved, this additional criterion is strictly contrary to the principle stated in the previous sentence.

Bi-uniqueness (see p. 80) is not insisted on in glossematics: thus German *Bund* and *bunt*, although both pronounced [bunt], may be assigned differing phonemic shapes /bund/ and /bunt/ respectively – the justification for this assignment would be that *Bund* has inflected forms which are pronounced [bundə], [bundəs] etc. while *bunt* has inflected forms [buntə], [buntəs] etc. (cf. criterion (a) above). In word-final position both /d/ and /t/ would be pronounced [t], and would therefore, by the additional criterion of the previous paragraph, form a phoneme class.

The extreme position adopted by the glossematicians is not a necessary consequence of the assumption that phonemic elements are abstract – in fact it is not a consequence at all, since at a later stage in the description, phonemic elements will certainly be characterized in phonetic terms.

Just as phonetically determined classes may be labelled by using distinctive features (cf. Table 1 above), so classes determined on abstract grounds may be labelled by using non-phonetic features (termed *cenemes* by the glossematicians). The cenemes of Table 2 consist of three sets of elements: (i) F and B, (ii) S and L, and (iii) X, Y, and Z; sets (i) and (ii) have fairly straightforward correlations with the phonetic distinctions front-back and short-long, while set (iii) has only a very complex relationship with phonetic features (mainly features of tongue-height). This latter possibility gives the 'abstract' approach the great advantage that type 3 variations (variations from speaker to speaker, see p. 78) can be fully incorporated within a phonemic system: many phonetically very diverse accents can be regarded as derived from the same underlying system of cenemes. This gives a good basis for making explicit what is meant by 'speaking the same language' (see p. 80): if A and B 'speak the same language', then, among other things, A's system of cenemes must be very much like B's, and furthermore the cenemic composition of each word of A's speech must be in most cases very much the same as that of the corresponding word of B's speech.

For further discussion of the glossematic approach see Fudge (1972) and Spang-Hanssen (1961); Togeby (1951: 7–88) presents a detailed application of the theory to French phonology. The parallel between an 'abstract' view of the phoneme and modern approaches in the philosophy of science is brought out by Shaumjan (1968): while allophones and distinctive features are entities with a physical basis, phonemes and 'differentors' (the abstract entities corresponding to distinctive features, cf. cenemes) are purely abstract and have the status of 'constructs' within the phonological theory – their purpose is to *account for* the complexities of the observed physical data (utterances by speakers of the language), and not directly to *describe* them. Furthermore, this insistence on a strict distinction between the (abstract) phonemic elements and the (at least partially concrete) phonetic elements would appear to be well suited to a psychologically real theory of speech production.

IV

We will now discuss the basic question: 'Is it legitimate to use grammatical information in establishing and stating phonological structure?' Proponents of the 'physical' view of the phoneme have usually answered with a decided negative, on the grounds that scientific investigation should start from observable data (in the case of linguistics, phonetic data), and, by applying *inductive* procedures (see p. 7) arrive at the abstract structures underlying the data (in linguistics, this means phonological structure first, and grammatical structure only *after* this has been established). Such structures are held to be valid to the extent that the steps leading to their discovery can be made explicit. This position reflects in a rather general way the positivistic intellectual climate of the 1930s and 1940s; on the other hand, it was glossematics, an 'abstract' approach, which was most influenced by the actual tenets of logical positivism (Fudge, 1972). In common with other 'abstract' approaches (notably the Firthian and the generative), validation of the structures arrived at is independent of the steps leading to their discovery – *deductive* procedures are applied to the structures (see p. 8), and the resulting phonetic predictions tested against further data: such procedures operate in essentially the reverse order from the inductive discovery procedures, and hence grammatical information is always available, if needed, in the phonological part of the description (see Figure 5).

As Figure 5 indicates, part at least of the task of phonology is to link grammar with phonetics. In view of its exclusion of grammatical facts from phonology, the 'physical' view might be expected to lead to difficulty in making the links represented by the upper pair of arrows in Figure 5. Even its most thoroughgoing adherents recognize that this is in fact the case (Bloch, 1950: 124–5; Joos, 1957: 348); to overcome this difficulty a further level of representation, 'morphophonemics', was introduced (Harris, 1951: 219–42). Bi-uniqueness (p. 80) is not required between phonemic and morphophonemic representations: thus German *Bund* and *bunt* (both /bunt/ according to the 'physical' view) would be morphophonemically /bunD/ and /bunt/ respectively, where /D/ means 'this segment is /t/ when word-final and /d/ otherwise'.

Proponents of the 'abstract' approach, however, would answer the basic question of this section by saying that, since phonology has to link phonetics with grammar, it is not only *legitimate* but also *necessary* for phonology to take account of grammatical considerations – for native speakers the various parts of the structure of their language are not insulated from one another but form a complete whole; moreover, and more importantly, it is only because the 'physical' approach fails to give proper weight to grammatical considerations that a separate

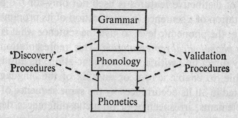

Figure 5. Diagram (greatly oversimplified) illustrating the relationship of phonology and grammar.

morphophonemic representation is needed. In fact, an 'abstract' phonemic representation is much more like a morphophonemic representation than like a 'physical' phonemic one.

The extreme glossematic view of phonology must also be judged to fall short – this type of phonology also fails to bridge the gap between grammar and phonetics, this time on the phonetic side (the lower arrows of Figure 5). For example, the largely non-phonetic procedures applied by Togeby (1951: 73–88) yield phoneme-classes (cenemes) which are not only counter-intuitive but also extremely difficult to link up with phonetic properties.

The most recent attempt at a grammatically oriented phonology, known as generative phonology, owes much to Sapir, as is expressly indicated by its leading proponents Noam Chomsky and Morris Halle (see, e.g. Chomsky & Halle, 1968: 76, fn. 23). In contrast to many older approaches, generative treatments begin by stating syntactic structure and only then pass on to phonology, which can thus make use of any syntactic facts which are relevant (cf. p. 90). For example, knowledge of constructions and knowledge of part-of-speech allocation are both needed in order to state the rules of stress for English (Chomsky & Halle, 1968: 15–24, 69–77).

Most generative treatments have taken some form of phonetic distinctive features as their basic elements; in Halle's early work, the Jakobsonian distinctive feature system (Jakobson & Halle, 1956) was adopted, while more recent work has led to far-reaching modifications of this (Chomsky & Halle, 1968: 293–329). This set of distinctive features is used not only for the phonetic representation of a sentence (a specification of its pronunciation), but also at the phonemic level to give the sentence what is usually called its *phonological representation*. This representation has no necessary direct link with actual pronunciation: its aim is, as far as possible, to enable a root or an affix of the language to be represented in all its occurrences by the same sequence of phonological elements, irrespective of phonetic differences depending on context (Firth and the glossematicians also explicitly adopted this principle).

The fact that there is no difference of kind between phonological representation and phonetic representation creates few problems in a 'natural' situation (like that of F and B, and L and S in Table 2, where phonemic patterning follows phonetic relationships), but is a source of real difficulty in 'unnatural' cases (e.g. X, Y and Z in Table 2, where each has a very complex relationship to phonetic properties).

The link between the two representations – phonological and phonetic – is established by a set of 'rules' which operate in a fixed order, adding, deleting, or modifying distinctive features. Table 3 gives a set of such rules which handles a very small part of the phonology of English, and Table 4 illustrates their operation; strictly speaking, they should be stated in terms of distinctive features – thus rule 2 would read [+ Voiced] → [− Voiced] in a certain context, rule 3 would read [+ Tense] → [− Tense] in a certain context, etc.

The difficulties arising in 'unnatural' situations are well exemplified by rule 6 of Table 3, which is actually incomplete: besides the rule ī → ā, we need rules ā → ē and ē → ī, and furthermore all three rules must apply simultaneously to give correct results. Incidentally rules 5 and 6 of Table 3 reflect the Great Vowel Shift in English, and it has been suggested that the types of rules which form part of a synchronic (p. 14) description are in general very similar to those which are needed to handle sound changes (see also pp. 304–10).

Phonology

The generative approach has the advantage of being able to handle type 3 variations (variations of pronunciation from speaker to speaker, p. 78) satisfactorily – phonetically different dialects of the same language would be accounted for by postulating different sets of rules (perhaps differing merely in their order of application) operating on the same phonological representation (Vasiliu, 1966; King, 1968; see also Kiparsky's chapter below, pp. 302–15).

1. $\left.\begin{matrix} k \\ t \\ d \end{matrix}\right\}$ $\begin{matrix} \rightarrow s \\ \rightarrow z \end{matrix}$ *before affixes beginning with* i

2. z → s *before* iv

3. ī → i *before* zion

4. $\left.\begin{matrix} s + i \rightarrow & \int \\ z + i \rightarrow & \mathbf{3} \end{matrix}\right\}$ *before a vowel*

5. zero → y *after a tense front vowel*

6. ī → ā

7. $\left.\begin{matrix} o \\ a \end{matrix}\right\}$ → ə *when unstressed*

Table 3. Some rules for English. A macron '–' over a vowel indicates that it is tense (long). Rule 1 may be read as follows: 'k and t are rewritten as s, and d as z, before affixes beginning with i', and the others analogously.

	logician	divide	divisive	division
Phonological representation	lodʒik+ian	divīd	divīd+iv	divīd+ion
After rule 1	lodʒisian	—	divīziv	divīzion
2	—	—	divīsiv	—
3	—	—	—	divizion
4	lodʒiʃan	—	—	diviʒon
5	—	divīyd	divīysiv	—
6	—	divāyd	divāysiv	—
7	lədʒiʃən	—	—	diviʒən

Table 4. Derivation of the phonetic representation of four English words from their phonological representations by the 7 rules of Table 3. The sign '—' indicates that the rule in question does not affect the form concerned.

Generative phonology as developed by Chomsky and Halle has been criticized for failing to distinguish between rules like 1, 2, and 3 of Table 3, which apply only in certain morphologically defined contexts, and those like 4, 5, 6, and 7 of Table 3, which are of general application: the former may legitimately be said to change one phonemic element into another phonemic element, whereas it is a matter of debate whether the same is true of the latter, which might be said to constitute phonology proper. The Chomsky and Halle model is expounded in more detail by Langacker (1968: 152–71), Chomsky (1964: 65–96; also Fodor & Katz, 1964: 85–112), and Harms (1968); for a very thorough application, see the treatment of English phonology by Chomsky and Halle (1968).

V

In general the relation between phonology and semantics is indirect, being mediated by syntax; however, we may single out two areas in which more direct links are discernible;

(i) The question of contrastive stress: the phonological difference between *Give me that* **book** and *Give me* **that** *book* does not correlate with anything syntactic, but rather with a situational factor. The corresponding problem for German is discussed from a generative viewpoint by Bierwisch (1968).

(ii) Questions of sound symbolism, onomatopoeia, and expressiveness, such as are described in Grammont (1933: 377–424): Fudge (1970*b*) suggests a possible framework in which some of these questions might be handled for English.

APPENDIX – PHONETIC SYMBOLS

Most transcriptions of English words in the chapter need no further elucidation. In non-English words, unless otherwise noted, phonetic symbols may be taken to imply a sound very much like their English value.

p. 76 [ˈpaβa] : [ˈ] indicates that the immediately following syllable is stressed. [β] resembles [v] except that the lower lip is brought close to the upper lip rather than close to the upper teeth.

p. 76 [qɔːl] : [q] differs from [k] only in that contact between tongue and soft palate takes place further back.

p. 77 [gel] : [e] is rather like the vowel of French *thé*.

[gæl] : [æ] is rather like the vowel of English *hat*.

p. 80 [bunt] : [u] is rather like the vowel of English *put*.

p. 83 [sœn] : [œ] is rather like the vowel of French *heure*.

[ŋ] is like the final consonant of English *sing*.

p. 85 [liŋk] : [ŋ] is phonetically the nasal counterpart of [k] and [g].

p. 88 [bundə] etc. : [ə] is rather like the first vowel of English *banana*.

5. RECENT DEVELOPMENTS IN MORPHOLOGY

P. H. Matthews

I have referred to morphology as 'a level of structure between the phonological and the syntactic' (p. 22). Another way of describing what is meant by 'morphology' is to say that it is complementary to syntax: morphology accounts for the internal structure, or 'form', of words (typically as sequences of morphemes) and syntax describes how these words are 'put together' in sentences. Matthews makes it clear, in the chapter which follows, that the relationship between morphology and syntax, in some languages at least, is rather more complex than this formulation would suggest, which, apart from anything else, trades upon ambiguities in the term 'word' (pp. 21, 109).

It can be argued that recent grammatical theory, especially in the 'post-Bloomfieldian' school of linguists where generative grammar had its beginnings, has generally been biased towards languages of the so-called 'agglutinating' type: languages in which inflection is marked by affixes that can be put into one-to-one correspondence with morphemes. English, as far as the regular patterns of inflection are concerned, is an agglutinating language. But there are also some notable instances of non-agglutinating structures in English, which have been much discussed in the post-Bloomfieldian literature (as Matthews points out) as test cases for grammatical theory.

One of the criticisms most commonly made of generative 'phonology' (as Fudge mentioned in the previous chapter: p. 94) is that it fails to draw a distinction between morphologically and phonologically conditioned processes. Much of what Matthews discusses below would no doubt be handled by the majority of generative grammarians in the phonological component of the grammar. But so far there has been no comprehensive treatment of morphology within a generative framework, other than by Matthews himself in a number of recent publications. A brief and non-technical account of part of his proposals is included in the present chapter.

Recent Developments in Morphology

1. THE theory of synchronic morphology may usefully be considered from three angles:

(1) What are the basic *units* of morphological structure, and what are the *relations* which obtain between them?

(2) How are these units *signalled* or *realized* in the phonological structure of the sentence?

(3) What are the *criteria* for determining the morphological analysis of any particular language?

In the 1940s and early 1950s the first two questions received comparatively simple answers (§2 below); on the other hand, the third question – the question of criteria, was the subject of extensive and prominent debate in linguistic journals. In more recent years, however, the discussion has tended to shift towards the opposite pole: the problem of criteria has been very largely set aside (though see §6, IV for certain exceptions), whereas the first two questions – concerning in effect the nature of morphological structure – have been answered with a number of subtler and more sharply varying formulations. For these reasons it is convenient to regard the mid-1950s as something of a turning-point in the recent history of morphological studies. We will therefore concentrate, in particular, on the work which has been published since that date.

2. An important article by Hockett (1954) forms the best starting-point. In this article, Hockett surveyed what was then the state of grammatical theory, and distinguished three very general concepts of linguistic structure. The first, to which he gave the label *Item and Arrangement* (abbreviated IA), is the one which had been dominant since the mid-1940s; it was on the merits and possible defects of this viewpoint that his argument accordingly turned. The second and third, to which he gave the labels *Item and Process* (IP) and *Word and Paradigm* (WP), were alternative approaches which had, in the immediately preceding period, been given rather less attention. Hockett argued that there were enough criticisms of IA to suggest that IP, in particular, deserved more serious consideration; however IP, when he attempted a closer formulation, revealed its own defects in turn. He therefore

refrained from any certain decision between these two approaches. The third viewpoint (WP) was mentioned, but not explored in a similar way.

What then were the characteristics of the dominant I A concept? If we take an English word such as *farmers*, it is possible to split the form as a whole into three independent segments: a segment *farm*, which also appears in *farm-ing* or *farm-s*; a second segment *er*, which reappears (again to indicate the 'do-er' or performer of some task or profession) in words such as *sing-er*, *sweep-er*, and the like; and a third segment *s* which reappears (again with the meaning of 'Plurality') in *car-s*, *log-s*, and so forth. The central observation of I A, in other words, is that certain word forms can show a 'partial phonetic-semantic resemblance' to other word forms (Bloomfield, 1935: 160; cf. 1926: §§II–III). Thus the form *farm-er-s* bears a partial resemblance to *farm-ing* with respect to one segment, and to *sing-er*, *log-s*, etc. with respect to others.

If we now turn to our first two questions (§1), it is at once clear why the I A answers were so straightforward. The *units* of morphology (Question 1) are simply the abstract grammatical constructs (see §3 below) which correspond to the recurring segments: in our example, the units which we might symbolize by FARM, -ER, and 'Plural'. These units are almost universally known as *morphemes* (compare already Bloomfield, 1935: 161). Likewise the *relation* between these units is that of simple sequence: thus in our example the morpheme FARM precedes the second morpheme -ER, and this precedes the third morpheme 'Plural'. Finally, the signals or phonological realizations of these units (Question 2) are the recurring segments themselves: these are commonly referred to as *morphs* (a term first used by Hockett, 1947) or *morphemic segments* (e.g. Harris, 1951: 156ff.). The complete morphological analysis of *farmers* might accordingly be shown by a diagram (Figure 6):

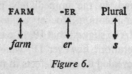

Figure 6.

in which the morphemes and morphs are paired off in the appropriate sequence, and the complete morphological analysis of the language would involve:

(1) A specification of the inventory of morphemes (the 'Items' of Hockett's 'Item and Arrangement' label);

(2) A specification of the sequences in which these morphemes can appear (the possible 'Arrangements'); and

(3) A specification of the morph or morphs (§3 below) by which each morpheme can be realized; – in other words, providing the link between the grammatical aspects of morphological structure (1 and 2) and the phonology.

A concept of this kind was already clear in the work of Harris (1942) and was repeated, with fairly slight qualifications, in the major American textbooks which appeared from 1957 onwards (Hockett, 1958: 123ff.; Hill, 1958: 89ff.; Gleason, 1961: 51ff.; Hall, 1964: 22ff.). But in the intervening years its attractiveness had been impaired by several criticisms. To take one example which became notorious in the literature, an English verb form such as *sank* is obviously comparable, in respect of grammar and meaning, to a further form such as *thanked*; both, that is to say, are the Past Tense forms of their respective verbs. But how does this comparability work out in IA terms? The word *thanked* can obviously be divided into two segments: *thank* (which reappears in *thank-s* or *thank-ing*) and *ed*, which one may regard as the signal for the 'Past Tense' itself. *Sank*, however, cannot be segmented according to a similar pattern: although it differs from the Present form *sink* in a way which can be paralleled for further verbs such as *drink/drank*, *sing/sang*, etc., it does so by an internal contrast between vowels and not by means of an external morph, such as *ed*, which could be assigned to 'Past Tense' as a morpheme. Various writers, notably Harris (1951: 167) and Nida (1948), attempted to speak of a change of vowel – *i* changing to *a*, as a morph of a special 'replacive' kind; but as others pointed out (Bazell, 1952: §II and eventually Hockett, 1954: §IV), this still makes nonsense of the principle of recurring segments. Bloch, in a lucid and rigorous article (1947), suggested that the best IA solution was to treat the entire word, *sank*, as the signal for the lexical element, SINK, alone; 'Past Tense' would then be realized by zero or by a zero morph at the end of the word. But this solution was also effectively criticized, immediately by Nida (1948) and subsequently in a thorough study by Haas (1957) of the misuses of 'zero' in linguistic literature. It was through this type of example, in particular, that Hockett and others were moved to investigate the possibility of alternative frameworks.

3. Let us now look at the development of IA, IP and WP in the period since Hockett's pivotal article. That of IA is associated mainly, though not entirely, with the so-called 'stratificational' theory of language propounded by Lamb (1966) and also by Gleason (1964); let us therefore begin with a brief exposition of the morphological aspect of this theory. If we examine the word forms of a language in detail we find, very soon, that the same morpheme can be realized sometimes by one morph and some-times by another: thus the so-called 'Past Participle' in English is signalled by *n* in a form such as [*I've*] *show-n*, but by *ed* in [*I've*] *play-ed*. It is for this reason that a distinction is drawn (see §2) between the abstract grammatical construct itself (FARM or 'Past Participle') and any of the one or more actual segments (*farm* or *ed*) which are involved. In addition, we find that the circumstances which dictate one morph or the other can be of two major kinds. The first type is that exemplified by *play-ed* as against *show-n*; certain verbs simply happen to have the *n* form, whereas the majority have *ed*. But if we examine further the segment written as *ed* a rather different picture emerges. If the preceding morph ends with a consonant *t* or *d*, then what we have is phonetically similar to the *id* in *hid*: thus *wait-ed* or *crowd-ed*. If it ends in a consonant such as (written) *ss*, *ck*, and several others then it is phonetically a *t*: thus *hiss-ed* and *hack-ed* end in the same way as *list* or *act*. Finally if it ends with a vowel or a consonant such as *n*, *b*, etc., it is phonetically a *d*: thus *boo-ed* or *wean-ed* end like *food* or *fiend*. It is not relevant, in other words, to consider the particular verb which happens to be involved; what is crucial is merely the phonological make-up of the end of the preceding morph.

This distinction was, as one might expect, well known in the earlier period: in the current terminology the *n* of *show-n* and the *ed*'s of *wait-ed*, *hiss-ed* and *wean-ed* were four different *alternants* (Harris, 1942) or *allomorphs* (Hockett, 1947) of the same morpheme, the *alternation* between the *n* and all the *ed*'s being *grammatically*, and those between the individual *ed*'s being *phonologically conditioned* (e.g. Gleason, 1961: 62). But Lamb's stratificational theory has gone further than its predecessors in two major respects.

I. In the first place, such examples are taken as the basis not merely for two sorts of alternation, but for a distinction between two quite separate levels of analysis. Already, in the earlier period, there had been some sporadic use of an intermediate unit called the *morphophoneme* (Swadesh & Voegelin, 1939; Harris, 1951: Chapter 14): one might, for example, establish a morphophoneme **D** (corresponding to written *ed*) as the regular form of 'Past Participle', and say that **D** alternates between the phonetic endings of *waited*, *hissed* or *turned* in the same way that the morpheme, as a whole, would alternate between **D** and the irregular *n* of *shown*. What Lamb has done, however, is to extend this formerly sporadic usage throughout the entire word form. For example in *waited* (phonetically [weitid]), not merely would [id] be the phonetic form of the morphophoneme **D**, but [t] would be the phonetic form of a morphophoneme **t**, [w] of **w**, and so on. The complete word would thus have a three-level (or three-*stratum*) analysis which might be diagrammed as in Figure 7:

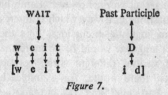

Figure 7.

– the highest level being represented in terms of morphemes (or *lexons* in Lamb's most recent terminology), and the second entirely in terms of this new intermediate unit, the morphophoneme (which Lamb has rechristened the *morphon*). This distinction of strata is most conveniently presented by Lamb (1964*b*) and may be exemplified, in particular, by Barker's grammar of Klamath (1964).

II. Secondly, Lamb has given particular attention to the nature of the conversion or *transduction* process from one stratum to another. Given a sequence of grammatical units (e.g. WAIT followed by 'Past Participle'), how precisely does the description of the language specify what its phonological form will be? Conversely, given a sequence of phonological units (e.g. [w e i t i d]), how precisely does it indicate the sequence of grammatical units which this might realize? In a comparatively early paper (1964*a*), Lamb addressed himself to the first question in particular; his answer involved two successive systems of rules (a *rule* is simply any kind of formal linguistic statement) which are very similar except that the first is concerned, of course, with the transduction from morphemes to morphophonemes and the second with the transduction from morphophonemes, in turn, into the phonology. Thus there would, for example, be a rule in the first system that the morpheme WAIT is always converted into the morphophonemes w e i t, and another that 'Past Participle' is converted to n if the preceding morpheme (note we are speaking in terms of grammatical conditions: see above) is one of a number such as SHOW, MOW (cf. *mow-n*), etc. Likewise there would be a rule in the second system that n, when standing at the end of the word and preceded by a morphophoneme such as w, is always converted to [n]; note that we are now speaking of conditions which are themselves expressed in terms of morphophonemes. In more recent work, however, Lamb has attempted to answer both questions in a way which is interesting and somewhat unusual in linguistic discussions. First the 'grammar' or description of a language would be no more than a network of connexions, of various different sorts, between the different individual units: there would, for example, be a connexion between 'Past Participle' and D, and another between, for example, n and [n]. Such a network of connexions may then be thought of in terms which are at least partly reminiscent of an electrical circuit. If an imaginary current were to activate, say, a connexion leading to WAIT, then this in turn would immediately activate the further connexions leading to w, e, i and t, and after that the still further connexions to [w], [e], [i] and [t]. Conversely, if the latter were activated first, then the current would pass through w, e, i and t to WAIT. In this way the distinction between transduction from the top to bottom levels of our diagram (Figure 7), and conversely from the bottom level to the top, is no more than a difference between the directions in which the 'current' happens to be passing.

The value of these proposals would be difficult to assess except as part of the wider 'stratificational' theory: the strata represented by morphemes and morphophonemes are only two out of six (Lamb, 1966: 18) suggested for language as a whole. Moreover, the network proposal has not yet been sufficiently explained and illustrated for other linguists to form a confident judgement. But critics have already queried, in particular, whether the morphophoneme is really a basic unit on a par with the morpheme, on the one hand, and the phonological units on the other. The latter two are simply a reflection of the feature of 'double articulation' (see p. 12 of Lyons's introductory chapter); language must involve at least two irreducibly primitive units, one of which is the basis of syntax and semantics and the other of phonology. But the morphophoneme may be no more than a pseudo-unit (compare Hockett, 1961: 31) which is invented to ease the transition from one 'real unit' to the other. Such an objection has indeed been brought against Lamb's theory as a whole: namely that his six strata are essentially pseudo-strata (Palmer, 1968; Hockett, 1968*b*). Nevertheless there is much in his work on morphology which might still be of value.

4. Let us now turn to Item and Process (this section) and Word and Paradigm (§5). Both these approaches may be seen, in the most general terms, as a denial of the principle of *discrete* or separate 'signals' which was the original basis for IA (§2). In the majority of our examples this principle of discreteness has been satisfactorily preserved: in *shown* or *waited* it is clear that *show* and *wait* belong exclusively to SHOW and WAIT, and *n* and *ed* to 'Past Participle'. But consider instead a Latin word such as *mensās*, the Accusative Plural of the Latin word for 'table'. If we compare this with a number of related words – *mensam* (Accusative Singular), *dominōs* (Accusative Plural of the Noun for 'master'), and so on, it is evident that at least the first four

elements (*mens*) belong to the 'table' morpheme, and at least the final element (*s*) to 'Accusative Plural': but to which should we assign the long vowel (symbolized by $\bar{a}$) which comes between? Is the word as a whole to be split into *mensā* ('table') and *s* ('Accusative Plural'), or into *mens* and *ās*? If the latter, then why do we find a similar *a* vowel recurring in *mensam* or *mensā* (Ablative Singular) as against the *o* vowel of *dominōs* or *dominō* (Ablative Singular for 'master')? If the former, then why do we find another long vowel – though an $\bar{o}$ this time, in *dominōs*? In such a case it is not obvious that the concept of discrete signals is a useful one to follow; would it not be better, to borrow a metaphor from Pike (1959; 1967: 546), if one thought of the word as a sequence of 'waves' in which the peak of one 'wave' (*mens*) corresponds to one morpheme, and the peak of the next (*s*) to another, but the 'trough' ($\bar{a}$) represents an inextricable merger between the two?

IP would provide one possible answer both to the problem which is illustrated by *mensās*, and also to that of *sank* which we sketched earlier (§2). So far as the units and relations are concerned (Question 1 in §1), the former may again be thought of as morphemes, and the latter once again as a relation of sequence : *sank*, for example, would again be grammatically of the form SINK followed by Past Tense. But when one turns to the second of our original questions (the question of how these units are realized phonologically, it is possible to distinguish three successive types of rule which would enter into an IP description

I. First, the vast majority of morphemes would be provided, at the outset, with some kind of intrinsic or *basic* phonological make-up. Thus, in the examples under discussion, English SINK would have the basic form [sink], the Latin morpheme MENSA (translated 'table') the basic form *mensa*, and the other Latin morpheme (Accusative Plural) might have a form *:s* in which the colon (see III below) would eventually account for the length of the preceding vowel. If we now take the grammatical representation of the words (SINK followed by Past Tense; MENSA followed by Accusative Plural), and write in the basic forms for morphemes wherever possible, what we will then get is a *basic representation* ([sink] followed by Past Tense; *mensa* followed by *:s*) which is already one step, in effect, towards the actual word forms which we want to specify.

II. Secondly, a small minority of morphemes, of which 'Past Tense' in English is one example, would have the capacity to alter their neighbours (or certain of their neighbours) in various specified ways. In the case of *sank* what would happen is that 'Past Tense', in itself, would disappear; but in doing so it would trigger off a *morphological process* (the process of changing [i] to [a]) which would operate on the preceding basic form to yield [sank] in place of [sink.] Likewise a Plural Noun such as *men* or *feet*, which is equally refractory from the IA viewpoint, would be derived by a further morphological process operating on the basic form in *man* or *foot*. By this technique, a form such as [sank] would still bear the traces of the 'Past Tense' element; but in the IP description there need be no actual or basic segment, as there would be in IA, belonging exclusively to this morpheme as such.

III. Finally, there would be a further set of processes (*morphophonemic processes* is perhaps the most usual term) which would cause the basic representations, resulting from I and II, to interact with each other. In many cases, of course, no process of this kind is needed: thus *sank* and *men* would already be completely specified after stage II. In many others, furthermore, the interaction would still leave the segments distinct: if, say, the form *hissed* is assigned the basic forms [his], for the Verb, HISS, and [D] (compare §3) for 'Past Tense', then the [D] merely interacts with the final [s] of [his] by converting itself to a still separable segment [t]. But there remain a wide range of cases, such as *mensās*, in which the interaction would result in a complete fusion between the elements: thus here the final short *a* of basic *mensa* would fuse with the initial *:* of *:s* (see stage I) in such a way that the resulting long vowel, *ā*, will resist any attempt whatever to split it between the successive morphemes. Likewise the *o* of basic *domino* (for the 'master' morpheme) would fuse with the same basic segment *:s* to yield the long vowel ending of *dominōs*. In this way the basic 'particles', to return to Pike's metaphor, yield actual 'waves' of precisely the type which the IA viewpoint declines to recognize.

This essentially dynamic approach to morphology is of respectable antiquity: stage III, in particular, corresponds to the rules of *sandhi* or 'joining' employed by the Ancient Indian grammarians (cf. Allen, 1962), to the sandhi techniques employed by Bloomfield in a well-known treatment of Menomini (1939), and to notions which have in general coexisted with IA (compare the illuminating introduction to Lounsbury, 1953) throughout the development of modern linguistics. But the real flowering of IP is due, above all, to the work of the 'generative' school in the past decade. Chomsky's first published discussion (1957: 32), sketchy though it is, already contains a departure from the then dominant IA framework; and if we turn to subsequent proposals, particularly by Halle (1959) or Chomsky and Halle (1968) for our stage III and Koutsoudas (1964; 1966: Chapter 3) for stage II, it is clear that IP concepts form an essential part of what has come to be known as 'generative phonology'. What, then, are the merits of this approach from the morphological angle?

On the credit side the advantages lie, as one may readily see, in greater generality; whereas IA can only handle the cases where segments are distinct (*show-n*, *wait-ed*, etc.), IP can handle both the discrete patterns and the non-discrete (*sank* or *mensās*) by essentially the same form of statement. But several linguists have objected to the formulations of 'dynamism', 'change', 'interaction', and so forth, by which this generalization is achieved. As Hockett pointed out in comparing IA and IP (1954:§7), a form such as *sink* is necessarily assigned some priority as against the derived form *sank*; but how can this notion of priority be interpreted – granted that we are concerned with a purely synchronic account of the word forms, and not with a diachronic account of their development (cf. synchrony *v.* diachrony in Lyons's introductory chapter p. 14), or with the way utterances are composed in the speaker's brain (cf. competence *v.* performance, p. 28), or the like? Adherents of the generative school would consider this objection misguided; others too, notably Pike in the references cited (1959; 1967: chapter 14), would maintain that both the segmental and the dynamic approach are useful in illuminating different aspects of language structure. But the argument has been restated with force by at least one recent writer (Lamb, 1966:

35 ff.). We are in fact concerned with a quite fundamental issue in linguistic theory, whose divisive effects are particularly visible in the morphological field.

5. The WP approach (at least as this term has been used since the late 1950s) would query the principle of 'discrete signals' on at least two rather different counts. We may illustrate both from Italian.

I. For the first, consider the Italian Noun forms set out in Figure 8:

Singular	Plural
donna 'woman'	*donne* 'women'
monte 'mountain'	*monti* 'mountains'
ragazzo 'boy'	*ragazzi* 'boys'
dito 'finger'	*dita* 'fingers'

Figure 8.

These forms are, of course, very easy to segment: *donn-a, donn-e*, and so on. But is it true that the endings 'signal' the Singular as opposed to Plural morphemes? What Figure 8 in fact shows is that there are three vowels which appear in Singular word forms (*a, e*, and *o*) and three which appear in Plurals (*a, e* and *i*); in other words the sets overlap, in that both *donn-e* and *mont-e* have an *e*, and both *donn-a* and *dit-a* an *a*. Faced with this distribution one can say that a word such as *donne* 'signals', as a whole, the complete series of morphemes DONN- ('woman') followed by 'Plural'; but surely the Plurality cannot be a function of *e* in isolation.

II. For the second consider a Verb form such as *canterebbero* '[If] they would, etc. sing'. This is traditionally the 3rd Person Plural of the Conditional; but where exactly could one find a distinctive and exclusive signal for each of these morphemes? A double *bb*, for example, appears only in forms which are both Conditional and 3rd Person (thus also *canterebbe* 'He would sing'); in that sense, therefore, it would be a likely phonological mark for both elements. But surely the preceding stressed *e* (thus *canterébbero*) is a second mark of Conditional in precisely the same sense; it consistently appears, that is to say, in Conditional forms such as *canteréi* 'I would sing', *canterémmo* 'we would sing', etc. And surely the final *ro* is a second mark of Person (contrast *canterei* and *canteremmo*), despite the fact that it marks 'Plural' (contrast again *canterebbe*) as well? The truth is that if we compare the paradigm for this verb as a whole, and we consider which of these morphemes is relevant to the distribution of each individual segment, the picture which emerges is the surprisingly complicated relation shown in Figure 9:

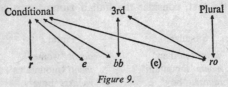

Figure 9.

in which not merely are the principal marks as above but, in addition, the *r* appears only in the Conditional or Future, and the 3rd Plural *ro* appears only in the Conditional or the Imperfective Subjunctive. On such a basis one can say that the three morphemes, – Conditional, 3rd Person and Plural as a whole – are signalled by the entire termination *-rebbero*, also as a whole; but can there be any realistic criterion for locating them, individually, in individual allomorphs?

Points of this kind are raised, in particular, in an important leading article by Robins (1959). For more recent discussion, one may refer to various scattered treatments by Pike (e.g. 1963 for Point I: also references in §6, II below); to some brief remarks by Chomsky (1965: 170 ff.); and, for point II, to an account of the Verb in Modern Greek (Matthews, 1967*c*) which provides an opportunity for comparison with an earlier IA analysis (Koutsoudas, 1962). How, then, might a WP description work out in detail? How far, in particular, might it simply resemble the way in which 'words' and 'paradigms' were handled in the earlier European tradition?

Where the basic units are concerned the tradition is partly, but only partly, satisfactory. It is satisfactory, from this viewpoint, in that elements such as 'Conditional' or '3rd Person' are treated as abstractions from words as wholes (cf. Robins, 1959: 128) and not from individual segments; more specifically, they may be regarded as *properties* of the various members of the paradigm. On the other hand it is unsatisfactory, as Lyons points out elsewhere (p. 21; also Lyons, 1963: 11f.), in that the term *word* has been used in too many different senses: thus the 'word' *canterebbero* (= *phonological word*) is the realization of a 'word' (= *grammatical word*) which belongs to the 'word' CANTARE (= *lexeme*) and which has, in addition, the properties Conditional, 3rd Person, and Plural. With the revival of interest in WP since Robins's article, the traditional concepts and their interrelations have now been largely clarified (Matthews, 1965c).

In the treatment of realizations (Question 2 in §1), the tradition has unfortunately less to offer. At worst the word forms in a paradigm have been listed with no explicit analysis, and at best there has been no more than a rudimentary division between 'stem' (e.g. *cant-* in the case of *canterebbero*) and 'ending' (e.g. *-erebbero*). There is, however, no reason why a WP description, while preserving the features which we have mentioned, should not in addition present a set of generalized rules for particular segments: for example, the rule that the *r* segment in the Italian Verb appears throughout the Future and Conditional. The question is: what exactly should these statements look like? According both to Robins (1959: 134f.) and to a detailed formulation by Matthews (1965b, 1966), a 'process' approach is most appropriate. Thus Matthews would begin by assigning a phonological *root* to each lexeme, e.g. the root *canta* to the lexeme CANTARE; this evidently corresponds, with allowance for the difference in units, to stage I in our account of IP (§4). He would then specify a series of morphological processes (§4, stage II), each of which may be triggered off by the properties of any grammatical word which is relevant; thus in Italian the addition of *r* (with stress on the following vowel) would be triggered by either of the properties 'Future' or 'Conditional', the further addition of *e* (stressed in consequence) would be triggered by Conditional alone, and so on. Finally, the resulting forms would again be affected by morphophonemic processes (§4, stage III), so that a conceivable basic representation *canta-r-é-bb-ro* (*bb* and *ro* being added by further processes) would have its second *a* altered to *e* by interaction with the following stress, and an *e* vowel brought in to separate the *bb* and *ro*. In large part, therefore, Matthew's proposal resembles a particularly thorough-going application of IP; the crucial difference, however, is that any property or set of properties may trigger off any number of successive processes within the same derivation.

This last formulation has unfortunately escaped critical comment; but presumably the objections to IP, if valid, would again apply. For WP in general there is, however, a problem which is more fundamental: namely that an approach which hinges on the word, and which abstracts from the word no more than a lexeme and a certain set of properties, will tend to be both pointless and unsatisfactory in many well-documented cases. It is unlikely, for example, that WP would have any advantage over IP in the description of English. Robins pays careful attention to this point, but suggests that it may simply be helpful to describe different types of language in different ways (1959: 137ff.). Matthews (1965*b*: 141f.) agrees, and refers to a similar suggestion for phonology by Lyons (1962) and to the important lecture by Bazell (1958) in which the morphological typology of languages is based on the quite different analytical problems which they tend to raise. But the usual requirements for linguistic theory are that it should be (1) as specific as possible but (2) universal, in the sense that any human language is covered: see Hockett (1954: §7.5) for a particularly clear statement on this point. It is not obvious that the sacrifice of requirement (2) would commend itself to the generality of linguists.

6. Finally, in view of the somewhat fashionable title of this volume, it is legitimate to guess at the issues which may come into prominence in the 1970s. First, of course, one may expect the reappraisal of I A, I P and WP to continue, with as much eventual agreement as one has the right to expect in these affairs. But in addition there are at least four related matters which would benefit from further discussion.

I. The first concerns the 'psychological reality' of the units, etc. which have been postulated. We know that a child's learning of English involves, among other things, the 'learning' of specific 'rules' for word formation (see the studies by Berko, 1958, or

Ervin 1964).) But can we be more specific about the ways in which the adult's 'rules' are organized and utilized? In particular, is the metaphor of 'signalling' (which we have used throughout this chapter) at all appropriate to the actual recognition of morphemes in a speech situation? It is possible, one hopes, to investigate such questions: partly by observation, partly by direct experiment with informants (e.g. by investigating the recognition of morphemes under conditions of noise or in incongruous grammatical contexts), and partly by computer simulation. But such investigations have not, to my knowledge, been seriously begun. In view of their possible bearing on the nature of 'double articulation' (§3 and III below), and the significance of double articulation, in turn, for psychological theories of speech-recognition, it seems important that they should be.

II. The second concerns the boundary between morphology and syntax. The traditional answer is that this is set by the word: thus in the example *Farmers have thought otherwise* the internal structure of *farmers* or *thought* is assigned to morphology, and their external relations (e.g. that of Plural *farmers* to the 'Plural' Verb form *have*) to syntax. But although many writers have maintained this division (Bloomfield, 1935: 207 is an early, and Dik, 1967: 353 a very recent example), it can nevertheless be questioned from two quite opposite angles. First from the viewpoint of IA: if one accepts that relations within the word are simply those of morphemic segments in sequence (compare §2), then there is in principle no difference between the patterning of, e.g. *farm-*, *er* and *-s* and that of *farmers have* and *thought*. It is for this reason in particular that many linguists (see Lyons's Introduction, p. 23) have declined to treat morphology as a 'level' on a par with phonology and syntax. However, a viewpoint opposed to IA does not necessarily lead to different conclusions. The morpheme, according to at least one proponent of IP, can only be defined as 'that unit of grammar the arrangement of which is specified by the syntax and the resulting sequences of which are used to predict the physical form of utterances' (Koutsoudas, 1963: 169). But the 'physical form of utterances' could be predicted from 'morphemes' which cut across the word entirely; to take a well-known example of Hockett's (1961: 51f.), might one not say that

The body was found by a troop of boy scouts is 'predicted' from the morphemes underlying *A troop of boy scouts found the body* plus, in addition, a further morpheme 'Passive'? The history of morphology since the 1930s has led to a progressively complex and non-patent relationship between the elements of grammar, on the one hand, and their phonological realization on the other (cf. Palmer, 1964); is there any reason why the domain in which an element may be realized should be kept within the traditional limits?

The answer, perhaps, is that the phenomena of 'realization' within the word are still very different from those which would obtain in larger units. But is this in fact a sufficient, or indeed a convincing, argument? That it is insufficient is implied by many accounts of European languages: in Latin, for example, a two-word form such as *amatus est* 'He has been loved' is regularly listed in paradigms alongside one-word forms such as *amavit* 'He has loved', and in recent studies of the English Verb (e.g. Palmer, 1965) *have thought* is established as the 'Perfective Aspect' in precisely the way that *thought* (in *Farmers thought otherwise*) is the 'Past Tense'. The Latin case, in particular, has been ably discussed (e.g. Bazell, 1953: I, C). That the argument is unconvincing would, moreover, be implied by a current of research (Pike, 1965, and Callow, 1968, are interesting recent studies) in which the insights of WP within the word are extended, in similar terms, to the phrase, etc. One can foresee a thorough re-examination of the morphology-syntax division in the coming decade.

III. The next point concerns a traditional division between the so-called 'inflectional' and 'derivational' aspects of morphology. In IA a word such as *farm-er-s* consists of three morphemes (§2); but is the *-er* element (which we have ignored in §§3–5) in fact the same sort of 'morpheme' as Plural? According to one established viewpoint it is not: FARM would be one lexeme (see §5) with the root *farm*; FARMER would be another, with a root *farmer* 'derived' from *farm* by the addition of a 'derivational' element *-er*; and Plural would be an 'inflectional' morpheme which supplies a particular 'form' (*farm-s* or *farmer-s*) in either paradigm. But how far is this division between inflectional and derivational morphemes either precise or valid?

Recent Developments in Morphology

This question has been brought into prominence by two developments. The first is the re-examination of WP, where Robins (1959: 125f.) has suggested that one might have 'derivational paradigms', e.g. *farm farmer*, in the same way that one already has 'inflectional paradigms', e.g. *farm farms* or *farmer farmers*; however, Matthews (1965*b*: 140, fn. 4) has disagreed with this, though in a somewhat offhand manner. The second is the attempt to handle the 'derivational' aspect in transformational terms where the literature is fuller but even less conclusive. According to the earliest proposal, this is simply a matter of transformations like everything else: thus *farmer* might be derived syntactically from *So-and-so farms, So-and-so has a farm*, or the like. But this gives rise to various difficulties: firstly, the patterns are often arbitrarily sporadic (e.g. *trumpet-er, violin-ist*, but neither *horn-er* nor *horn-ist*); secondly, there are irregularities and discrepancies of meaning not found in the 'inflectional' field (compare, e.g., the meanings of *solicit-or* and *solicit* or *push-er* and *push*); next there are forms which seem to be 'derived' from others which are non-existent (e.g. *barrister* but not *barrist*; *broker* but not *broke*); finally it is not always possible to put an exact limit to the pattern (thus *the bearer of this letter*; but is, e.g. *the bringer of this letter* acceptable or not?) These difficulties are now well known: see reviews by Schachter (1962) and Matthews (1961) of the earliest transformational account of compounding (Lees, 1960: Chapter 4), and more recent discussions by Zimmer (1964), Dik (1967) and Botha (1968). But there is no consensus as to their solution. The discussion has, in effect, revived a classic discrepancy of criteria for 'grammatical units': are they a unit based essentially on phonological composition (e.g. *solicit-* and *-or*), or a unit based on function within wider units (e.g. *solicitor* as a whole)? Many linguists have tended to seize on either the former (the *morpheme*) or the latter (the *idiom* in the sense of Householder, 1959) as the grammatical primitive *par excellence*; but the discrepancies (recognized in particular by Bolinger, 1948; Bazell, 1953, etc.) remain. One hopes that some more recent remarks by Chomsky (1965: 184ff.) will provoke a further discussion within the generative framework.

IV. Finally we come to the problem of criteria in general

(Question 3 in §1). The classic problem of morphology in the 1940s was that of 'defining the morpheme': of developing an organized methodology, or in the extreme case a formal procedure, which would enable grammatical units to be identified in a maximally controlled and objective manner. So far as a formal procedure is concerned, this approach was in effect destroyed by Chomsky (1957); Harris (1955) is perhaps the last important paper in that genre. But its destruction has unfortunately led to a reluctance to discuss criteria in any form. There are scholars such as Haas (cf. Haas, 1954) who have pursued the definition of units on a looser or more flexible basis; the discussion by Strang (1964) is another which deserves mention at this point. However, comparatively little progress has been visible in the past decade. Many others would agree with Chomsky in declining any 'definition' whatever; the morphemes established by a grammar can only be justified as a part of the total description of the language. But the problem of evaluating the description remains, and for this the evaluation of morphological rules must be one facet. Again, it is to be hoped that the matter will receive a fresh examination in the 1970s.

6. GENERATIVE SYNTAX

John Lyons

Many of the chapters in this book presuppose general understanding of Chomsky's theory of generative grammar. My main purpose in the first part of this chapter has therefore been to provide a concise account of the principles of generative syntax for readers with no previous background in the subject. I have paid special attention to the system introduced by Chomsky (1957, 1965). In the final section, I have given a summary, with references, of some of the more recent work by other scholars, much of which is critical of Chomsky's (1965) system.

Constituent Structure

ALL current syntactic theory, and not only generative syntax, gives recognition, in one way or another, to the notion of constituent structure. It will be convenient, therefore, to begin this chapter by explaining what is meant by this.

Consider the following English sentence: *My friend came home late last night*. It is made up of seven words; and the words are arranged in a particular order. Since we are not concerned here with morphological analysis, we will say that the seven words in this model sentence are its ultimate constituents. This sentence and in general any sentence of the language may be represented as a particular arrangement of the ultimate constituents, the minimal grammatical elements, of which it is composed. Every sentence has therefore what we will refer to as a *linear structure*.

It should be noted at this point that alternative arrangements of the same words may yield an equally acceptable English sentence (e.g. *Last night my friend came home late*) or a non-sentence (e.g. **Friend home last my came late night*). And the permutation of words may or may not affect the meaning of the resultant sentence: *Last night my friend came home late* is more or less equivalent to *My friend came home late last night*, but *Brutus killed Caesar* is very different in meaning from *Caesar killed Brutus*. For the moment at least, we will assume that every different arrangement of the same words is a different sentence, whether or not the meaning is affected by the permutation of the constituent words.

It is intuitively obvious that sentences have another kind of syntactic structure superimposed, as it were, upon their linear form. Anyone who knows English will recognize immediately that in our model sentence, *last night* forms a phrase, as do *my friend* and *came home*; and that *night my* or *late last* do not. The phrases *my friend*, *came home* and *last night* are also constituents (though not ultimate constituents) of the sentence. Let us express this fact by putting brackets around them: (*My friend*) (*came home*) *late* (*last night*). We can now ask whether there are any larger phrases of which one or more of these two-word phrases are constituents. At least two possibilities suggest themselves: ((*came home*) *late*) and (*late* (*last night*)). That both of these alternatives are reasonable (and that the choice between them rests upon alternative interpretations of the function of the word *late* – whether it 'modifies' the verb phrase *came home* or the temporal adverbial *last night*) becomes clear if we consider such sentences as *My friend came home late*, on the one hand, and *My friend died late last night*, on the other. Having noted this instance of *structural ambiguity* (to which notion we shall return presently), let us decide arbitrarily for the former of the two alternatives. One might argue for the further grouping (((*came home*) *late*) (*last night*)). But we will assume that the constituent structure of our illustrative sentence is correctly represented as ((*My friend*) ((*came home*) *late*) (*last night*)). The brackets indicate that the sentence can be analysed into three *immediate constituents* – *my friend*, *came home late* and *last night*; that each of these phrases can be analysed into its immediate constituents – *my* and *friend*, *came home* and *late*, and *last* and *night*; and finally that *came home* has as its immediate constituents *came* and *home*.

Various notations have been used by linguists to represent the constituent structure of sentences. Particularly common in recent work is the use of *tree diagrams*, as illustrated for the model sentence in Figure 10. It should be noted that this tree diagram is equivalent to (conveying no more and no less information than) the system of brackets employed in the previous paragraph.

Far more obvious instances of *structural ambiguity* can be found than the one referred to above in the analysis of our model sentence. A classic example is the phrase *old men and women*, which can be interpreted either as *old* (*men and women*) or (*old*

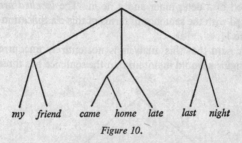

my friend came home late last night

Figure 10.

men) *and women*. Another is *John or Bill and Tom* – (*John or Bill*) *and Tom* or *John or* (*Bill and Tom*). Yet another is *the German history teacher*. Each of these ambiguous phrases is representative of an indefinitely large class of similarly ambiguous phrases that could be constructed on the same pattern. The theoretical importance of these, and a host of other examples that could be cited, lies in the fact that their ambiguity cannot be accounted for in terms of the meaning or the linear arrangement of their ultimate constituents. Although additional and independent reasons could be given for the introduction of the notion of constituent structure into the theory of grammar, we need not go into these here.

The notion of constituent structure, as it has been developed so far in this section, is relatively weak. We have said nothing about the syntactic function of the ultimate and intermediate constituents of sentences other than that they are *bracketed* together in 'layers' of 'phrases'. We must now extend our conception of constituent structure by introducing the notion of *labelling*. For this purpose, we will take a sentence of somewhat different structure: *My friend will open the door*. A fairly traditional, though not entirely uncontroversial, analysis of this sentence might run as follows: it is a sentence (S), which is composed of a noun phrase (NP) and a verb phrase (VP); the noun phrase (*my friend*) is composed of a determiner (Det) and a noun (N), and the verb phrase is composed of a verb (Verb) and a noun phrase; the verb (*will open*) is composed of an auxiliary (Aux) and what we may call, informally, the 'nucleus' of the verb (there is some ambiguity in the use of the term 'verb': the verb nucleus will be symbolized as 'V'), and the noun phrase (*the door*) within the predicate is composed of a determiner and a noun. The *labelled bracketing* associated with the sentence in terms of this classification is given in Figure 11.

I have said that this analysis is not entirely uncontroversial. Some linguists would maintain that the sentence has three, rather

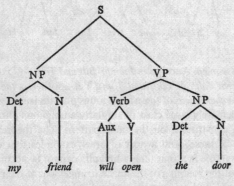

Figure 11.

than two, immediate constituents (*my friend, will open* and *the door*). We will return to this question later. Here it is worth noting a more important point of controversy. Let us grant that, whether we adopt a binary or ternary analysis, *my friend* is the subject and *the door* is the object in the sentence we are discussing; and let us follow Chomsky (1965: 68) in calling such terms as 'subject' and 'object' *functional* labels, and such terms as 'noun phrase' (and 'noun', 'verb', etc.) *categorial* labels. Many linguists (e.g. Halliday, 1961; Pike, 1966; cf. also Elson & Pickett, 1962; Longacre, 1965) have developed systems of syntactic analysis in which phrases like *my friend* are given both a functional and a categorial classification. Against this, Chomsky (1965: 68–74) has argued that the functional classification of noun phrases as subject or object can be derived from the constituent structure. Under the binary analysis of the sentence (which is the one adopted by Chomsky) the subject is that NP which is directly 'dominated' by (i.e. is an immediate constituent of) S and the object is that NP which is directly 'dominated' by VP. In other words, subject and object are recognized at different levels of constituent structure; and their explicit functional labelling is redundant. This is undoubtedly correct, provided that we accept the binary analysis and grant priority to the categorial classification.

But Chomsky's definition of functional terms is not immune from criticism. Since sentences have both a linear and a constituent structure, the functional classification of *my friend* and *the door* could be derived equally well from their position relative to the verb, or indeed from the fact that the subject noun combines with VP and the object noun with Verb; and it might be argued that there is some redundancy in a system which allows for the definition of such notions as subject and object in different ways. The points that have been raised here will be taken up later in our discussion of recent work in transformational grammar. At this stage, let us merely note that the issue is far more complex than it is made to appear in a good deal of the polemical work of the last few years (notably in Postal, 1964*a*).

Phrase-Structure Grammars

We will now move on to consider how constituent structure might be assigned to sentences within a particular system of *generative grammar* (cf. p. 23). Given certain principles of application (which we will explain below), the following set of rules will generate the sentence *My friend opened the door* and assign to it what we are assuming to be the correct constituent structure:

(1) S → NP VP

(2) VP → Verb NP

(3) NP → Det N

(4) Verb → Aux V

(5) Det → {*my*, . . . , *the*}

(6) N → {*friend, door*, . . .}

(7) Aux → {*will*, . . . , *can*}

(8) V → {*open, eat*, . . .}

This system of rules (which is of course grossly inadequate for the generation of more than a small fraction of the sentences of English) is a simple, context-free, *phrase-structure grammar*. The arrow can be taken as an instruction to *rewrite* the symbol that appears to its left as the symbol or string of symbols that appears to its right. (The system is *context-free*, because there are no contextual conditions imposed upon the applicability of any of the rules.) It will be observed that the righthand part of rules (5)–(8) gives a set of elements (under our simplifying assumptions, the ultimate constituents – or syntactic *primes* – of the sentences generated by the grammar), only one of which is to be selected in the application of each rule. This is the significance of the brace brackets enclosing the sets of words or *lexical items* (cf. p. 21). Only a sample has been given of each set of lexical items. You may also have noted (although we shall not develop this point) that I have drawn a notational distinction between the *closed* sets introduced in rules (5) and (7) and the *open* sets introduced in rules (6) and (8). For our present purpose, this distinction between 'open' and 'closed' sets can be interpreted as a distinction between sets with a large number of members and sets with a small number of members.

The rules are to be applied as follows: (i) We start from what is designated as the *initial symbol*. This is S (standing for 'sentence'), which occurs on the left of rule (1). It is rewritten as the *string* of symbols NP VP, which are bracketed together and labelled as S by the operation of the rule. (ii) We now inspect the bracketed string so far generated, S(NP VP), and see whether any of the symbols in it can be rewritten by one of the rules. At this stage of the *derivation*, we can apply either rule (2) or rule (3). It does not matter which of the two rules are applied first, since we make it a condition that the order in which the rules are applied is irrelevant, provided that this does not make a difference to the constituent-structure assigned to the sentence. Rule (3) will have to be applied twice; and it is immaterial whether we proceed by way of (2)–(3)–(3) or (3)–(2)–(3), or indeed (2)–(4)–(3)–(3) or (2)–(3)–(4)–(3), etc. The result is the same S(NP(Det N) VP(Verb (Aux V) NP(Det N))). (iii) Eventually, after two applications of rules (3), (5) and (6) and one application of each of the other rules in the system (and assuming that the appropriate selection has been made in the application of rules (5), (6) and (7)), we come to the point at which no further rules are applicable; and we have generated the sentence *My friend will open the door* with the desired constituent structure. The constituent structure assigned to the sentence (as represented in Figure 11) may be referred to as a *phrase marker*.

Phrase-structure grammars are by no means the only systems of generative grammar that will assign constituent structure to sentences. And phrase-structure grammars themselves fall into various subtypes according to the various conditions that are imposed upon the format and application of the rules. What we have illustrated is a particularly simple kind of grammar; and it will serve as an introduction to our discussion of Chomsky's system of transformational grammar.

Syntactic Structures (1957)

It has been claimed that 'One of the advantages of a transformational grammar is that it enables us to relate superficially distinct sentences and distinguish superficially identical sentences' (p. 26). Let us grant, provisionally, that *The door will be opened by my friend*, though clearly distinct from *My friend will open the door* in terms of its surface structure, is identical with it in deep structure. The relationship between these two sentences was traditionally described in terms of the notions 'active' and 'passive'.

Chomsky's formulation of the active-passive relationship in *Syntactic Structures* (1957) made use of a *transformational* rule, which we may give as:

$$NP_1 - Aux - V - NP_2 \rightarrow NP_2 - Aux + be + en - V - by + NP_1$$

This rule differs in a number of ways from the phrase-structure rules exemplified in the previous section. Not just one symbol, but a string of symbols, appears to the left of the arrow; and the operation that is performed by the rule is rather complex – involving the permutation of the two NPs and the insertion of the elements *be*, *en* (the 'past participle' suffix, realized as *en* in such forms as *taken*, but more regularly as *ed*, in forms like *opened*, etc.) and *by* at particular points in the resultant string. (There is also the distinction between the dashes and the plus-signs, to which we will return presently.)

Transformational rules, in Chomsky's (1957) system, presuppose and depend upon the previous application of a set of phrase-structure rules and have the effect, not only of converting one string of symbols into another, but (in principle) of completely changing the associated phrase marker. Let us assume that the passive transformation, as it has just been formulated, operates upon the string *my + friend — will — open — the + door* and that this string has been generated by means of the phrase-structure rules given in the previous section. The rule applies under the condition that the string in question is *analysable* (without residue) into NP — Aux — V — NP (the use of subscripts to distinguish the two NPs in the formulation of the rule is an informal device for indicating the operation of permutation). If we look at the representation of the phrase marker that is given in Figure 11, we will see that *my + friend* is *dominated* by a node labelled NP, *will* by the node Aux, *open* by the node V, and *the + door* by a node NP: the whole string *my + friend — will — open — the + door* is therefore 'analysable' as NP — Aux — V — NP in the intended sense, and the rule is applicable. It would have the effect of converting the 'input' string into *the + door — will + be + en — open — by + my + friend*; and subsequent rules would apply, permuting *en* and *open*, converting *en* to *ed*, etc., to produce the passive sentence *The door will be opened by my friend*.

But what is the phrase marker that is associated with *the + door — will + be + en — open — by + my + friend* by the operation of the rule $NP_1 — Aux–V — NP_2 \rightarrow NP_2 — Aux + be + en — V — by + NP_1$? Here we touch, though cannot dwell upon, one of the major theoretical problems in the formalization of transformational grammar. Since the 'output' string of one transformational rule may serve as 'input' to a subsequent transformational rule, it will require to be analysable in terms of its associated phrase marker. The plus-signs were used above (as they were used by Chomsky in *Syntactic Structures*) to give part of the information that is required in order to construct the phrase marker for the output string of the passive transformation.

They tell us that *be* + *en* are to be 'attached' to Aux (rather than V) and that *by* is to be 'attached' to NP. This information is clearly insufficient for us to be able to construct the phrase marker in all its details. The problem referred to here is that of assigning *derived constituent-structure* by means of some general principles or conventions associated with the different kinds of transformational operations.

The problem of assigning derived constituent-structure provides us with a nice illustration of the beneficial effects of *formalization*. It would never have been recognized as a 'problem' if the attempt had not been made to describe precisely the conditions under which particular grammatical transformations operate. In certain instances, it is clear enough what the derived constituent structure of a string should be if it is to be subject to the application of a subsequent transformational rule; in other instances, it is not. For example, it is reasonably certain that NP_2 should be the 'subject' in the derived constituent-structure of a passive sentence, as NP_1 is the 'subject' in the phrase marker underlying the corresponding active sentences. (As evidence for this statement one may cite a number of phenomena, including the fact that a particular NP may serve simultaneously as the subject of an active and a passive sentence when the two are coordinated: e.g. *My friend was run over* (*by a car*) *and died instantly*.) But it is not so obvious where the constituents *by* and NP_1 should be placed in the derived phrase marker underlying a passive sentence. In principle, this problem could be solved (other than arbitrarily) in either of two ways. By investigating a wider range of data, one might find empirical evidence to support a decision. Alternatively, in default of empirical evidence, one can apply such general conventions as have been associated with particular formal operations on the basis of those instances where the same operations yield an empirically justifiable result. In either event the linguist is forced to look for a non-arbitrary decision and to weigh the consequences from both the formal and the empirical point of view. For further discussion of the problem and the proposals that have been made to solve it, at least, partially, the reader is referred to one of the standard textbooks (Bach, 1964; Koutsoudas, 1967; Ruwet, 1967). Chomsky's own treatment of this question, which goes back to 1955, has never been published in full and is not generally accessible.

Aspects (1965)

In the years that followed the publication of *Syntactic Structures* (1957), Chomsky's system of transformational grammar underwent a considerable number of modifications: and in 1965, in *Aspects of the Theory of Syntax*, he presented a more comprehensive theory, which differed from his earlier theory in a number of respects. As described in *Aspects*, the grammar of a language (and 'grammar' must now be taken in its widest sense: cf. p. 23) consists of three sets of rules: syntactic, semantic and phonological. The syntactic rules generate the sentences of the language, assigning to each both an *underlying* phrase marker (which represents the *deep structure* of the sentence) and a *derived* phrase marker (which represents the surface structure). The meaning of the sentence is derived (mainly, if not wholly) from its deep structure by means of the semantic rules of interpretation; and the phonetic realization of the sentence is derived from its surface structure by means of the phonological rules. It will be observed that in this conception of grammar, as in that of Katz and Postal (1964), syntax is 'generative' (reflecting the 'creative' or 'productive' aspect of language: cf. p. 12), while phonology and semantics are 'interpretive' (assigning a phonetic and semantic 'interpretation' to the abstract structures generated by the syntax). Since phonology and semantics are discussed from this point of view in the chapters by Fudge and Bierwisch (pp. 91–94 and 166–84), we will say nothing more about them here.

The syntax falls into two parts: the rules of the *base* and the *transformations*. It is the base 'component' that generates the deep structures and the transformational component that converts these into surface structures. The transformational component is therefore 'interpretive' in much the same way as the phonological and semantic rules are; and all the 'creative' power of the system is located in the base. The base itself consists of two parts, or 'subcomponents': the *categorial* subcomponent and the *lexicon*. The categorial subcomponent contains a set of rules similar (with certain important differences which will be mentioned in due course) to the phrase-structure rules of the earlier system; the lexicon lists, in principle, all the lexical items of the language and associates with each the syntactic, semantic and phonological information required for the correct operation of the rules.

It will be clear from this brief account of what we may call an *Aspects*-type grammar that it is a very complex system. We cannot hope to discuss it in any detail. It was necessary, however, to mention some of its main characteristics here, since at least a

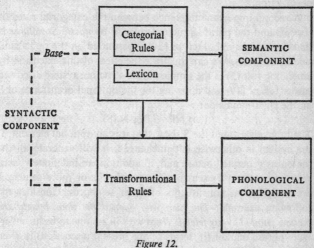

Figure 12.

general appreciation of the way in which the various sections of an *Aspects*-type grammar are related is assumed in a good deal of current linguistic research. The diagram in Figure 12 should be helpful in this respect.

There are a number of ways in which the categorial rules of *Aspects* differ from the phrase-structure rules of the earlier system. First of all (as will be clear from the previous paragraph), they do not introduce lexical items into the underlying phrase marker (by contrast with rules like rules (5)–(8) on p. 119): this is done by means of a special 'lexical substitution' rule, which selects items from the lexicon according to certain conditions, the details of which we need not go into at this point. Roughly speaking, we may say that the categorial rules generate a phrase marker which contains a number of lexical 'slots', with each of which there is associated a set of syntactic *features*: these 'slots' are then 'filled' from the lexicon with items that are there listed as having features compatible with the syntactic specification. (For example, the word *man* might be inserted in a position that requires a noun with the features 'singular', 'human', 'common', etc.). We will explain the distinction between 'categories' and 'features' in the next section.

A second important difference between the categorial rules of *Aspects* and the phrase-structure rules of *Syntactic Structures* is that the initial symbol (cf. p. 120) is permitted on the right-hand side of the rules. We can illustrate the effect of this extension by amending rule (3) of the simple phrase-structure system discussed earlier (cf. p. 119) and allowing for the optional occurrence of S on the right-hand side:

$$\text{(3a) NP} \rightarrow \text{Det N (S)}$$

The brackets around the S show that it is an optional element. If the system is otherwise left unchanged, it will generate all the sentences generated before and, in addition, an indefinitely large set of more complex sentences, in which one or more sentences are *embedded* as constituents of other sentences. Consider the following example: *The man who opened the door bought the picture painted by my friend*. What we will assume to be its underlying phrase marker (in terms of the present discussion) is given in Figure 13. (For simplicity of reference we have attached subscripts to the different occurrences of S.) Assuming that *ed* (an abstract representation of 'past tense') is included with *will* and *can* and that the lexical items *man*, *picture*, *buy* and *paint* are listed appropriately, this phrase marker will be generated by the amended set of rules. (The reader may wish to verify this for himself.)

Certain transformations must be carried out on the underlying phrase marker. These we will assume include the following: (i) S_3 is transformed into the corresponding passive ('The picture was painted by my friend'); (ii) *the man* in S_2 is replaced with *who*, and *the picture* in S_3 with *which* or *that*; (iii) *which/that ed be* ('which/

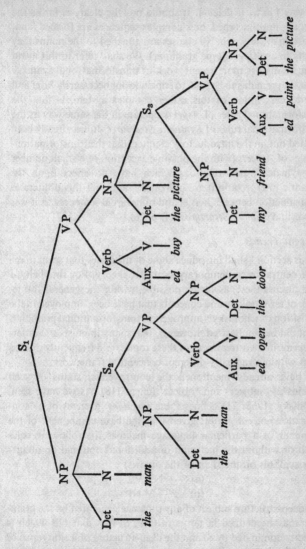

Figure 13.

that was') in S_3 is deleted. It should now be clear, as far as the essentials are concerned, how complex sentences are formed (and, in particular, how relative clauses are attached to the nouns they qualify in an *Aspects*-type grammar). We shall refer to this again when we discuss more recent work in transformational syntax.

All that remains to be said, to conclude our necessarily brief and general description of this rather complex system, is that the transformational rules of *Aspects* operate in the same way as the transformational rules of *Syntactic Structures*. It has already been pointed out, in the introductory chapter, that the transformational rules of *Aspects* (with the possible exception of a small number of 'stylistic' transformations which have no effect upon the semantic interpretation) are obligatory, and that this obliterates the distinction between kernel and non-kernel sentences as it was drawn in *Syntactic Structures* (cf. p. 26).

Current Trends

In this section I shall introduce some of the issues that seem to me to be central in contemporary syntactic theory. For simplicity, I shall discuss these, as far as possible, within the general framework of terminology and concepts that have been employed in the exposition of Chomsky's approach to transformational grammar. It should be emphasized, however, that many linguists use different terms in their treatment of these topics, and frequently discuss them within a radically different conceptual framework.

I have already mentioned the controversial status of such notions as 'subject' and 'object' (cf. p. 118). As we have seen, Chomsky (1965: 71) defines these *functions* in terms of a 'configuration' of *categories*: given that the base component of the grammar of a particular language includes the following rules (with or without the inclusion of additional optional or obligatory symbols on the right of the arrows)

(a) S → NP VP
(b) VP → V NP

the deep-structure subject of any sentence generated by the grammar may be defined in terms of [NP, S] (i.e. that NP which is directly dominated by S) and the deep-structure object in terms of [NP, VP] (i.e. that NP which is directly dominated by VP). It was pointed out above that these 'configurational' definitions will operate independently of the order in which the symbols occur in the string of symbols introduced by S and VP: and that Chomsky's system would also allow us to define the subject as that NP which occurs to the left of VP, and the object as that NP which occurs to the right of V. One may conclude, therefore, that either the relative order of constituents, or direct domination by a higher-level constituent, is irrelevant for the definition of the deep structure subject and object. Since the notion of 'domination' is fundamental to the definition of the scope of transformational rules, and can be applied equally well in the analysis both of languages with a relatively 'free' word order (e.g. Sanskrit, Latin, Russian) and of languages which, like English, make syntactic use of 'fixed' word order (cf. *John killed Bill; Bill killed John*), many linguists have argued that, as far as the definition of 'subject' and 'object' is concerned, the relative order of NP and VP in rule (a) and of V and NP in rule (b) is irrelevant. More generally, it has been suggested that there is no need for the linear ordering of elements in deep structure (cf. Staal, 1968). Chomsky's own arguments in favour of ordering are far from conclusive (1965: 123–7).

It could also be argued that the definition of 'subject' and 'object' should take precedence over the definition of categorial terms like NP, VP, V, etc. Proposals along these lines have been made by Seuren (1969), within a modified version of Chomsky's system of transformational grammar which, in this respect, has much in common with the non-transformational 'tagmemic' approach of Pike and his associates (cf. Pike, 1967; Longacre, 1965).

A number of linguists, working independently of one another, have made the more radical suggestion that notions like 'subject' and 'object' are relatively superficial and can be given no direct interpretation at the deepest level of syntactic analysis. Halliday gives an account of his views on this question in the following chapter (pp. 146–58), and relates his proposals to those of Fillmore (1968), Anderson (1968*a*), and others. The general tendency of this work, it will be seen, is to derive the superficial constituent structure of sentences from a 'deeper' *syntactic* specification in which the determinant elements are such items as 'agentive', 'instrumental', 'locative', 'dative', 'causative', and so on. According to this point of view, in a sentence like *My friend opened the door with the key*, the noun phrase *my friend* would be 'agentive', *with the key* would be 'instrumental' and *the door* would be 'neutral' ('objective', in Fillmore's terms, 'affected' in Halliday's: see p. 157 below). Two points should be made in connexion with what Halliday calls the 'functional' analysis of sentences. First of all, notions like 'agentive', 'locative', 'causative', 'instrumental', etc. can be given a direct semantic interpretation: we have already referred to the influence of semantic considerations in contemporary syntax (cf. p. 27). Secondly, 'functional' notions of this kind have frequently been invoked by linguists in the past, more or less informally, in their analyses of a wide range of languages throughout the world. One may reasonably hope, therefore, that it will eventually prove possible to extend a more precisely formulated system of syntactic description based upon these notions to all human languages. Needless to say, a considerable amount of work remains to be done before we can be at all confident of the success (or failure) of this venture.

A good deal of current syntactic theory, though by no means all, is influenced by the attempt to discover 'deep' semantically interpretable and universal features which are overtly (or 'superficially') manifest in a variety of ways in different languages. Proposals have also recently been made by a number of scholars to explain some of the 'deeper' syntactic phenomena that have been discovered by appealing to notions previously discussed by logicians and philosophers of language. Boyd and Thorne (1969), and independently Ross (cf. McCawley, 1968: 155) and Householder (1970), have related Austin's (1962) notion of 'performative' verbs to the 'modality' of sentences (their status as statements, commands, predictions, etc.). Bach (1968) has provided an analysis of noun phrases (although the evidence is mainly from English the analysis is expressly intended to be applicable to other languages), according to which a sentence like *The professors signed a petition* has the underlying structure suggested by 'The ones who were professors signed something which was a petition'. This analysis, for which he gives a number of arguments, can be compared to the kind of analysis that many logicians might give in terms of operators and variables. Seuren (1969) also draws upon the 'operators' of formal logic in his discussion of negation, modality and quantification, as does McCawley (1968) in his discussion of a range of topics involving the relationship between syntax and semantics.

In the previous section, we saw how relative clauses are attached to the nouns or noun phrases they qualify in a grammar of the type outlined by Chomsky (1965). In the generation of the sentence *The man who opened the door bought the picture painted by my friend*, two relative clauses are formed: *who opened the door* (S_2) and *which* (or *that*) *was painted by my friend* (S_3). The substitution of *who* for *the man* in the string underlying S_2 and of *which* (or *that*) for *the picture* in the string underlying S_3 depends upon the general principle operative in English, that *who* is the form of the relative pronoun that is used when the 'antecedent' noun or noun phrase denotes a human being (technically, is assigned the *feature* [+Human]: see below) and *which* (or *that*) is the form that is used otherwise (there are certain complicating factors which we need not discuss here). At this point we are concerned with a more general, and theoretically more important, condition that must be fulfilled whenever a relative pronoun of any form is substituted for an underlying noun phrase. This is the condition that the noun phrase for which the pronoun is substituted must be *identical* with the 'antecedent' noun phrase in the matrix string to which the pronoun 'refers'. The important theoretical question is this: in what sense are the noun phrases said to be identical? What is the nature of the relevant *identity condition*?

First of all, it should be noted that it is the same condition of identity as that which holds more generally for pronominal substitution in a transformational grammar of the kind described by Chomsky (1965). In the second clause of the sentence *When the man opened the door, he got the shock of his life* the pronoun *he* is substituted for the underlying noun phrase *the man* (we are neglecting of course the alternative interpretation in which *he* refers to some person not mentioned in the sentence); and *he* 'stands for', or is equivalent to, *the man* in the first clause, in the same way that a relative pronoun 'stands for', or is equivalent to, an antecedent noun phrase. Similarly, the reflexive pronoun *himself* 'stands for' *the man* in *The man killed himself*; and it is derived by a substitution transformation conditional upon the identity of the subject noun phrase and the object noun phrase in the underlying string (*the man killed the man*).

In earlier transformational work based on Chomsky (1957) the condition for pronominal substitution was formulated solely in terms of what might be called *lexical identity*. By this I mean that two noun phrases were deemed to be identical if, and only if, they consisted of the same lexical items. Whether they were *referentially identical* (i.e., whether they denoted, or referred to, the same person or thing) was held to be, in principle, irrelevant. It was later suggested (cf. Chomsky, 1965: 145–7) that pronominalization should be made conditional upon *strict identity*, where 'strict identity' includes both lexical and referential identity. One of the principal reasons for introducing into the grammar this notion of coreferentiality is that it makes it possible to account syntactically for the fact that in a sentence like *The man killed the man* (as distinct from *The man killed himself*) 'the two phonetically identical Noun Phrases are necessarily interpreted as differing in reference' (Chomsky, 1965: 145). The way in which Chomsky proposed to handle sameness and difference of reference for the purpose of pronominalization was to assign arbitrarily to all the noun phrases in the deep structure of a sentence *markers*, or (as we shall call them) *indices*, indicating whether they were referentially identical with other occurrences of the same noun phrases in the same sentence or not. Using subscript numerals for the referential indices (Chomsky's proposal is that the indices should be treated formally as *features*: see below), we can represent the underlying structure of our model sentence for relativization (the introduction of relative pronouns into the sentence) roughly as follows (this informal representation should be interpreted in terms of the phrase marker given in Figure 13):

(*the man$_1$* (*the man$_1$ opened the door$_2$*) *bought the picture$_3$* (*my friend$_4$ painted the picture$_3$*)).

The second occurrence of *the man* is strictly identical with the first (it is both lexically and referentially identical), and is therefore replaced by *who*; the second occurrence of *the picture* is strictly identical with the first, and is replaced by *which* (or *that*). Had the referential indices on the two occurrences of *the man* or the two occurrences of *the picture* been different – and it must be remembered that they have been assigned arbitrarily in the generative process – the relative transformation would have failed to operate (it would have 'blocked'); and the deep structure in question would have been rejected as ungrammatical. In the case of a deep structure like *the man killed the man* (to give a very informal representation), the resultant sentence would be either *The man killed himself* or *The man killed the man* according to whether the two noun phrases were referentially identical or not.

It will be observed that in assigning referential indices to the noun phrases in the model sentence above we tacitly followed the convention that the same index was not used for different noun phrases. In Chomsky's conception of the role of referential indices (according to which the syntactic component of the grammar is generative and the semantic component 'interpretive': cf. p. 124), this convention is unnecessary and unmotivated. Since the identity condition for pronominalization requires both sameness of reference and sameness of lexical items, we could have assigned the same index to *the man*, *the door*, *the picture* and *my friend*; and the relative pronouns would still have been correctly substituted for their antecedent noun phrases.

A different treatment from Chomsky's has been suggested in what we may refer to as post-*Aspects* transformational grammar. McCawley (1968*a*) has proposed, as part of his general thesis that semantics is prior to syntax (see below, p. 180), that the referential indices required for pronominalization should be interpreted as standing for, or identifying, the particular persons or things (including 'imaginary objects', etc.) that the speaker intends to refer to, every distinct referent 'in the speaker's mental picture of the universe' (1968*a*: 138) being provided with a different index. If this proposal is adopted (cf. also Sampson, 1969), it is clear that there is no need to insist upon strict identity as a condition for pronominalization: the relevant identity condition can be formulated solely in terms of sameness of referential index.

McCawley's proposal is especially interesting, as he says, if it is taken in conjunction with Bach's (1968). It was pointed out above that Bach's analysis of *The professors signed a petition* presupposes an 'underlying form' rather like 'The ones who were professors signed something which was a petition' (1968: 97). We can reformulate this, using x and y as variables, as 'Those x such that x were professors signed a y such that y was a petition'. There is a striking resemblance between this kind of analysis and that which would normally be given by logicians in terms of the predicate calculus. Bach's discussion relates mainly to referential indices operating as variables ('quantified' in various ways – by means of *some*, *all*, the definite article, etc.), McCawley's to the use of referential indices as constants. For example (on the assumption that *my friend* is intended by the speaker to refer to a specific person), a sentence like *My friend killed himself* would be derived from a structure something like (x_1 (x_1 *was my friend*) *killed* x_1), where x_1 is the referential index denoting the person the speaker has in mind. One of the points to note about this analysis is that unlike Chomsky's it does not depend upon there being a second occurrence of *my friend* in the deep structure. A further important feature of what we may refer to as the Bach-McCawley analysis is that, combined with the logician's notion of 'scope', it can account for the ambiguity of such sentences as *She wants to marry a man with a big bank account*: the ambiguity in question is that which depends upon whether the man referred to is a specific individual or not (cf. Bach, 1968: 106). Whatever may be the fate of these proposals by Bach and McCawley, and of the other attempts mentioned above to relate formal logic to generative syntax (and the authors would probably admit that they are no more than tentative), there can be no doubt that the problems they seek to resolve are problems that linguists, as well as logicians and philosophers, must eventually come to grips with. For some further, cautionary discussion of the relationship between logic and linguistics the reader is referred to the chapter by Janet Dean Fodor (pp. 198–214).

One of the most controversial topics in current discussions of generative grammar has to do with the place at which *selectional* (or *collocational*) restrictions are accounted for and the manner in which they are formulated. Consider the following 'sentence'

Sincerity may admire the boy. Granted that this is in some sense abnormal, or deviant (this is the significance of the asterisk that has been prefixed to it), and that its deviance results from the collocation of *sincerity* with *admire* (cf. Chomsky, 1965: 75), the question is: How do we account for this fact in a systematic presentation of the grammar of the language? Chomsky's (1965) answer depends upon the distinction that he draws between *categories* (which we already have met: see p. 118) and *features*. Since this distinction is of considerable importance in recent generative syntax and is invoked in other chapters of the present volume, I will begin by explaining what is involved in a relatively non-technical way.

Among the rules of the categorial component of an *Aspects*-type grammar, we might find the following (cf. Chomsky, 1965: 85):

(1) NP → (Det) N (S)
(2) N → [+N, ±Common]
(3) [+Common] → [±Count]
(4) [−Common] → [±Animate]
(5) [+Animate] → [±Human]
(6) [−Count] → [±Abstract]

Rule (1) is a phrase-structure rule of the kind we have discussed in previous sections: it rewrites the *category* that appears to the left of the arrow as the string of (one or more) *categories* that appears to the right of the arrow. Such rules are called *branching rules* in Chomsky (1965). Rules (2)–(6) are *subcategorization rules*; and their function is to develop the category N into a set of *features*. The subcategorization rules given here can be interpreted as follows: every member of the category 'Noun' has the property (or feature) of being a 'Noun' and the property of being either 'Common' or 'non-Common' ('plus Common' or 'minus Common'); all categories that have the property 'plus Common' must be either 'plus Count' (i.e. countable) or 'minus Count'; and so on. The set of features that results from the application of the subcategorization rules is called a 'complex symbol' (abbreviated elsewhere in Chomsky, 1965, as CS). One such complex symbol might be [+N, −Count, +Abstract]; another might be [+N, +Count, +Animate, +Human].

Given this formalization of the syntactic properties relevant to the subclassification of nouns, we can organize the lexicon appropriately, with entries of the following form:

(a) *sincerity*: [+N, −Count, +Abstract]
(b) *boy*: [+N, +Count, +Common, +Animate, +Human].

These entries may be read as 'the lexical item *sincerity* is an uncountable, abstract noun' and 'the lexical item *boy* is a countable, common, animate, human noun'. Now, assuming for the sake of the argument that the deviance of **Sincerity may admire the boy* is correctly accounted for by saying that the verb *admire* occurs only with human nouns in the subject position, we can formulate a *selectional rule* to this effect in terms of the feature [+ [+Human] Aux ——]. It should be stressed that in Chomsky's (1965) system this is a *single* feature, to be interpreted as 'having the property of occurring in the third position of a string of symbols, the first position of which is occupied by a complex symbol having (amongst others) the feature [+Human] and the second position of which is occupied by the category Aux'. If the reader consults the illustrative phrase structure rules and subcategorization rules that have been given in the previous sections of this chapter, he will see that this is equivalent to saying 'taking as its subject a noun phrase, the head noun of which is human'. We need not go further into the details of Chomsky's technique of subcategorization: for a critical examination of the formalism see the review by Matthews (1967*b*). From what has been said, it will be clear that Chomsky treats selectional restriction as a matter for syntax, rather than semantics. (He does, however, remark (1965: 72) that 'it should not be taken for granted, necessarily, that syntactic and semantic considerations can be sharply distinguished'.)

It is often said that selectional restrictions are semantic, rather than syntactic, in origin. Indeed, one might claim that this is the more traditional view, according to which deviant sentences like **Sincerity may admire the boy* might be described as 'grammatical, but meaningless'. (For an illuminating discussion of this question in relation to earlier transformational syntax, see Bazell, 1964.) This view, or something approximating to it, has also been maintained in the recent literature of generative grammar. Prior to the appearance of *Aspects of the Theory of Syntax*, Matthews (1961, 1965*a*) proposed that the phrase-structure rules and transformational rules of the syntactic component should generate strings consisting not of lexical items but of syntactic categories (and certain grammatical elements); and that the lexical items should be inserted in place of the categories by the operation of a separate set of *collocational rules* operating with reference to the relevant properties ('Human', 'Abstract', etc.) specified in the lexicon. The essence of Matthews's proposal is that although lexical insertion is made after all the transformational rules have applied, his collocational rules are defined with respect to what we may be permitted to call 'deep' functional relations: 'subject': 'predicate', 'subject': 'complement', 'predicate': 'complement', etc. (Matthews uses the term 'kernel colligation' to refer to what we are calling complexes of 'deep' functions.) He also points out, correctly (1965*a*:46), that the analysis presented by Lyons (1963) rests upon a somewhat similar conception (although the author of this work failed to appreciate the implications of his departure from the system of *Syntactic Structures*, which he claimed to be following). Matthews makes further brief references to his notion of 'collocability' in the course of his review of *Aspects* (Matthews, 1967*b*).

A rather different view of selectional restrictions has been taken by those scholars who advocate a 'semantically based' model of transformational grammar. The suggestions that have been made differ considerably in detail (cf. Anderson, 1968*b*; Chafe, 1967; Lakoff, 1968; McCawley, 1968*a*, *b*), and it would be impossible even to summarize them here. What they have in common is their rejection of 'deep structure' in the form in which this has been defined by Chomsky (1965). They argue that all the 'generative' power of the grammar is located in the semantic component, the rules of which operate prior to the operation of the now purely 'interpretive' rules of the syntactic component (see p. 124 for this distinction of 'generative' and 'interpretive'). Fundamental to the argument is the observation that pairs of sentences which differ with respect to their 'superficial' syntactic structure and the lexical items contained in them may still be semantically equivalent (or at least semantically related to one another) in much the same way as pairs of sentences (e.g. corresponding active and passive sentences) in a 'syntactically based' transformational grammar. For example, Lakoff (1968) has claimed that pairs of sentences like *John used the key to open the door* and *John opened the door with the key* manifest the same selectional restrictions (for the positions occupied here by *John*, *key*, *open* and *door*) and should be derived from the same underlying semantic representation. Anderson (1968*b*) has made the same claim with respect to pairs of sentences like *John bought the car from Harry* and *Harry sold the car to John*. What is common to the semantic representation underlying the latter pair of sentences might be indicated by the following paraphrase: 'That x, such that x was a car, passed from (the possession of) y_1, who was called John, to (the possession of) y_2, who was called Harry, by means of purchase'. (I have also incorporated in this paraphrase the Bach-McCawley proposal referred to above.) The potential semantic difference between the two sentences might be accounted for by assigning to either 'John' or 'Harry' the function (or role) 'agentive'. Presumably, 'car', 'purchase' and perhaps also 'possession' would be analysable in terms of more specific semantic features. The point to be noted is that *lexicalization* takes place, according to these proposals, after the operation of at least some transformational rules, lexical items being substituted for syntactically structured complexes of semantic features.

At the time of writing, it is unclear how far a comprehensive and systematic description of a language could be carried along these lines. It should be added that Chomsky has recently described the claims made for 'semantically-based' grammar as vacuous, on the grounds that it is nothing more than a 'notational variant' of the theory of transformational grammar outlined in *Aspects* (cf. Chomsky, forthcoming). Whether or not this is so (and it is by no means certain that Chomsky is correct in his evaluation of the relationship between 'generative' and 'interpretive' semantics), concentration upon the complex interrelations that exist between syntax and semantics, and the attempts that are being made to formalize these by the 'generative semanticists', cannot but contribute to our understanding of the structure of language.

It has not been possible to mention in this final section more than a few of the general trends in contemporary syntactic research that appear to be extending the 'horizons' of the subject, and most of the references have been to work which is of its nature speculative and in much of its detail, no doubt, ephemeral. In conclusion, I should stress two points, of which anyone actively engaged in linguistics is, or should be, aware. First of all, it must be appreciated that a considerable amount of research is going on all the time into the grammatical structure of various languages, which, though it does not command the same general interest or have the same immediate effect as the more obviously theoretical work, must eventually be taken into account in the further development of syntactic theory. The current concern with 'deeper' and more 'abstract' syntax on the part of many theoreticians makes it all the more important to examine as wide a range of languages as possible. Much of the work so far published which purports to demonstrate the 'universality' of certain 'deeper' analyses of English makes only the most cursory reference to the structure of other languages. (This comment applies also to the more speculative sections of my own book: Lyons, 1968.)

The second point is this. The differences between the various 'versions' of post-*Aspects* generative syntax are now at least as striking as those that exist between 'Chomskyan' syntax as a whole and other 'non-Chomskyan' systems of syntactic analysis. Chomsky himself has remarked of the work that derives immediately from his own: 'At present the field is in considerable ferment, and it will probably be some time before the dust begins to settle and a number of issues are even tentatively resolved' (1968: 54, fn. 6). If and when the dust does settle, it may be even less useful to distinguish between 'Chomskyan' and 'non-Chomskyan' grammar than it is now.

7. LANGUAGE STRUCTURE AND LANGUAGE FUNCTION

M. A. K. Halliday

*In this chapter Halliday distinguishes three grammatically relevant
'language functions', and illustrates them from English: (i) the
'ideational', (ii) the 'interpersonal' and (iii) the 'textual'. The
first refers to what is commonly called the 'cognitive meaning', or
'propositional content', of sentences; the second to distinctions
such as those of 'mood', or 'modality' (e.g. the differences between
statements, questions and commands); and the third to the way in
which the grammatical and intonational structure of sentences
relates them to one another in continuous texts and to the situations
in which they are used. It is in terms of the 'textual function' that
Halliday describes certain kinds of so-called 'stylistic' variation
(e.g. the use of an active or passive sentence to express the same
'cognitive meaning').*

*As I pointed out in the previous chapter (p. 129) and as Halliday
himself mentions below, his account of the 'ideational' component
of grammatical structure in terms of 'transitivity functions' has
much in common with Anderson's (1968a) or Fillmore's (1968)
treatment in terms of 'deep cases'. According to Halliday the
distinction between transitive and intransitive verbs is becoming
more and more 'marginal' in English: 'action clauses . . . seem to
be organized on an ergative basis' (p. 157).*

*Halliday's criticism of the distinction between 'competence' and
'performance' as either 'unnecessary' or 'misleading' (p. 145) may
be compared with what Campbell and Wales have to say in a later
chapter. Unlike Halliday, they do not reject the distinction between
'an idealized knowledge of a language and its actualized use'. They
propose instead that the notion of 'competence' (or 'idealized
knowledge') should be extended beyond purely 'grammatical
competence' to include what they call the speaker's 'communicative'
ability (which seems to correspond quite closely with Halliday's
'textual function').*

Also worth noting is Halliday's claim that 'each tone group represents what the speaker decides to make into one unit of information' (p. 162). This would seem to be supported by what Laver says about speech production: that the tone group 'is handled in the central nervous system as a unitary behavioural act' p. 69).

I. THE FUNCTIONS OF LANGUAGE

WHY is language as it is? The nature of language is closely related to the demands that we make on it, the functions it has to serve. In the most concrete terms, these functions are specific to a culture: the use of language to organize fishing expeditions in the Trobriand Islands, described half a century ago by Malinowski, has no parallel in our own society. But underlying such specific instances of language use, are more general functions which are common to all cultures. We do not all go on fishing expeditions; however, we all use language as a means of organizing other people, and directing their behaviour.

A purely extrinsic account of linguistic functions, one which is not based on an analysis of linguistic structure, will not answer the question; we cannot explain language by simply listing its uses, and such a list could in any case be prolonged indefinitely. Malinowski's ethnographic account of the functions of language, based on the distinction between 'pragmatic' and 'magical', or Bühler's well-known tripartite division into the 'representational', 'expressive' and 'conative' functions, show that it is possible to generalize; but these generalizations are directed towards sociological or psychological inquiries, and are not intended primarily to throw light on the nature of linguistic structure. At the same time, an account of linguistic structure that pays no attention to the demands that we make of language is lacking in perspicacity, since it offers no principles for explaining why the structure of language is organized in one way rather than in another.

Here, therefore, we shall consider language in terms of its *use*. Structural preoccupations have been dominant in linguistics for some time; but the usefulness of a synthesis of structural and functional approaches has long been apparent from the work of the Prague linguists (Vachek, 1966) who developed Bühler's ideas, especially in the study of grammar. The particular form taken by the grammatical system of language is closely related to the social and personal needs that language is required to serve. But in order to bring this out it is necessary to look at both the system of language and its functions at the same time; otherwise we will lack any theoretical basis for generalizations about how language is used.

It is perhaps most helpful to begin with the notion of an act of speech, regarding this as a simultaneous selection from among a large number of interrelated options. These options represent the 'meaning potential' of language. In speaking, we choose: whether to make a statement or ask a question, whether to generalize or particularize, whether to repeat or add something new, whether or not to intrude our own judgement, and so on. It would be better, in fact, to say that we 'opt', since we are concerned not with deliberate acts of choice but with symbolic behaviour, in which the options may express our meanings only very indirectly: in the same sense we may be said to 'opt' between a long vowel and a short one, or between a straight arm and a bent one (where the meaning is likewise mediated through the symbolic significance of the distinction between a handshake and a salute). The system of available options is the 'grammar' of the language, and the speaker, or writer, selects within this system: not *in vacuo*, but in the context of speech situations. Speech acts thus involve the creative and repetitive exercise of options in social and personal situations and settings (Firth, 1968; Pike, 1967; Ellis, 1966).

It is fairly obvious that language is used to serve a variety of different needs, but until we examine its grammar there is no clear reason for classifying its uses in any particular way. However, when we examine the meaning potential of language itself, we find that the vast numbers of options embodied in it combine into a very few relatively independent 'networks'; and these networks of options correspond to certain basic functions of language. This enables us to give an account of the different functions of language that is relevant to the general understanding of linguistic structure rather than to any particular psychological or sociological investigation.

Language Structure and Language Function

1. Language serves for the expression of 'content': that is, of the speaker's experience of the real world, including the inner world of his own consciousness. We may call this the *ideational* function, though it may be understood as easily in behavioural as in conceptual terms (Firth, 1968: 91). In serving this function, language also gives structure to experience, and helps to determine our way of looking at things, so that it requires some intellectual effort to see them in any other way than that which our language suggests to us.

2. Language serves to establish and maintain social relations: for the expression of social roles, which include the communication roles created by language itself – for example the roles of questioner or respondent, which we take on by asking or answering a question; and also for getting things done, by means of the interaction between one person and another. Through this function, which we may refer to as *interpersonal*, social groups are delimited, and the individual is identified and reinforced, since by enabling him to interact with others language also serves in the expression and development of his own personality.

These two basic functions, to each of which corresponds one broad division in the grammar of a natural language, are also reflected in Bernstein's studies of educational failure (e.g. Bernstein, 1970). Bernstein's work suggests that in order to succeed in the educational system a child must know how to use language as a means of learning, and how to use it in personal interaction; these can be seen as specific requirements on his control of the ideational and interpersonal functions of language.

3. Finally, language has to provide for making links with itself and with features of the situation in which it is used. We may call this the *textual* function, since this is what enables the speaker or writer to construct 'texts', or connected passages of discourse that is situationally relevant; and enables the listener or reader to distinguish a text from a random set of sentences. One aspect of the textual function is the establishment of cohesive relations from one sentence to another in a discourse (Hasan, 1968).

All these functions are reflected in the structure of the clause. In this chapter we attempt to show, by reference to English, what a clause is: how it serves for the realization of a number of very general meanings, or semantic options, relating to the interpersonal, ideational and textual functions of language; and how these are expressed through various configurations of structural 'roles' – functional elements such as 'process' and 'actor' that derive from these basic functions. For a more detailed exemplification we shall consider an aspect of ideational meaning, the system of transitivity; the remaining areas, which have the same formal properties, will be referred to only briefly. Any one clause is built up of a combination of structures deriving from these three functions (for the sake of brevity we shall leave out the logical component in linguistic structure, which is somewhat different in its realizations).

II. LANGUAGE AND EXPERIENCE

Since normally every speech act serves each of the basic functions of language, the speaker is selecting among all the types of options simultaneously. Hence the various sets of structural 'roles' are mapped onto one another, so that the actual structure-forming element in language is a complex of roles, like a chord in a fugue: for example *Sir Christopher Wren*, in the clause *Sir Christopher Wren built this gazebo*, is at once actor and subject and theme (see 13 below). Each of these three represents a value in some configuration – some melodic line, so to speak – such as 'process plus actor plus goal'. And all such configurations are meaningful, since what we have called the basic functions of language, looked at from another point of view, are simply different kinds of meaning.

So for example there is a difference in meaning between (li) and (lii):

(li) She would marry Horatio. She loved him.
(lii) She would marry Horatio. It was Horatio she loved.

The difference concerns the organization of the second clause as a piece of information, and it derives from the textual function. There is also a difference between (li) and (liii):

(liii) She would marry Horatio. She did not love him.

But we cannot say that this difference is 'greater' or 'more meaningful' than that between (li) and (lii); it is merely of a different kind. The speaker does not first decide to express some content and then go on to decide what sort of a message to build out of it – whether to turn it into a statement or a question, whether to make it like (li) or (lii), and so on. If he did, the planning of each sentence would be a totally discrete operation and it would be impossible ever to answer a question that had actually been asked. Speech acts involve planning that is continuous and simultaneous in respect of all the functions of language.

Linguistics is not as a rule concerned with the description of particular speech events on individual occasions (although it is possible to write a theoretical grammar of just one instance if the need arises; it usually does not). It is concerned rather with the description of speech acts, or texts, since only through the study of language in use are all the functions of language, and therefore all components of meaning, brought into focus. Here we shall not need to draw a distinction between an idealized knowledge of a language and its actualized use: between 'the code' and 'the use of the code', or between 'competence' and 'performance'. Such a dichotomy runs the risk of being either unnecessary or misleading: unnecessary if it is just another name for the distinction between what we have been able to describe in the grammar and what we have not, and misleading in any other interpretation. The study of language in relation to the situations in which it is used – to situation types, i.e. the study of language as 'text' – is a theoretical pursuit, no less interesting and central to linguistics than psycholinguistic investigations relating the structure of language to the structure of the human brain.

We shall consider each of the functions in turn as it is reflected in the structure of the English clause, beginning with what we have called the 'ideational'. To the adult – though not, be it noted, to the child – the predominant demand that we make on our language (predominant, at least, in our thinking about language; perhaps that is all) is that it allows us to communicate about something. We use language to represent our experience of the processes, persons, objects, abstractions, qualities, states and relations of the world around us and inside us. Since this is not the only demand we make on language it is useful to refer to it specifically; hence 'ideational function', 'ideational meaning' etc. (other terms that have been used in a similar sense are 'representational', 'cognitive', 'semantic', 'factual-notional' and 'experiential').

Let us consider the expression of processes: of actions, events, states and relations, and the persons, objects and abstractions that are associated with them. For this purpose we will focus our attention on one unit of linguistic structure, namely the clause. In any language, a vast number of different processes can be distinguished; but these are reducible to a small number of process types, and the grammar of every language comprises sets of options representing broad categories of this kind. The most familiar, and simplest, model is that which groups all processes into the two categories of 'transitive' and 'intransitive'.

Associated with each type of process are a small number of functions, or 'roles', each representing the parts that the various persons, objects or other classes of phenomena may play in the process concerned. For example, in

(2) Sir Christopher Wren built this gazebo

we have a 'transitive' clause containing three roles: an 'actor', a 'process' and a 'goal'. (The specification of this clause, assuming just these categories, would involve (i) selection of the option 'transitive', from the system transitive/intransitive; which would then determine (ii) the presence of the functions 'process', 'actor' and 'goal'; these being realized (iii) by *built*, *Sir Christopher Wren* and *this gazebo* respectively.)

III. TRANSITIVITY FUNCTIONS: PROCESS AND PARTICIPANT ROLES

The roles which appear in the expression of processes are of different kinds. First there is the process itself, usually represented by a verb, e.g. *built* in (2). Then there are the participant functions, the specific roles that are taken on by persons and objects, e.g. *Wren* and *gazebo*; and finally there are what we may call the circumstantial functions, the associated conditions and constraints such as those of time, place and manner (Fillmore, 1968, where the two together are referred to as 'cases'; Halliday, 1967/68).

It has been customary to recognize three participant functions in English, namely 'actor', 'goal' (or 'patient'), and 'beneficiary'. Various subdivisions and modifications have been proposed, such as the distinction between goal and 'object of result' (Lyons, 1968: 439; cf. 'factitive' in Fillmore, 1968: 25) as in

(3i) The Borough Council restored this gazebo
(3ii) Sir Christopher Wren built this gazebo

where *this gazebo* is goal in (3i) but object of result in (3ii); in (3ii) the gazebo comes into existence only as a result of the process of building. Similarly, the beneficiary may be the recipient of an object, as *Oliver* in (4i), or the recipient of a service, as *Frederick* in (4ii):

(4i) I've given Oliver a tie
(4ii) I've made Frederick a jacket

These subclassifications are not made arbitrarily; they account for systematic distinctions in the grammar, e.g. the related prepositional form is *to Oliver* but *for Frederick* in (4), and in (3) *restore* but not *build* can be substituted by *do to* (*what they did to this gazebo was restore it*). But there may be many, often contradictory, criteria to choose from (see below, IV); moreover the more categories one sets up, the more indeterminate instances will arise – for example, is *I've brought Percival a pullover* like (3i) or (3ii)?

The same function may often be expressed in more than one way, e.g. *Oliver, to Oliver* above. Similarly, *General Leathwall* is actor throughout (5i, ii, iii):

(5i) General Leathwall won the battle
(5ii) The battle was won by General Leathwall
(5iii) General Leathwall's winning (of) the battle ...

This is what makes it necessary to distinguish 'logical' from 'grammatical' categories (Sweet, 1891: 10ff., 89ff.). In Sweet's terms, *General Leathwall* is the logical subject in (5i–iii), though it is the grammatical subject only in (5i). Conversely in *the book sells well*, *the book* is grammatical subject but 'logical direct object'. The concepts of actor, goal and beneficiary are represented in Sweet's account as 'logical subject', 'logical direct object' and 'logical indirect object' respectively.

The linguistic expression of processes, and of the participants (and, by extension, the circumstances) associated with them, is known by the general term *transitivity*. Transitivity comes under what we have called the 'ideational' function of language. Actor, goal and beneficiary are structural functions, or roles, in transitivity; and just as the same transitivity function may be realized in more than one way, as in (5), so also the same constructional form may express different transitivity functions. Thus *by the fire* is actor in (6i), place in (6ii):

(6i) it was singed by the fire
(6ii) it was stored by the fire.

This also illustrates the conflict of criteria. In (6i), *by the fire* might be considered instrument rather than actor, on the grounds that it is inanimate. Fillmore (1968) distinguishes actor and instrument as, respectively, the 'typically animate perceived instigator of the action' (his 'agentive'; cf. VIII below) and the 'inanimate force or object causally involved in the action'; the latter may also be grammatical subject, and if not may also be expressed by *with* as in (7):

(7i) the key opened the door/John opened the door with the key
(7ii) the door was opened with the key.

But *with* is not normally used where the action is unintentional (*the window was broken with the ball* is odd), nor can it be substituted in (6i). We need here a further distinction between instrument and (natural) force, the latter not being subject to any external intent.

We might therefore list, as participant roles,

(a) actor ('logical subject'): prepositionally *by*
(b) goal ('logical direct object')

(c) beneficiary ('logical indirect object'): prepositionally *to/for*
(d) instrument: prepositionally *with/by*

with the possibility for further distinctions such as

(b) goal: goal, resultant [ex. (3)]
(c) beneficiary: beneficiary, recipient [ex. (4)]
(d) instrument: instrument, force [ex. (6i), (7)]

where 'force' may simply be equivalent to (inanimate) actor.

IV. OTHER TRANSITIVITY FUNCTIONS:
CIRCUMSTANTIAL ROLES

The three main types of transitivity role – process, participant, circumstance – correspond, by and large, to the three major word (or word group) classes found in most languages: verb, noun, adverb. In English, typically, processes are expressed by verbal groups, participants by nominal groups and circumstances by adverbial groups – the last often in the form of prepositional phrases. There are also incongruent forms of expression, with functions of one type expressed by classes primarily associated with another type, as in (8):

(8) dinner of roast beef was followed by a swim.

Here the processes of eating and swimming are expressed by nouns; the temporal relation between them by the verb *follow*; and of the two participants, one is omitted and the other (*roast beef*) is made to qualify *dinner* (contrast *in the evening they ate roast beef and then swam*).

The circumstantial functions seem less central to the process than do the participant functions; this is related to their inability to take on the role of subject. But this peripheral status is not a feature of all circumstantial elements, which can be subdivided into an 'inner' and 'outer' type. Within the function 'place', in

(9i) he was throwing stones at the bridge
(9ii) he was throwing stones on the bridge

at the bridge (the 'inner' type) seems more central to the process than *on the bridge*: we can say *what was he throwing stones at?*

and not (in this sense) *what was he doing at the bridge?* (on the other hand, we can say *what was he doing on the bridge?* and not *what was he throwing stones on?*) However, the sense of 'inner' and 'outer' is contributed to by various factors not all of which coincide. For example, in (10) the place element is obligatory in (i) but optional in (ii):

(10i) he put all his jewels in the wash
(10ii) he lost all his jewels in the wash.

In (11), there is a difference of clause type; (i) is a relational clause (see VII below) whereas (ii) is an action clause (Fillmore, from whom (11) is taken, gives this as an instance of dependency between functions: the place element is 'outer' if an actor is present and 'inner' otherwise):

(11i) John keeps his car in the garage
(11ii) John washes his car in the garage.

V. INHERENT FUNCTIONS

The distinction between obligatory and optional roles helps us to relate transitivity functions to a system of *clause types*. As, however, this involves recognizing that an 'obligatory' element may in fact be absent, we shall use the term 'inherent' rather than 'obligatory'. An inherent function is one that is always associated with a given clause type even if it is not necessarily expressed in the structure of all clauses of that type. (We are not here talking about ellipsis, which is a matter of textual structure.)

Consider a pair of clauses such as (12):

(12i) Roderick pelted the crocodile with stones
(12ii) the crocodile got pelted.

The verb *pelt*, as it happens, is always associated with three participant roles: a pelter, a pelted and something to pelt with; and this holds for (ii) as well as for (i) (cf. Svartvik, 1966, on 'agentless agentives'). Similarly there are inherently benefactive clauses without a beneficiary, such as *we're giving a silver coffee-pot.* So

(12iii) Roderick pelted the crocodile

is '(inherently) instrumental', and although no instrument is mentioned the receiver interprets the process as having an instrumental role associated with it.

The same verb may occur in clauses of more than one type. But within one type there may be different sets, and different alignments, of participants; this is the function of the system of 'voice' – of the choice between active and passive, though the actual patterns are more elaborate than this. The options in the voice system (simplifying somewhat) are (a) middle/non-middle (see next paragraph); if non-middle, then (b) 'active'/'passive' (not exactly equivalent to active and passive in the verb; see Halliday, 1967/68: I 39ff., where they are referred to as 'operative' and 'receptive'); if 'active', then (c) plus/minus goal; if 'passive', then (d) plus/minus actor. The reason for choosing one rather than another of these options lies in the textual function of language (see XI and XII below); but which options are available to choose from depends on transitivity.

Voice is concerned with the roles of actor and goal (but see VIII below), both as inherent and as actualized roles. A 'middle' clause is one which has only one inherent participant, which for the moment we will continue to refer to as the 'actor'; examples are *Hector sneezed, the cat washed*. A 'non-middle' clause is one which has two, an actor and a goal, but one or the other may not be actualized: if 'active', there may be no goal, e.g. *Mary is washing* ('the clothes'), and if 'passive', no actor, e.g. *the clothes have been washed* ('by Mary'). All actions are classified into those involving one participant role and those involving two; there are then different ways of presenting the situation in those cases where there are two.

The point was made earlier that the notion of 'participant' derives from the more fundamental concept of syntactic function, or 'role'. The basic elements of transitivity structure are the various roles associated with processes; and two or more such roles may be combined in one participant, as in a reflexive clause such as *John is washing* ('himself') where *John* is both actor and goal at the same time. The elements that operate as actor, goal, etc. also play a part, simultaneously, in other structures of the clause, expressing aspects of the interpersonal and textual functions of language. The principle of combining a number of roles in a single complex element of structure is fundamental to the total organization of language, since it is this that makes it possible for the various functions of language to be integrated in one expression. We return to this in IX below.

VI. TRANSITIVITY CLAUSE TYPES: ACTION CLAUSES

All the clauses so far considered have been concerned with actions or events, and have involved an 'actor' as inherent role. Let us refer to this type as *action* clauses. Action clauses all have corresponding equative forms as in example (32) below, having *do* or *happen* in them, such as

(13i) what Lionel did was (to) jump off the roof
(13ii) what happened to Lionel was that he fell off the roof.

The following table shows the full range of possibilities of voices in action clauses, together with the roles associated with each of them:

voice (clause)	roles	voice (verb)	example
middle	actor	active	the gazebo has collapsed
'active'	actor, goal	active	the Council are selling the gazebo
'active'	actor (goal)	active	the Council won't sell
'passive'	goal	active	the gazebo won't sell
'passive'	goal, actor	passive	the gazebo has been sold by the Council
'passive'	goal (actor)	passive	the gazebo has been sold

(The 'active' and 'passive' rows are bracketed together under the label **non-middle**.)

The roles in parentheses are inherent but not expressed.

Not all clauses are of the 'action' type. English appears to recognize three main types of process: action, mental process, and relation. Mental process clauses, and clauses of relation, are associated with what are at first sight rather different sets of participant roles.

VII. TRANSITIVITY CLAUSE TYPES:
MENTAL PROCESS CLAUSES, RELATION CLAUSES

In mental process clauses, such as

(14) I liked your hairstyle

we cannot really talk of an actor and a goal; it is not possible to say, for example, *what I did was like your hairstyle*, or *what I did to your hairstyle was like it*. The inherent roles are those of a human, or at any rate animate, being whose consciousness is impinged upon, and some phenomenon which impinges upon it. Let us refer to these as the 'processer' and the 'phenomenon'. The voice potentialities are now somewhat different; among the non-middle (two participant) clauses there are two types, those having the phenomenon as subject in active voice (15i), and those having the processer (15ii). In the first type, the passive form is much more frequent than the passive in action clauses; in the second type it is much less so:

(15i) the gift pleased her/she was pleased by (with) the gift
(15ii) she liked the gift/the gift was liked by her.

This is because the passive is a means of bringing the element governed by *by* into prominence as the focus of information (see XII below); in (15ii) the *by* element, i.e. *her*, is the processer, and in English this tends to be the 'given' element in the situation (*she* must have been referred to already in the text), and thus does not appropriately carry such prominence.

Mental process clauses express (a) perception, e.g. *see, look*; (b) reaction, e.g. *like, please*; (c) cognition, e.g. *believe, convince*; (d) verbalization, e.g. *say, speak*. They are distinct in that the 'phenomenon' – that which is perceived, reacted to, etc. – is not limited, as are the participants in action clauses, to the class of 'things', namely persons, objects, abstractions and the rest of the phenomena on the plane of experience.

What is perceived or felt or thought of may be a simple phenomenon of this kind, but it may also be what we might call a 'metaphenomenon': a *fact* or a *report* – a phenomenon that has already as it were been filtered through the medium of language. Here words as well as things may participate in the process.

For example, in (16) all the 'processed' entities are simple phenomena, or 'things':

(16i) I noticed Helen over there [person]
(16ii) I noticed a discrepancy [abstraction]
(16iii) I noticed a quarrel (going on)/them quarrelling [event]
(16iv) I noticed what (the thing that) she was wearing [object].

In (17) and (18), however, they are metaphenomena; facts in (17), reports in (18):

(17i) I noticed what (the fact of what) she was wearing
(17ii) it worries me that you look so tired
(18i) I notice the bank rate's going up again
(18ii) he says the bank rate's going up again.

We could insert *the fact* (*that*) in (17) and *the report* (*that*) in (18i); not however in (18ii), which is a clause of verbalization, since such clauses accept only reports, and 'reported speech' is the meaning of clauses of this type. The difference between fact and report is that a 'fact' is a representation at the semantic level, where the truth lies in the meaning – (*she regretted*) *that he had gone away*; whereas a 'report' is a representation at the lexicogrammatical, or syntactic, level, where the truth lies in the wording – (*she said*) *that he had gone away*.

In relational clauses, the 'process' is simply a form of relation between two roles. One type is the attributive, such as

(19i) Marguerite is a poet
(19ii) Marguerite looks desperate

where the relation is one of class membership: 'Marguerite belongs to the class of poets,' '. . . the class of people who look desperate'. This is a relation between entities of the same order of abstraction but differing in generality.

The other type, exemplified by (20)

(20i) Templecombe is the treasurer
(20ii) the treasurer is Templecombe

has two functions, resembling the two terms of an equation, where the one serves to identify the other, as in $x = 2$. Here the two entities are alike in generality but differ in abstraction: the identifying element may be of a higher order of abstraction, as in (21i), where *the treasurer* expresses Templecombe's function, or of a lower order, as in (21ii) where *the fat one* expresses Templecombe's form, how he is to be recognized:

(21i) (which is Templecombe?) Templecombe is the treasurer.
(21ii) (which is Templecombe?) Templecombe is the fat one.

(21i) could be interpreted in the sense of (21ii) if the committee were in view on the platform; there is in fact partial ambiguity between these two sub-types.

These two major types of relational clause, the attributive and the equative, differ in various respects. The attributive are non-reversible (e.g. we can say *that man is a poet* but not *a poet is that man*), have the role 'attribute' which may be an adjective and is usually indefinite, express class inclusion, are usually questioned by *what?* or *how?* and are expressed by the verbs *be*, *get*, *turn*, *keep*, *remain*, *seem*, *sound*, *look*, etc. The equative are reversible (i.e. have a 'voice' system), have the role 'identifier' which must be a noun and is usually definite, express class identity, are usually questioned by *who?* or *which?* and are expressed by the verbs *be*, *equal*, *represent*, *resemble*, *stand for*, etc.

It is interesting to note that, in relational clauses, quite unlike clauses of action or mental process, the verb is regularly unstressed. This is a symptom of its much weaker function in the clause. Contrast the pronunciation of *equals* in (22i) and (22ii):

(22i) England Equals (Australia's Total of) 512 [action]
(22ii) $2^9 = 512$ [relation]

VIII. THE ERGATIVE

As far as the ideational component of grammar is concerned, the English clause shows the three principal types – action, mental process and relation – and associates with each a set of different inherent roles, or structural functions. The system of clause types is a general framework for the representation of processes in the grammar; possibly all languages distinguish three such categories. We need to ask, at this point, whether the structural functions can be generalized across clause types; whether, for example, an actor in an action clause can be shown to be equivalent to a 'processer' (one who does the thinking, etc.) in a mental process clause. This may be approached through a reconsideration of the functions in action clauses, a reconsideration which such clauses demand anyway.

If we look at examples like (23i and ii)

(23i) the sergeant led the recruits
(23ii) the sergeant marched the recruits,

they appear to be clearly distinct, (i) being transitive, with actor and goal, (ii) causative, with initiator and actor. However, there is a problem with (23iii):

(23iii) the sergeant trained the recruits

Is it like (23i) or like (23ii)?

Actually it is like both; (23i) and (23ii) are not really different as far as transitivity is concerned. In English no very clear distinction is made between doing something to someone and making someone do something, so that (23iii) can be interpreted in either way without any sense of ambiguity. This is why so many verbs are labelled 'vb trans. & intrans.' in the dictionary.

The concepts of actor and goal are not well suited to describing this situation, since with these we are forced to describe (23i) and (23ii) differently. The distinction between them is by no means entirely unreal, since there are verbs like *lead* which are normally transitive (two inherent participants) and others like *march* which are normally intransitive (one inherent participant). But with a large number, especially of the more frequently used verbs, either form seems equally normal: there is nothing to choose, as regards the more typical use of the verb *bounce*, between *he bounced the ball* and *the ball bounced*. In addition there are a number of verbs which, while themselves clearly transitive or clearly intransitive, group into pairs differing only in transitivity, so that *Mary put out the fire* is to *the fire went out* as *Polly lit the fire* is to *the fire lit*.

It has been pointed out by various linguists (Anderson, 1968; Fillmore, 1968; Halliday, 1967/68: §3) that action clauses in English seem to be organized on an ergative rather than on a transitive (or 'nominative') basis. This means that, with any action clause, there is associated one inherent role which is that of the participant affected by the process in question. Fillmore describes this as the 'semantically most neutral' function, and labels it the 'objective'; I used the term 'affected', which I will retain here. In (23) *the recruits* has the role of 'affected' in every case, even though it is goal (if an actor–goal analysis is used) in (23i) and actor in (23ii); in general, the affected is the goal in a transitive and the actor in an intransitive clause.

We have now turned what was the borderline case, such as (23iii), into the most central clause type. This is the type in which both middle (one-participant) and non-middle (two-participant) forms are equally normal; it may be considered the 'favourite' clause type of Modern English. The transitive and intransitive types – those with non-middle as norm and with middle as norm respectively – are the marginal ones, and they seem to be becoming more marginal as time goes on.

Hence all the examples in (24i) have the same structure, with a process and an affected. Those in (24ii) also have a 'causer' (Fillmore's 'agentive'):

(24i)
they're being led
they're being trained/they're training
they're being marched/they're marching
(24ii)
he's leading them
he's training them
he's marching them.

These two ways of representing processes, the transitive and the ergative, are very widely distributed; possibly all languages display one or the other, or (perhaps always) both, in different mixtures. In English, the two occur side by side. The transitive system asks 'does the action extend beyond the active participant or not?'; the ergative, 'is the action caused by the affected participant or not?' The ergative component is more prominent now than it was in Middle English, and this appears in various ways, for example, the change from impersonal to personal forms in mental process clauses (formerly *methinks, it likes me*). In the modern form *I like, I* cannot be explained as an actor (among other things we cannot say *what he does to jam is like it*); but it can be shown on various grounds to have the function 'affected'.

As this suggests, the ergative pattern, whereby a process is accompanied by an obligatory 'affected' participant and an optional 'causer', is more readily generalizable than that of actor and goal. It extends beyond action clauses to those of mental process, and perhaps even to clauses of relation as well. We want to say that *Paul* has the same function in both (25i) and (25ii)

(25i) Paul fears ghosts
(25ii) ghosts scare Paul

– not that they are identical in meaning, but that the transitivity roles are the same. This is not possible in actor-goal terms. But in an ergative system there is considerable evidence for regarding *Paul* as the 'affected' participant in both cases. The ergative, therefore, represents the more general model of the transitivity patterns of modern English – that is, of the options available to the speaker of English for talking about processes of all kinds.

IX. OTHER DIMENSIONS OF CLAUSE STRUCTURE

So far the discussion has been confined to the expression of ideational meanings. We have not yet considered the structure of language in its other functions, the 'interpersonal' and the 'textual'. Both these functions are manifested in the structure of the clause.

Certain problems that have arisen in the history of the investigation of subject and predicate provide an insight here. A sentence such as (26i) presents no problem in this respect: *my mother* is clearly subject and the rest predicate. But in (26ii) there seem to be three candidates for the status of subject, *these beads, my mother* and *I*:

(26i) my mother gave me these beads
(26ii) these beads I was given by my mother.

The solution was to recognize different kinds of subject. For Sweet, *my mother* was 'logical subject', *I* was 'grammatical subject'; *these beads* came to be known as 'psychological subject'. In (26i), all three coincide. The notion of subject conflates three distinct roles which, although they are typically combined into one element, are nevertheless independent of one another. We may think of this as governed by a 'good reason' principle: many linguistic systems are based on this principle, whereby one option (the 'unmarked' option: see p. 17, above) will always be selected unless there is good reason for selecting otherwise (cf. Jakobson, 1963: 268ff.).

These three 'kinds of subject' relate to the functions of language as described above. The logical subject is the actor; this is a transitivity role, deriving from the ideational function. The other two have different sources, though they are no less meaningful. The grammatical subject derives from the interpersonal component in language function; specifically, it has to do with the roles taken on by the performer and receiver in a communication situation. The psychological subject belongs to the textual component; it is concerned with the organization of the clause as a message, within a larger piece of discourse. The next two sections will examine these in turn.

X. MOOD

As we have said, one function of language is to provide for interaction between people, by allowing the expression of statuses, social and individual attitudes, assessments, judgements and the like; and this includes participation in linguistic interaction. Language itself defines the roles which people may take in situations in which they are communicating with one another; and every language incorporates options whereby the speaker can vary his own communication role, making assertions, asking questions, giving orders, expressing doubts and so on. The basic 'speech functions' of statement, question, response, command and exclamation fall within this category (though they do not exhaust it), and these are expressed grammatically by the system of *mood* (cf. Sweet, 1891: 105), in which the principle options are declarative, interrogative, (yes/no and wh– types), and imperative etc. The difference between *he can* and *can he?* is a difference in the communication role adopted by the speaker in his interaction with a listener.

The notion 'grammatical subject' by itself is strange, since it implies a structural function whose only purpose is to define a structural function. Actually, just as the 'logical subject' is a function defined by transitivity, so the 'grammatical subject' is a function defined by mood. If we consider an example such as (27)

(27) Tigers can climb trees. – Can tigers climb trees? – They can climb trees, can't they? – No they can't.

we find that one part, *tigers can*, has the function of expressing mood throughout; it also typically carries the positive/negative option. It consists of the finite element of the verb, plus one nominal (noun or noun group) which is the 'grammatical subject'.

The function of the 'grammatical subject' is thus a meaningful function in the clause, since it defines the communication role adopted by the speaker. It is present in clauses of all moods, but its significance can perhaps be seen most clearly in the imperative, where the meaning is 'I request you to . . .'; here the speaker is requiring some action on the part of the person addressed, but it is the latter who has the power to make this meaning 'come true' or otherwise, since he can either obey or disobey. In the usual form of the imperative, this modal entity, or 'modal subject' as we may call it, is the listener; and the only option is plus or minus the speaker himself, as in *let's go home* as opposed to (*you*) *go home*. Hence, in a passive imperative such as *be guided by your elders*, although the actor is *your elders*, the modal subject is 'you'; it is the listener who accedes, potentially, to the request, fulfilling the modal function defined by the speaker's role.

XI. THEME

The basic unit of language in use is not a word or a sentence but a 'text'; and the 'textual' component in language is the set of options by means of which a speaker or writer is enabled to create texts – to use language in a way that is relevant to the context. The clause, in this function, is organized as a message; so in addition to its structure in transitivity and in mood, it also has structure as a message, what is known as a 'thematic' structure. (It was linguists of the Prague school who first studied this aspect of language, cf. Mathesius, 1928; Firbas, 1959, 1964; Svoboda, 1968 and references therein.)

The English clause consists of a 'theme' and a 'rheme'. The theme is another component in the complex notion of subject, namely the 'psychological subject'; it is as it were the peg on which the message is hung, the theme being the body of the message. The theme of a clause is the element which, in English, is put in first position; in (28 i–v) the theme is the item outside the brackets, what is inside being the rheme:

(28i) I (don't know)
(28ii) yesterday (we discussed the financial arrangements)
(28iii) his spirit (they could not kill)
(28iv) suddenly (the rope gave way)
(28v) people who live in glasshouses (shouldn't throw stones).

As we have seen, theme, actor and modal subject are identical unless there is good reason for them not to be (cf. (26) above). Where they are not, the tendency in Modern English is to associate theme and modal subject; and this is the main reason for using the passive. The passive has precisely the function of dissociating the actor from this complex, so that it can either be put in focal position at the end or, more frequently, omitted, as in (29):

(29i) this gazebo was built by Sir Christopher Wren
(29ii) this gazebo is being restored.

The typical theme of a declarative clause is thus the modal subject (or 'grammatical subject' – *this gazebo* in both cases); in interrogatives, however, the picture is different. If we ask a question, it is usually because we want to know the answer, so that the typical theme of an interrogative is a request for information. Hence we put first, in an interrogative clause, the element that contains this request for information: the polarity-carrying element in a yes/no question and the questioning element in a 'wh–' question, as in (30)

(30i) didn't (Sir Christopher Wren build this gazebo?)
(30ii) how many gazebos (did Sir Christopher Wren build?).

In English there is a definite awareness of the meaning expressed by putting something in first position in the clause. The theme is the point of departure for the message; a paradigm form of it is the headword in a definition, e.g. *a gazebo* in (31):

(31) a gazebo is a pavilion or summerhouse on an eminence, open for the view.

In addition to the selection of a particular element as the theme, the speaker has other options in thematic structure open to him (Halliday, 1967/68: §2); for example, any clause can be split into two parts by the use of nominalization, as in

(32) the one who built this gazebo was Sir Christopher Wren

where the theme is the whole of whichever part comes first – here *the one who built this gazebo*.

XII. INFORMATION STRUCTURE

Thematic structure is closely linked to another aspect of the textual organization of language, which we may call 'information-structure'. This refers to the organization of a text in terms of the functions 'given' and 'new'. These are often conflated with theme and rheme under the single heading 'topic and comment'; the latter, however, is (like the traditional notion of 'subject') a complex notion, and the association of theme with given, rheme with new, is subject to the usual 'good reason' principle already referred to – there is freedom of choice, but the theme will be associated with the 'given' and the rheme with the 'new' unless there is good reason for choosing some other alignment.

In English, information structure is expressed by intonation. Connected speech takes the form of an unbroken succession of distinctive pitch contours, or 'tone groups'; each tone group represents what the speaker decides to make into one unit of information. This is not necessarily the same length as a clause, though it often is so. The information unit consists of an obligatory 'new' element – there must be something new, otherwise there would be no information – and an optional 'given' element; the main stress ('tonic nucleus') marks the end of the 'new' element, and anything that is 'given' precedes it, unless with good reason – which means, here, unless it is a response to a specific question, either asked or implied. The function 'given' means 'treated by the speaker as non-recoverable information': information that the listener is not being expected to derive for himself from the text or the situation.

(33) illustrates the interaction of information structure with thematic structure (information unit ('i.u.') boundaries are marked by //; main stress is indicated by bold type; 4 = falling-rising tone, 1 = falling tone):

(33) //4 **this** gazebo //1 **can't** have been built by Wren//
(clause: theme . . .   rheme . . . .)
(i.u.(1): new . . . .; (2): new . given . . . .)

meaning 'I am talking (theme), specifically, (new) about this gazebo: the fact is (rheme) that your suggestion (given) that Wren built it is actually (new) quite impossible'. No such suggestion need actually have been made, for this clause to occur; one of the features of the 'given–new' structure is its use for various rhetorical purposes, such as bullying the listener. Given and new thus differ from theme and rheme, though both are textual functions, in that 'given' means 'here is a point of contact with what you know' (and thus is not tied to elements in clause structure), whereas 'theme' means 'here is the heading to what I am saying'.

The functions of given and new link up in turn with the functions in transitivity. It was noted earlier (see III above) that a number of participant roles may be expressed in either of two ways, either directly or through the mediation of a preposition, for example the beneficiary in

(34i) I've offered Oliver a tie
(34ii) I've offered the tie to Oliver.

The members of such a pair have the same ideational meaning but differ in information. Typically, the prepositional form of the beneficiary is associated with the function 'new', the other form with the function 'given'; and if we assume here the expected intonation pattern, then in (34ii) *Oliver* is new and *the tie* is given, the implied question being 'who did you offer the tie to?', while in (34i) *a tie* is new and *Oliver* is given, answering 'what have you offered to Oliver?' (note that one of the meanings of definiteness – not the only one – is 'given', hence the likelihood of *the tie* in (34ii)).

A general principle underlies the existence of these two informationally distinct forms, one with a preposition and one without, for expressing participant roles. The textual function of language requires that, for effective communication, new information should be made grammatically explicit. New lexical content has to be backed up, as it were, by adequate quanta of grammar; specifically, it has to be made clear what is the ideational function of any new material in the discourse, and here it is the preposition that indicates the role of the unfamiliar element. The use of a preposition to specify function in the clause in just those cases where the element in question is typically 'new' (compare the use of *by* with the actor in a passive construction) illustrates how the 'texture' of discourse is achieved through the interplay of varied grammatical resources expressing different facets of the total meaning.

XIII. CONCLUSION

The subject, in its traditional sense, is thus a complex of four distinct functions, three in the structure of the clause (cf. Lyons, 1968: 343–4):

1. actor ('logical subject'): ideational;
2. modal subject ('grammatical subject'): interpersonal;
3. theme ('psychological subject$_1$'): textual.

together with a fourth function which is in the structure of the 'information unit':

4. given ('psychological subject$_2$'): textual.

These coincide unless there is 'good reason' for them not to do so; thus in (35i) *the Borough Council* is actor, modal subject and theme, whereas in (35ii) *the Borough Council* is actor, *this gazebo* is modal subject and *next year* is theme:

(35i) the Borough Council will restore this gazebo next year
(35ii) next year this gazebo will be restored by the Borough Council.

No mention has been made of subject and predicate as a logical relation. We might introduce 'predication' as another dimension of clause structure, with *the Borough Council* in (35i) being also 'subject in predication' and the rest predicate; but the subject in this sense would be identical with the modal subject. The subject–predicate structure is entirely derivable from mood, and has no independent significance (cf. Fillmore, 1968: 17; and Fillmore's reference, ibid., to Tesnière, 1959: 103–5). As a form of generalization, it may be useful in that it expresses the fact that actor, modal subject and theme are regularly associated; but it obscures the equally important fact that they are distinct and independent structural roles.

The multiple function of language is reflected in linguistic structure; this is the basis for the recognition of the ideational (including logical), interpersonal and textual functions as suggested here. It is not necessary to argue that one function is more abstract, or 'deeper', than another; all are semantically relevant. The investigation of these functions enables us to relate the internal patterns of language – its underlying options, and their realization in structure – to the demands that are made on language in the actual situations in which it is used. As performers and receivers, we simultaneously both communicate through language and interact through language; and, as a necessary condition for both of these, we create and recognize discourse (the textual function is thus instrumental to the other two). A speech act is essentially a complex behaviour pattern which in most instances combines the ideational and interpersonal functions, in varying degrees of prominence. These very general notions in turn encompass a broad range of more specific patterns relating to the creative and the repetitive aspects of language in use.

8. SEMANTICS

Manfred Bierwisch

As I said in the Introduction, there has been a very noticeable renewal of interest in semantic theory among linguists in the last few years, one of the main reasons for this being the development of generative grammar with its emphasis upon distinction between 'deep structure' and 'surface structure' (pp. 26–7). Much of the work published by linguists has been influenced by the 'componential' approach to the analysis of meaning: that is to say, by the attempt to describe the structure of vocabulary in terms of a relatively small set of very general elements of meaning (called 'components', 'markers', or 'sememes') and their various possible combinations in different languages. The chapter by Bierwisch falls within this category of 'componential' semantics (although he does make mention of an alternative approach in terms of what Carnap called 'meaning postulates').

All semanticists would agree that, whatever else might be included within a study of meaning, it should certainly deal, on the one hand, with the way words and sentences are related to objects and processes in the world and, on the other, with the way in which they are related to one another in terms of such notions as 'synonymy', 'entailment' and 'contradiction'.

Not everyone will accept as 'plausible' the hypothesis 'that all semantic structure might finally be reduced to components representing the basic dispositions of the cognitive and perceptual structure of the human organism' (p. 181); indeed, it is expressly rejected by some of the other contributors to this volume. Nevertheless, it is a hypothesis that has been put forward on a number of occasions by linguists in recent years (notably, though somewhat tentatively, by Chomsky); and it deserves consideration.

Bierwisch takes for granted some familiarity with Chomsky's (1965) system of generative grammar (pp. 124–38).

Semantics

1. *The Goals of Semantics*

THE semantic analysis of a given language must explain how the sentences of this language are understood, interpreted, and related to states, processes, and objects in the universe. This general task, which might be summarized by the question 'What is the meaning of a sentence S of the language L?' cannot be approached directly, but must be broken down into a set of more basic questions. One particular set of these can be illustrated by the following examples:

(1) His typewriter has bad intentions.
(2) My unmarried sister is married to a bachelor.
(3) John was looking for the glasses.
(4) (a) The needle is too short.
    (b) The needle is not long enough.
(5) (a) Many of the students were unable to answer your question.
    (b) Only few students grasped your question.
(6) (a) How long did Archibald remain in Monte Carlo?
    (b) Archibald remained in Monte Carlo for some time.

A semantic analysis of English must explain that (1) is a semantically anomalous sentence, that (2) is a contradictory sentence, that (3) is semantically ambiguous, that (4a) and (4b) are paraphrases of each other, or synonymous sentences, that (5a) follows from (5b), that (6a) implies or presupposes (6b). An account of semantic properties and relations of this kind requires more than an analysis of the meaning of single words. Though the ambiguity of (3) follows from the ambiguity of *glasses*, no such simple explanation is possible for the relation between (4a) and (4b) or (5a) and (5b). In other words, in order to understand the meaning of a sentence and its semantic relations to other expressions, one must know not only the meaning of its lexical elements, but also how they interrelate. This in turn depends on the syntactic structure of the sentence. The semantically relevant syntactic properties consist of rather abstract grammatical relations. Thus in sentences like

(7) (a) It was difficult to find the right page.
    (b) To find the right page was difficult.
    (c) The right page was difficult to find.

the syntactic relations relevant for the semantic interpretation are the same, in spite of their surface differences. Only such deep-structure relations, which are not in general present in the syntactic surface structure, are essential for semantic interpretation. Thus the syntactic theory must indicate that in (7a)–(7c) *the right page* is the direct object of *find*, and *someone finds the right page* is the subject of *was difficult*.

In short, a semantic theory must: (i) make reference to the syntactic structure in a precise way; (ii) systematically represent the meaning of the single words (or, more generally, of the lexical elements, which include also lexicalized phrases like idioms, isolated compounds, etc.); and (iii) show how the structure of the meanings of words and the syntactic relations interact, in order to constitute the interpretation of sentences. Finally, it must indicate how these interpretations are related to the things spoken about.

2. *The Analysis of Word Meanings*

All approaches to the semantic analysis of natural languages are based on the insight that the meanings of lexical items are not unanalysable or undefinable wholes. This insight has been made explicit in essentially two ways. The first is based on meaning postulates, the other on semantic components into which the lexical meanings are analysed. Meaning postulates, or semantic rules, formally introduced in Carnap (1956), might be illustrated by the following examples:

(8) (a) *boy* → *male*   (b) *girl* → *female*

A rule like (8a) says that *boy* implies *male* or, what amounts to the same, that sentences like *A boy is male* or *If x is a boy, then x is male* are analytic. Meaning postulates might also involve logical constants like 'and', 'or', 'not', etc.:

(9) (a) *man* → *male* and *adult*
   (b) *woman* → *female* and *adult*
   (c) *boy* or *girl* → not *adult*
   (d) *female* → not *male*
   (e) *man* or *woman* or *boy* or *girl* → *human*

The meaning of a lexical element is therefore specified, roughly speaking, by the set of all the meaning postulates in which it occurs. More precisely: the meaning of a lexical element of L is defined implicitly by the set of all meaning postulates associated with L. (An empirical investigation of part of the Greek vocabulary based on essentially these principles is given in Lyons (1963).)

The second approach is that of componential analysis, which underlies the linguistic theories developed by Katz and Fodor (1963), Weinreich (1966), Bierwisch (1969) and others. It defines the meaning of a lexical element explicitly in terms of semantic components. These components are not part of the vocabulary of the language itself, but rather theoretical elements, postulated in order to describe the semantic relations between the lexical elements of a given language. These components are connected again by logical constants. Thus we get the following oversimplified example:

(10) (a) *boy*: ANIMATE and HUMAN and MALE and not ADULT
    (b) *girl*: ANIMATE and HUMAN and FEMALE and not ADULT
    (c) *man*: ANIMATE and HUMAN and MALE and ADULT
    (d) *woman*: ANIMATE and HUMAN and FEMALE and ADULT

A system of such explicitly defined lexical elements might be supplemented by a set of implicational rules of the following type:

(11) (a) HUMAN → ANIMATE   (d) MALE → ANIMATE
    (b) MALE → not FEMALE   (e) FEMALE → ANIMATE
    (c) FEMALE → not MALE

These implicational rules automatically complete a redundancy-free entry like (12a) to its fully specified form (12b):

(12) (a) *boy*: HUMAN and MALE and not ADULT
    (b) *boy*: ANIMATE and HUMAN and MALE and not FEMALE and not ADULT

Rules of this type not only simplify the necessary dictionary specifications; they also express relevant generalizations about the semantic structure of the vocabulary described.

There is obviously a close connexion between the two types of analysis just illustrated. In fact, as far as only systems of a particular kind are considered, a componential analysis of the type illustrated by (10) and (11) can be directly converted into a system of meaning postulates, and vice versa. Notice, however, that the status of elements like *male* in (8) and (9) is quite different from that of MALE in (10) and (11): while *male, adult, human* belong to the language described, this is not the case with respect to the components MALE, ADULT, ANIMATE, etc. The relationship between implicit and explicit definition in more complicated cases has not been systematically investigated so far. For the present exposition I will assume, quite gratuitously, that both explications are at least formally equivalent, in the sense that for each set of meaning postulates there is a componential analysis of the vocabulary involved defining the same semantic relations, and vice versa. The subsequent discussion is based on the framework of componential analysis.

3. *The Dictionary as a System of Concepts*

In terms of componential analysis, the meaning of a word is a complex of semantic components (or features, or markers) connected by logical constants. This assumption immediately allows us to define certain semantic properties and relations of lexical entries. Thus a word is semantically ambiguous if it has more than one complex of semantic features assigned to it. Two entries E_1 and E_2 are synonymous, if their meanings consist of the same components connected by the same logical constants. E_1 is a hyponym of E_2 (i.e. E_1 is included in E_2) if the meaning of E_1 contains all the components occurring in the meaning of E_2, but not vice versa. Thus *woman* might be a hyponym of *adult*, since the former but not the latter contains e.g. the component FE-MALE. E_1 and E_2 are antonyms, if their meanings are identical except that the meaning of E_1 has a component C where that of E_2 had C', and C and C' belong to a particular subset of mutually exclusive components.

Sets of lexical entries whose meanings have certain features in common form a 'semantic field'. A famous example is that of kinship terms, whose elements share the feature configuration 'ANIMATE and HUMAN and RELATIVE'. The verbs of motion are another example.

There are also subfields, e.g. that of male relatives including *father*, *brother*, *son*, *uncle*, etc., or that of lineal *v.* collateral kinship. On the other hand there are more inclusive fields, e.g. that of social roles, which includes, besides a subset of the kinship terms, elements like *friend*, *colleague*, *teacher*, etc. It follows therefore that semantic fields are relative, and not absolute. The notion of semantic fields was introduced by Trier (1931) in order to account for the observation that the meaning of lexical elements is specified only by their relatedness to and their difference from other relevant elements. By redefining this conception of the semantic field in terms of semantic components, we might indicate precisely the organization of particular fields and the relations among their members.

Besides having components in common, the elements of the vocabulary are connected to each other by other relations. One of these is the pertinence relation of which a particular instance is the relation between part and whole. The words *arm*, *hand*, *finger*, for example, denote parts of the human body, so that their meaning must contain a component that relates them appropriately to all entries whose meaning contains the feature HUMAN. Another instance of the pertinence relation is class membership. Thus an entry like *member* must be connected by a certain feature to words like *set*, *class*, *club*, *party*, in short to all entries shown by appropriate features to represent different types of sets or groups.

A different type of relation among the elements of the vocabulary is established by restrictions on their combinability. Thus verbs like *talk*, *think*, *dream* only allow subjects with the feature HUMAN; *drink* requires an object with the feature LIQUID; the adjective *blond* requires a subject specified by such appropriate features as human hair. Restrictions of this kind are called 'selection restrictions', as they indicate which lexical elements may be selected in order to form a semantically well-formed combination of two or more syntactically combined lexical elements. They specify, so to speak, possible semantic affinities among lexical entries. How these conditions are to be represented will be indicated briefly below.

In general, one might define a complex of semantic components connected by logical constants as a concept. The dictionary of a language is then a system of concepts in which a phonological form and certain syntactic and morphological characteristics are assigned to each concept. This system of concepts is structured by several types of relations. It is supplemented, furthermore, by redundancy or implicational rules of the kind illustrated under (11), representing general properties of the whole system of concepts. This last assumption accounts for the fact that it is much easier to come to understand a new concept in a system whose general structure has already been acquired than an isolated element of a completely unknown system. At least a relevant part of these general rules is not bound to particular languages, but represents presumably universal structures of natural languages. They are not learned, but are rather a part of the human ability to acquire an arbitrary natural language. I will return to this aspect in section 8.

4. *Relational Components*

So far we have treated semantic components as if they represented nothing but properties. That this cannot be true becomes obvious if we try to analyse transitive verbs like *hit*, *meet*, *love*, or verbs with two objects like *give*, *take*, *borrow*, etc., because they imply relations between a subject and an object, etc. But even relational nouns such as *father, mother, brother, friend, colleague,* etc. cannot adequately be described without relational components. We must therefore introduce semantic components representing relations between two and perhaps more terms. Let us illustrate such relational features by means of certain kinship terms. Instead of the apparently non-relational component RELATIVE mentioned above, we need certain relations, the central one being X PARENT OF Y with its inverse relation Y CHILD OF X. In order to clarify the connexion between relational and other components, we will also provide features representing properties with the appropriate variable. Thus we get the following (oversimplified) lexical entries:

(13) (a) *father*: X PARENT OF Y and MALE X
(b) *mother*: X PARENT OF Y and FEMALE X

(c) *son:* X CHILD OF Y and MALE X

(d) *brother*: X CHILD OF PARENT OF Y and MALE X

In (13d) we have used a composition of relational components that might be defined as follows ('$=_{def}$' means 'equals by definition'):

(14) X CHILD OF PARENT OF Y $=_{def}$ there is a Z such that X CHILD OF Z and Z PARENT OF Y and X $\neq$ Y

(13) must be supplemented by an additional redundancy rule, expressing that the elements related by PARENT OF are animate. The first member of this relation must presumably be marked furthermore as being adult:

(15) X PARENT OF Y $\rightarrow$ ⟨ANIMATE X and ANIMATE Y and ADULT X⟩

Thus (13a) automatically expands into (16):

(16) *father:* X PARENT OF Y and MALE X and ⟨ANIMATE X and ADULT X and ANIMATE Y⟩

The components enclosed in angled brackets specify implicit conditions for the correct application of a lexical entry. They express at the same time the selection restrictions mentioned above. Thus *father* requires an animate subject if it occurs as predicate noun. This can be seen from the anomaly of sentences like *This suitcase is Bill's father.*

A less obvious example of relational components is provided by adjectives like *long, high, wide, light,* etc., and their antonyms *short, low, narrow, easy.* A sentence like *The table is high* might be paraphrased as *The table is higher than a certain norm.* The norm involved in this paraphrase is bound to the class of objects to which the subject of *high* belongs. According to this analysis, which is due to Sapir (1944: 93), the positive form *high* turns out to be a special case of the comparative *higher than*, with the expected norm providing a standard of comparison. A more detailed analysis reveals furthermore that adjectives like *high, long, wide, tall,* etc., do not relate directly to objects, but rather to particular dimensions of objects. Thus *This table is high* might be paraphrased more precisely as 'This X is a table and Y is the height of X and Y is greater than the normal value of Y'. The meaning of *high* therefore contains at least two relational components: Y HEIGHT OF X and Y GREATER Z where Z represents the norm in the basic form of the adjective, while it is replaced by the dimension compared with Y in the comparative *higher*. The converse relation SMALLER now immediately characterizes the antonyms *low*, *short*, *narrow*, etc. The component Y HEIGHT OF X must further be analysed into the general relation Y DIMENSION OF X and additional characteristics of the three orthogonal dimensions of space. Characteristics of this kind are distributed in a fairly complicated manner on several adjectives, as can be seen from the following examples indicating how spatial adjectives apply to the two or three dimensions of particular objects:

(17) | | | | |
|---|---|---|---|
| *stripe*: | *long* | *wide* | —— |
| *board*: | *long* | *wide* | *thick* |
| *door*: | *high* | *wide* | *thick* |
| *table*: | *high* | *long* | *wide* |
| *cupboard*: | *tall* | *wide* | *deep* |
| *river*: | *long* | *broad* | *deep* |
| *nail*: | *long* | | *thick* |
| *pole*: | $\left\{ \begin{array}{c} long \\ high \end{array} \right\}$ | | *thick* |
| *tower*: | *high* | | *wide* |

The features specifying the different dimensions must therefore agree in a definite way with the corresponding dimensional features of the nouns modified by the adjectives in question. They function like the selectional restrictions mentioned above or conditions on conceptual congruity. Thus the meanings of *long* and *high* and their antonyms are roughly as follows:

(18) *long*: Y GREATER N and ⟨Y DIMENSION OF X and MAXIMAL Y⟩

short: Y SMALLER N and ⟨Y DIMENSION OF X and MAXIMAL Y⟩

high: Y GREATER N and ⟨Y DIMENSION OF X and VERTICAL Y⟩

low: Y SMALLER N and ⟨DIMENSION OF X and VERTICAL Y⟩

The argument N (for this sense of the term 'argument', see the Glossary) here abbreviates the normal value of Y mentioned above. Again the components enclosed in angles represent selection restrictions, indicating that the qualified object X must have dimension Y with the required property. If this condition is not met, we get a semantically anomalous sentence as, e.g., *The cigarette is high*, since one does not normally talk about the height of a cigarette.

The feature MAXIMAL occurring in *long* and *short* might be further reduced to the already required relation GREATER by the following definition:

(19) MAXIMAL Y $=_{def}$ there is no Z such that Z GREATER Y

By this definition a maximal dimension is not necessarily greater than all other dimensions. It is sufficient that it is not shorter than any other one. We thus can account for the fact that a sentence *This square is just as long as it is wide* is neither anomalous nor contradictory. A more detailed discussion of spatial adjectives and related matters can be found in Bierwisch (1967) and Teller (1969).

5. *The Composition of Semantic Components*

So far we have considered only examples in which semantic components are connected by logical constants like 'and'. The concatenation of relations in cases like (13d) is no exception in principle, since this can be reduced by definition (14) again to components connected by 'and'. There are however crucial phenomena in the semantic structure of natural languages that cannot be represented by this simple type of connexion. This can be illustrated by several verbs analysed in Bendix (1966). Let us assume that the meaning of *have* as it occurs in sentences like *John has many books* can be represented by a single component X HAVE Y. The meaning of *give* in *Peter gives John many books* can then be analysed as Z CAUSE (X HAVE Y) where the component Z CAUSE P represents something like 'Z is the one who brings about the state indicated by P'. Hence CAUSE is a relational component, whose second argument is not an individual (or several individuals, for that matter), but a whole proposition made up from a semantic component with its arguments. A similar component is CHANGE TO: that is, part of the meaning of *got* in *John got many books*. This meaning of *get* could then be represented as X CHANGE TO (X HAVE Y). Some other verbs, whose meaning is based on the same components, have been analysed by Bendix as follows:

(20) X *lends* Z to Y: X HAVE Z and not Z IS OF Y and X CAUSE
 (Y HAVE Z) and not Z CHANGE TO (Z IS OF Y)
 X *takes* Y *from* Z: Z HAVE Y and X CAUSE (X HAVE Y)
 X *gets rid of* Y: X HAVE Y and X CAUSE (not X HAVE Y)
 X *keeps* Y: X HAVE Y and not X CHANGE TO (not X HAVE
 B)

The component IS OF occurring in *lend* represents a rather abstract instance of the pertinence relation mentioned above. It might be mentioned in passing that *have*, *give*, *get*, the verbs in (20), and some others constitute a particular semantic field, connected by the component HAVE. It is obvious from these examples that the internal organization of a field of this type might be of a fairly complex nature. Components like CAUSE and CHANGE TO can furthermore be used recursively in combination with other components. Assume, for example, that we abbreviate the meaning of *alive* or *living* by ALIVE X. Then the meaning of *die* can be represented as X CHANGE TO (not ALIVE X), and the meaning of *kill* becomes approximately X CAUSE (Y CHANGE TO (not ALIVE Y)). The same combination of CAUSE and CHANGE TO occurs in transitive verbs like *lengthen*, *raise*, *shorten*, *broaden*, etc. Thus if we rely on the analysis of *long* given above, the meaning of *lengthen* would be roughly as follows:

(21) X *lengthens* Y: X CAUSE (Y CHANGE TO (Z' GREATER Z))
 ⟨Z EXTENSION OF Y and MAXIMAL Z⟩

Z' here abbreviates the changed value of Z. Notice that there are many verbs in English whose transitive and intransitive use differs in meaning in the same way as *kill* and *die*, viz. by the presence or absence of the component CAUSE. Thus the meaning of *He applies the rule to this case* and *The rule applies to this case* differ essentially by the occurrence of X CAUSE (. . .) in the former, but not in the latter sentence. Similarly, if we erase X CAUSE from (21), we get the intransitive meaning of *lengthen*.

Lexical entries like those in (20) and (21) exemplify a further, important point in the internal organization of lexical entries. The arguments X, Y, Z of these entries stand for syntactic constituents combined with the verbs in a definite way. Thus we must indicate that in the meaning of *give*, represented as X CAUSE (Y HAVE Z), the argument X refers to the subject *Peter*, Y to the indirect object *John* and Z to the direct object *many books* in the sentence *Peter gives John many books*. In order to provide the necessary information, the arguments associated with semantic components in lexical entries will be indexed for the grammatical relations in question. As mentioned above, these grammatical relations are based on the syntactic deep structure. If we abbreviate the relations 'subject of the sentence', 'direct object of the main verb' and 'indirect object of the main verb' by s, d, and i, respectively, the meaning of *give* will then be X_s CAUSE (X_i HAVE X_d). Notice, that not all arguments refer to specified syntactic constituents. Thus the dimensions Z occurring in (21) cannot be expressed by a particular syntactic element. Hence this argument remains without a grammatical index. Finally particular selection restrictions might be associated with each of these syntactically indexed arguments. Thus the meaning of *kill* might now be:

(22) *kill*: X_s CAUSE (X_d CHANGE TO (not ALIVE X_d)) and $\langle$ANIMATE $X_d\rangle$

Further restrictions like '$\langle$CONCRETE $X_s\rangle$' or '$\langle$HUMAN $X_s\rangle$' would indicate that only concrete or human beings might be the agents of an act of killing.

6. *The Relation between Syntax and Semantics*

We have discussed so far the internal structure of the meaning of lexical elements, and several relations within the dictionary that follow from this intrinsic structure. It turned out at the same time that certain syntactic properties must also be incorporated in the representation of word meanings. Thus the syntactically indexed arguments of a verb indicate the required or permissible noun phrases and their syntactic function. The selection restrictions impose further conditions on these co-constituents. Hence an essential part of the syntactic behaviour of a lexical element can be derived directly from its semantic representation. We will now briefly show how the semantic interpretation of a sentence is connected with its syntactic structure.

The first explicit and systematic solution of this problem was proposed by Katz and Fodor (1963) and Katz and Postal (1964). It is based on the theory presented by Chomsky (1965) according to which a grammar has a base component that generates syntactic deep structures, each of which consists of a string of lexical elements on which a hierarchy of syntactic categories are imposed so that such relations as 'subject of the sentence', etc., can be derived (cf. pp. 118–19 above). Each lexical element contains a phonological representation, certain syntactic and morphological features and a semantic representation. A deep structure of this kind is then transformed by rules that are for the most part unique to particular languages into appropriate surface structures which are finally mapped into phonetic representations.

The semantic representation of a sentence as a whole is derived from the syntactic deep structure by certain universal operations that combine the meanings of the lexical elements of a deep structure according to the relevant syntactic relations. Several proposals have been made for the formulation of this procedure. I will follow here the version suggested in Bierwisch (1969). This proposal relies on the fact that all noun phrases, except for predicate nominals in sentences like *Alexander is an unlucky fellow*, are referential constituents, i.e. are constituents of the sentence which refer to objects rather than describing them, and are therefore marked with a reference index, say an arbitrary natural number. Two noun phrases with identical indices refer to the same (set of) object(s), those with different indices refer to different objects. Thus in *When they$_1$ came in, Paul$_2$ asked the students$_1$* the pronoun *they* is coreferential with *the students*. Given these referential indices, the semantic interpretation of a deep structure is then derived by two operations. The first of these interrelates the semantic components by means of appropriate arguments. Thus an argument X_s of a verb or an adjective or a predicate noun is replaced by X_i, if i is the referential index of the subject noun phrase. An argument X_d is replaced by X_j, if j is the referential index of the direct object. And so on for all syntactically indexed arguments in the lexical elements. The second operation connects the meanings of the individual words by logical constants, mainly (but not only) by 'and'. Thus we would get (23b) as the semantic interpretation of (23a) if we abbreviate the specific semantic components of *dog* as DOG:

(23) (a) [[the boy]$_{NP1}$ [kills [the dog]$_{NP2}$] $_{VP}$]$_S$
   (b) HUMAN X_1 and MALE X_1 and not ADULT X_1 and X_1
       CAUSE (X_2 CHANGE TO (not ALIVE X_2)) and ANIMATE
       X_2 and DOG X_2

I have oversimplified the matter in several respects. I have ignored, in particular, the fairly complex problems involved in quantifiers like *all*, *many*, *some*, in definite and indefinite determiners, etc. The meaning of these elements must be incorporated in the semantic representation of sentences essentially in the form of certain operators which further specify the referential arguments X_i, X_j, etc. It should be clear, however, that in principle the meaning of a sentence can be derived in a definite form on the basis of the meaning of its words and its syntactic deep structure, and that this derived meaning represents the crucial properties of its cognitive content in a plausible way. If appropriately refined the semantic structures arrived at in this way will presumably turn out to be nothing but a suitably adapted realization of the principles of formal logic. Hence the logical rules of transformation and deduction apply to semantic representations, explaining how we are able to carry out logical operations in natural language (cf. the chapter by Janet Dean Fodor). The principles according to which semantic representations are organized must furthermore be assumed to be universal, i.e. the same for all languages. Thus it is not the types of semantic components and of their possible interrelations that differ from language to language, but only the particular combinations that form the specific concepts listed in the dictionary. It might finally be mentioned that recently a somewhat different model for the relation between syntax and semantics has been proposed. According to this theory of 'generative semantics', sketched for example in

McCawley (1968), the grammar first specifies a semantic structure for each sentence. This semantic representation is then converted into a syntactic structure in roughly the following way: if a particular configuration of semantic elements is identical to the semantic representation of a lexical entry E, this configuration is replaced by the phonological form of E. If all semantic components of a given semantic representation are replaced in this way, we get a string of words which is syntactically organized according to the relations that originally connected the meanings of the lexical elements in the semantic representation. Thus, instead of deriving (23b) from (23a), in the theory of generative semantics we derive a syntactic structure like (23a) from some equivalent of (23b). In other words, the semantic representation of a sentence receives a syntactic interpretation by applying to it the dictionary and certain transformational rules. Since there are many unsolved problems here, I will not pursue the theory of generative semantics any further. In some important respects it is equivalent to the theory of interpretive semantics sketched out above: it expresses in general the same facts in a different form.

7. *The Interpretation of Semantic Components*

With semantic representations of the type outlined so far, we can explain many semantic properties and relations. Thus two sentences S_1 and S_2 are synonymous – or paraphrases of each other – if their semantic representations are identical. A sentence is semantically anomalous, if its semantic interpretation contains a contradiction between a selection restriction and some other semantic component. S_1 is entailed by S_2 if the meaning of S_1 is part of the semantic representation of S_2. In general, we can now deal in a systematic way with questions of the type illustrated by the examples (1)–(6). Notice, incidentally, that relations like paraphrase, entailment, etc. are suitable generalizations of lexical relations like synonymy, hyponymy, etc. This is a natural consequence of the fact that the semantic representations of sentences are in principle of the same character as lexical meanings.

We will now turn briefly to the complicated question of how sentences are related, by means of their meaning, to states, processes, and objects in the universe. This problem can be divided into two parts: the mechanism of reference and the interpretation of semantic components. As to the first problem, we should remember that the semantic representations that we have devised contain referentially indexed arguments. These arguments are variables representing possible (sets of) objects. They indicate identity or difference of reference, they do not represent, however, particular objects. In other words, every referentially indexed variable must be replaced by the representation of particular objects, if a sentence is intended to refer to particular objects in specific situations or contexts. Thus a sentence like *He asked him* might refer to two particular persons in one context, to two other persons in another. The sentence as such is not ambiguous, however. The sentence *If he comes, I will ask Bill*, on the other hand, is ambiguous with respect to reference, since *he* and *Bill* can have the same or a different referential index. In general, then, a semantic theory must provide the means for relating sentences to particular objects and situations, while the representation of the objects themselves is not part of the semantic structure of a language. We are left then with the interpretation of the semantic components that have been treated so far as purely formal elements expressing interrelations between semantic structures. It seems natural to assume that these components represent categories or principles according to which real and fictitious, perceived and imagined situations and objects are structured and classified. The semantic features do not represent, however, external physical properties, but rather the psychological conditions according to which human beings process their physical and social environment. Thus they are not symbols for physical properties and relations outside the human organism, but rather for the internal mechanisms by means of which such phenomena are perceived and conceptualized. This then leads to the extremely far-reaching, though plausible, hypothesis that all semantic structures might finally be reduced to components representing the basic dispositions of the cognitive and perceptual structure of the human organism. According to this hypothesis semantic features cannot be different from language to language, but are rather part of the general human capacity for language, forming a universal inventory used in particular ways by individual languages. Basic components of this type might be X GREATER Y representing the general ability of comparison, X DIMENSION OF Y based on the three-dimensional space orientation, VERTICAL Y reflecting the special role that the vertical dimension plays for human beings. HUMAN X, ANIMATE X, X PARENT Y, X CHANGE TO P, X CAUSE P and other components that we have used by way of illustration might also be candidates for such a universal interpretation – or might else be reduced to true basic elements. All these basic elements are not learned in any reasonable sense of the term, but are rather an innate predisposition for language acquisition. They have to be actualized or released by experience during the process of language acquisition, but as a possible structure they are already present in the learning organism. Hence what is learned during the process of language acquisition, is not the semantic components, but rather their particular combinations in special concepts, and the assignment of phonemic forms and morphological properties to these concepts. (For a somewhat different view, see the chapter by Campbell and Wales, pp. 242–60.)

If we interpret the semantic components in this way, their purely formal character is related to the cognitive and perceptual equipment of the human organism. This then provides the necessary interrelation of semantic structures with the surrounding universe, which is perceived and categorized according to these inherent conditions of the organism. This mediated relation between semantic structures and real situations also explains the fact that we are able to talk about things that are not present in the situation, or are purely fictitious, that we are able to form concepts corresponding to nothing in the real world.

It should be obvious from these considerations that semantic components are abstract theoretical entities representing complex psychological structures and mechanisms. Their names must not lead us to the impression that they are themselves lexical entries of any natural language. It is in this respect that the componential analysis might differ substantially from the perhaps formally equivalent theory of meaning postulates. As I mentioned in section 2, the theory of meaning postulates does not introduce theoretical elements that are not part of the language to be described. As far as the considerations connected to the interpretation of semantic components are reasonable, the theory of componential analysis attempts a more detailed answer to the question of how sentences are semantically related to the extralinguistic environment. It should be noted, however, that in all other respects, in particular as far as the interrelation of syntax and semantics are concerned, the theory of meaning postulates and that of semantic components are confronted with the same problems.

8. *Some Wider Perspectives*

It goes without saying that we have greatly oversimplified the problems raised by the question 'What is meaning?' We have not only ignored several problems of detail, we have also left out of the present discussion certain substantial questions that a full theory of meaning must take into consideration. I will now mention at least some of them.

First of all, we have dealt only with problems of cognitive content or denotative meaning. We have ignored, in other words, all problems of stylistic variation or connotative values. Although it is a fairly obvious fact that two sentences may say the same thing, though in a different way (i.e. with different stylistic connotations), little is known about how this can be systematically explained. Notice that it is not sufficient to assign stylistic values to particular lexical entries, since stylistic phenomena might very well be the function of the particular semantic and syntactic interaction of the basic elements. In any case, every theory of meaning that tries to incorporate such problems must be based on a systematic account of the problems of cognitive meaning.

Secondly the semantic interpretation of a given sentence might depend in part on the particular linguistic or extralinguistic context in which it occurs. In other words, a sentence that is ambiguous if taken in isolation might have only one interpretation if it occurs in a particular universe of discourse. Hence we might expect a semantic theory to explain how one of the several meanings associated with a particular word or sentence is selected in accordance with a particular universe of discourse.

We must know, for example, that *group* has one meaning when used in mathematical textbooks, another in sociological discussions, and still another in everyday discourse. Although little progress has yet been made in the systematic treatment of these problems, they do not seem to pose difficulties of principle. A semantic description must in any case provide a representation of all meanings possibly associated with a given sentence in a particular language. The question to be answered is therefore the following: how is this language divided into certain sub-languages according to the different universes of discourse to which it might be applied? If viewed in this way, the problem of context is similar to that of stylistic variation in the sense that stylistically different sub-languages are used in different contexts.

Finally it should be noted that the semantic analysis of a given natural language poses enormous difficulties because of the great complexity and apparent vagueness of the relevant phenomena. Problems of this kind are relevant not only for the adequate description of particular languages, but also for the development of the general theory, since a general theory is valid only in so far as it is based on empirical facts. Semantic analysis must therefore start with small, clear sub-systems, developing thereby the necessary basic concepts. Such islands might then be extended to larger complexes and more intricate problems. In this way, we may finally reveal also the basic structure underlying the apparently vague and imprecise phenomena of meaning in natural languages. This process is in its very beginning. It will certainly lead to important modifications of the hypotheses sketched in this outline. But there is good reason to assume that a precise theory of meaning is possible, and that such a theory will provide at the same time important insights into the nature of cognitive processes.

9. GENERATIVE GRAMMAR AND STYLISTIC ANALYSIS

J. P. Thorne

'Stylistics', as Thorne points out below, is a word that is applied to various kinds of linguistic analysis. One reason for this variety of interpretation is that different scholars draw upon different theories of linguistic structure (to the extent that they have any definite theoretical commitment). Another reason is that the word 'style' (from which of course 'stylistics' is derived) is often used to refer to a number of rather different aspects of language. This point was mentioned in the Introduction (p. 19).

Thorne is primarily concerned with the analysis of literary texts. He sets his discussion within the framework of Chomsky's (1965) version of transformational grammar (see pp. 124–8); and, like Bierwisch in the previous chapter, he makes particular appeal to the notion of 'deep structure' and 'selection restrictions'. The main burden of his argument is that many of the impressionistic terms of stylistics ('complex', 'terse', etc.) can be related to the formal properties of language as described by generative grammar. A further point he makes is that 'most stylistic judgements relate to deep structure' (p. 189).

THE name 'stylistics' is given to studies of many different kinds (cf. Bailey & Burton, 1968). About the only thing they all have in common is that they involve in some form or another an analysis of the linguistic structure of texts. One can, of course, comment on the linguistic structure of a text without having a formal knowledge of grammar, but obviously such a knowledge is very useful. Any advance in grammatical studies is, therefore, likely to have some effect on stylistics. The purpose of this chapter is to suggest that there are special reasons for thinking that the introduction into linguistics of the notion 'generative grammar' will have an effect upon stylistics.

To see why this should be so it is necessary first to understand

185

what a generative grammar is intended to be. In constructing a generative grammar of a language the linguist is attempting to construct a model of the native speaker's 'linguistic competence'; that is, of what he knows about the structure of his language. An obvious and important manifestation of linguistic competence is the English speaker's ability to recognize that some word strings, like *The children are asleep*, are well-formed (i.e. 'grammatical') English sentences while others, like *Asleep children the are*, are not. That is to say, anyone who speaks English possesses knowledge which enables him to recognize on hearing the first of these utterances that it has the syntactic structure of an English sentence and, on hearing the second, to recognize that it does not. This, in turn, is connected with the fact that he will understand the first while the second will appear meaningless to him. A generative grammar as described by Chomsky (1965), is organized in such a way that the output of the syntactic component of the grammar is the input to an interpretative semantic component. This aspect of linguistic competence can be accounted for quite naturally, then, by setting up the grammar in such a way that only well-formed sentences are generated (and, therefore, interpreted). But between these extremes of well-formedness occur sentences of varying degrees of grammaticalness (cf. Chomsky, 1965*b*; 148–60). For example, a sentence like *The houses are asleep*, while clearly not ungrammatical in the sense in which *Asleep children the are* is ungrammatical, is nevertheless not completely well-formed. These 'semi-sentences' pose a serious problem for the linguist. Their ungrammaticalness is the result, not of their having no syntactic structure, but of their having a syntactic structure that differs from that of any well-formed sentence. By the same token they can be interpreted, even though the interpretation has to be distinguished as 'figurative'. To solve this dilemma Katz (1964) has proposed that the linguist's task should include, not only the construction of a grammar that generates and interprets all and only the well-formed sentences in a language, but also the construction of a 'counter-grammar' that will generate and interpret all the semi-sentences of that language.

Another aspect of linguistic competence to which linguists

have paid particular attention is termed 'acceptability' (cf. Ross, 1967). In the sense in which the term is being used here the sentences *An old man came in who suffered with asthma* and *An old man who suffered with asthma came in* are equally acceptable, whereas in the case of the sentence *An old man with asthma came in* and *An old man came in with asthma* the former is more acceptable than the latter. To take some other examples, the sentences *I called most of the girls up* and *I called up most of the girls* are equally acceptable but the sentence *I called up the girls who lived there* is more acceptable than the sentence *I called the girls who lived there up*. These last examples are important because they illustrate very clearly that the crucial factor here is not the mere length of certain elements in these sentences but their syntactic structure. This aspect of linguistic competence is accounted for by specifying output conditions (in the case of the sentences cited above these relate to the domains of certain optional permutation transformations), all sentences generated by the grammar but failing to meet these conditions being unacceptable sentences.

Linguists have tended to be preoccupied by the phenomena of grammaticalness and acceptability. But these are not the only structural phenomena that an adequate grammar should reflect. Another, to which some attention has been paid is illustrated by sentences like *The dog chased the cat that killed the rat that ate the corn* and *The rat the cat the dog chased killed ate the corn*. Both of these contain more than one underlying sentence. These happen to be the same in each case. It is therefore particularly interesting that the second sentence is more difficult to understand than the first. It seems somehow to be more complex. The relevant structural facts are that the first sentence is a right-branching structure while the second is self-embedding. That is to say, the tree-diagram (see p. 116) for the first sentence shows that in each case the embedded sentence forms part of the predicate of its matrix sentence, whereas the tree-diagram for the second shows that each embedded sentence forms part of the subject of its matrix sentence. Sentences that have a self-embedding structure always appear more complex than corresponding sentences with right-branching structures. It could be argued that a grammar which failed to specify the structural characteristics of this pheno-menon would be open to criticism in exactly the same way as one which failed to specify the structural characteristics of gramma-ticalness or acceptability.

Generative grammarians are not the first to be interested in the phenomenon of complexity. In fact, traditionally the char-acterization of a sentence as 'complex' would be accounted a stylistic judgement. The term 'complex' itself forms part of the traditional vocabulary of stylistics. The same is true, in effect, of judgements concerning grammaticalness and acceptability. Both 'ungrammatical' and 'unacceptable' can be related to traditional stylistic terms. The connexion between certain kinds of ungram-matical structures and certain kinds of figurative expressions has already been noted. Some of the examples of unacceptable sentences given above could serve in a handbook on style as examples of how not to construct sentences. Conversely, if terms like 'loose', or 'terse', or 'emphatic' (to take other examples from the traditional vocabulary of stylistics) have any significance as descriptions of style – and surely they do – it must be because, like the description 'complex', they relate to certain identifiable structural properties. If this is less obviously the case with other stylistic terms it is only because the relationship is less clear, not because it does not exist. What the impressionistic terms of stylistics are impressions of are types of grammatical structures. The ability to form these judgements is just as much a manifestation of linguistic competence as the ability to form judgements about grammaticality and acceptability.

The main reason, then, for suggesting that generative grammar might prove to have an important influence on stylistic studies is that they are both concerned with essentially the same kind of phenomena. This is because the basic postulates of both studies (generative grammar explicitly, traditional stylistics implicitly) are mentalistic (in the sense of Katz, 1964). In both cases the most important data are responses relating to what is intuitively known about language structure. It can be argued that only a mental-istic grammar can provide an adequate basis for stylistics. It follows from the same argument that the failure of pre-Chomskyan linguistics to provide such a basis can be traced to its extreme anti-mentalist tendencies. This resulted in linguists' attention being restricted almost entirely to those structural facts which can be directly related to what is observable in language. Generative grammar (see p. 23) is important to stylistics because, in addition to these 'surface structure' facts, it is concerned with the so-called 'deep structure' aspects of language, that is, those facts about linguistic structure which cannot be directly related to what can be observed. Most stylistic judgements relate to deep structure.

Obviously there is no reason why there should not be quite general studies of a phenomenon like terseness in just the same way as there are quite general studies of a phenomenon like acceptability. But presumably stylistics will continue to be mainly concerned with characterizing the structural properties of particular texts – especially literary texts. In describing the style of a particular text as 'terse' or 'complex' one is, of course, indicating the general impression one receives. Thus a passage which most people would describe as 'terse' usually turns out to contain a majority of – but not necessarily only – sentences which involve deletion rules in their generation. Particularly interesting cases of this kind of overall impression are those which lead us to describe the style of a passage as, say, Shakespearian or Jamesian, or which lead us to ascribe a text to a certain author. The fact that we can recognize successful parodies as being parodies of particular writers emphasizes the fact that it is structural considerations that form the basis for these impressions.

A study of the basis for these kinds of judgements is given in Ohmann (1964). Ohmann shows very clearly how an author's style can be related to his predilection for certain grammatical structures. Among the passages he examines is the following extract from Faulkner's *The Bear* (1942: 255–6):

the desk and the shelf above it on which rested the letters in which McCaslin recorded the slow outward trickle of food and supplies and equipment which returned each fall as cotton made and ginned and sold (two threads frail as truth and impalpable as equators yet cable-strong to bind for life them who made the cotton to the land their sweat fell on), and the older ledgers clumsy and archaic in size and shape, on the yellowed pages of which were recorded in the faded hand of his father Theophilus and his uncle Amodeus during the two decades before the Civil War, the manumission in title at least of Carothers McCaslin's slaves . . .

Ohmann describes the style of this passage as 'complex, highly individual and difficult . . . also . . . quite typically Faulknerian'. His analysis shows the structural correlates of this style to be a high proportion of (1) relative constructions, particularly those deleting the relative pronoun and the verb *to be*; (2) compound structures formed with the conjunction *and*; (3) comparative constructions. To support his claim that these represent the key structures in Faulkner's writing Ohmann also analyses characteristic passages from three other modern English prose writers showing that none of them reveal Faulkner's preference for this particular combination of structures.

It is probably true that most writers – perhaps all writers – maintain a preference for certain structures throughout the whole of their work. It is also true, of course, that a writer can vary the kinds of structures he employs in order to produce corresponding variations in style. Often a stylistic effect can be produced by just a slight shift in syntactic structure. Take for example the following passage from Raymond Chandler's novel *The Lady in the Lake* (1952: 139–40):

An elegant handwriting, like the elegant hand that wrote it. I pushed it to one side and had another drink, I began to feel a little less savage. I pushed things around on the desk. My hands felt thick and hot and awkward. I ran a finger across the corner of the desk and looked at the streak made by the wiping off of the dust. I looked at the dust on my finger and wiped that off. I looked at my watch. I looked at the wall. I looked at nothing.

I put the liquor bottle away and went over to the washbowl to rinse the glass out. When I had done that I washed my hands and bathed my face in cold water and looked at it. The flush was gone from the left cheek, but it looked a little swollen. Not very much, but enough to make me tighten up again. I brushed my hair and looked at the grey in it. There was getting to be plenty of grey in it. The face under the hair had a sick look. I didn't like the face at all.

I went back to the desk and read Miss Fromsett's note again. I smoothed it out on the glass and sniffed it and smoothed it out some more and folded it and put it in my coat pocket.

I sat very still and listened to the evening grow quiet outside the open windows. And very slowly I grew quiet with it.

The two most frequently occurring words in this passage are *I* and *and*. This superficial observation relates to the fact that most of the sentences have deep structures conforming to the pattern *I Verb Phrase and I Verb Phrase*. The number of underlying sentences joined together in this way being anything up to five. In each case the corresponding surface structure is formed by the deletion of the repeated first person pronoun. In fact, nearly every underlying sentence in this passage repeats some element from a previous sentence. Thus while 'repetitive' is undoubtedly an accurate description of the style of this passage its linguistic basis can be properly established only with reference to the deep structure of the sentences in it, a very general condition of English grammar determining that most of the repeated elements should not appear in their surface structures. This highly repetitive style plays a major part in creating the mood of aimless, nervous agitation the passage conveys. The last sentence stands apart from the rest of the sentences in the passage. Not merely because it announces a change of mood. Grammatically too, it forms an exception. It is the only sentence where the sequence *and I* occurs in a surface structure. This is because this sentence connects to the previous one, not only by repeating the subject (*I*) of its matrix but also by repeating the verb phrase (*grow quiet*) of its underlying constituent sentence. Several sentences repeat the verb phrase of a previous sentence, but this is the only case where a repeated verb does not have the subject *I* in both of its occurrences. Moreover, in its first occurrence the subject is inanimate (*evening*). How effective the resulting zeugma is can be judged by substituting another verb for the second occurrence of *grow quiet* (say, *relaxed*). At least part of its effectiveness comes from the fact that this sentence which announces a change of mood, a change from alienation to reconciliation, connects syntactically with the rest of the sentences in the passage in a different way from that in which they connect with each other.

So far we have been discussing aspects of linguistic structure that are common to both prose and poetry. Stylisticians have always been attracted to the question of whether or not it is possible to identify aspects of linguistic structure which distinguish prose from poetry. The problem is very old and very difficult. For the most part those writers, of any period, who have interested themselves in this problem have looked for features over and above the phonological features of rhythm and rhyme. But some of them have seen these features as providing an essential insight into the way in which the organization of the language of poetry differs from that of prose, claiming that what distinguishes poetry from mere verse is that in the case of the former these phonological regularities are matched or reinforced by grammatical regularities. This view is summarized in Mac Hammond's (1961: 482) statement that 'syntax is poetic when grammatically equivalent constituents in connected speech are juxtaposed by coordination or parataxis, or are otherwise prominently accumulated'. The phenomenon of 'parallelism' in poetry has been studied by among others Jacobson (1960, 1966) and Levin (1962). Implicit in some of these studies is the idea that not only with regard to the phonological component of the grammar but with regard also to the syntax and semantics the poet works under the restraint of self-imposed rules; that is, rules which do not form part of the grammar of a natural language. An attempt to restate this view of poetry within the larger context of the view of language structure provided by generative grammar is contained in Thorne (1965). (See also Hendricks, 1969; Fowler, 1969; Thorne, 1969).

The discussion centres around two observations. The first is that ungrammatical sentences tend to occur far more frequently in poetry than in prose. (The proportion tends to vary from the works of one poet to the next and, even more strikingly, from the poetry of one period to the next, but this remark is true, broadly speaking, of the work of all poets and all periods.) Recognition of these deviant sentences forms an essential element in our response to poetry. The second is that although, inevitably, we recognize these deviant sentences as being deviant, it is sometimes also the case that they are felt not to be deviant within the context of the poem. One of the poems studied (Thorne, 1965: 59) is Donne's 'A Nocturnall Upon S. Lucies Day'. The first stanza of the poem contains the clause (*mee*) *who am their Epitaph* where the deep structure would be equivalent to that of the sentence *I am their epitaph*. This is a semi-sentence. It breaks selectional rules which specify that noun phrases on either side of the copula *to be* should be marked in the same way for the feature *animacy*, that is either both should be plus animate or both should be minus animate. (Cf. *I am a student*, *I am a desk, *The desk was a student*, *His desk was an old oil drum*.) In succeeding stanzas there occur the sentences *I am every dead thing*, *I . . . am the grave of all*, and *I am None*, all of which break this same rule. (One could also add here *I am . . . of the first nothing the Elixir grown* which involves a different kind of structure but the same selectional rule being broken.) At the same time the poem also contains the sentences *All these seem to laugh* (where *these* refers back to *the sunne* and *th'hydroptique earth*) and *Yea plants, yea stones detest and love*. In these sentences too, a selectional rule is broken – verbs which demand an animate subject taking here an inanimate subject. In short the poem has sentences which have inanimate nouns where one would usually expect to find animate nouns and animate nouns (or rather the animate first person pronoun) where one would expect to find inanimate nouns. These irregularities are regular in the context of the poem. It seems likely that these linguistic facts underlie the sense of chaos and breakdown of natural order which many literary critics have associated with the poem.

One way of representing these facts is simply to do what has just been done, that is, simply to list those structures in the poem which are deviant, indicating in each case which rules have been broken. Another way involves stating the rules which would actually generate these structures. Most of the rules would form part of the grammar of Standard English (that is, a grammar which would generate only well-formed sentences), but it would be necessary to give special rules for the first person pronoun, which in the language of the poem always selects an inanimate predicate (interestingly enough the sentence which might look as though it is an exception to this rule has a subjunctive copula, *Were I a man . . .*) and for verbs like *laugh* and *love*, which in the language of the poem can select inanimate subjects. There is a good reason for preferring the second approach. It suggests a quite interesting hypothesis about what it is poets (or at least some poets) are trying to do when they write poetry and, therefore, also about what it is that distinguishes some kinds of poetry from prose. Behind the idea of constructing what is in effect a grammar for the poem lies the idea that what the poet has done is to create a new language (or dialect) and that the task that faces the reader is in some ways like that of learning a new language (or dialect).

There is room here only for one more example to illustrate this approach to the stylistic analysis of poetry. The poem is by Theodore Roethke (1957: 55).

Dolour

I have known the inexorable sadness of pencils,
Neat in their boxes, dolour of pad and paperweight,
All the misery of manila folders and mucilage,
Desolation in immaculate public places,
Lonely reception room, lavatory, switchboard,
The unalterable pathos of basin and pitcher,
Ritual of multigraph, paper-clip, comma,
Endless duplication of lives and objects.
And I have seen dust from the walls of institutions,
Finer than flour, alive, more dangerous than silica,
Sift, almost invisible, through long afternoons of tedium,
Dropping a fine film on nails and delicate eyebrows,
Glazing the pale hair, the duplicate grey standard faces.

From the point of view of this approach the most interesting feature of this poem is the ungrammatical constructions; *the inexorable sadness of pencils, dolour of pad and paperweight, misery of manila folders and mucilage*. These provide a particular problem for the analyst. There is, of course, nothing to stop one constructing a grammar which would assign quite arbitrary analyses to these or any of the constructions in the poem. This would be equivalent to making the claim that they were meaningless. But although they are deviant they are clearly not meaningless. They can be understood. The whole point of constructing a grammar which would generate these constructions is that it provides a way of stating clearly the interpretation that one finds for them.

The grammar that one constructs for a poem must therefore meet one of the conditions for a 'counter-grammar'. Although it contains rules which are not rules of Standard English, they must relate to rules of Standard English (cf. Katz, 1964: 412). Now constructions like *the ... sadness of pencils*, etc. are, presumably, nominalizations of underlying sentences of the form *The pencils are sad, The paperweight is dolorous, The manila folders are miserable*. Obviously these are deviant sentences. The problem is that there are at least two ways of accounting for their ungrammaticalness. This is because adjectives like *sad* and *miserable* select either animate nouns like *boy* and *girl* or certain subcategories of abstract nouns like *experience, occasion* and *spectacle*. Thus if one wants to say that nouns like *pencil, paperweight, manila folder*, etc. constitute a special subcategory of nouns in the language of the poem, one then has to decide whether the rule which governs their distribution relates to that governing the distribution of nouns like *boy* and *girl*, etc. or that governing the distribution of nouns like *experience, spectacle*, etc. in Standard English. A decision that is not open to one is to make the distribution of *pencil, paperweight*, etc. coincide with that of both of these subcategories, since this would mean that one had still not indicated the way in which one understood phrases like *the sadness of pencils*; the semantic interpretation of *sad boy* being, of course, different from that of *sad experience*. (Roughly speaking, in the first case the relationship is like that of verb to object, in the second like that of subject to verb.) The problem is typical of the kind of problem one encounters in attempting to construct grammars for poems and to some extent justifies the exercise. In making choices about the grammar one is choosing between readings of the poem.

In discussing the grammars both of the Donne poem and the Roethke poem the rules we have been concerned with have all been deep-structure rules. This is important in view of what it suggests about what it is these poets are trying to achieve, because (in terms of the grammatical model we have adopted) the deep structure of a sentence determines its meaning. For these poets the point of creating a new language, therefore, seems to be that it enables them to say not only things that can be said in Standard English, but in a different way, but also things that cannot be said in Standard English at all – though they can be understood only by someone who understands Standard English. Donne has created a language in which the word *I* is still the animate first person. But to attribute the regular occurrence in the language of the poem of sentences like *I am a grave* (and, by implication, the absence of sentences like *I am a man*) to a difference in the deep grammar of this pronoun is to attribute to it a different meaning (cf. Putnam, 1962: 222–3). The words *stone* and *plant* still retain all the features that together make up their ordinary meanings. But if the grammar of the language of the poem is such that *Stones love* is a well-formed sentence in it, then they too have changed their meaning. Similarly, in the language of Roethke's poem *pencil*, *pad*, etc. are still the names of pieces of stationery, but at the same time they acquire new meanings because they have (under one reading) acquired the selectional range of words like *experience* and *occasion*.

This has a bearing on the declared inability of many people to understand poems like these. It also explains why it is impossible to paraphrase some of the sentences in these poems. We have been concerned exclusively with selectional rules. Deviation from selectional rules seems to have always been the main source of 'witty' writing in English. This is particularly the case for selectional rules involving the features animate, inanimate, concrete, and abstract. There are comparatively few good jokes in English arising from dislocation of rules concerning the features, masculine and feminine. Poets do also invent their own surface-structure rules, of course. But on the whole it seems to be the case that poems in which the grammar differs from that of Standard English only in the surface structure are usually bad poems. Take the following lines of Longfellow:

> Have I dreamed? Or was it real,
>   What I saw as in a vision,
> When to marches hymeneal
>   In the land of the Ideal
> Moved my thought o'er Field Elysian?

The superficial strangeness of these lines is associated with the *ad hoc* transformations that have to be postulated for the analysis of the sentences in them. Their basic banality (their prosaicness) is associated with the fact that the deep structure of these sentences would be generated by rules which form part of the grammar of Standard English.

10. FORMAL LINGUISTICS AND FORMAL LOGIC

Janet Dean Fodor

There is some evidence of the influence of logic upon linguistics in two of the previous chapters. A number of terms and concepts derived from modern logic are used by Bierwisch in his account of the 'componential' approach to semantics (pp. 166–84); and mention is made, in the chapter on syntax, of the way in which such scholars as Bach (1968), McCawley (1968) and Seuren (1969) have drawn upon the logical notion of 'quantification' in their analysis of the 'deep structure' of sentences (pp. 26, 124).

After a general discussion of the relationship between logic and linguistics, Janet Dean Fodor considers whether the 'deep structure' of sentences can be identified with their 'logical form'. She concludes that, while this may in principle be possible, in practice it solves few problems. Different systems of logic assign different forms to sentences. We must therefore decide which system is best for the linguist in that it permits the simplest set of rules for relating deep structures to the surface forms of sentences.

Readers without any background in formal logic may find that one or two points made in this chapter elude them (e.g. the reference to alternative systems of formalization on p. 209). But they should have no difficulty in following the main thread of the argument.

THE recent, and apparently growing, trend among linguists to ransack textbooks of logic might be merely an intellectual fashion, destined like all fashions to fade. But it would be foolish, if not insulting, simply to dismiss it in this way, especially as the interest has not been entirely one-sided. Philosophers, too, are becoming increasingly keen, despite the inaccessibility of some of the material, to acquaint themselves with the results of linguistic research (see, for example, Vendler, 1967). When two disciplines start to become conscious of each other, this awareness may reveal something of interest about the nature of the problems, whether substantive or methodological, which they then find themselves confronting. The boundaries between disciplines are notoriously complex and untidy, and all we can hope to do here is to delineate roughly some of the many interconnexions between logic and linguistics, and then to consider to what extent and in what ways we might expect them to gain by contact with each other. And whether or not the benefits are really all on one side, we may perhaps, as linguists, be forgiven for revealing a selfish preoccupation with what the study of formal logic has to offer us.

It is not difficult to find parallels between a generative grammar of a natural language and a system of formal logic. The syntactic rules of a grammar license the move from one syntactic representation of a sentence to another just as the inference rules of logic (e.g. that 'P' can be inferred from 'P & Q') license the move from one logical formula to another. In both types of system the derivations are quite mechanical, in the sense that whether or not a certain rule applies to a formula can be determined by reference solely to the configuration of symbols in the formula and in the formal statement of the rule. Syntactic derivations therefore formally resemble proofs in logic, and, in line with this, the initial symbol 'S' of the base component of the grammar can be regarded as the analogue of the axioms of the system of logic. The surface structures generated by grammatical rules can be likened to the theorems of a logical system. Despite certain differences (such as the absence in a logical system of the distinction between terminal and non-terminal vocabularies, which is usually made in grammatical systems) both surface structures and theorems are what result when the rules of a system are applied to its axioms.

These parallels could probably be extended, but they are not especially interesting. Any two axiomatic systems will show formal similarities of this kind. In fact even for chess there is an 'axiom' (the initial positioning of pieces on the board) and a set of 'transformational rules' which license moves from one configuration of the pieces to another. More revealing of the relationship between grammars and systems of logic is a comparison of the *functions* of the representations and rules which the two types of system employ. Logical inference rules map formulae into formulae, preserving truth: a false statement must never be derivable from a true one. The mapping which syntactic rules produce might be said to preserve grammaticality, although we should have to be quite ingenious in framing our definition of grammaticality for this assertion to have a clear sense. In a grammar of the kind envisaged by Katz & Postal (1964), in which deep syntactic structures contain all that is relevant to the semantic interpretation of sentences, the transformational rules of the syntax preserve meaning, and therefore *a fortiori* preserve truth, but still it is not clear what phrase-structure rules could be said to preserve. In any case, the primary function of syntactic rules is to define the grammatical sentences of a language. The set of well-formed formulae of a system of logic also constitutes a language, an artificial language, explicitly designed, often for some special purpose, and far more restricted in its scope than a natural language such as English or Latin or Vietnamese. It is what are called the formation rules of the logical system that define which of all possible strings of symbols are to count as grammatical in this abstract language, and it is therefore these rules which are the functional counterpart of the syntactical rules of a linguistic system. Although we have called them formation rules, they are usually framed as conditions in the following form: if so-and-so is a well-formed formula, then such-and-such is also a well-formed formula. There must also, of course, be at least one non-conditional definition of a well-formed formula so that these recursive rules have somewhere to start from. For example one statement of the formation rules of the propositional calculus contains, among others, the rules:

Any propositional variable (i.e. 'P', 'Q', 'R', ...) is a well-formed formula (abbreviated to *wff*).

If 'P' is a *wff*, then '∼P' is a *wff*.

If 'P' and 'Q' are both *wffs*, then 'P & Q' is a *wff*.

We shall discuss formation rules and compare them with phrase-structure and syntactic-transformation rules in more detail later on. For the moment we should simply note that, as far as their function is concerned, it is the formation rules, and not the inference rules, of a system of logic which are the counterpart of syntactic rules in linguistic descriptions.

Is there, then, any counterpart in a grammar to the inference rules of logical systems? It might be thought that the answer to this should be 'no', on the grounds that inference rules are concerned with deduction, with the validity of types of argument, and most linguists would agree that the way in which people use the sentences of their language for the purposes of argumentation is not a question which falls strictly within the domain of linguistics, and is certainly not something that we should expect the grammar of a language to characterize. Nevertheless, even though we still know very little about the proper organization of the semantic component of a grammar, it is arguable that something along the lines of inference rules will play a part in a complete description of a natural language. One of the things that a complete description must contain is a specification of the meaning of each grammatical sentence, and, as Strawson says, 'To know the meaning of a ... ["statement-making" sentence] is to know under what conditions someone who used it would be making a true statement; to *explain* the meaning is to *say* what these conditions are. One way of giving a partial account of these conditions is to say what some of the entailments of the sentence are' (Strawson, 1952). (Strawson makes it clear that this account must be adapted appropriately to cover sentences which are used to give orders, ask questions, make promises, and so on, as well as those used to make assertions.) It is thus reasonable to suppose that the semantic component must provide representations of sentences which determine the entailments of these sentences. But, since the entailments of a sentence may be infinite, these representations cannot consist of an *enumeration* of the entailments, and the semantic component will have to contain rules corresponding to the inference rules of logic, which will generate the set of entailments from some finite, formulaic representation of a sentence. Beyond this, there is very little to be said at present. Whether or not, for example, there should be a distinct 'logical component' or whether these rules will be an integral part of the semantic component, is a question that we cannot begin to answer until we know a good deal more about other aspects of the semantic component than we do at present.

The meanings which logical symbols have, by virtue of the way they interact with formal inference rules to determine entailments, do not necessarily define one unique interpretation for the formulae of the system. Within the constraints imposed by the nature of inference rules, the system may be susceptible of a number of distinct interpretations, and other rules ('semantical rules') have to be given in order to specify such an interpretation. Putting together all of these observations, then, we can say that linguistic descriptions and logical systems both contain rules which define a set of well-formed strings of the symbols in their respective vocabularies, and both contain rules which provide interpretations for each of these strings. The two types of system might therefore be viewed as doing much the same kind of job, although for different kinds of language. The logician may first devise a system of rules and then study the language which they define, while the linguist constructs his rules so that they define the language which he has decided to study, but both are concerned with a formal statement of the syntax and semantics of a language, whether it be a natural or an artificial one.

Can we, then, say anything revealing about the relationship between the two types of language? We have already seen that systems of formal logic cover a much narrower range of meaning than natural languages. Far fewer semantic distinctions and semantic relationships can be expressed in logical formulae than in the sentences of English, for example. What is gained in return for this restriction of the expressive range of the language studied is determinacy and generality of the relationships within that range. But although the systems of logic which have so far been devised and studied are in fact limited in range, it is not clear that there is in principle any limit to the aspects of meaning which a system of logic *could* represent. Recently, for example, systems which take account of the tense and modality of verbs have been developed (see Prior, 1968; Lewis & Langford, 1959; Hughes & Cresswell, 1968), although previously the effects of these upon the entailments of sentences had to be handled intuitively or not at all. Logicians are generally not interested in the meanings of lexical items, such as *dog, tarnished, wrestle*, but only in some 'grammatical' words like *and, or, if, not, all, the*. The tendency is very naturally to concentrate upon those features which are most general and not limited to discourse on particular topics, such as hi-fi systems or trout fishing, but which keep recurring in discourse on all subjects. Also quite naturally, the logician tends to study those aspects of meaning which are of general philosophical interest. It is not surprising to find that there is a logical system designed to explicate the logical behaviour of the words *necessary* and *possible*, or of *know* and *believe* (Hintikka, 1962), but no system, so far, concerned with the behaviour of the words *finger* and *toe*.

Logicians are anxious not to be confused with lexicographers, but the words *know* and *believe* will, surely, if there is any real distinction to be made between 'lexical' and 'grammatical' words, fall into the former category. In any case, certain aspects of the meanings of other lexical items have long been accepted as legitimate topics for the logician to study; for example, the various properties of relational terms – transitivity, reflexiveness, symmetry. These properties are important in determining the set of valid arguments into which a relational term can enter. The argument *John is related to Mary, therefore Mary is related to John* is a valid argument, but *John is the father of Mary, therefore Mary is the father of John* is not. To describe the logic of relational words does not, it is true, involve giving a complete analysis of their lexical content, but it does require that some particular aspects or 'components' of their meaning are abstracted out and represented explicitly so that the inference rules can apply to them. It is often said that logic is only interested in the entailments which sentences have by virtue of their form and not of their content, but there are no special syntactic properties of relational words in English from which we could read off such properties as transitivity or reflexiveness. We simply have to consider the meaning of each word and decide into which sub-class it falls. Furthermore these properties are not usually expressed in logic by any interesting configurational property of formulae but simply by means of subscripts on the symbol standing for a relational word. Since it is always possible to represent 'content' as 'form' by some minor notational elaboration such as this, the content-form distinction does not effectively exclude any semantic fact from representation in logical formulae.

If no aspects of the meanings of words are *in principle* excluded from consideration by the logician, but at worst are low on his list of priorities because they are neither very general nor philosophically interesting, then it is no longer so obvious that there is a difference between the types of language which are studied in linguistics and in logic. The logician begins by singling out some small area to which he can approximate with quite simple and general representations and rules, and then slowly extends his compass from there to other areas of the language and to the finer details of those he has already studied. The linguist confronts the whole vast tangle of a natural language head on, extracts certain superficial regularities, and works back from there into the problems that arise in connexion with abstract underlying syntactic and semantic patterning. It is pleasant to dream that on one glorious day they will meet in the middle and between them have solved all the puzzles about the nature of language.

It hardly needs saying that this account of the relationship between the two subjects is an oversimplification. Some logicians would argue that ordinary conversational language is so fuzzy, so vague, imprecise, or downright illogical, that it could never be completely described by a precise system of logical symbols and rules. Even the sentence connectives such as *and* and *or* in English carry implications which are either unsystematic or else difficult to capture in formal rules governing their counterparts in logical notation. (See Strawson, 1952: 78–92, for detailed comparisons.) On the other hand it has also been argued (by Grice, forthcoming) that these extra implications of the English words are to be explained by reference to the way in which the words are employed in actual conversation, and should not be included in a description of the meanings of the words themselves.

This may be the point at which to correct a misleading impression that may have been given in the preceding discussion. By no means all of formal logic is concerned with characterizing the logic of ordinary language. The development of modern symbolic logic has been intimately bound up with the desire to formalize the foundations of mathematics, and systems of logic were prized mostly for the light they could throw upon mathematical concepts. Logicians are also interested in formal logical systems for their own sake rather than for the sake of their applications. They are interested in determining and comparing general properties of different systems, such as consistency and completeness, in comparing the effect upon the set of theorems of adding or discarding some axiom or rule, and so on. This is exactly like the mathematical linguist who studies the general properties of types of grammar, how the set of sentences generated varies with the type of rule the grammar contains, and so on, with only a glancing interest in how these grammars relate to those of actual languages. Furthermore, even when a logician does set about characterizing some of the logical properties of a natural language, he may well go only a short way with this and devote most of his time and attention to the philosophical implications of the system he has constructed, such as the ontology it presupposes or its bearing upon some well-known paradox or philosophical puzzle. Other logicians (for example, Quine, 1960) see their task not as capturing the complex logic of ordinary language but as constructing some alternative to it, a consistent and precise language with which to supplant ordinary language for the purpose of serious talk on scientific matters. It must be emphasized, therefore, that both in what precedes and in what follows, our discussion of the relationship between linguistics and logic is confined to that corner of logical endeavour which is concerned with explicating the logical relationships exhibited in ordinary language. (For a classic study, see Reichenbach, 1947.)

There is one important way in which the languages studied in logic and linguistics do not coincide, even in principle. The formulae employed in logic are designed to represent the facts about the meaning of a sentence which are relevant to the validity of arguments in which the sentence occurs; it is often said that such a formula represents the 'logical form' of a sentence. Logical formulae cannot be representations of the sentences of a language in the sense of there being one symbol for each word of a surface structure, with configurations of words taken over unchanged as configurations of symbols – or rather, if they were, then there would be no point at all in translating the sentences into a special logical notation. In actual fact, surface structures almost never express logical form unambiguously and perspicuously, and the systems of notation devised by logicians to make logical form explicit do serve a real purpose. The 'sentences' of the language studied by the logician, that is, the well-formed formulae of his system, are therefore not identical with the surface structures of a natural language. In one sense, logic is not concerned with surface structures at all, for statements about logical properties and relations are supposed to be independent of the facts about particular languages. An account of the logic of the words *believe* and *know*, for example, is not essentially connected with the English language, because for any language which happened to contain words meaning what *believe* and *know* mean in English, the logical behaviour of those words would be described by the systems of rules set up for *believe* and *know*. In this sense it is incidental to the logician exactly how the concepts and propositions he studies are expressed in any particular natural language, and, since surface structures are language-specific, logic is not essentially concerned with surface structures.

On the other hand, one reason given for studying formal logic is that it will enable us to assess the validity of ordinary everyday arguments which are not couched in logical symbols. First we translate the premises and conclusion of the informal argument into formal logical symbols, and then we apply the rules and principles of the logical system to determine whether the formula representing the conclusion is indeed entailed by the conjunction of the formulae representing the premises. But the ultimate usefulness of a system of formal logic in cutting through the uncertainties and unclarities of everyday reasoning will depend crucially upon how precisely the formulae of the logical system can be related to the sentences of the ordinary language. It is little use knowing that an argument expressed in formal notation is valid if we cannot be sure that we have translated correctly between the formulae it contains and the sentences of the informal argument whose validity we wish to assess.

Formal Linguistics and Formal Logic

No precise and explicit translation rules relating a natural language and a system of logic have ever been formulated. In logic textbooks the principles of translation are presented informally, and only general hints and rules of thumb are given. Formulae may be loosely associated with characteristic syntactic patterns, but these associations are intended only as a rough and ready guide, and the student must rely upon his own intuitions to supplement and correct them. He must decide for himself when a sentence is ambiguous, what its alternative senses are, when two sentences are sufficiently similar in relevant respects to warrant representing both by the same propositional variable, how to supply the proper referent of a pronoun, and so on. The fact that generations of students in introductory logic courses have picked up the art of translation without too much difficulty suggests that the task of formulating an explicit set of translation rules is a possible one. It would be rather implausible to maintain that the implicit principles with which someone operates in exercising his skill at translation could never be explicitly characterized.

Nevertheless in carrying out such a translation one draws upon virtually everything one knows about one's language, one's knowledge of the meanings of words and also of how types of syntactic structure determine the way in which the meanings of words combine to define the meanings of phrases and sentences, and so we should not be surprised if it turns out that practically every rule of the grammar of the language must be known before the translation rules can be formally stated. This, of course, is where linguistics has something to contribute to logic, for in writing the grammar of a natural language, we peel away surface variations and ambiguities in sentence structure, and provide formal, explicit, and non-redundant representations of what we might call their 'real' structure. In these underlying structural representations, the grammatical relations which are relevant to meaning are marked, items which are relevant to interpretation but missing from surface structures are supplied, and various bits and pieces of surface structures which are irrelevant to meaning are omitted. A large part of the translation problem is thereby solved, for the logician can now relate his representations of logical form to these underlying structures, which do bear some consistent relationship to the meanings of sentences. He can leave it to the linguist to provide explicit rules which interrelate these structures with the apparently chaotic surface structures of the language.

There are those who are tempted to press this argument further and make a much stronger claim about the interrelationship of underlying linguistic structures and representations of logical form. In its broadest terms the purpose of a grammar is to correlate the meanings of sentences with their sounds. For this purpose we obviously need a representation of the meaning of each sentence and a representation of its pronunciation. The latter is a phonetic representation, and we know quite a lot both about what information it should contain and also about how this information should be expressed. At the other edge of the grammar, few linguists have ventured to specify even what kinds of information should be contained in a semantic representation, let alone in what form it should be expressed. We do know that semantic representations must be mappable, by a set of explicit, and preferably general, rules onto syntactic representations. But now the linguist confronted with the task of specifying these semantic representations and mapping rules seems to be in the same boat as the logician who has to provide translation rules between representations of logical form and syntactic structures – except, of course, that the logician already has his representations. He settled on these by considering certain entailment relationships between sentences and how to capture them in explicit inference rules, for since inference rules are structure-dependent, formulation of the rules will automatically determine how meanings are to be expressed structurally. The strong claim about the relationship between logical formulae and linguistic representations which one might be led to by these observations, is that representations of logical form are identical to the semantic representations of linguistic descriptions, and the translation rules which the logician must state to relate his formulae to sentences of a natural language are identical to the linguistic rules which map semantic representations onto syntactic ones.

The claim is therefore that logic and linguistics will converge not only in what facts about the meanings of sentences they represent, but also in the details of how they represent them. The primary concern of the logician is how these meaning representations interact with inference rules to determine entailment relations between sentences. The primary concern of the linguist is how meaning representations can be mapped onto syntactic and ultimately phonetic representations. The suggestion is that these two considerations will lead to the same conclusions about the form in which meanings should be stated.

Even in its strong form, however, this claim about the relationship between logical and linguistic representations is too vague to be assessed; for even if it is true that the semantic representations provided by a grammar will be identical to the formulae of a system of logic, this says very little until we specify *which* system of logic we have in mind. A number of logical systems have been formulated, and a great many others which no-one has in fact yet described are possible. Even if some could be excluded as obviously inappropriate for the representation of sentences of ordinary language, there will still be a choice to make. For the logician, the existence of more than one type of logical system dealing with the same subject matter is not disturbing (although he may be interested in comparing and contrasting some of their formal properties), but many linguists argue that there must be just one correct grammar for any language, and that, given any two proposals, it should be possible to determine which of them is the more correct, either on the basis of further empirical data, or else by reference to their relative simplicity or conformity to general universal principles concerning linguistic structures. If this is so, the linguist must at the very least *select* from among the various alternative systems which logicians make available, and even then there is no guarantee that the system which is best suited to his purposes has yet been formulated.

To add to this, it is not at all clear when two logical systems differ significantly and when their difference is merely a matter of using one notation rather than another completely equivalent to it. (Is there, for example, a significant difference between Polish notation and the familiar Russell-Whitehead notation for the propositional calculus? Presumably not. Is there a significant difference between a system which employs variables and a system, such as that devised by Quine (1966: 227–35), which uses instead a variety of operators on predicates to represent exactly the same aspects of meaning? Perhaps here there is a difference, but no-one has stated the criteria which are relevant to answering such questions.) The task of selecting the appropriate logical system for purposes of linguistic description is clearly going to be somewhat hampered if we cannot be sure when two logical systems are related in such a way that talk of selecting between them even makes sense. So, quite apart from the obvious fact that logicians have not yet invented formal notations for a vast number of semantic phenomena that would have to be accounted for in a complete linguistic description, the assumption that semantic representations are identical to representations of logical form merely imposes some rather general constraints on the nature of the semantic component, and tells us very little in practice about what semantic representations are like.

Nevertheless since something is always better than nothing and in the area of semantics we are preciously close to having nothing, a system of formal logic can serve as a very useful starting point in thinking about how to represent meaning in linguistic descriptions. By considering the ways in which the logical system both is and is not suitable as a model for linguistic description we may be led to some general conclusions about the kind of semantic representation that is required. How, then, would one set about evaluating a proposed system as a model for linguistic description? Possibly psychological data, if it were obtainable, should be regarded as relevant. It is not easy, though, to imagine what kinds of psychological observation would support even a relatively straightforward hypothesis about semantic structures. In logic, the symbol corresponding to the English word *or* can be defined in terms of the ones which correspond to *and* and *not*. (Alternatively *and* can be defined in terms of *or* and *not*.) It is conceivable that some linguistic facts might be found which suggested that in the ultimate vocabulary of the semantic component of a linguistic description there is nothing corresponding to the logical symbol for *or*, disjunction being represented instead by the appropriate combination of conjunction and negation. But even if there were differences between *and*-sentences and *or*-sentences according to the various criteria for ease of comprehension or production, there would almost certainly be too many other explanations for such differences for any secure conclusions to be drawn about the psychological validity of a proposed semantic notation.

One criterion which will certainly be relevant to selecting the form in which semantic information is expressed is the simplicity of the rules which interrelate semantic representations and syntactic ones. At this point, however, we can no longer completely ignore, as we have up to now, the formal properties of the rules which effect this mapping, for example the difference between generative theories of semantics and interpretive theories (see p. 137 above), or between theories which regard only deep structures as relevant to semantic interpretation and those in which surface structures are also interpreted, and so on. For the criterion of simplicity might favour different forms of semantic representation depending on how the mapping is defined in detail and evaluations of the respective merits of alternative proposals. will therefore be relative to a particular linguistic theory. The important point, however, is that the form of semantic representations and the nature of the grammatical rules cannot be decided upon independently, any more than semantic representations and inference rules can be chosen independently.

As a simple illustration of this interdependence we may consider the consequences of assuming that the deep structures of a grammar may contain elements formally analogous to the quantifiers and variables of the predicate calculus. The predicate calculus is a well-developed branch of formal logic, and, especially with the extensions to it which are currently being studied, is probably the best candidate available at present as a model for linguistic description. It is therefore of interest to investigate some of the implications of assuming that deep structures resemble the formulae of this system.

It can be demonstrated, for example, that such structures could not be generated by means of a system of phrase-structure rules, at least on the reasonable assumption that one of the conditions these structures must meet is that no variable may be

bound by more than one quantifier. The set of structures to be
generated will thus contain those analogous to the formulae

(x) Fx

(∃x) (Fx & Gx)

(x) (∃y) Rxy

etc., but none like

(x) & (∃y) z

F (∃x) y

(x) (∃x) Fx

(∃x) (Fx & (x) Gx).

If it is assumed that the base (or 'deep') structures of a natural
language contain analogues to the quantifiers and variables of the
predicate calculus, with scope defined as it is in the predicate calculus, then it follows that the rules of the base component must
somehow impose this constraint. Any rule which has the effect of
introducing a quantifier into a structure must be restricted in such
a way that it does not do so when the variable that the quantifier
would bind is already bound by some quantifier present in the
string. This constraint cannot, however be stated within the format of phrase-structure rules.

Phrase-structure rules are of the form: XAY → XZY where X,
Y and Z are variables ranging over strings of grammatical symbols, and A is a variable ranging over single grammatical symbols
(see pp. 119–21 above, and cf. Postal, 1964*a*, Chapter 3, for some
further constraints on phrase-structure rules). The point of the X
and Y here is to specify the context in which the symbol A may be
'rewritten as' the string Z. (If X and Y are both null, the rule is
called a 'context-free phrase-structure rule'; if either X or Y is not
null, the rule is called 'context-sensitive'.) The form of a phrase-
structure rule thus allows *positive* contextual restrictions – if such-
and-such a symbol (or symbols) is present in a given string, then
the rule may apply to that string. We cannot, however, with a rule
of this form, require that some symbol or other be *absent from* a
string as a condition of the applicability of the rule. The only way
in which a negative condition of this kind could be stated is indirectly, by listing as positive contextual conditions upon the
applicability of the rule all contexts *other than* the one that has to

be excluded. Another way of putting this is to say that it is not possible to indicate in a phrase-structure rule that it is debarred from applying in some context; we can only state the contexts in which the rule does apply.

The condition mentioned above that is to be imposed upon rules introducing quantifiers into base structures is a negative condition. A rule may introduce a quantifier only if there is not already present in the structure some quantifier binding the variable it would bind. There is no way of stating this condition if only positive contextual constraints can be imposed. This can be demonstrated informally in the following way. To state the condition using *positive* contextual specifications only would require finding some symbol or set of symbols, say W, such that if W is present in a string, then a rule which introduces a quantifier to bind some variable v is applicable to that string. But there can be no such set of symbols W. For the presence of W in a string must guarantee that the position into which the quantifier is to be inserted is not within the scope of a quantifier binding v. Otherwise the introduction of the quantifier would be illegitimate, and W would not be doing the work required of it. The rule may apply to any well-formed structure U containing W. But if U is well-formed, so is, for example, the string (v) (U&Fv), or its analogue in linguistic notation. This string also contains W since it contains U, but it violates the constraint on the legitimate introduction of a quantifier over the variable v, for the whole formula is within the scope of a quantifier binding v. Therefore the presence of W is not, after all, a sufficient condition for the applicability of the rule. This argument holds however we select W; therefore the constraint on quantifier introduction cannot be stated using positive contextual conditions only, and therefore it cannot be stated in a phrase-structure rule.

To demonstrate that deep structures formally analogous to the formulae of the predicate calculus cannot be generated by a phrase structure system is not, of course, to demonstrate that such structures cannot be part of a linguistic description. What has been shown is simply that any grammar which does employ structures like these must also contain some more powerful type or rule which imposes the necessary constraints on variables and quantifiers. Within the framework of transformational grammar, there are in fact a number of ways in which this might be done. Quantifiers and variables might, for example, be treated as lexical items, to be introduced into structures by the lexical insertion transformation. If this transformation, as defined by Chomsky (1965), were extended somewhat in power, then it could be used to impose the necessary constraints on quantificational structures. Alternatively, deep structures containing redundant quantifiers might be generated by the phrase structure rules, but 'filtered out' at some point during the transformational derivation. Each of these approaches involves using a rule with transformational power to impose the constraints, and they are therefore not subject to the argument about phrase structure rules given above.

It is worth bearing in mind, however, the other alternative of giving up the hypothesis that quantifiers and their scope should be represented in the grammar of a natural language as they are in the predicate calculus. This is certainly an elegant system for representing scope relationships but it is not the only possible one, and some other might suit the needs of the linguist better. What we ultimately have to maximize is the simplicity and generality of the grammar as a whole, and we cannot automatically assume that any given system of logic, however simple and elegant it is in itself, will necessarily contribute to this.

11. COMPUTATIONAL LINGUISTICS

M. F. Bott

The possibility of translating automatically from one language into another is sometimes discussed at a purely technological level – in terms of such factors as increasing the speed and storage capacity of computers, miniaturizing their components, and so on. One of the points made by Bott in his chapter (and it would be echoed by anyone who has ever worked in the field of computational linguistics) is that the technological aspects of mechanical translation are almost trivial by comparison with the difficulty of providing the computer with all the information required for the successful identification and interpretation of utterances. It is not even clear that the completely automatic analysis of texts is feasible: partly for the reason mentioned by Bott, that translation may depend upon an encyclopaedic knowledge of the 'real world' (p. 225); and partly because there is no guarantee, as transformational grammars are at present formalized, that there can be an algorithm for deciding how a sentence is related to its 'deep structure'.

This does not mean that Bott's 'theoretical optimism' (tempered as it is with caution) is unjustified. Computational linguistics (of which mechanical translation is only the best known and most glamorous aspect) has had a considerable, and on the whole beneficial, influence on the development of linguistic theory in recent years. It has forced linguists working with computers to formulate their rules more precisely than they might have done otherwise; and this striving for precision has frequently been carried over into the non-computational analysis of texts.

The reader will note that the chapters in this book dealing with the physiological, neurological or psychological 'mechanisms' underlying the use of language tend to use terms and concepts drawn from computer science ('storage', 'programming', etc.). By thinking in such terms scholars are encouraged to formulate 'realistic' and testable hypotheses. They are not thereby committed to the view that there is any very close parallel between the way in which linguistic operations might be simulated by computer and the way in which they are carried out by human beings.

I. INTRODUCTION: COMPUTERS

SINCE their first appearance, in the late 1940s, computers have become increasingly familiar to the general public, through newspaper and magazine articles of a more or less sensational nature. More recently, the tone of such articles has become more rational and informative so that the intelligent general reader is well aware of the use of computers both in the automation of routine clerical tasks and in the more sophisticated spheres of scientific research and industrial, commercial and governmental planning and control. Accordingly, we shall content ourselves here with a brief, functional description of the computer, oriented towards its application in the linguistic field.

Christopher Strachey has defined a computer as 'a machine for processing symbols', and this seemingly simple definition is indeed broad enough to cover all the tasks that a modern digital computer can perform. To expand the definition slightly, it implies that a computer is a machine which, when presented with a string of symbols which we call the *input*, will process them according to a fixed set of rules, previously stored in the computer and called the *program*, to produce another string of symbols called the *output*. Thus a computer programmed to perform arithmetic operations might process the string of eight symbols: $12 + 37 - 16$ to produce as output the string consisting of the two symbols: 33. It is important to realize that the set of rules for performing even such comparatively simple sequences of operations as those involved in evaluating arithmetic expressions is extremely complicated; every operation must be broken down into the application of a series of rules of the type: 'if the character just read was a 2, and if the character stored in position X is a 3, put 5 in position Y'.

When preparing a task for a computer, the most intellectually demanding part of the job is normally the preparation of a set of rules which completely define what is to be done (this is particularly true of linguistic problems); these rules are often formulated in normal, everyday language. The most laborious task is turning these rules into the precise and detailed format required by the computer. The whole operation is often compared to preparing instructions for a reliable, tireless, but totally unintelligent robot; a more illuminating analogy, due to Judith Matthewman, is the preparation of a knitting pattern. The concept of the garment as a whole is clear; producing the detailed and accurate instructions for knitting the garment, using the small number of basic operations involved in knitting, is an extremely difficult and time-consuming task.

The way in which the computer, as defined by Strachey, is realized in actual hardware is of no great moment as far as the theoretical possibility of performing linguistic operations is concerned. Provided that we can specify the operation completely and exactly in terms of transformations of a string of symbols, we can programme a computer to perform that operation. However, one cannot altogether escape from practical considerations if one is concerned with linguistic data processing, and it is therefore appropriate to give a very brief functional description of the organization of a typical modern computer.

The central parts of the machine are the *control unit* and the *core store*. The store is divided into numbered units called *bytes* (or characters, or, on machines of a rather different type, words); each byte is capable of storing a number between 0 and 255, but this number may also be interpreted as an alphabetic character in some coded form, or as part of an instruction in a program, according to the way in which the machine treats it. This is controlled by the control unit which, according to the demands of the program, selects instructions from the store and then performs the required operation. The number of bytes in the store may vary from less than a thousand, on very small machines, to more than a million on very large installations. The essential point about the core store is that all bytes are equally accessible, and that the information held in a byte can be retrieved, ready for some operation, in about two-millionths of a second.

In addition to the core store, the machine is usually provided with some sort of auxiliary storage (called *backing store*); this usually consists of magnetic tape or discs, on which data is recorded in ways analogous to those used for tape-recorder tape or gramophone records. A magnetic tape or disc may be used either for temporary storage during the operation of a program, or as semi-permanent storage which can be taken away from the computer after the completion of one job and used to hold information until it is again required for use on the machine. These provide cheap means of storing large quantities of information (a magnetic tape can hold about twenty million characters) but they have the disadvantage that the information cannot be accessed randomly, especially on magnetic tape.

Input data, that is, the strings of symbols to be processed, is usually prepared on punched cards or punched paper tape, using a special machine with a keyboard similar to that of an ordinary typewriter; however, when a key is depressed, a pattern of holes is punched in the card or paper tape, which represents the character in question. The computer is equipped with a reader which, in response to a signal from the control unit, senses the row of holes and transfers the corresponding character in coded form into some specified byte. The computer is equipped also with card or paper-tape punches which enable information to be transferred from the core store on to these media; there is normally also a *lineprinter* which enables information from the store to be printed in a directly readable form.

Typically, in linguistic applications of computers, we are dealing with fairly large quantities of data and so the normal sequence of operations is that this data is prepared on punched paper tape or cards and then transferred to magnetic tape before processing; the program then takes the data from this tape, thus avoiding the frequent errors which are unfortunately associated with card equipment. The output is also usually written onto magnetic tape from which it may be printed, punched on to cards or paper tape or retained for further processing.

II. CONCORDANCES AND WORD INDEXES

Because of the basic simplicity of the problem, one of the most successful applications of the computer to language research has been the production of concordances and word indexes. A word index of the text consists of a list, in alphabetical order, of all the words in a text, each word heading being followed by a list of references to each occurrence of the word in the text, using some appropriate reference system, e.g. page and line number, or stanza number, according to the nature of the text. A concordance is essentially the same except that, in addition to the reference, a context (e.g. the line in which the word occurs) is given for each occurrence. A concordance is thus considerably bulkier than a word index of the same text and hence, because of publishing costs, a word index often has to be produced where a concordance would be more valuable. Concordances and word indexes are of considerable value to the literary scholar and the philologist; until the coming of the computer, however, they were only available for a small number of works of the best-known authors. Although, as we shall see, such works produced by a computer are in various ways inferior to those produced by hand, most scholars would feel that this is more than compensated by their vastly increased availability.

The first, and by far the most laborious, part of the work is the initial preparation of the data in a form that can be read by the machine, that is, cards or paper tape. When this is being done, care must be taken to ensure that all the information which will be required by the program is punched onto the cards or tape; this means, for example, that conventional signs of some sort must be established to mark divisions in the tèxt, such as end of stanza or end of page. At this point the computer is normally used to transfer the information from cards onto magnetic tape; this tape is then printed and the text proof-read. A computer program is used to correct the errors on tape, which is then printed and rechecked. This process must usually be repeated several times before a reasonably error-free text is obtained.

The input data is now ready for processing and, in order to show how a program to construct a word index works, we assume that the text consists only of punctuation marks (.,;:?!) and upper-case letters A to Z, and that the only reference required to the words is the line number of the lines in which they occur. Such a text would have been indexed by hand by reading through it and copying each word, with its line number, onto a separate card; in this way we shall have obtained as many cards as there are words in the text, and we then proceed to sort these cards into alphabetical order of headwords, and, within this, numerical order of line number. If we imagine ourselves instructing the unintelligent robot to perform the first part of this process, the instructions will have something like the following form:

(1) Take a blank sheet of paper and write the number 1 on it (this will be the line number).

(2) Read characters until you find either a letter or a new-line character.

(3) If you completed instruction (2) by finding a new-line character, cross out the number on the sheet of paper and replace it by the number that was there, plus one, and then go back to instruction (2); otherwise go on with instruction (4).

(4) Take a new card and write on it the character that you last read.

(5) Read another character.

(6) If it is a letter, copy it on to the current card and go back to instruction (5); if not, go on to instruction (7).

(7) Copy on to the card the number on the sheet of paper, and put the card on to the output pile.

(8) If the character last read was not a new line, go back to instruction (2); if it was a new line, erase the old line number and replace it by the old one, plus one, and then go to instruction (2).

This list of instructions for the first stage of the process is substantially complete, except that no provision is made for recognizing the end of the text, so that our robot will be a little at a loss when he finds that there is nothing more to read. The computer program for performing the first stage of the index performs essentially the same operations, but it must be borne in mind that the basic computer instructions correspond to much smaller steps, so that each of the instructions given above would require some twenty or thirty computer instructions. The remainder of the process, which need not be described in detail, requires that we sort the individual output items into lexicographical order and arrange to print them in some suitable format. The format of this final output is very important because, instead of conventional printing techniques, it is normal to reproduce the computer output photographically, thus reducing production costs.

In view of the tendency to try to use computers for tasks which might be better done by hand, it is instructive to examine the economics of producing a word index by computer. Suppose that we are dealing with a poem of the length of, say, *Paradise Lost* (some 12,000 lines). To transfer this to punched cards will take about twenty working days for a skilled punch operator, say £100; this figure could be four or five times as large if the text is in an unfamiliar language with large numbers of diacritics. A total of at most two hours time on a medium-sized computer will be required, £150. Overheads of one sort or another (stationery, maintenance of the card punches, etc.) may account for a further £50, giving a total of £300 so far. This leaves two major items unaccounted for (leaving aside printing costs): the cost of the program, and the work of the scholar who supervises the production of the index, and who must take on a considerable part of the work involved in checking the text after it has been punched. The actual cost of producing the program may vary, depending on its sophistication, from £500 to about £5,000. However, a well-designed program can be used for the production of any number of indexes, not just that of the text for which it was originally written. Thus one might give a nominal cost of, say, £100 for programming, giving a total of £400. In addition, there is some three months' work for the scholar, which is probably unquantifiable. This must be set against some two years' work for the scholar to produce the index by manual methods.

The above analysis is not intended to be definitive, nor is the problem of producing a word index one of great linguistic interest; indeed, the linguistic content is minimal. Its purpose is to illustrate the type of problem which may be tackled, the way in which the problem must be analysed before using the computer, and the sort of economic analysis which must be performed in order to establish whether the use of the computer is justified.

Machine-produced concordances and word indexes are inferior in a number of ways to those produced by hand methods; many of these failings, such as the inadequate appearance of photographically reproduced computer output, may be remedied as the technology improves. However, the most important failing is that no attempt is made to separate words which are orthographically identical, but distinct in grammatical function or in meaning. Thus in an index of an English text, under a heading such as *charge* or *that*, there would be subsumed occurrences of these words with all the many different meanings and functions which they may have. To overcome this is a problem of an entirely different magnitude from that of producing the concordance or word index in the first place; the reader who doubts this may try producing a set of instructions for the robot, comparable to those given above, which also assign syntactic categories to each word in the input text, as it is encountered. This problem is very important to mechanical translation and we shall, therefore, deal with it in the following section.

III. MECHANICAL TRANSLATION

The problem dealt with in the last section was an example of the application of the computer to work of purely linguistic or literary interest. Computational linguistics is a term which covers both work of that kind and also the application of linguistics to problems which are basically concerned with computing; that is, where the aim is to produce a computer program which will perform some required task more efficiently, more quickly or more economically than it could be performed by human beings. Much more work has been done in this aspect of computational linguistics (for the obvious reasons that government and other grant-giving organizations are more interested in work of this type) and although the aim has not, therefore, been pure linguistic research, there has been a considerable fall-out to linguistics. The most widely publicized work of this kind has been mechanical translation, and more effort has been put into this than into any other branch of computational linguistics.

Historically, interest in mechanical translation seems to have been first stimulated by a famous memorandum circulated by Warren Weaver in 1949, in which he suggested that automatic computers might be used at least to assist in 'the solution of world-wide translation problems'. Early work on the problem was characterized by a very naïve approach to the difficulties involved. It was assumed that the computer could be made to perform the same operations as were presumed to take place when the translation was performed by a human translator; in other words, each word in the input language text would be looked up in a bilingual dictionary (which could easily be stored on magnetic tape), an equivalent would be chosen from amongst the translations provided by the dictionary, and, at the end of, say, a sentence, the equivalents selected would be rearranged according to the requirements of word order in the output language. It was rapidly realized, however, that the task of selecting the appropriate equivalent from the bilingual dictionary, and of rearranging these in a suitable order, raised problems of extreme difficulty.

At this point, two different views of the objectives of mechanical translation research became apparent. One school of thought (particularly associated with Bar-Hillel), directed themselves towards what is sometimes called 'fully automated, high-quality translation', believing that this long-term goal could be attained by a large investment of effort in basic research. The second school might be said to have taken an engineer's view of the problem, that is they felt that efforts should be concentrated on reducing the total cost of the translation process, by a suitable combination of human and mechanical effort. With this in mind, Reifler suggested, in 1950, a translation process in which the original text would be scanned by a *pre-editor*, who needed only a knowledge of the input language and who would insert appropriate diacritical marks into the input text so as to assist the mechanical selection of output language equivalents. After mechanical processing, the computer output would be processed by a *post-editor*, having knowledge only of the output language, who would 'clean up' the resulting translation. A modification of this process was suggested by Oettinger in 1954, in which the pre-editor was eliminated, the machine output listing all the dictionary equivalents for each input word, with the original word order, the whole burden of rearrangement and selection now falling on the post-editor.

Both of these schemes are clearly workable and, if applied to technical material, would have the desired results of freeing highly qualified translators for more important or more difficult texts. However, the main reason why no such scheme has been implemented on a commercial scale is that, economically, it would not make sense. Even a person with only a moderately good knowledge of the input language can, when dealing with a subject with which he is familiar, translate accurately at very good speed. Using Oettinger's scheme, the text is processed at least three times: the initial key-punching, the post-editing and the final typing. Each of these operations will take roughly as long as the translation process performed by the human translator, and at least one of the persons involved (the post-editor) must be intelligent and knowledgeable about the subject matter of the text, and, therefore, highly paid. Further, a not inconsiderable amount of computer time will be required.

So far, then, no large-scale commercial application of computers to translation exists. It should be clear, however, that there are various factors which may change the economics of the process. Optical-character readers, which read direct from the printed page into the computer, are becoming available and can cope with the typographic diversity of scientific articles. In some applications a machine-readable version of the input text is available as a by-product of some other process. Factors such as these, together with the diminishing costs of computer power and the increasing sophistication of translation programs which are therefore less demanding on the post-editor, mean that we may well see machine-aided translation in use on a large scale by translation agencies within the next ten years.

The increasing sophistication of the translation programs to which we have referred is due to the realization that it is possible to automate the process of syntactic analysis. The initial impetus for work of this kind came from the grammatical models of Chomsky, although it must be emphasized that these models were in no way developed with computational applications in mind. Since, however, one of Chomsky's prerequisites for a grammatical theory is that it should provide an automatic means for generating all the sentences of a language, his models are naturally suitable for use on a computer, in that a computer can be programmed to generate sentences according to the rules of the grammar. (This of course, is far from true of traditional grammars which require the intervention of the user's intelligence or linguistic intuition.) From this, it is at least a plausible supposition that there should be an algorithm (i.e. an automatic procedure) for deciding how a sentence has been generated by a grammar: in fact, it can be shown on theoretical grounds that this is always possible for a context-free phrase-structure grammar (one in which the context does not impose selectional restrictions on individual items).

Programs have been written which successfully perform this sort of analysis, but this still leaves considerable problems to be solved. Producing a descriptively adequate grammar for a language is an extremely time-consuming task, and when such a grammar has been produced, the parsing program will normally produce several different parsings for a given sentence, reflecting the syntactic ambiguity inherent in the sentence. For example, the sentence *Traffic jams are caused by slow lorries and buses carrying heavy loads* has at least four possible parsings according to whether *slow* is taken as qualifying *lorries* only, or *lorries and buses*, and to whether *carrying heavy loads* qualifies *buses*, or *lorries and buses*. Other parsings are also possible. A human reader resolves these ambiguities by context, by his knowledge of what is likely, and by his knowledge of the 'real world'. We do not know how to make a computer simulate this process; indeed we cannot yet really conceive how this sort of encyclopaedic knowledge could be held in a computer. At this point, a solution of our problems seems to depend on developments in other disciplines concerned with the way in which the human brain organizes its information.

In spite of the problems caused by multiple parsings, however, syntactic analysis can help a great deal in mechanical translation; many things that would be ambiguous in a straight word-for-word translation can be resolved by the analysis, and problems of word order in the output language can be solved if we know how to map phrase markers in the input language on to phrase markers in the output language. If we accept the hypothesis that all languages exhibit basically the same deep structures, then we have theoretical grounds for supposing that mechanical translation should be possible by using this kind of analysis. In other words, given a grammar of the input language and an algorithm for determining the deep structure of sentences in the language, we should be able to use this deep structure, together with the transformations in a grammar of the output language, in order to generate the translated sentences. However, against these theoretical grounds for optimism we must set the enormous practical problems of producing the grammars required, our present very inadequate knowledge of what constitutes deep structure and the problem of genuine lexical ambiguity. In view of this, one cannot foresee fully automatic high-quality translation as a possibility for many years to come.

IV. DOCUMENT AND INFORMATION RETRIEVAL

After mechanical translation, the most widely publicized area of research in computational linguistics has probably been information retrieval. The impetus for this work has come from an urgent practical problem: scientific and technical information is now published at such a rate that it is frequently impossible for a scientist to keep abreast of all the material published which concerns his work. Indeed, it is often cheaper and quicker to do an experiment oneself than to search through the literature to discover whether it has been done previously elsewhere. The basic aim of automation in this field, then, is to enable a research worker to present a computer with a request for information on a certain specific topic, and then to be provided with all the published material available. This material may be presented in the form of references to the original publications, in which case the process is more correctly referred to as *document retrieval*, or the actual information may be presented, which constitutes information retrieval proper.

A number of satisfactory document-retrieval schemes are now in operation for various specialized fields. In most of these systems, the person requesting the information is required to present his request in the form of a number of key words, chosen from some predefined set, possibly indicating their relative importance; the machine then searches through its catalogue in which each document is recorded, together with the set of key words to which it is relevant. As a first attempt, the machine will produce references to all the documents which are relevant to all the key words; if requested, it will then continue by producing those documents which are relevant to all but one of the key words, and so on.

Systems such as the one just described work very well on a small scale in highly specialized fields of interest. However, there are two problems which stand in the way of their being used on a larger scale. The first is again concerned with the structure of knowledge: an article entitled 'Agrarian Reform in Underdeveloped Countries', and an article entitled 'The Economics of Rice Production in a Peasant Economy', might both be relevant to a request for information on agriculture in South-East Asia. If, however, the articles were indexed under the key words 'agriculture, reform, underdeveloped' and 'rice, peasants', respectively, then the retrieval program would need to know that South-East Asia is underdeveloped, that rice is grown there, that the economy is a peasant one and that rice is relevant to agriculture. In small-scale systems this problem does not arise, since the user will be able to scan through the key words himself, and effectively build these relationships into his request; in more general systems, however, it can cause serious difficulty.

The second problem concerns the indexing of documents: producing lists of key words to which new documents are relevant absorbs a lot of time from technically qualified staff. We can, therefore, try to use the computer itself for this work; this is normally known as automatic indexing or automatic abstracting. A lot of effort has gone into this problem with, as yet, little result. It is clearly very difficult to make the machine in any sense 'understand' the material which it is processing, but it is also difficult to see how the desired result can be achieved without this. Current research work concentrates on statistical methods, determining the frequencies with which the various key words occur in the text, perhaps in certain crucial positions, and attempting to index the text from these; the result of this work is rather better than might superficially be expected, but it is still a long way from what is required.

On information retrieval proper, we have said nothing, since, apart from one or two very restricted types of application, the problems are still very far from any meaningful solution.

V. CONCLUSION

There are naturally many areas of computational linguistics which we have not been able to deal with here, and we have been unable to do more than outline the problems in those fields that we have covered. The interested reader is, therefore, referred to Borko (1967) for a much more comprehensive description of current research in this field, and for a full bibliography.

12. THE BIOLOGY OF COMMUNICATION IN MAN AND ANIMALS*

J. C. Marshall

It has often been argued, and perhaps more frequently assumed without argument in recent years, that human language must once have evolved from some more 'primitive' form of communication akin to one of the 'signalling' systems employed by other animal species, and there is no need to stress the importance of this question for the more general biological theory of evolution.

In this chapter Marshall gives a summary of the available evidence and draws the conclusion that the evolutionary hypothesis, as it relates to language, far from being confirmed by recent research, is without empirical foundation. Language is radically different from all known forms of animal communication, and, 'in spite of the vast accumulation of knowledge, scholars are still unable to propose a biological theory of language' (p. 241).

The Unavailability of the 'Natural History' of Language

THE systematic study of language as a *biological* phenomenon has but a short history (although Marx, 1967, summarizes its more remote beginnings). The publication of Darwin's *The Origin of Species* in 1859 encouraged scholars to see that both the form and function of higher animals could be explained in terms of natural law. Shortly after Darwin's work became available, the comparative linguist Schleicher wrote *Die Darwinsche Theorie und die Sprachwissenschaft* (1863), an ambitious, albeit highly speculative extrapolation of evolutionary ideas to the domain of the origin and development of languages. Darwin himself (1871) emphasized that 'The faculty of articulated speech does not in itself offer any insuperable objection to the belief that man has developed from some lower form'. Of more direct biological significance was Broca's claim (1863) to have discovered a

* I am most grateful to R. C. Oldfield, R. J. Wales and Mary Marshall for their critical comments on an earlier version of this chapter.

'language centre' in the brain. Broca observed that patients with damage to the third frontal convolution of the left cerebral hemisphere suffered severe impairment of their linguistic abilities and were sometimes reduced to uttering only a few words or stereotyped phrases. Broca postulated that this area, which has close anatomical links with parts of the motor cortex intimately concerned with the control of vocalization, was the seat of articulate language.

Acceptance of a broadly biological approach to language was later furthered by Darwin's observations on similarities in *The Expression of the Emotions in Man and Animals* (1872) and by the work of many early clinical neurologists who, following Broca, attempted to localize specific aspects of linguistic ability in particular areas of the brain. The stage seemed set for the construction of a biological theory of language. However, the magnitude of the task soon became apparent. Correlations between the site of brain lesions and the presence, nature and extent of associated behavioural deficits are considerably less than perfect. Today, the very concept of strict localization of function is controversial. An early critic, Hughlings Jackson (1874) noted that 'to locate the damage which destroys speech and to locate speech are two different things'. Study of the origin and development of language in our species encountered an even more serious problem – the paucity of data against which theoretical claims could be tested.

Careful descriptive work by anthropological linguists showed that there are no extant 'primitive' languages, but only complex languages spoken by technologically primitive peoples. Similarly, whilst languages are subject to historical change, there is no evidence to suggest that such change results in their becoming more complex in any general sense. Of course, the span of time for which pertinent data are available is very brief. There is no evolutionary or cultural record of the development of communication from hominids to reconstructions of proto-Indo-European. Fossil evidence concerning the size and shape of jaw and cranium in extinct higher primates tells us little or nothing about their mode of communication. Whilst there are many species whose social behaviour is regulated by 'informative' signs, no animal other than man communicates with 'language-like' expressions. By 'language-like' in this context, I mean a system of signals whose structural properties fall, at least partially, within the domain of theories of phonological, syntactic and semantic universals, as these are currently formulated. Although many animal signals are undoubtedly 'structured', the notion of parsing the alarm cries of birds and apes into the types of constituent suitable for the description of sentences is not reasonable. Alternative approaches to bridging the gap between man and other animals have included attempts to teach interesting subparts of natural languages to chimpanzees. Past efforts in this direction have been failures, although such studies continue unabated (cf. Kellogg, 1968) and eventual success cannot be ruled out on *a priori* grounds.

Although the theory of language is unlikely to encompass animal signs, some authors (e.g. Sebeok, 1968) believe that a unified account of 'information exchange' in animal species, including man, may be feasible. What, then, is involved in the claim that whilst many animals 'communicate' with each other, only *homo loquens* talk to each other?

Structure and Function in Animal Communication

Students of animal behaviour have often noted the extreme difficulty of restricting the notion of communication to anything less than every potential interaction between an organism and its environment. Any situation which reliably elicits one of a set of 'similar' responses is, to that extent, 'informative'. The following interactions have often been regarded as communicative in this broad sense.

Aggressive exchanges between hermit crabs involve stereotyped postures and movements of the chelipeds and ambulatory legs (Hazlett & Bossert, 1965). The crabs respond selectively to the different types of 'signal' and the displays can thereby be ranked in terms of their relative aggressiveness: extending a major cheliped is more effective than raising a single ambulatory leg in causing the second crab to retreat or duck back into its shell. Visual displays are also found in fish. In spring, male sticklebacks will defend their territory against other males intruding into it. The effective stimulus which releases aggressive behaviour is the sight of the red belly and throat of an intruding stickleback; the size and shape of the intruder are, within limits, relatively unimportant (Tinbergen, 1951). The sight of red patches evokes deterrent behaviour only when the stickleback is within its own territory. Thus a normal function of such inter-actions is to space out animals into areas within which sufficient food can be found to feed both parents and young.

Acoustic signals are common. Familiar examples are the alarm and mating calls of birds. Alarm cries which evoke flight or rushing to cover are typically squeaky, high-pitched whistles. The acoustic properties of these calls are such that their source is difficult to locate. Since the calls are given upon sighting potential predators, the biological utility of squeaks is obvious enough. By contrast, many of the calls which play a role in the selection of a mate, courtship and parental duties involve sudden pitch and amplitude changes. These calls can be located fairly easily (Marler, 1957). Much of the social behaviour of higher primates is regulated by vocal signals which sometimes appear to convey quite specific information. Vervet monkeys produce at least six, more or less distinct, alarm calls. The different calls are evoked by the sighting of a different kind of predator (e.g. leopards, snakes, eagles), and each in turn elicits a different form of escape be-haviour in monkeys hearing the call (Marler, 1965).

Chemical signals ('pheromones') are implicated in the social behaviour of many animals. Fire ants which have located a food-source exude a scent trail when returning to the nest. Other ants are attracted by the chemical and follow trails back to the food. The pheromone loses its potency after a short time, thereby ensuring that paths to finished sources of food will not remain attractive (Bossert & Wilson, 1963).

Tactile signals have been discovered. Honey bees execute complex dances upon returning to the hive after successful foraging expeditions (Von Frisch, 1950). The dances appear to code the distance and direction of the food source. This informa-tion is communicated to other bees as they jostle against the foragers who have returned and 'join in' the dance, prior to their own foraging. In the 'waggle dance', the orientation of the run during which tail-wagging occurs indicates the direction of food and the number of runs per unit time codes the distance of the source. This interpretation has, however, been challenged. The actual communication channels involved may be primarily acoustic and olfactory (Wenner, 1968). The structure of the dance may be a correlated but not a causal variable in determining the behaviour of foraging bees.

Although I have described but a small sample of informative exchanges, their great variety should be apparent. It is, indeed, this variety of function, structure and underlying physiological mechanism which makes it unlikely that any single theory will cover all cases of animal communication. Some degree of systematization is, however, possible.

Following Tinbergen (1951), ethologists have distinguished communicative exchanges from other regular patterns of behaviour by means of the concept of a 'sign stimulus'. A sign stimulus is part of an animal's appearance or behavioural repertoire which reliably elicits a particular type of response from another animal of the same species. The primary function of sign stimuli is the elicitation of behaviour which serves to ensure the continuation of the species. Sign stimuli have evolved, then, as specific 'releasers' of adaptive behaviour patterns. It is by invoking the evolutionary concept of adaptation, that Tinbergen distinguishes 'communicative' from other stimulus-response relationships. For example, some spiders discriminate between prey and leaves in their webs by virtue of the fact that struggling prey produce in the web a different mechanical waveform from that associated with inanimate objects (Parry, 1965). Spiders ignore the leaf wave-form but rush to the area of maximum intensity of the wave-form caused by their prey. Because the *signals* emitted by the fly are clearly not adaptive from the fly's point of view (although struggling to get out is useful behaviour), Tinbergen's definition would not classify the exchange as communicative. The spider, of course, may have a different point of view!

Sign stimuli which involve movement (including movement of sound-producing organs) are thought to have developed from 'intention movements', especially those involved in attack, escape and orientation, and 'displacement activities'. Displacement activities, such as preening, are often performed in situations of conflict where an animal is motivated towards incompatible actions. Displacement activities then appear irrelevant to the situation. Incomplete parts of functional or displaced acts are relatively flexible expressive movements which may become modified by genetic and micro-evolutionary changes into stereotyped signals (sign stimuli). This change is called 'ritualization'. Ritualized displays may become 'emancipated' from the stimulus situations which originally evoked them. Tinbergen (1952) has argued that 'displacement preening' in male ducks was originally an irrelevant activity which occurred when there was conflict between the male's motivation to attack or flee from the female. Evolutionary changes have modified the form of the display, making it more conspicuous, and it has been brought under the control of purely sexual mechanisms as part of the courtship pattern.

The most striking differences between animal signs and language behaviour are to be found, then, in the rigid, stereotyped nature of the former and in the fact that they are under the control of independently specifiable external stimuli and internal, motivational states. The vocalizations of monkeys and apes do permit greater flexibility of expression, as they vary semi-continuously along acoustic parameters, but their communicative significance would appear, nonetheless, to be restricted to expressions of emotional states. As Marler (1965) writes, the graded nature of the cries 'permits a subtlety of portrayal of slight shifts in motivation that would be impossible with more stereotyped signals'. Even the alarm calls of the vervet monkey which seem, superficially, to be 'naming' the type of predator are more plausibly regarded as expressing no more than the relative intensity of the fearful and aggressive emotions aroused by the various predators (cf. Altman, 1968). Thus Andrew (1963) has suggested that vocalization in primates is to be interpreted in terms of the patterns of facial expression and muscular tension associated with particular emotive situations. Vocalization is seen, then, as an accidental by-product of bodily 'gestures', the structure of which may lead to become ritualized in the way that other movements are. An emotive interpretation of primate calls is also suggested by the observation that vocalizations can be obtained by electrically stimulating sites in the limbic system of monkeys. This brain area is known to be crucially implicated in the mediation of emotional behaviour (Robinson, 1967).

So far, I have used the words 'informative' and 'communicative' interchangeably. Yet the two notions are not equivalent when applied to human behaviour. My dropping a piece of priceless china may 'inform' you, or 'indicate', that I am clumsy. But unless I 'intended' my action to so inform you, we would not regard it as 'communicative'. We have behavioural criteria for regarding animal signs as informative. The criteria are the existence of (a) correlations between 'states of the world' and selective responses (putative 'signals') made by an animal; (b) further correlations between the signals and other selective responses made by a second animal. It is not necessary to invoke the notion of an 'intention to inform' in discussing such examples of sign-behaviour. What, then, would count as behavioural criteria of an intention to inform? Essentially, we need criteria which indicate that an animal *recognizes* and *intends* that its behaviour shall have an effect upon the behaviour of another animal. The clearest cases are probably those which reveal an 'intention to misinform'. Anecdotal evidence suggests that some higher animals can mislead by 'lying', in various ways, rather than by simply making mistakes. Lorenz (1954) provides many charming examples, including the following story about one of his dogs which attempted to conceal the fact that it had mistaken his master for a stranger:

I had just opened the yard gate, and before I had had time to shut it the dog rushed up barking loudly. Upon recognizing me, he hesitated in a moment of acute embarrassment, then pushing past my leg he raced through the open gates and across the lane where he continued to bark furiously at our neighbour's gate just as though he had been addressing an enemy in that garden from the very beginning.

Experimental evidence for behaviour of this nature would, I think, support claims that an animal understood the notion of communication. Without such demonstrations, the most that could be said is that certain signals are informative. Whilst

Lorenz' dog may plausibly be regarded as communicating, one might still hesitate to call his behaviour 'language-like'.

Proto-linguistic systems should be capable of expressing propositions which are either true or false of particular external 'states of affairs'. A common propositional form consists of an identifying designation of which a general term is predicated, e.g. *That leopard* is *spotted*. Identifying designations are often used to 'pick out', refer to, or mention individuals. Somewhat loosely, we can regard such expressions as 'naming' a person, object, event or place. Although animals can recognize individuals and respond appropriately to given states of affairs, there is no evidence that animal signs ever name individuals. In order for vervet monkey calls to qualify as 'names', a particular call would have to be associated with a particular object irrespective of the emotion aroused by the perception of that object. In the human case, the expression 'leopard' is appropriately used in referring to members of the class of leopards. Whether one is attracted or repelled by leopards is irrelevant. Similarly, one can propose criteria which must be met if responses to signals are to count as understanding propositional information. If bee dances communicate propositions (e.g. 'The food is to the North-West'), it is necessary that bees should be able to learn to disregard dances performed by a bee (perhaps an artificial one, controlled by an ethologist) which consistently imparted false information (Bennett, 1964). That is, we need an apian analogue of the boy who cried 'Wolf'. It is unlikely that bees possess the requisite capabilities. Without this kind of evidence, it seems misleading to regard the informative signs of animals as 'primitive' forms of symbolic communication systems.

'Primitive' Stages of Language

If, as I have argued, the study of animal signs does not throw light upon the development of language, which avenues of investigations are open to us? Two sources of data suggest themselves. Karl Bühler (1935) noted that 'The child provides the only opportunity that we have to observe language in its nascent state'. And Roman Jakobson (1941) pointed out the converse approach: 'Pathological speech disturbances of a central nature provide the only opportunity that we have to observe language in dissolution'.

Although sophisticated studies of language development in both normal and retarded children are now available (McNeill, 1969; Lackner, 1968), such work has concentrated upon the acquisition of 'code elements' and orders rather than on conceptual categories and relations (see Campbell & Wales pp. 242–60 below, for alternative approaches). That is, scholars have *assumed* that the kinds of proposition that the child expresses and the kinds of speech acts he performs are closely similar to those of adults. For example, let us assume that very young children understand the notion of denying a proposition in roughly the same way that adults do. A child says 'No play'. On the basis of a 'context of situation', which is embarrassingly little understood, we claim that what the child *probably* means is 'I am not playing'. According to this account, language acquisition consists of learning that the logical subject of such propositions must be overtly expressed (by means of the pronoun *I*), that an auxiliary verb is required, that the *Negative Element* must be positioned between the auxiliary and the main verb etc. etc. What the child eventually learns is the adult *code*. But studies of code learning leave the really difficult problems untouched.

To explain how the child comes to say 'I know that my father has left' rather than 'Allgone Dada' is to provide only a partial solution of the language-acquisition problem. We also need an account of the mechanisms which underlie our ability (in whatever code has been acquired) to 'make statements', 'ask questions', 'issue commands' and recognize the relevance of *particular* remarks to particular situations.

Many studies of language disorders have been directed toward describing the dissolution of control over code elements in much the same way that developmental investigations have emphasized their acquisition. For example, many patients with an 'expressive' dysphasia (frequently associated with anterior lesions of the left cerebral hemisphere) speak fairly fluently in short bursts. They are then held up while they 'search' for the specific word which is on the tip of their tongue but whose realization eludes them. In this state, they often produce circumlocutions and semantically related words which show that they 'know' the item they are looking for: 'Last week, I broke my . . . um . . . tells the time . . . um . . . clock . . . watch, my watch'.

The spontaneous utterances of such patients are normally appropriate to the situation. Often, their performance on non-verbal intelligence tests is little impaired and their comprehension of statements, questions, commands and instructions is quite adequate. A subject that I saw recently produced many examples of behaviour of the following nature. The typed stimulus 'The baby — all night' was placed in front of the subject and he was asked to say, as quickly as possible, a word which could replace the dash, thereby making a sensible sentence. He read the material out loud, correctly, and immediately said 'Now, what does a baby do?', a remark that can be taken as showing that the patient knew that a main verb was required. It was three minutes later, after innumerable ums, ahs, grimaces and other expressions of effort, that he managed to say 'cried'. Dysphasic symptoms of this kind seem to be a severe form of a difficulty which occasionally affects us all (Brown & McNeill, 1966; and for a general discussion of 'word-finding', Oldfield, 1966).

In other cases of expressive disability, rate of speaking is greatly reduced and utterances are often produced in a telegrammatic style, lacking many closed-class items. The slowing down of speech does not seem due to a general disturbance of articulatory coordination. Rather, as Lenneberg (1967) reports, the problem lies in 'an inability to "plan for the motor events" that are necessary for speech'. The conceptual substrate of language and language use therefore seems to be still more or less intact. As one of Head's patients remarked, 'silent thought was easy, but vocal thought was muddling' (Head, 1926). The conditions described above can be seen as relatively pure coding disorders, and we can study the particular elements and types of syntactic construction which cause special difficulty (Luria, 1964).

However, when patients manifest more pronounced disabilities, we encounter problems similar to those previously noted with respect to developmental studies. The linguistic output of some patients is so reduced and distorted that it becomes difficult to know whether (a) their grasp of logico-linguistic relations has disintegrated; or (b) whether it is solely their ability to produce 'realizations' of the code that has been disturbed. Consider, for example, the following sample of spontaneous speech that Goodglass (1968) describes as 'typical of severe motor aphasia with agrammatism'. The passage is a reply to a question about why the patient had returned to hospital: 'Yes ... ah. ... Monday ... ah ... Dad and Peter Hogan, and Dad, ... ah ... Hospital ... and ah ... Wednesday ... Wednesday, nine o'clock and ah Thursday ...'.

Does the patient 'know' what an appropriate answer is? Although he is obviously unable to *express* well-formed sentences, what evidence would support (or fail to support) claims that the patient 'knows' that the noun phrases he produces should have other syntactic forms associated with them in certain grammatical relations? No really convincing criteria are currently available, although it is clear that studies of the structure of gesture and pantomime in dysphasic subjects would be pertinent and valuable (Alajouanine & Lhermitte, 1964). The ability to respond to complex commands with appropriate non-verbal behaviour would indicate that the patient is able to carry out basic forms of inner propositional thinking and does not therefore suffer from 'receptive' disability. But when 'expressive' loss is found in conjunction with some degree of 'receptive' language disorder, as is often the case, the difficulty of testing claims about the structure of thought processes becomes only too apparent.

Determinants of Language Acquisition

Behavioural repertoires are acquired as a function of complex interactions between innate principles of organization and learning processes whose content is determined by particular environments. Lenneberg (1966) notes that language develops in children according to a relatively fixed schedule: 'There is a very orderly progression from pure crying to additional cooing sounds, then babbling and the introduction of intonation patterns.' This is followed by 'holophrastic' speech in which individual words seem to convey propositions and then the rapid acquisition of the syntactic structures of the particular language to which the child is exposed. Systematic progression in the face of haphazard exposure to a verbal environment suggests that innate schema, determined by genetic and maturational factors, impose fairly strong constraints upon the mechanisms of language acquisition. 'Even if the maturational scale as a whole is distorted through retarding disease, the order of developmental milestones, including onset of speech, remains invariable' (Lenneberg, 1964).

Wide variations in the number of nerve cells in the brain are not crucially correlated with the ability to acquire language. Thus it seems unlikely that the *number* of 'computing elements' available for the processing and storage of information in man and other higher primates is of significance in explaining why man alone talks. Rather, it would seem that the *structural organization* of the human brain is peculiarly adapted to language learning. Geschwind (1964) points out that the major anatomical connexions in sub-human primates are between brain areas concerned with sensory data and the limbic system which is 'involved in the motor and sensory aspects of feeding, drinking, elimination, aggression, flight and reproduction.' In man, on the other hand, connexions between different sensory modalities (vision, audition and somaesthesia) may be relayed through a non-limbic brain area, the angular gyrus region. Geschwind thus proposes that the development of language skills, in particular object naming, is dependent upon man's 'ability to form non-limbic cross-modal associations' (but cf. Lenneberg, 1967: 217–18, for a sceptical appraisal).

The existence of a 'critical period' when the brain is specially 'tuned' to language acquisition seems plausible. Up to the age of puberty, the prognosis for full recovery from dysphasic disorders resulting from traumatic lesions to the left hemisphere is quite good. When such injuries are sustained by very young children (between two and three years old), the child may lose his linguistic abilities entirely but re-acquire proficiency by passing through the same developmental schedule, from babbling onwards, that had previously been completed. During infancy both cerebral hemispheres are implicated in language acquisition. If the left hemisphere is damaged, the right is capable of supporting language skills and mediating further language learning.

However, if the left hemisphere has not been injured, the major mechanisms of language behaviour in the adult are, typically, located in the left (or 'dominant') hemisphere; that is, 'a progressive decrease in involvement of the right hemisphere' takes place (Lenneberg, 1967). Thus, after puberty, the prognosis for recovery from dysphasia-inducing traumatic lesions to the left hemisphere becomes steadily worse, although complete recovery from symptoms produced by cerebro-vascular accidents is not uncommon.

Lenneberg (1967) has reported a wealth of biological data relevant to language. These range from studies of the peripheral anatomy of the speech organs to the correlations between symptoms of language dissolution and injury to particular brain areas; from the genetic substrate of certain inherited language disorders to the physiological correlates of vocalization, and from the functional organization of the central nervous system to the structural, chemical and electro-physiological changes which define the maturation of the brain during the period of first-language acquisition. But in spite of the vast accumulation of knowledge, scholars are still unable to propose a biological *theory* of language – a formal model of a brain mechanism consistent with the physiology described by Lenneberg and the type of psychological data summarized in the chapters by Campbell and Wales (pp. 242–60) and Johnson-Laird (pp. 261–70). Advances in knowledge have only shown even wider areas of ignorance.

13. THE STUDY OF LANGUAGE ACQUISITION

Robin Campbell and Roger Wales

By the acquisition of language is meant the process whereby children achieve a fluent control of their native language. The term 'acquisition' is used rather than 'learning', because 'learning' tends to be employed by psychologists in a more specific sense than is perhaps appropriate. It is a matter of controversy whether the acquisition of language can be accounted for within current versions of psychological theories of 'learning'.

The study of language acquisition has been strongly influenced by the theory of generative grammar. Chomsky (1968) has argued that the speed with which children are able to infer the grammatical rules underlying the speech they hear about them, and then to use these rules for the construction of utterances they have never heard before, suggests that children are born with a knowledge of the (allegedly universal) formal principles which determine the grammatical structure of the language. This is the 'rationalist' hypothesis (the hypothesis of 'innate ideas'), as opposed to the 'empiricist' hypothesis, which, in its strongest form, says that all knowledge comes from experience.

Chomsky's restatement of the doctrine of innate ideas has provoked a lot of discussion among psychologists, philosophers and linguists; and it is criticized in this chapter by Campbell and Wales. They argue, as others have done, that Chomsky and many of the psychologists influenced by him have failed to give sufficient attention to the environmental factors involved in the development of what they call 'communicative competence'. See also Hymes (1970).

I have already referred to this notion of 'communicative competence' in my introduction to the chapter by Halliday (p. 140; see also p. 287). The present chapter also contains much that is relevant to Kiparsky's discussion of the role of language acquisition in language change (pp. 310 ff.).

The Study of Language Acquisition

1. THE first attempt we know of to record the linguistic development of a child was that of the German biologist Tiedemann (1787); and his interest was in initiating the collection of normative data on the development of children. The greatest stimulus to the serious and careful study of the acquisition of language by children stems from Darwin's theory of evolution, which suggested the continuity of man with other animals. Darwin himself contributed a pioneer study (1877), as did Taine (1877). But it was in the superb, detailed study of the German physiologist Preyer (1882), who made detailed daily notes throughout the first three years of his son's development, that the study of child language found its true founding father. With Sully (1895) and Shinn (1893) following closely on Preyer, a substantial tradition of careful descriptive work was established, easily traceable from the early decades of this century in the journal *Pedagogical Seminary*, through the massive work of the Sterns (1924, 1928) and Leopold (1939–49), up to the exciting recent attempts to refine the descriptive process by appropriating the tools developed by the generative grammarians (e.g. Brown & Frazer, 1963). This tradition was largely unaffected by the behaviourist movement in psychology.

It seems appropriate to begin this chapter by referring to the historical origins of the study, because there is currently a tendency to forget that the scientific study of child language has an important and thoroughly respectable heritage of observation and theoretical discussion. Recognition of the existence of this tradition and its influence may not only save us from the mere reworking of old questions but may also lead us to adopt a more moderate and informed position with respect to a number of contemporary claims and controversies. For example, the contemporary practice of vilifying behaviourism for its misleading and inept attempts to explain language acquisition seems largely irrelevant. The important issue is how to go beyond the achievements of Leopold and the Sterns, scholars who owed nothing to behaviourism.

Let us therefore allow Sully to describe the kinds of questions and issues which continue to determine the range and nature of our interest in child language:

To the evolutionary biologist the child exhibits man in his kinship to the lower sentient world. This same evolutionary point of view enables the psychologist to connect the unfolding of an infant's mind with something which has gone before, with the mental history of the race (1895: 8). If, reflects the psychologist, he can only get at this baby's consciousness so as to understand what is passing there, he will be in an infinitely better position to find his way through the intricacies of the adult consciousness. It may be, as we shall see by and by, that the baby's mind is not so perfectly simple, so absolutely primitive as it at first looks (1875:7). In this genetic tracing back of the complexities of man's mental life to their primitive elements in the child's consciousness, questions of peculiar interest arise. A problem, which though having a venerable antiquity is still full of meaning, concerns the precise relation of the higher forms of intelligence and of sentiment to the elementary facts of the individual's life experience. Are we to regard all our ideas as woven by the mind out of its experiences, as Locke thought, or have we certain 'innate ideas' from the first. Locke thought he could settle this point by observing children. Today when the philosophic interest is laid not on the date of the appearance of the innate intuition, but on its originality and spontaneity, this method of interrogating the child's mind may seem less promising. Yet if of less philosophical importance than was once supposed, it is of great psychological importance (1895:7–8). The awakening of this keen and varied interest in childhood has led, and is destined to lead still more, to the observation of infantile ways. Pretty anecdotes of children which tickle the emotions may or may not add to our insight into the peculiar mechanism of children's minds (1895:10). The observation which is to further understanding, which is to be acceptable to science, must be scientific. That is to say, it must be at once guided by foreknowledge, specially directed to what is essential in a phenomenon and its surroundings or conditions, and perfectly exact. If anybody supposes this to be easy, he should first try his hand at the work, and then compare what he has seen with what Darwin or Preyer has been able to discover (1895:11).

Thus from the first the study of language acquisition was set in the context of the investigation of the child's total development. Further, the original interest arose out of serious questions about the nature of man and his behaviour: there was more at stake than mere description. Nevertheless, priority was given to the careful description of what the child was doing. This was followed by attempts to elucidate what sort of thing language acquisition was, and only then by speculation about the explanations of these phenomena. We will now use these aims as a platform from which to discuss contemporary issues.

In the pursuit of these aims Leopold (1949) and those before him took the communicative act as their basic psychological unit. Description was a matter of accurately recording not only the form of a child's utterances, but also the context in which they were made and the meanings (so far as they could be determined) of the constituent 'words'. Perhaps because of this, but more probably because they did not have such clear ideas about syntax as we have today, these early workers tended to terminate their accounts at about the beginning of the third year of the child's life, by which time most children have begun to produce utterances of two or three distinct words.

The principal focus of more recent research, however, has been the period stretching from the beginning of such syntactically structured speech. This reorientation is due almost completely to Chomsky's work in syntactic theory (see pp. 23–8). The main aim of this chapter will be to argue that an extremely important guiding principle of the early work has been sacrificed in this reorientation and to suggest some ways in which it might be restored to its former methodological prominence. Limited space prevents us from giving a detailed review of empirical work on language acquisition, but many excellent reviews are available elsewhere: cf. Richter (1927), Leopold (1948), McNeill (1966, 1969), Ervin-Tripp (1966). Details of much recent work can also be found in the following collections of articles: Bellugi & Brown (1964), Smith & Miller (1966), Slobin (1970), Reed (1970), Hayes (1970).

Contrary to what one might expect, our knowledge of language acquisition has not been greatly advanced by the recent spate of empirical work. Furthermore, it is our belief that no real theoretical understanding of the acquisition of syntax will be obtained unless, paradoxical as this may seem, the methodological distinction between *competence* and *performance* drawn by Chomsky (the man who, more than any other, has shown the shallowness, indeed the irrelevance of almost all behaviourist accounts of language acquisition) is drastically revised. We will now indicate how and why we think this distinction should be revised.

2. In the first half of Fodor and Garrett (1966) there is an excellent discussion of the distinction between competence and performance, in the course of which the authors distinguish one clear sense of the distinction which they, like us, regard as 'eminently honourable'. This is the sense in which competence in any sphere is identified with capacity or ability, as opposed to actual performance, which may only imperfectly reflect underlying capacity. This sense of the distinction has been honoured by psychologists in the past (e.g. Lashley, Hull, and many psychologists concerned with education) and likewise by certain social psychologists concerned with the study of attitude and opinion, etc. (e.g. Lazarsfeld). It applies in the construction of so-called 'performance' models of language users; that is to say, 'performance' models are in fact models of competence (in this weak sense of competence). However, when Chomsky talks of competence he is usually referring to a far 'stronger' notion, although it is not clear exactly what is meant by this stronger notion. We shall try to clarify the stronger notion in what follows.

The diverse capacities of human beings are subject to a variety of limitations, and some of these limitations may be described as 'non-essential'. For instance, our arithmetical capacity is limited by the amount of information we can store and manipulate at any one time; our capacity to walk is limited by the amount of time we can go without food or rest. In both these cases, the limiting factors are very general, applying, in the case of the former, to all mental activities and, in the case of the latter, to all physical activities. Hence we may, if we so choose, omit these limiting factors from our theoretical account of arithmetical or locomotive abilities: they are non-essential (i.e. non-specific) to these abilities. Similarly, by omitting any account of the role of memory or the various low-level sensori-motor capacities involved in the perception and production of speech, we can considerably simplify our characterization of linguistic abilities, and thereby arrive at the stronger notion of linguistic competence.

We have distinguished two senses of the term 'linguistic competence', the 'weaker' and the 'stronger'. We shall refer to these as *competence*$_1$ and *competence*$_2$ respectively. So far our discussion has been relatively uncontroversial, and it would be generally agreed that the clarification of the notion of 'competence' has far-reaching consequences for the psychological investigation of language and for the study of language acquisition in particular (cf. Moravcsik, 1967, 1969). But we must now distinguish a third sense of 'competence'.

Although generative grammarians, in particular Chomsky, claim that their work is an attempt to characterize the nature of $competence_2$ (that is, the nature of those human abilities that are specific to language), their main effort has in fact been directed towards a more restricted sort of competence, which we will call $competence_3$, from which by far the most important linguistic ability has been omitted – the ability to produce or understand utterances which are not so much *grammatical* but, more important, *appropriate to the context in which they are made* (on this point, the crux of this chapter, see also Schlesinger, 1969). By 'context' we mean both the situational and the verbal context of utterances. It is interesting to note that in at least one place Chomsky allows that part of this ability belongs properly to linguistic competence: 'an essential property of language is that it provides the means for ... reacting appropriately in an indefinite range of new situations' (1965: 6). In passing, it is also worth remarking that the gloomy, negativistic and questionable conclusions of Fodor and Garrett (1966) on the nature of the relationship between grammar and 'performance' models lose their relevance once it is realized how crucial this notion of contextual appropriateness is to the use of language, since neither the type of grammar motivating the empirical studies they discuss, nor the studies themselves, incorporate contextual information.

Of those linguistic abilities explicitly accounted for by recent transformational work, it is the ability to produce and understand indefinitely many novel sentences that has received the greatest attention (see p. 12 above). Chomsky frequently refers to this ability and for him at least it is this productivity and creativity implicit in the normal use of language that most needs explaining. Chomsky's many remarks on this point are well grounded, and he has quite properly criticized twentieth-century 'structural' linguistic and behaviourist psychology for ignoring this important aspect of language use. But one can go too far in the opposite direction. Much of what we say and write is constrained, in important ways, by the particular circumstances in which we are speaking or writing. Recent work on language acquisition and use has tended to neglect this fact.

Before continuing, we should emphasize that it is not our intention to question the productivity or creativity of language use: what we are insisting upon is the *limited* nature of the productivity to be explained. Nor do we wish to take issue with the validity of choosing, as a methodological decision, to limit the study of *language* to the level of context-less sentences. It should be recognized, however, that although a limitation of this kind may serve linguistic ends, its inevitable effect upon the psychology of language is as stultifying as that of the much-abused behaviourist approaches. The history of psychology shows that there is a very great danger of leaping from one extreme position to another when in fact the correct view of the phenomena lies somewhere in between. (A good recent example might be the incremental *v.* all-or-none learning controversy: cf. Simon, 1968.) We are therefore arguing that an adequate psychology of language must take account not only of the creative aspects of language use but also of the important role played by contextual factors.

At this point it is worth while referring to a related issue which has been grossly oversimplified in recent psycholinguistic literature. It is only too easy to infer from a casual reading of Chomsky's devastating review (1959) of Skinner or Bever, Fodor and Weksel's (1965) critique of Braine that not only have traditional learning theories very little to say on the subject of language acquisition, but also that no learning is involved at all in the process of acquiring a language and that everything is accounted for by innate predispositions. We are beyond doubt innately predisposed to 'structure information' in certain ways. As Chomsky (1965) has pointed out, even the most militant brand of empiricism presupposes some sort of innate determination. However, it is equally certain that every behavioural acquisition depends to some extent on the interaction of these predispositions with the environment. It is a matter of methodological emphasis whether one directs attention to the environmental variables or to the predispositions. However, it seems clear to us (and to this extent we are in line with traditional approaches) that it is the environmental variables that should be made the primary object of study, since they are more accessible to investigation.

There are considerable parallels between the two issues just discussed: in each there is a question of emphasis at stake, not a question of fact. In both cases it is necessary to take account both of the contribution of the individual and the contribution of the context or environment in which he acts or learns.

For the sake of future reference, let us call the two restricted types of language competence referred to above *communicative competence* (corresponding to competence$_2$) and *grammatical competence* (corresponding to competence$_3$). The rest of this chapter will be devoted to considering how the acquisition of communicative competence can be described and explained. We claim little originality for the view that communicative competence is the primary goal of the psychology of language – in this respect we are the heirs of a long tradition. This theoretical commitment is also in accord with current developments in psychology and linguistics. It can be related, for example, to the numerous recent attempts to enlarge the notion of 'grammaticality' by taking into account such contextual matters as relations between speaker and hearer (e.g. Fillmore, 1966; Boyd & Thorne, 1969) and referential relationships (e.g. Postal, 1968; Dik, 1968). It can also be related to the current tendency for linguists to describe the deepest levels of grammatical structure in semantic terms (cf. Chafe, 1967, 1968; Anderson, 1968; McCawley, 1969). Clearly, semantically based transformational grammars hold out greater promise for the characterization of communicative competence than do grammars of the type discussed in Chomsky (1965). From these very general considerations, we turn now to more specific issues. We will begin by considering how the preceding suggestions might affect the way in which communicative competence is studied from a developmental point of view. We will then deal with the controversial issue of *explaining* its acquisition.

3. Many recent descriptions of syntactic development, notably that of Roger Brown and his associates (e.g. Brown & Fraser, 1963; Klima & Bellugi, 1966) have failed to take account of situational variables and freely admit this as a defect. Even if one's goals are limited to describing the range of grammatical structures that a child is capable of producing at a particular stage of development, there is still no escape from the necessity of specifying contexts. We can see this in the following way. Let us suppose that during a particular period of development a child is never observed to produce any passive sentences. Suppose further that certain contextual considerations are satisfied whenever such sentences are produced by adults (not an implausible suggestion: for a discussion of some of the factors relevant to the choice of the passive in English see Svartvik, 1966). Then the absence of passive sentences from our sample of the child's language at this stage may be attributable either to a lack of capacity to produce this particular structure or to the absence of occasions for its production. Without the relevant contextual information, there is clearly no possibility of deciding between these two alternatives. Some support for this observation is provided by an unpublished analysis of comparative expressions in the speech of a group of pre-school children aged three-and-a-half to four. The corpus consisted of daily observations in the experimental nursery of the Edinburgh S.S.R.C. Cognition Project over a period of six months. From this analysis (collated by Julian Dakin) it is clear that comparative expressions occur much more frequently in 'competitive' situations where two or more children are vying with each other in various tasks – for example in threading strings of beads, building sandcastles, etc. Clearly, the language of a single child at home is less likely to show such structures.

The approach we are recommending would therefore involve sampling not only as much speech as possible but also as diverse a range of situations as possible, some sort of situational record being made at the same time as the speech record. The obvious alternative to this would be to construct different situations experimentally rather than simply wait for them to develop 'naturally'. Here we come up against serious problems. We cannot decide in advance what contexts are most likely to provide suitable occasions for the utterance of a particular structure. We can however, study children's comprehension in various situations and note whether it approximates to adult comprehension in all of these; and, to the extent that it does, we can then try out eliciting contexts which work with adults with the hope that they will be close to the appropriate eliciting context for children.

At Edinburgh, we have made a detailed study of comparative expressions in pre-school children following roughly these lines. Unfortunately, the finding quoted above came too late to be used experimentally in an 'eliciting' context. In one study the eliciting context was a series of cardboard soldiers of increasing or decreasing stature. The child was first presented with two soldiers and asked to tell the experimenter about them. Questioning followed until some mention was made (or, failing that, provided by the experimenter) of their different sizes. On addition of each subsequent soldier to the series the child was asked 'And what about him?' This technique produced a full range of adjectival forms – so-called positives or absolutes (*He's big*, *He's a big soldier*, etc.), full comparatives (*He's bigger than him*, etc.), superlatives (*He's the biggest soldier*, etc.) as well as several 'functional' comparisons (*He's too big*, *He's wee enough*, etc.) which would not have been appropriate adult utterances. In another study the eliciting context involved the justification of a choice of one from a set of depicted objects varying in size for a particular purpose. Here the range of expressions was more restricted: most of them included superlatives, but 'functional' comparisons and so-called absolute adjectives were also found. Notably, almost no full comparatives were found. We say 'so-called' absolute adjectives, since another study of comprehension of expressions containing absolute adjectives (conducted with Robert Grieve) has shown convincingly that, even at the age of three or so, children interpret such constructions comparatively. The details of these various studies are not relevant here (cf. Donaldson & Wales, 1970; Wales & Campbell, 1970; Wales, 1970). These results have been mentioned merely to illustrate the effects of varying the 'eliciting' context. So far as we know, studies of this type have not been conducted in the past.

There are two kinds of investigation which we would wish to distinguish from our own. Firstly, a few recent studies (e.g. Frazer, Bellugi & Brown, 1963) have tested children's production and comprehension of grammatical contrasts like singular *v.* plural, past *v.* present, etc. Strictly speaking, this technique does not measure production at all, since the child has merely to choose between two proffered oral descriptions of a picture: he does not have to describe it himself. Nor does this technique test comprehension satisfactorily, since the child has to choose between only two alternative 'depictions' of each expression. Our approach, by contrast, has been to take a particular structure, and to vary both its lexical content and the context in which it is to be comprehended.

The second group of studies we wish to refer to and compare with our own are those associated with the name of Piaget. It is often said that many studies of children's thinking in the tradition of Piaget could be reinterpreted as studies of their linguistic comprehension. While we subscribe to this general view, we would point out that one could in principle distinguish such studies in terms of the differing demands they make on cognitive and linguistic capacity. In those studies traditionally regarded as testing cognitive capacity it is assumed (possibly quite often wrongly) that the demands made upon linguistic capacity are correspondingly slight. At any rate, we are very much aware of this difficulty and for that reason we have endeavoured to make our tasks as simple as possible. Using this method with pre-school groups, we have discovered many facts which appear surprising in a Piagetian framework. For instance, expressions containing *more* are understood in the same way as the corresponding expressions containing *less*. For example, children confronted with two model trees on which model apples can be hooked tend to respond in the same way to the instruction 'Make it so that there are less apples on this tree than on this one', as they do to 'Make it so that there are more apples on this tree than on this one' (cf. Donaldson & Balfour, 1968). In a classification task we have also observed that expressions containing *the same . . . as* are interpreted in the same way as the corresponding expressions containing *different . . . from.*

By defining communicative competence (competence$_2$) as only those human abilities that are specific to language, we have made the assumption that, although it is difficult to distinguish linguistic from cognitive competence, this is an important issue. This follows equally from Chomskyan notions of linguistic competence. The success of formal linguistics certainly buttresses the assumption that linguistic capacity is theoretically separable from other cognitive capacities. The experimental study of children's linguistic comprehension seems to provide an excellent testing-bed for this assumption.

4. We turn now to the problem of *explaining* the acquisition of communicative competence. As will be clear from the preceding sections, we believe that much more attention must be paid to the linguistic environment (construed here as the communicative environment) of the developing child than has been given in the recent past, without however reverting to arid stimulus-response formulations (e.g. of behaviourist explanations). Although some studies of phonological aspects of the communicative environment and their relationship to the child's phonology have been reported (cf. Eunice Pike's, 1949, study of intonation contours), very few studies of syntactic or semantic aspects have been made (we shall refer to them below). Among the questions that might be investigated are the following: (a) Is there a tendency among parents to simplify their speech when addressing children? And, if so, what form does this simplification take? (b) How do parents react to non-comprehension or mis-comprehension and how do they modify their subsequent questions or constructions? (c) What sources of information are available to the developing child about the well-formedness and appropriateness of his utterances or the accuracy of his comprehension? (d) How often does this or that construction occur in the speech of parents? (e) In what contexts are these constructions used? (f) To what extent do parents correct, repeat, expand or elaborate the speech of children and what form does their intervention take? Clearly, one could go on asking questions of this type indefinitely.

In some cases we have partial answers, in others the answer has been assumed. For instance, in a brilliant paper, Brown used as his starting point such assumptions about the use of everyday common nouns in concrete situations as the following (1958: 15): 'the frequencies to which we are now appealing have not, of course, been recorded. We are explaining imagined preferences in names by imagined frequencies of names.' As an example, he suggests that 'when pineapples are being named, the word *pineapple* is more frequent than the word *fruit*'. On the other hand, Bresson (1963) has argued that the early learning of what such nouns refer to cannot be satisfactorily explained by appealing to the situational pairing of these nouns with their referents, since such words are rarely used in the presence of the object they refer to: one tends instead to point to the object or to use a more general term or a pronoun. If either of these apparently contradictory assumptions is correct, it must impose important constraints on the way in which we learn language; but we cannot know whether either of them *is* correct until some kind of empirical tests have been carried out.

Almost alone among current students of child syntax, Brown, in his more recent work, has shown a clear awareness of the importance of describing the communicative environment (cf. Brown, 1968; Brown & Hanlon, 1970). He has shown, for example, that, for the families on which he has data (Brown & Hanlon, 1970), 'approval and disapproval are primarily linked to the truth value of the proposition which the adult fits to the child's generally incomplete and often deformed sentence. ... While there are several bases for approval and disapproval they are almost always semantic, or phonological. Explicit approval or disapproval of either syntax or morphology is extremely rare in our records and so seems not to be the force propelling the child from immature to mature forms.'

Consider now question (c) above. It has often been suggested in recent psycholinguistic literature that the major source of linguistic information open to the child (the 'primary linguistic data' in the sense of Chomsky, 1965: 25) is the corpus of utterances to which he is 'exposed' and that this set of utterances is meagre and fragmentary. On this assumption, it is quite understandable that so much innate predetermination has been claimed. But we feel that the 'primary linguistic data' is merely one among many such sources of information; and that it may be of relatively minor importance. For instance, Lenneberg (1967) notes that normal children of congenitally deaf parents are very little retarded in their linguistic development (although the speech of their parents is highly abnormal). This might be taken as evidence that there is a considerable innate predetermination; it seems to us to show merely that certain sources of linguistic information have been overvalued.

What then are the other sorts of information? The most salient perhaps is feedback from the child's everyday communicative acts. If his questions, wishes, demands, and so forth are comprehensible and appropriate to the occasion, they will be followed by the desired consequences. There is, however, an important methodological difficulty here: it is no straightforward matter to determine what is a wish, demand or question in the speech of children. As Chomsky (1959) pointed out with respect to Skinner's (1957) analogous notion of *mand*, it is fatuous to attempt to define such communicative acts in terms of their consequences. We must somehow divine the speaker's *intentions*.

This point is relevant to another observation made by Brown and Hanlon (1970): that there is apparently no relationship between the well-formedness of children's utterances and comprehension on the part of the parents. In fact, Brown only succeeds in distinguishing comprehension or misunderstanding, on the one hand, from *lack* of comprehension, on the other. Clearly we need to find ways of distinguishing *correct* interpretations of the child's utterances from incorrect interpretations. Brown himself seems to regard this difficulty as probably insuperable, since 'any message the investigator can make out, the family can also make out, and so the child will in fact already be communicating any idea we can be sure he has'. That is, where true misunderstanding occurs it is unlikely that we, as investigators, will be able to spot it, since the parent has failed to do so. But the child presumably can. It may well be, therefore, that we should examine all three components of the communicative act: the child's question or demand, the parental response to this and the child's response to the parent's action. Brown implicitly suggests a second possible approach when he remarks that he was only able to identify one instance of

genuine misunderstanding in his corpus: Child: *What time it is?*
Parent: *Uh-huh, it tells what time it is.* In view of his comments
quoted above on the difficulty of spotting instances of genuine
misunderstanding, it is surprising that Brown fails to see the
significance of his identification of this exchange as such an instance. Clearly, it is only because he has succeeded in isolating a
class of utterances of the above type as primitive question forms
corresponding, in this case, to the well-formed *What time is it?*,
that he has identified this interchange between child and parent as
an instance of misunderstanding. It will be clear from this example how complex the study of language acquisition must be, if
it is to be conducted in an informative manner.

Despite his largely negative findings (which need to be qualified
in the light of the remarks we have just made about misunderstanding), Brown still holds the view that 'the empiricist position
has possibilities that have not yet been explored' (1968: 290). He
discusses three-termed 'interaction patterns' consisting of a question or demand from the child (or mother), a response by the
mother (or child) indicating partial or complete incomprehension,
and a complete or partial restatement of the original question or
demand by the child (or mother). At Edinburgh we have examined similar data, obtained from transcripts of many experimental
sessions with pre-school children. Brown argues that the middle-
term of the exchange, *Eh?*, *What?*, etc., is understood by the
child as a directive to repeat what he has just said. This is not
borne out in our data, where the 'repeated' version of the first
utterance is normally significantly altered (cf. Child: *Isn't a torch
got a battery not a different as that?* Experimenter: *Eh?* Child:
Isn't a battery in a torch not the same as that?) The child is
attempting to produce a paraphrase or to correct his syntax or to
elaborate in some way on what he previously said. The *value* of
the resulting information (when comprehension is finally secured)
is far from clear, since it depends on what the child is attempting.
But it does illustrate some interesting possibilities.

Clearly, there are many ways in which a child might learn
whether his utterances are well-formed or not (apart from the
rather unlikely one of comparing them with stored representations of model utterances to which he has been 'exposed'). The

current neglect of environmental factors in favour of 'innate ideas' (cf. Chomsky, 1969) is doubly unfortunate in view of the common tendency to equate linguistic universals with innate predispositions and to overlook the possible contribution of similarities of environment and upbringing. The proper course to adopt in the investigation of language acquisition is to specify first the nature of the linguistic environment, and thus identify the possible sources of information available to the child about his language, and then to discover, presumably by experimentation, which of these possible sources are used. When that has been done, and not before, it will be time to speculate about the genetic contribution of the individual to language acquisition.

5. In the previous section we limited our discussion of language acquisition to external environmental factors. In this final section, we shall discuss briefly the role of internal factors in the development of the system of language in children. This area of cognitive psychology has been neglected until recently, except in the work of Piaget (cf. Flavell, 1963), who has long urged the necessity of recognizing certain, presumably innate, principles of internal organization ('processes of equilibration', to use his term) in all areas of cognitive development.

Of course, as we have just emphasized, before claiming that a certain change of behaviour is the expression of an endogenous reorganization of some kind, it is methodologically desirable to demonstrate that it is not the result of learning (in the conventional sense). However, there is a certain type of developmental progression frequently observed to occur in young children which effectively guarantees that the development in question is not the result of learning. These are progressions where the child first of all does something 'correctly' and then, with every appearance of systematicity, later proceeds to do it 'wrongly'. Clearly, this development cannot be explained by environmental factors, since there is no adult model for the wrong behaviour. Nor can it be considered simply as one of a series of approximations to the adult model, since the erroneous behaviour is preceded by a stage in which the child behaves correctly. Perhaps the best-known example of such a progression is the over-regularization of the rule for past-tense inflection in English, which has been noted by many of the earlier workers mentioned in section 1 and recently by Ervin (1964). If one examines the child's acquisition of the past-tense forms of the strong verbs in isolation from the rest of the verb system, they can be seen to display this particular developmental sequence. However, although it is in such sequences that the *existence* of innate principles of organization is most clearly revealed, it seems to us that whenever we find that the child's use of language is (a) systematic (that is, reasonably constant and predictable over a period) and (b) anomalous (that is, strikingly different from the adult usage), we have evidence of the *workings* of such innate principles. We can see this by asking why the child's communicative competence has developed in this particular way. It cannot be the *direct* result of external factors, because of the anomalies, so it must be the result of some sort of endogenous systematic change. The particular form of the anomalous usage then tells us something about the character of these endogenous processes.

It is not hard to find the above characteristics. For example, a frequent topic in traditional work on language acquisition was the interplay of extension and restriction of the range of application of the child's earliest words (cf. Sully, 1895; Lewis, 1951; Leopold, 1949: 149). It often happens that a child's usage of a particular word is initially over-extended as compared with adult usage. Each such over-extension, when systematic, tells us something about the way in which the child organizes his experience. The subsequent changes in the application of such words are a potentially rich source of information about organizational principles. The older writers quoted many cases of endogenous restriction: it was often noted that when a new word, with a range of application overlapping that of a previously acquired word, was learned, the application of the earlier word became restricted, *without benefit of instruction or correction*. Although this principle works efficiently with *incompatible* terms, it leads to interesting over-restrictions when one term is a *hyponym* of the other. (By 'hyponymy' is meant the inclusion of the meaning of one term in the meaning of another: e.g. *tulip* and *rose* are hyponyms of *flower*. Cf. Lyons, 1968: 453.) Such over-restrictions are clear expressions of endogenous change, since they satisfy our definition of systematic error.

At Edinburgh we have obtained some data on the development of a sub-system of English adjectives, the adjectives used to describe variations of size (i.e. *big, tall, fat*, etc., and their antonyms). The adjective *big* stands in a peculiar semantic relationship to the others. Although the relation between each of *tall, fat, long*, etc. and *big* is not strictly one of hyponymy it has similar properties, since the range of application of these terms is smaller than that of *big* and the range of application of *big* overlaps with each of their ranges. Now we have observed an interesting progression in the application of these adjectives with a number of children (too small, unfortunately, on which to base hard and fast conclusions). Initially, *big* (or its antonym *wee*) is used with reference to almost all differences of size. As the other more specialized adjectives are learned, however, *big* may fall out of use or may be restricted to cases of complex differences in size (e.g. to cases where the objects being compared both vary along two or more dimensions).

If our interpretation is correct, a further question arises: suppose that this over-restriction of the range of application of superordinate or quasi-superordinate terms is the result of an innate organizing principle which resolves overlapping ranges in this way, how does the child progress to adult usage? This is a serious problem, since, while over-extension of the range of application leads directly to overt errors, over-restriction does not do so. We have no clear ideas about this and our speculations have already run too far ahead of the facts. However, it is interesting to note that Piaget has often argued that an understanding of class-subclass relationships is a crucial acquisition which marks a fundamental reorganization of the child's thought and occurs usually around seven to eight years of age. Moreover the type of diagnostic test which he favours for assessing this understanding consists in, for instance, showing the child three tulips and five roses and then asking *Are there more roses or more flowers?* At lower age-levels children tend to reply that there are more roses. If children typically organize their vocabulary in the way we have suggested, then this result is hardly surprising.

This brings us right back to our remarks in section 3 on the subject of distinguishing linguistic abilities from other cognitive abilities. The generative grammarians have insisted upon the methodological advantages for linguistics of making such a distinction. We have argued that in any study of the acquisition and use of language this distinction needs to be revised in various ways – in ways which give explicit recognition to the communicative function of language. In doing so, we have been attempting to bridge the gap between traditional views of language acquisition and views that are dominant at the present time. We have also tried to relate the psychology of speaking to the psychology of thinking.

14. THE PERCEPTION AND MEMORY OF SENTENCES

P. N. Johnson-Laird

This chapter relates closely to Fry's chapter on the reception and perception of speech (pp. 29–52). Johnson-Laird begins by assuming that it is in principle possible to establish 'a comprehensive account of the way spoken sounds are identified as words', and then moves on to consider, from the psychological point of view, 'how the meanings of words are combined to form the meanings of sentences'. There is a sense, therefore, in which Johnson-Laird can be said to start at the point where Fry leaves off. But of course it is not as simple as that. As Fry emphasizes, the identification of spoken sounds as words is partly dependent upon the listener's recognition (or prediction) of the grammatical structure of the utterance he is 'processing'; so that a full account of the way in which we recognize the words that have been spoken presupposes the solution of the 'further problem' of how these words are combined into meaningful phrases and sentences. Some of the evidence cited by Johnson-Laird also supports this conclusion: that, at certain times at least, 'the perceptual mechanism is more preoccupied with grammatical analysis than with monitoring the incoming sounds' (p. 262).

Of particular interest in this chapter is Johnson-Laird's argument (based on the evidence obtained from experiments of various kinds) that 'deep structure', in the sense of Chomsky (1965), has no direct psychological validity. A further point (which links the chapter with the one immediately following by Clark) is the suggestion that sentences are remembered not as strings of words with a certain syntactic structure, but as complexes of 'semantic markers' (or 'components': see p. 169). One might perhaps interpret this as further evidence for the view that 'semantically based transformational grammars hold out greater promise for the characterization of communicative competence than do grammars of the type discussed in Chomsky (1965)', as Campbell and Wales suggest on p. 249, and as many scholars have suggested recently.

Perception and the Surface Structure of Sentences

Suppose that it were possible to give a comprehensive account of the way spoken sounds are identified as words, what further problems of linguistic perception would remain? The principal problem I believe would be to explain how the meanings of words are combined to form the meanings of sentences. Since this depends in some way upon syntax, linguistic perception must involve a form of syntactic analysis. At the very least, a sentence is likely to be analysed into its grammatical constituents to yield what is called its *surface structure*.

One aspect of such a process has been examined in an ingenious experiment by Garrett, Bever and Fodor (1966). They constructed pairs of sentences that had identical endings but different beginnings:

(1) In order to catch his train George drove furiously to the station,

(2) The reporters assigned to George drove furiously to the station.

The identical endings have a different surface structure because the major boundary between clauses occurs immediately before *George* in (1) but immediately after it in (2). (This may be readily checked by reading aloud the two sentences and trying out pauses at these two points.) Tape-recordings were played to students so that in one ear they heard a sentence and, in the other, a click timed to occur in the middle of a word, e.g. *George*. After each presentation, they wrote down the sentence and indicated where the click had occurred. There was a reliable tendency for it to migrate from its objective position towards the major syntactic boundary. This suggests that in the region of such boundaries the perceptual mechanism is more preoccupied with grammatical analysis than with monitoring the incoming sounds. No doubt there are often acoustic cues (such as pauses) to boundaries, but this was not so in the experiment because the endings of the pairs of sentences were acoustically identical. Parsing therefore seems to consist of an active search for intrinsic structure rather than the passive registration of extrinsic structure, with the consequence that major constituents like the clause gain sufficient perceptual integrity to repel extraneous noise. Of course, the clicks could have migrated, not during the process of perception, but subsequently while responding. Hence it would be particularly interesting to know whether a difference can be detected in the position of the click when it occurs in different places in two identical sentences presented one after the other. It ought to be difficult to distinguish a click in a major boundary from one in an adjacent word.

If the cues to surface structure are not necessarily acoustic, just *what* are they? Knowledge of the properties of lexical words (nouns, verbs, etc.) is undoubtedly important. For instance without an appreciation of the transitive nature of *picking* and the intransitive nature of *falling* it would be impossible to differentiate the structures of *They are picking apples* and *They are falling apples*. But since, even without having read Anthony Burgess's novel *The Clockwork Orange*, we can parse apparent nonsense like

(3) *The* gloop*y* malchick*s* scat*ted* razdraz*ily to the* mesto,

we must rely heavily on our ability both to recognize grammatical words and affixes (italicized in (3)) and to predict structure from them. The initial occurrence of *the* is bound to suggest that a noun will follow later to complete the noun phrase and, ultimately, a verb phrase to complete the sentence. Such predictions are almost certainly set up by the parsing mechanism and tested against the incoming sentence. This would explain why it is easier to make up a suitable ending for an incomplete sentence than to make up a suitable beginning (Forster, 1966), and why a solecism, such as an inversion in word order, is more disruptive at the beginning of a sentence (Marks, 1967). When a prediction remains unfulfilled for too long, the sentence becomes excessively laboured, e.g. *The modern multi-channel automatic digital strain-gauge measuring system using carrier-frequency techniques was described*. Yngve (1960) has even argued that languages are organized to prevent the occurrence of such sentences. This seems unlikely, even if there were a special dispensation for scientific prose. However, there is some evidence that sentences with a mild increase in predictive load are more difficult to remember (Martin and Roberts, 1966).

But it would seem, theoretically, that comprehension ought to be affected rather than recall as such.

Important as these predictive aspects of performance are, their role should not be overemphasized, as perhaps it has been by those psychologists who see syntactic relations as 'associative links' between one word and the next. Even the most sophisticated analysis of surface structure would be an inadequate basis for understanding. There are sentences, such as *The policeman's arrest was illegal*, which are ambiguous yet which may be parsed only in a single unequivocal way. Examples like this show that sense is not just a simple function of surface structure. Meaning must be mediated by an underlying *deep structure* which specifies the functional relations between constituents. Thus the ambiguous example derives from two alternative deep structures, one specifying that the policeman arrested someone, and the other that someone arrested the policeman.

Since we do not have to wait for the end of a sentence before we begin to understand it, structure and meaning must be analysed together. Indeed, Thorne (1968) has suggested that for many sentences the number of possible parsings becomes quite unmanageable unless deep-structure relations are taken into account from the start. An important consequence of this contemporaneity is that processing is likely to cease once *one* satisfactory meaning has been discovered. An ambiguity would be noticed spontaneously only when some difficulty arose in the initial attempt to derive a plausible interpretation. Moreover, surface structure may suggest one meaning rather than another, so that an ambiguous sentence may in practice seldom receive one of its latent interpretations. I have found, for example, that sentences such as:

(4) Every child loves some toy. (active voice)
(5) Some toy is loved by every child. (passive voice)

which are identically ambiguous (is it the same toy or not?), are usually given different interpretations. Placing *some* at the beginning of affirmative or negative sentences made one interpretation (the same toy) much more likely than the other, so a purely surface characteristic can exert a decisive effect on interpretation. Furthermore, the ambiguity of the sentences was not noticed spontaneously except when they were juxtaposed in a reasoning task (Johnson-Laird, 1969*a*, *b*).

There are other variables, of course, which crucially affect the perception of sentences (cf. Wales & Marshall, 1966). One type of processing interacts with another. Hence the intelligibility of words spoken against a background of noise is greater if something is known about their meaning (Bruce, 1956); if they are combined to make a *meaningful* sentence (Millar & Isard, 1963); if they occur in a sentence with a relatively simple surface structure (Compton, 1967); and if the syntactic pattern of the sentence, surface or deep, is not unexpected (Mehler & Carey, 1967).

Of course, it is quite possible to perceive a sentence, in the sense of identifying its component words, without being able to understand it: its vocabulary may be obscure, its syntax intricate, or it may violate certain restrictions on the use of words – as in much poetry and existentialist philosophy. Experiments have for the main part concentrated upon the effects of syntax upon comprehension. But in a series of pioneering studies Wason (1959, 1961) was able to show that negative statements are harder to understand and to evaluate than affirmatives. Jones (1966) has similarly shown that negative instructions lead to more mistakes and to a slower rate of performance. Otherwise, we know very little about those factors which make meaning intrinsically easy or hard to grasp. Studies are greatly handicapped by the lack of a comprehensive account of semantics. Another stumbling-block is the assumption that it is impossible to explain how the context of a sentence influences its meaning and reference. The crucial point, however, is that apparent ambiguity, vagueness or obscurity direct the listener to those aspects of context relevant to rendering the sentence unambiguous. In this way a sentence may be said to define its own context.

The Psychological Reality of Deep Structure

It is obvious that the principal aim of linguistic perception is to grasp meaning, and we have seen that a necessary prerequisite for this is an analysis of deep structure. It is perhaps this intermediate role of deep structure – midway between manifest surface structure and latent meaning – that has tempted psychologists to raise the question of its psychological reality. It does seem a somewhat implausible luxury because its supposed effects could be due to meaning itself, or to 'some artificial, non-syntactic, non-semantic permutation invented by the subject' (Miller & McKean, 1964). Yet arguments aimed at demolishing deep structure are as futile as experiments aimed only at establishing its empirical existence. The real problem is to reconcile its linguistic necessity (on the assumption that it is necessary) with the exigencies of human information processing. Paradoxically, the solution to this problem may not be best served by too close a reliance upon linguistic theory. Current conceptions of deep structure are widely divergent and unlikely to be correct. Moreover, the simple importation of linguistic theory into models of syntactic processing may lead psychologists to specify only algorithmic procedures, whereas the listener in his 'effort after meaning' may adopt a more irregular and heuristic approach. Indeed, he may have to do this in order to cope with the innumerable solecisms, false starts, and slips of the tongue, that occur in ordinary speech (Goldman-Eisler, 1964).

It may be helpful to inquire just how deep structure would be retrieved by the listener. He probably uses two sorts of cue. The first sort stem from surface structure and his implicit knowledge of how this is related by *grammatical transformations* to deep structure. For example, these cues will reveal that certain sentences are in the passive voice, and enable the appropriate alteration to be made in the semantic roles of the two noun phrases. It is implausible that the passive would in fact be 'detransformed' into an active sentence. This would involve permuting the noun phrases and so it could only start after the entire sentence had been spoken. It would also imply that *Some toy is loved by every child* should be given the same interpretation as *Every child loves some toy*.

The surface cues to the passive voice are obvious, but cues to other constructions may be less conspicuous if the sentence is of a greater transformational complexity. Fodor and Garrett (1967) have argued that this should make comprehension more difficult. They found that sentences like *The man the dog bit died* were harder to paraphrase than ones like *The man whom the dog bit died*. The pronoun provides a clear cue to the fact that *the man* is the object of *bit*.

The second sort of cue to deep structure arises from the listener's knowledge of the properties of lexical words. He cannot grasp the deep structure of many sentences unless he knows the structural meaning of lexical items they contain. Consider the sentences: *John promised the man to escape* and *John persuaded the man to escape*. If the listener were unfamiliar with *promised* and *persuaded*, he would not know that the subject of *escape* was *John* in the first sentence, but *the man* in the second sentence. Deep structure is supposed to be a prerequisite for meaning, yet here its analysis seems to depend upon an aspect of meaning. The resolution of this apparent circularity suggests one potential solution to the general problem of the psychological nature of deep structure. Its analysis must be envisaged as polarized into two separate components, parallel to the two sorts of cue that have been discussed. Thus one component is intimately associated with parsing surface structure, and the other with interpreting lexical words. In this way, deep structure loses its independent psychological status – though its function is none the less real, and the arguments against its psychological reality may be reconciled with those for its linguistic necessity.

Memory and the Meaning of Sentences

A sentence has structure and meaning and this makes it easier to remember than the same set of words in random order. But a sentence is a small element of discourse in real life and if we remember anything about it at all, we remember its sense rather than its syntax. Only for a very short interval of time is it recalled with complete precision. During this time memory seems to function like an 'echo box', so that we can even recall its original intonation. There is good evidence that verbal material is represented in acoustic form in 'short-term' memory even when it is *visually* presented (Conrad, 1964). This may also happen with sentences – at least until they are interpreted.

In his classic statement of the aims and early achievements of contemporary psycholinguistics, George Miller (1962) suggested that the deep structure of a sentence may be temporarily held in memory. This hypothesis has been tested by Savin and Percho-nock (1965) using the following ingenious technique. The subject is presented with a sentence followed a few seconds later by a list of eight unrelated words. He then attempts to recall both the sentence and the list of words. Provided he is successful with the sentence, the number of words he correctly recalls from the list gives an indirect measure of the amount of 'space' taken up in memory by the sentence. The fewer the number of words recalled, the greater the amount of space that must have been pre-empted by the sentence. An experiment using this technique showed that passives took up more space than actives, interrogatives more space than declaratives, and emphatics (*The boy HAS hit the ball*) more space than their unemphasized correlates. In general, the amount of space required by a sentence was a function of the number of transformational 'footnotes' such as Passive, Interro-gative, and Emphatic, specified in its deep structure. Such 'foot-notes' should tend to be forgotten, and Mehler (1963) reports just such a result with, for instance, passives tending to be recalled as actives.

Unfortunately, the subjects in these and most other recent studies have known that they were going to have to recall sen-tences word for word. This knowledge, together with repeated experience of the task, may easily lead to the adoption of a special strategy to remember syntactic detail. In my view this is exactly what happened. And I want to propose, partly as the result of an unsuccessful experiment, that *all* forms of syntactic structure are normally lost to memory within a few seconds. My experiment was designed to discover the locus of the tendency for passives to be recalled as actives. Was it to do with perception or memory? In the event, the promised phenomenon did not materialize. When the subjects were confronted with an unexpected test of their ability to recognize the sentences of a brief spoken story, they recalled actives as passives just as often as they recalled pas-sives as actives. Yet their memory for meaning was extremely good. I abandoned the technique as 'unsuitable'. But interest-ingly enough Sachs (1967) has obtained the same result in studies where the subjects did not know *which* sentence in a spoken pas-sage was the test item. She found that after about 12 seconds her subjects could no longer recognize whether the original sentence was in the active or the passive. But their ability to recognize changes in meaning persisted for the longest test interval she used: about 54 seconds.

If deep structure as I have argued has no independent psychological status, it is difficult to see how it could directly enter memory. And it is evident that it is not normally recalled. Using more complex sentences than the earlier studies, Clark and Clark (1968) have even confirmed this when subjects knew that verbatim recall was required. However, a simple but stringent test would involve the detection of paraphrases of the original material. Fillenbaum (1966) reports that subjects are poor at recognizing changes such as the substitution of *closed* for *not open*, but rather better at recognizing non-synonymous substitutions such as *cold* for *not hot*. This has been confirmed in an independent study by Cornish and Wason (1969). Subjects were given a series of brief descriptions to help them to identify an unknown object, followed by an unexpected test of their memory for these 'clues'. But the most suitable material would involve paraphrases of the following variety: *James liked one particular painting very much and the painter sold it to him, One particular painting pleased James very much and he bought it from the painter*. If subjects confuse these statements, then it is clear that they have no memory for deep-structure relations but a good memory for meaning.*

No one knows how meaning is represented within memory, but there is no evidence to show that any form of syntactic structure is directly involved. This is puzzling because if syntax is not necessary for storing meaning why should it be necessary for communicating it? The answer may be that the elements from which meaning is composed – the so-called 'semantic markers' – are utilized in cognitive processes other than language (e.g. the formation of concepts). Hence their organization would not be specifically linguistic. If meaning is represented by an amalgamation of the semantic markers which correspond to lexical items, then forgetting should involve these markers rather than grammatical constituents or words. It should lead to a simplification in meaning. And this is precisely what Clark has observed in several

* Such confusions do occur (cf. Johnson-Laird & Stevenson, 1970).

experiments (e.g. Clark & Card, 1969). There was a tendency for a sentence such as *The girl isn't as bad as the boy* to be recalled as *The girl is better than the boy*, showing that the 'feature' that both the girl and boy are bad has been forgotten (see below, pp. 273–9).

It is natural to wonder whether the sentence is the largest unit normally involved in the recall of language. It is possible that from the meanings of sentences in a connected discourse, the listener implicitly sets up a much abbreviated and not especially linguistic model of the narrative, and that recall is very much an active reconstruction based on what remains of this model. Where the model is incomplete, material may even be unwittingly invented to render the memory more meaningful or more plausible (Bartlett, 1932) – a process which has its parallel in the initial construction of the model (Gomulicki, 1956). A good writer or raconteur perhaps has the power to initiate a process very similar to the one that occurs when we are actually perceiving (or imagining) events instead of merely reading or hearing about them. Hence it is likely that the study of linguistic memory shades imperceptibly into the study of memory in general.

15. WORD ASSOCIATIONS AND
LINGUISTIC THEORY

Herbert H. Clark

'Associationism' has long been very influential in psychology. As far as language is concerned, this is the doctrine that, whenever two words occur together or in close proximity, an 'associative' link is formed between them in the mind of the hearer, and the more frequently they occur together the stronger the 'association'. This theory is at least superficially attractive (because, as Clark says below, it is 'simple'); and it seems to explain the fact that, when people are presented with one word as a stimulus and asked to produce as a response the 'first word that comes into their head', there will be a fair degree of consistency in the results (provided that the responses are made without reflexion or hesitation). It is after all a fair assumption that all speakers of a language have met the words with which they are familiar (or at least the most common words) in the same contexts. There is, however, an alternative explanation. This is that we are able to produce associations as a consequence, a side-product as it were, of our ability to understand and produce utterances; and that these associative links between words do not play any fundamental role in the acquisition or use of language. This is the point of view taken by Clark.

The reader will find this chapter easier to follow if he has read the chapters on generative syntax (especially pp. 134–8, dealing with selection restrictions and subcategorization) and semantics (pp. 166–84).

It will be noted that Clark, unlike Johnson-Laird in the previous chapter, accepts the psychological validity of 'deep structure' (in the sense of Chomsky, 1965). However, the rules he proposes in order to account for word associations do not appear to depend crucially upon this fact.

THE free-association game has been played for centuries. It requires only a stimulus, a referee, and a player who is willing to follow the simple rule, 'Say the first thing that comes to mind when the stimulus is presented to you.' When the game is further restricted to single words as both stimuli and responses, it is more properly called the word-association game. It is this game that will be the subject of the present chapter.* Unlike conversation or the other language games we play daily, the word-association game is an artificial, derivative phenomenon, important not because it is interesting in itself, but because it reveals properties of linguistic mechanisms underlying it. Our ability to produce associations is presumably derived from our ability to understand and produce language. For this reason, language must play a central role in the explanation of these associations.

Word associations have not always been thought of in this way, and even now most psychologists treat word association in the way the British empiricists have done for several centuries. For these psychologists, two words become 'associated' with each other when the two are experienced in temporal contiguity. Quite recently, however, this simple, hence attractive, theory has been severely criticized for a variety of reasons (Chomsky, 1959; McNeill, 1966; Clifton, 1967). Most important among these reasons is that 'association theory' cannot account for language comprehension and production: language, the critics say, should not be thought of as a consequence of built-up associations; rather, word associations should be thought of as a consequence of linguistic competence (cf. p. 246).

Word associations have characteristically different effects depending on the rules the player has followed. When the player is allowed to take his time, he generally reacts with rich images, memories, or exotic verbal associations, and these give way to idiosyncratic, often personally revealing, one-word responses. But when he is urged to respond quickly, his associations become more 'superficial', less idiosyncratic, and more closely related in an obvious way to the stimulus; these responses are much more predictable in that they are the ones almost everyone else gives to

*The preparation of this chapter was supported in part by Public Health Service research grant MH–07722 from the National Institute of Mental Health. I thank Eve V. Clark and William C. Watt for their valuable discussion and comments.

the stimulus. But if he has to respond even more quickly, the player will ignore even the meaning of the stimulus and produce 'clang responses', words that sound like or rhyme with the stimulus. Of these three categories, it is the second that is most dependent on linguistic competence. But there are important differences even among these fast, meaningful responses. The common associations – i.e., the responses other people are most likely to give – are produced more quickly than the uncommon ones. This suggests that we can attach greater importance to the fastest, most frequent associations, for hypothetically they are the product of the basic association mechanisms.

Even the most preliminary analysis of the word-association game reveals its kinship with language comprehension and production. The game has three identifiable stages: (1) the player must 'understand' the stimulus; (2) he must 'operate' on the meaning of the stimulus; and (3) he must produce a response. It is the unique second stage that clearly sets this game apart from normal language mechanisms. It contains an 'associating mechanism', which, through its 'associating rules', fixes the response at the third stage. I will go into these associating rules in some detail, but only after examining what is known about understanding and producing sentences, the counterparts of the first and third stages in word association.

According to one current linguistic theory (Katz & Fodor, 1963; Katz & Postal, 1964; Chomsky, 1965), the meaning of a sentence consists essentially of its deep-structure relations plus the dictionary entries of the lexical items inserted into this deep structure (cf. pp. 124–8 above). There also is some psychological evidence to suggest that comprehension involves coming to know the deep-structure relations between the lexical items in a sentence (Miller, 1962; McMahon, 1963; Gough, 1965, 1966; Clark, 1969). In production, on the other hand, the speaker might begin with an abstract semantic characterization of what he intends to say, then construct a surface structure in keeping with this characterization. Psychological evidence supporting this view comes from experiments that require subjects to recall sentences presented previously. Typically, subjects are found to reconstruct sentences anew from certain fragments of the deep structure and semantic features they have retained from the original sentence, not from fragments of surface structure (Mehler, 1963; Fillenbaum, 1966; Sachs, 1967; Clark & Clark, 1968; Clark & Stafford, 1969; Clark & Card, 1969).

When this view of comprehension and production is incorporated into the first and third stages of the word-association game, the requirements of the second stage become much clearer. Consider the stimulus *man*. At stage one, comprehension entails setting up a list of features that completely characterizes this surface realization, perhaps as follows: [+Noun, +Det—, +Count, +Animate, +Human, +Adult, +Male] (for the notation and the concept of syntactic *features*, cf. p. 135). At stage two, some associating rule is applied. If the rule were 'change the sign of the last feature', the associating mechanism would alter [+Male] to [—Male]. And then, at stage three, production would form the realization of the altered feature list [+Noun, +Det—, +Count, +Animate, +Human, +Adult, —Male] as *woman*.

Surface structure, however, is only an imperfect indicator of deep structure, and analogously the surface form of a one-word stimulus is particularly ambiguous. At stage one, the surface realization *man* could be assigned several abstract characterizations: (1) *man* meaning 'male adult human', (2) *man* meaning simply 'human' (3) the verb *man* meaning 'attend to', and so on. With these different meanings, the same stage-two associating rule will give quite different results. Whereas the rule 'change the sign of the last feature' produced *woman* from the first *man*, it might produce *animal* or *beast* from the second *man*. Ambiguity of the surface form is one of the most important problems in word association.

I will now consider various important associating rules. In keeping with traditional studies of word associations, I will treat 'paradigmatic' and 'syntagmatic' responses separately. 'Paradigmatic' responses are those that fall in the same syntactic category as the stimulus; 'syntagmatic' responses are those that fall into other categories (cf. p. 16). For example, a paradigmatic response to the noun 'tree' might be the noun 'flower'; a syntagmatic response to the same word might be the adjective 'green'.

For adults, paradigmatic responses are far more prevalent than syntagmatic ones, so they will be discussed first.*

The Paradigmatic Rules

THE MINIMAL-CONTRAST RULE. If a stimulus has a common 'opposite' (an antonym), it will always elicit that opposite more often than anything else. These responses are the most frequent found anywhere in word associations. As McNeill (1966: 555) remarks, 'It appears that for adjectives at least, and possibly for nouns also, the most frequent paradigmatic response tends to be a word with a maximum number of features in common with the stimulus. The paradigmatic response then forms a *minimal contrast* with the stimulus.' Stated in terms of features, the rule would go as follows: 'Change the sign of only one feature.' (Although not stated in this form, this rule is equivalent to the law of contrast of the early British empiricists.)

The most compelling evidence for this rule comes from the so-called 'polar' adjectives (*long* v. *short*, *good* v. *bad*, etc.). Deese (1964) found that the most frequent association to each of 80 such adjectives was its antonym. At the first stage, the feature list for *long*, for example, would end with [+Polar] (Bierwisch, 1967). The second-stage associating rule would change [+Polar] to [−Polar], and the third stage result would be *short*. Nouns, too, often show alterations of only one feature. Among animate nouns, the sign of the feature [±Male] is reversed, giving *male-female*, *man-woman*, *boy-girl*, *he-she*, *him-her*, *aunt-uncle*, etc. (and vice versa) as most frequent responses. Antonymous prepositions, e.g. *up-down*, *above-below*, and *to-from*, strongly elicit each other with a change of the feature [±Polar] (Clark, 1968), and so do verb 'converses', e.g. *give-take*, *sell-buy*, *go-come*, and so on. Other frequent single-feature contrasts include [±Plural] in verbs (*is-are*, *was-were*, *has-have*, etc.), [±Past] among strong verbs (*is-was*,

---

*In the rules that follow, there is much in common with proposals by McNeill (1966), Clifton (1967), Perfetti (1967, 1968) and Marshall (1968), who share the present point of view; but these rules would have been impossible to formulate without the extensive word-association norms now available (Palermo & Jenkins, 1963; Fillenbaum & Jones, 1964; Entwisle, 1966) as well as some of my own (Wright & Clark, unpublished data).

are-were, *has-had*, *take-took*, etc.), [±Nominative] among pronouns (*he-him*, *she-her*, *they-them*, etc.), and [±Proximal] among
the deictic words (*here-there*, *this-that*, *now-then*, etc.). Obviously,
the minimal-contrast rule accounts for a large number of the
commonest responses in word associations.

We can strengthen the minimal-contrast rule considerably,
however, by noting that it is not a single rule, but rather a hierarchy of rules. In many of the 'minimal pairs' just illustrated, the
changed feature was not a random one, but the last feature in the
list. (This, of course, assumes that features can be ordered in a
motivated way: cf. Bierwisch, pp. 167–84 above and 1967.) *Man*
most frequently elicits *woman*, not *boy*, indicating a change in
[+Male] (the final feature), not in [+Adult] (the penultimate
feature). Similarly, the changed feature among antonymous adjectives and prepositions was [±Polar] also the final feature.
Features not coming in the final position are also changed, but
less often. *Man* does elicit *boy*, and it does so more often than it
elicits *girl*, which results from changes on two features. Table 1
shows several examples of a major contrast (on the final feature),
a minor contrast (on the penultimate feature), and a double contrast, along with their proportions of occurrence in word association norms. A series of minimal contrast rules might therefore be
proposed in the following form: 'Change the sign of one feature,
beginning with the bottommost feature.' Allowed to apply several
times, it would result in the previously illustrated responses, as
well as those in Table 1.

THE MARKING RULE. This rule, a particularization of the
minimal-contrast rule, was suggested by some remarks of Greenberg (1966: 53). He pointed out that there was a greater tendency
to change a feature from, rather than to, its *marked* value in
word-association data. (For the distinction between the 'marked'
and the 'unmarked' terms of an opposition, cf. p. 17. In the
assignment of values in the examples given below, I have for
simplicity followed Greenberg, 1966, although I recognize that
certain of these assignments are debatable.) Consider the feature
[±Plural] for nouns. A plus signals the addition of the morpheme
'Pl', usually /z/; a minus signals the morpheme 'Sg', usually zero.

Word Associations and Linguistic Theory

Table 1. Stimuli with major, minor, and double contrasts as responses with their percentage of occurrence in word association norms.

Features	Stimuli	Major Contrast		Minor Contrast		Double Contrast	
[±Child,	man	woman	62	boy	8	girl	3
±Female]	woman	man	53	girl	9	boy	1
	boy	girl	70	man	5	woman	0
	girl	boy	60	woman	5	man	1
	father	mother	65	son	15	daughter	2
	mother	father	67	daughter	5	son	0
	son	daughter	42	father	28	mother	3
	daughter	son	40	mother	10	father	7
[±Nominative,	he	she	42	him	8	her	10
±Female]	she	he	31	her	17	him	5
	him	her	65	he	5	she	2
	her	him	25	she	12	he	2
[±Nominative,	we	they	48	us	20	them	0
±Proximal]	us	them	30	we	37	they	5
	they	we	20	them	38	us	8
	them	us	22	they	7	we	3
[±Past,	is	are	19	was	14	were	0
±Plural]	are	is	21	were	5	was	2
	was	were	21	is	18	are	0
[±Deixis,	here	there	67	now	6	then	0
±Temporal	there	here	37	then	3	now	2
±Proximal]	now	then	38	here	4	there	1
	then	now	36	there	10	here	0

[+Plural] is therefore the marked value, and [−Plural] the unmarked. In word-association data, then, it should be commoner to find, say, *dogs-dog* than *dog-dogs*, and it is. Comparative adjectives also elicit their positive forms (*better-good*) more often than the reverse (*good-better*), and past participal verbs their infinitive forms (*brought-bring*) more often than the reverse (*bring-brought*). Marshall (1968) extended this rule to unmarked and marked adjectives (e.g., *long* and *short*, respectively) (cf. Lyons, 1968: 466). An examination of 16 pairs of adjective stimuli that have only one antonym (data from Deese, 1964) generally supports his extension, with 14 of the 16 pairs consistent with the rule. Also, if we take the accusative case to be unmarked with respect to the nominative case (Lyons, 1968: 356), the rule holds, with the stimulus-response pairs *I-me*, *he-him*, *she-her*, *they-them*, etc., occurring more often than the reverse pairs. Again, if the suffix *-less* is marked with respect to *-ful*, the rule holds once more, as in pairs like *careless-careful*, *thoughtless-thoughtful*, and *useless-useful*. And there are other cases which confirm this.

On the other hand, *man* is generally considered to be unmarked with regard to *woman* (Greenberg, 1966: 25), and *he* with regard to *she*, *him* with regard to *her*, and so on. Yet *man* elicits *woman* more consistently than *woman* does *man*; the same is true for *he* and *she*, *her* and *him*, and certain others. To save the marking rule, *man* would have to be shown to be marked, and *woman* unmarked. This, however, would go against the very foundations of marking found in Greenberg (1966) and elsewhere. The marking rule therefore cannot be retained as a general rule.

Some results which seem to agree with the marking hypotheses can furthermore be explained in an alternative way by considering the surface ambiguity of the stimuli. The unmarked adjective *deep*, for example, could be assigned either of two senses at stage one: (1) 'in depth', as in *three feet deep*, or (2) 'opposite to shallow', as in *The river is deep*. But *shallow* has only one sense, 'opposite to deep'. If the minimal-contrast rule is invoked at stage two, *deep* will at times produce words like *high*, *far*, etc., from sense (1) and at other times *shallow* from sense (2); *shallow* on the other hand, will always produce *deep*. The consequence is that *shallow* should elicit *deep* more often than the reverse, which agrees with the data. Thus the minimal-contrast rule, taken together with the surface ambiguity of unmarked adjectives, might account quite simply for the asymmetry in associations between unmarked and marked words.

THE FEATURE-DELETION AND -ADDITION RULES. There also appear to be rules that either delete features from, or add features to, the end of the feature list. As Marshall (1968) points out, the deletion rule should have precedence over the addition rule, since there are many possible features that might be added, but those to be deleted are exactly specified. Deletion of features generally produces superordinates, like *fruit* from *apple*, while addition of features produces subordinates, like *apple* from *fruit*.

Both superordinates and subordinates occur often in word associations, but subjects generally offer superordinates more quickly than subordinates (Woodworth & Wells, 1911; Karwoski & Schacter, 1948). Another example of feature deletion is the dropping of [+Cause] from such verbs as *kill* yielding *die* (Lyons, 1968: 381ff.). Again, this feature is more often dropped than added, as in pairs like *kill-die, teach-learn, feed-eat, show-see*, etc. (Wright & Clark, unpublished data). If we assume that for *listen-hear*, *listen* is identical to *hear* except for an additional [+Volitive] and that the same is true for *look-see*, then the precedence of deletion over addition is again confirmed (Wright & Clark, unpublished data). The feature-deletion and addition rules, like the minimal-contrast rule, actually consist of a hierarchy of rules, with single deletions and additions preferred to multiple operations.

Word associations often include near synonyms, like *house-home, odour-smell, seem-appear, thing-object*, etc. One sense of *home* appears to contain all the features of *house* plus some extras indicating that it is someone's usual residence, but other synonyms differ in different ways. Although partial synonyms have not been characterized in any consistent form in terms of feature theory, it is clear that they usually have feature lists differing on only a few, possibly optional, features. The feature-deletion and addition rules, then, also produce synonyms. But the minimal-contrast rule has priority over these rules, for if the stimulus has a full antonym, it is always more frequently given as a response than is a partial synonym (cf. e.g. Clark, 1968: 430).

With many stimuli, applying the minimal-contrast and feature-deletion and addition rules produces semantic representations that have no surface realization in English. In such cases, the rules must be applied repeatedly. The result that does finally have a surface realization could be semantically far removed from the stimulus. Nevertheless, we should find certain of the most basic features of the stimulus untouched. This leads to the following general rule.

THE CATEGORY-PRESERVATION RULE. A long-standing observation in word-association literature is that stimuli tend to elicit paradigmatic responses (Thumb & Marbe, 1901; Deese, 1962; Fillenbaum & Jones, 1965). This is not too surprising given the previous rules, since the responses produced by those rules are always paradigmatic. But there are seeming exceptions. Common adjectives elicit other adjectives almost invariably, but uncommon adjectives do so less consistently (Deese, 1964). As Deese pointed out, this happens because the common adjectives mostly belong to antonym pairs and have minimal contrasts, whereas the uncommon ones do not. The category-preservation rule is therefore a negative one: 'Do not change features high on the list,' such as the feature [+Noun] or [+Adjective]. The rule is, in fact, only another aspect of the rules stressing that features at the bottom of the list should be altered first.

This rule need not be restricted to the highest feature alone, e.g. the feature [+Verb]. The next few features down, according to Chomsky (1965), are the subcategorization feature, like [+——NP] for transitive verbs, and the selectional feature, like [+——Det[+Animate]] for transitive verbs that accept only animate objects (for the distinction between *subcategorization* and *selection*, cf. p. 135 above). According to the category-preservation rule, the feature [+Verb] should be preserved most often, [+——NP] less often, and [+——Det[+Animate]] least often. Evidence for this ordering is found in the word associations to common English prepositions (Clark, 1968). The category feature [+Preposition] was preserved most often, with paradigmatic responses occurring more often than anything else. But subcategorization features were also often preserved, since prepositions within the subcategories of place, manner, direction, etc. tended to elicit each other. Finally, selectional restrictions like [+——Det[−Animate]] and [+——Det[−Abstract]] were also often preserved; prepositions with similar objects tended to elicit each other. These three effects were of approximately decreasing importance, just as the category-preservation rule would predict.

Paradigmatic responses, therefore, appear to be produced by a fairly homogeneous set of rules, perhaps ultimately by one very general rule. This *simplicity-of-production rule* might be stated as follows: 'Perform the least change on the lowest feature, with the restriction that the result must correspond to an English word.'

Expanded, this rule defines 'least change' in such a way that the operations of (1) changing the sign of a feature, (2) deleting a feature, and (3) adding a feature, are of increasing difficulty. And the rule defines 'lower feature' in the way specified and illustrated above. The reason people do not always choose the easiest rule to apply is because that rule results in a semantic representation with no possible surface realization in English; unsuccessful applications of simpler rules therefore force people to use more and more complex rules.

The Syntagmatic Rules

Syntagmatic responses are found much less often than paradigmatic responses in word associations; and they are more difficult to characterize in rules. But there are two related rules that appear to account for the bulk of the syntagmatic responses.

THE SELECTIONAL FEATURE REALIZATION RULE. The list of features for a word often contains selectional features that partially characterize the meaning of the potential context of that word. The adjective *young*, for example, has selectional restrictions on the nouns it can modify, as specified in the feature [+Det[+Animate]be——]. Many responses to *young* are merely specific realizations of this feature – e.g. *boy*, *child*, *girl*, *man*, and *people*. To produce these responses, the respondent took the partial feature list [+Noun, +Animate] filled it out with other features, and gave the result; the features added were often other features of *young*, since some responses were words with the feature [−Adult] – *boy*, *girl*, and *child*. The rule that accounts for these responses might be stated as follows: 'Take the features specified by a selectional feature, adding as many features as necessary for a surface realization; in addition, restrict yourself to the "significant" part of the selectional feature, the portion specifying a lexical word.'

The selectional feature realization rule accounts for the differences in the number of syntagmatic responses people give to nouns, verbs, adjectives, and so on. Notice that in the theory put forward by Chomsky (1965) nouns have no selectional features, although verbs, adjectives, and other categories do. So nouns should elicit relatively few syntagmatic responses in comparison to the other categories. As confirmation, we see that in Deese's (1962) large sample of stimuli and responses nouns produced only 21 per cent syntagmatic responses, while verbs produced 48 per cent, adjectives 50 per cent, and adverbs 73 per cent. Several further predictions of this sort can be verified in data from Fillenbaum & Jones (1965). First, the selectional features for adjectives specify the nouns they modify. So adjectives should elicit nouns most often, and they do, with nouns accounting for 80 per cent of the syntagmatic responses. Similarly, the selectional features for verbs specify the subjects and objects that govern the verb. So nominals (nouns and pronouns) should occur most often here also, and they do. Verbs likewise select for the particles and prepositions that occur with them, as in *get along*, *seem like*, and *try out*; these responses also occur quite often. Prepositions select for their objects, so prepositions should elicit nominals most often as their syntagmatic responses. This is also confirmed (cf. also Clark, 1968). It is within prepositions that the dominance of the previous minimal-contrast rule over the selectional feature realization rule is best illustrated. Some prepositions have a common antonym, hence the minimal-contrast rule can be successfully applied to them. These prepositions tend to elicit far fewer nominals than other prepositions do (Deese, 1965; Clark, 1968). This implies that the selectional feature realization rule is usually applied only after certain other rules have failed.

THE IDIOM-COMPLETION RULE. The stimulus *cottage* often elicits *cheese*, completing the common idiomatic phrase *cottage cheese*. Likewise, *whistle* elicits *stop*; *white*, *house*; *stove*, *pipe*; *justice*, *peace*; *how*, *now*; *so*, *what*; and so on. The rule that generates these responses is a close cousin of the selectional feature realization rule, for it seeks out a selectional feature that has only one realization. The rule might be stated: 'Find an idiom of which the stimulus is a part and produce the next main word.' Without better semantic specification of idioms, this rule will have to stand as it is.

This rule might also be appealed to to explain many apparently paradigmatic responses. *Ham* elicits *eggs*, *bread* elicits *butter*, and *needle* elicits *thread*, probably not so much because the responses are paradigmatic, but because they are completions of common idioms. But carried too far, this reasoning might be used to explain the associations *here-there*, *high-low*, *now-then*, *man-woman*, etc, in exactly the same way. Instead, the phrase *here and there* appears to be common just because *here* and *there* are simple contrasts, and it is the latter fact that explains their frequent occurrence in word associations. This interpretation is further supported by Marshall's (1968) observation that, for example, *low* elicits *high* more often than *high* elicits *low*, in spite of the fact that the normal order of the two words is *high and low*. The rule usually applied in these cases is therefore the minimal-contrast rule, not the idiom-completion rule.

Syntagmatic responses are influenced in important ways by the normal left-to-right production of sentences. *Cottage* often elicits *cheese*, but *cheese* rarely elicits *cottage*; and the same is true of other idioms. The idiom-completion rule therefore works left to right, not right to left. Also consider adjective stimuli with the selectional feature [+Det [−Abstract] be——]. If the selectional feature realization rule is to add as few extra features as possible to [+Noun Phrase, −Abstract], it should often produce pronouns. But it does not. Almost all nominal responses to adjectives are full nouns. Nouns would be produced, of course, if the adjectives were taken to be in their normal pre-nominal position, where pronouns are impossible. So here again, normal left-to-right order dictates to some extent the form responses will take. Also, in the case of transitive verbs, their features restrict subjects and objects both, yet responses to transitive verbs tend to be objects rather than subjects (Clark, 1964); furthermore, the objects of transitive verbs can be produced more quickly than their subjects in restricted word-association tasks (Cattell, 1887).

Nevertheless, syntagmatic associations are not merely continuous fragments of normal speech, as writers such as Saporta (1959) have assumed, but rather responses that bear only an abstract relationship to normal speech. First, note that many stimulus-response pairs would never be found in normal speech – e.g., *about-house*, *bread-butter*, *on-table*, etc. – for there is a missing function word in between stimulus and response. People prefer to give lexical rather than function words as responses. And the distance between syntagmatic associations and speech is also demonstrated in a comparison of (a) the nominal responses to prepositions with (b) the objects of the same prepositions in sentences people had composed (Clark, 1968). Whereas the nominal responses are pronouns 48 per cent of the time, the objects are pronouns only 4 per cent of the time. In word association, the rule that produces a realization for [+——[−Abstract]], for example, does so by adding as few other features as possible, so the responses are often semantically 'empty' pronouns, like *it, them, him, her,* etc. In full utterances, on the other hand, speakers tend to fill in the feature list, producing nouns as objects. So the nominal responses and the true objects of a preposition reflect the same selectional restrictions, but the selectional feature realization rule, when applied with time limitations, is more likely to produce simpler realizations in the form of pronouns.

Thus, although syntagmatic responses first *appear* to be different from paradigmatic responses, they are produced by rules that belong to the same class of rules stated for paradigmatic responses – the simplicity of production rule. To repeat that rule, 'Perform the least change on the lowest feature, with the restriction that the result must correspond to an English word.' To include syntagmatic responses, we must consider the operation of isolating selectional features and filling out their feature list to be a possible 'least change', an operation more difficult, however, than changing feature signs or deleting or adding features. The various expansions of this rule are obvious.

Concluding Remarks

By listing several paradigmatic and syntagmatic rules, I have been assuming that the process of word association is not a homogeneous one, but rather a set of alternative processes. There is independent support for this claim in the data of Moran, Mefford and Kimble (1964). They found three classes of people in word association. Those in the first class gave mostly 'contrasts' (*big-little, man-woman*) and 'co-ordinates' (*yellow-blue, apple-orange*), to use their terms, and responded very quickly. Those in the second class preferred to give 'synonyms' (*big-large*) and 'superordinates' (*apple-fruit*) and responded less quickly. The people of these two classes were quite similar compared to those in the third class, who gave mostly 'functional' associations (*red-apple, needle-thread*) and did so quite slowly. Obviously, the three classes can be characterized by their reliance on the different associating rules – the minimal-contrast rules, the feature-deletion and addition rules, and the syntagmatic rules, respectively. This is strong evidence for the independence of the separate rules, or rather of the separate *operations* within the general 'simplicity of production' rule.

The rules presented here are for adults. Several important studies (Ervin, 1961; Palermo & Jenkins, 1963, 1965; Entwisle, 1966) have shown that children, in contrast to adults, give mostly syntagmatic responses, even for those stimuli that have common antonyms. And from about five to nine years of age, children go through a 'syntagmatic-paradigmatic shift', where they move from giving mainly syntagmatic to giving mainly paradigmatic responses. The shift occurs at different times for different syntactic categories, with nouns first, adjectives second, verbs third, and adverbs last (Entwisle, 1966). An ingenious explanation for these early associations has been devised by McNeill (1966), who assumes that the young child has only partly formed feature lists. Therefore, when the child attempts to find a minimal contrast, he ends up by contrasting on syntactic category features, rather than semantic features, as adults do. It seems more likely, however, that the young child does not have a minimal-contrast rule until he has the lower binary features he can apply it to. Instead, with his incomplete feature lists, he merely uses one of the syntagmatic response rules on the selectional features he already has for use in producing utterances. Unfortunately, we can only speculate in this area until more is known about the child's linguistic competence and about the relation of adult competence to word associations.

In this brief account of the word-association game, I have tried to show that any successful explanation of word associations must be formulated in terms of syntactic and semantic features. In such a theory, the explanation will consist of rules that operate on features of a stimulus to produce features of an utterable response. Examination of the data now available suggests what several of these rules must be, but further work waits on more extensive studies of the semantic features in the lexicon. Because of the limited scope of this review, I have had to omit discussion of many very important studies – e.g. Deese's work (1964, 1965), which shows the extent of very subtle semantic information in word associations; these studies often contain rich and orderly data but have no ready explanations. Since the word-association game is so easy to play, we know plenty about the scores. We now need to find out more about the rules.

16. SOCIOLINGUISTICS

J. B. Pride

Sociolinguistics, as Pride says below, is not simply an amalgam of linguistics and sociology (or indeed of linguistics and any other of the social sciences). It embraces, in principle at least, every aspect of the structure and use of language that relates to its social and cultural functions. It will be clear from the present chapter that this is a very wide brief!

It is frequently suggested that there is a conflict between the sociolinguistic and the psycholinguistic approach to language; and furthermore that generative grammar (which, according to Chomsky, 1968: 1, is a branch of cognitive psychology) must necessarily adopt the latter. I do not believe that this is so.

The two points of view, the 'sociolinguistic and the psycholinguistic, can certainly be distinguished at the moment (and linguists tend to favour the one or the other according to their particular interests). But ultimately they must be reconciled. The ability to use one's language correctly in a variety of socially determined situations is as much and as central a part of linguistic 'competence' as the ability to produce grammatically well-formed sentences. Whether the theory of generative grammar can be extended to account for the full range of linguistic competence remains to be seen. But it is interesting to note that Campbell and Wales, who write as cognitive psychologists in an earlier chapter, do in fact advocate the necessity of widening the notion of competence to take account of at least part of what might be called the 'social context' of speech (pp. 250–57). I have already mentioned this point in connexion with Halliday's rejection (from what we may call a 'sociolinguistic' standpoint) of Chomsky's notion of competence (p. 140).

THE study of language as part of culture and society has acquired the now commonly accepted label 'sociolinguistics'. But any single name for such a vast field of inquiry would be misleading if interpreted too literally. Just as the study of culture and society cannot be the prerogative of any one discipline, so that of their linguistic aspects cannot properly be represented as some kind of amalgam of sociology and linguistics. It is instructive to consider the spread of expressions which have been used at one time or another, including: 'the sociology of language', 'social linguistics', 'sociological linguistics', 'anthropological linguistics', 'linguistic anthropology', 'ethnolinguistics', and 'the ethnography of communication'. Furthermore, what may be the most fruitful growing points for future development (namely, where linguistics meets with social anthropology and social psychology) are not likely to be terminologically recognized at all, for obvious reasons (although 'the social psychology of language choice' comes quite near to the latter).

One does not of course explain what sociolinguistics *is* by merely enumerating the various disciplines which go into its making, but rather by giving some indication of how they are made to relate to each other. To begin with, the opportunity for reciprocal validation (in both theory and description) is obvious enough in all interdisciplinary work. The linguistic study of social dialects, for example, presupposes some prior understanding of social structure as seen from the point of view of the sociologist. The social-psychological study of interpersonal relationships can take advantage of observations of linguistic patterning among, say, forms of address. And so on. But mutual borrowing and interchange of information is not the end of the matter. The sociologist will not normally be heard to say, for example, 'hand it to the linguist and see what he can do with it', nor vice versa, though Fischer (1958) for one maintains that this would be a good idea. The real point is that sociolinguistics recognizes a unique *subject matter* which in many if not in all respects amounts to a fusion of forms of behaviour each of which (were they separable in any case) would otherwise be tackled independently by distinct disciplines (Pride, 1970*b*).

Language interpenetrates with almost all walks of life and varieties of experience. It does not exist 'for its own sake'. Nor does it exist mainly for the sake of broadly referential communication (see Lyons, 1968: 424ff.) Rather, it very often serves for what Sapir called 'communion', the reflection or clarification or consolidation or alteration of interpersonal relationships and socio-cultural values, and may in many cases be their only detectable sign. Stylistic choice within both bilingual and monolingual repertoires is usually full of social as well as other types of meaning. The linguistic behaviour known as 'code-switching' for example (as between say Standard and dialectal English in this country, or between Spanish and English among Puerto Ricans in New York) may on occasion amount to a rather subtle (if somewhat unconscious) form of social behaviour which by no means merely reflects something else in the situation which is independently observable in its own terms. The notion of 'phatic communion', or verbal behaviour which is almost wholly aimed at establishing or reinforcing conventional social relationships (especially an appropriate degree of relaxation, as for example in talk of the weather among English people), is in a sense *too* well known, since a very great deal of one's everyday use of language carries many other social meanings besides. *Nice day isn't it* is no more a largely social utterance than say *I see* spoken in any one of so many meaningful ways. It is difficult to escape the conclusion that language *is* very frequently the whole social behaviour of the moment.

The interpenetration of language with so many areas of human experience is well reflected in the difficulty of arriving at satisfactory criteria for the demarcation of boundaries between one language and another and one dialect and another (and, moreover, between one variety of style and another), hence for the definition of all such terms. Labov (1964, 1966, 1967) shows for example how in certain respects the assumption of linguistically discrete boundaries between social dialects does not seem to hold for New York speech. He shows how in this setting variations in the pronunciation of the 'phonological variables' represented by small capitals in such words as c*ar*, ba*D*, o*ff*, T*Hing*, and T*His*, form extensive and unbroken articulatory continua, and are statistically related both to the level of carefulness or casualness in each particular interaction and to measures of socio-economic stratification. Not only this, but Labov's initial espousal of discrete socio-economic boundaries (derived from an already existing sociological survey of parts of New York) is broadened in his later work to include the equally relevant factor of social mobility (Labov, 1967). The latter, it is important to note, influences people's choice of language not only in respect of economic, educational and other observable forms of mobility, but also in respect of subjective evaluations of the desirability or correctness of the various pronunciations. People in the same age-group and of the same mobility type are remarkably similar in the way they evaluate the desirability of various pronunciations, far more so than in their actual speech. Evaluations of this sort therefore help the analyst in interpreting or explaining behaviour. For example, the close correspondence between 'lower middle class upward mobility type' and 'upper middle class' speech particularly in non-casual relationships is matched by even stronger subjective endorsement of the norms in question on the part of the former than on the part of the latter. In certain respects, therefore, if not in all, social dialects in New York resolve themselves into unbroken continua on the linguistic side, closely related to mobility types and levels of interpersonal relationship; which cut across discrete socio-economic class boundaries on the sociological side; and these patterns and processes of change are to some extent explained by the existence of stable evaluative norms. Such findings suggest to Labov that language cannot properly be regarded as a 'structured integrated system' (Labov, 1964: 188).

In a somewhat wider context Gumperz (1962, 1964a, b, 1967) has discussed aspects of the linguistic scene in the Indian subcontinent, these are different in detail from those found by Labov, but lead him to a broadly similar conclusion. Village dialects, he writes, form 'a continuous chain from Sind to Assam', with mutual intelligibility between adjacent areas but not between relatively distant areas (Gumperz, 1962: 83). Switching between Hindi and Punjabi in Delhi (Gumperz, 1964a) gives rise to mixed styles of speech which illustrate how languages can 'seem to merge' in 'stable bilingual communities' to the point at which it seems irrelevant to speak of 'interference' between distinct 'standard' forms of speech (Gumperz, 1967). Gumperz suggests that phenomena of this sort may not be wholly distinct from those found in the development of pidgin languages. Pidgins are essentially utilitarian trade languages which come into being to serve the communicative needs of buying and selling, loading and unloading, etc., and result from processes of reciprocal imitation or 'rudimentary language learning'. These too pose the same problem of basic linguistic identity (Hall, 1966).

Possible criteria for demarcating boundaries among languages and dialects, or indeed for demonstrating the occasional irrelevance of boundaries, are numerous. Those favoured by descriptive linguistics concern various types of structural distance which may themselves yield quite different boundaries: syntactical boundaries may not be identical with lexical boundaries for example. But these are only the most obvious and should be measured against others which include the following: sociolinguistic observations of performance ('who speaks what language to whom and when': Fishman, 1965), assessments of mutual or non-reciprocal intelligibility (Wolff, 1959), beliefs of language users (Hoenigswald, 1966), political or other institutional considerations, attitudes of one sort or another (Ferguson, 1959) historical or 'diachronic' as well as non-historical or 'synchronic' relationships, and so on. There is probably no simple or single key to the complex incompatibilities found among these various criteria. For example, faced with the problem of devising standardized orthographies for structurally related dialects in Nigeria, Wolff (1959) not unnaturally assumed that mutual intelligibility would be found to be largely predictable from the results of contrastive structural analysis. But in many cases this proved not to be so. Indications of non-reciprocal intelligibility pointed rather to the play of local economic and power relationships, along with feelings of 'ethnic self-sufficiency', giving rise to 'pecking orders of intelligibility'. Similarly, Stankiewicz (1957) points out that at the time of writing the Slovaks were better understood by the Russians and Serbians than by the Czechs, even though the phonemic and grammatical patterns of Slovak and Czech differ less than those of Slovak, Russian and Serbo-Croatian. Stankiewicz concludes that both intelligibility tests and native intuition are 'unreliable', and falls back upon structural (particularly phonological) criteria, advocating the pursuit of 'structural dialectology'. Weinreich (1954) made the same basic assumption earlier, but paid more attention to semantic than to other levels of structural analysis.

These examples could easily be multiplied, but what is important to realize is that they are not examples of absence of system in language, but rather indications of probably very complex systems which take in more than purely structural relationships. A good deal of light can be thrown on the nature of the problem of identifying factors other than the purely structural which are relevant to the discrimination – both by the linguist and by the language user – of dialects, varieties, and styles of language, by investigating different kinds of code-switching behaviour in which the alternatives are unambiguously distinct languages. In such cases one can be more reasonably sure of what is being switched with what, whereas in the case of dialects, etc., the problem of demarcation is more difficult.

Broadly speaking, studies of code-switching between languages (as indeed many other areas of sociolinguistic investigation) are of two main types: those which make the assumption that verbal behaviour in all or in most important respects can be predicted from observable 'situational' determinants, and those which assume that it cannot. The large-scale sociolinguistic survey might appear bound to accept the possibility and importance of predictability, in order to present objectively verifiable results valid for a wide community; but this is an open question. Fishman's important study of patterns of bilingualism (Spanish and English) in a section of the Puerto-Rican population of New York City (Fishman, 1968*b*) deserves attention from this as from many other points of view. Here as elsewhere (Fishman, 1966), Fishman maintains that factors such as prestige, feelings of language loyalty, interpersonal relationships concerning power and intimacy and the like, however important for the language user himself, cannot easily be empirically verified, and tend to mean different things to different people in different settings (see also Nader, 1962). Accordingly, he makes what amount to three basic theoretical decisions: first, to place the concept of 'domain' at the forefront of analysis; second, to resolve domains primarily into constituent 'role relations'; and third, to seek out correlations between these two categories and choice of language.

Domains in Fishman's sense are institutionally given 'spheres of activity' or 'occasions on which one language (variant, dialect, style, etc.) is habitually employed rather than (or in addition to) another' (Fishman, 1966: 428). Everyday examples might be the family, the neighbourhood, governmental administration, the school, etc., each to some extent characterized by its particular set of role relations, such as parent-child in the family, policeman-pedestrian in the neighbourhood, and so forth. Domains are not necessarily easy to identify: 'the appropriate designation and definition of domains of language behaviour . . . calls for considerable insight into the socio-cultural dynamics of particular multilingual settings at particular periods in their history' (Fishman, 1966: 429).

The final objective of analysis goes beyond domain and role relationships however, to the 'confident prediction' of the language and variety of language most likely (say) 'to be employed by a *cleric* preaching to *parishioners* on a specific *religious topic* in the *place of worship*'. It might fairly be pointed out however that one should ask to what extent code-switching behaviour among Puerto Ricans in New York appears in fact to be *un*-predictable from its observable 'situational context', and might therefore be better described in terms of non-observable factors which enable the analyst not so much to predict as to understand. There are in fact many indications in Fishman's study of code-switching behaviour which takes place against a situational background which does not observably change at all (see especially Hoffman, 1968). Relevant factors are such things as: reprimanding a child versus discussing educational goals and aspirations with him, expression of anger versus warning of impending anger, argument versus discussion, group-therapy situations versus situations which do not threaten personal dignity, 'kidding and joking and impressing the opposite sex at parties', humour, ethnic feeling, asking for a favour, advances in intimacy, the expression of courtesy or respect, and so forth. If such factors account (as they clearly do in the present case) for recurrent code-switching behaviour *within* specific domains and role relationships and settings, then it follows that the latter do not adequately enable one to describe or explain that behaviour. One way out of this impasse might be to subject the results of domain investigation to factor-analysis in the hope of uncovering more generalized constraints which might throw light on these more problematical code-switching behaviours. Fishman argues as much when he refers to the operation of two complementary sets of domains which answer to or 'enact' two corresponding 'cultural identifications' or 'value clusters' for the given society. These are namely the 'high culture' and the 'low culture', the one emphasizing distance and power relationships, formality and ritual, the other ethnicity, spontaneity, comradeship, intimacy, etc. The question is now therefore whether the rather mixed bag of non-observable factors indicated above can properly be resolved into these two major value clusters; but one imagines they cannot. It is certainly true that a given framework of observables (stipulating *who* are the language users in question, *where*, and so forth: Hymes, 1964*b*; Whiteley, 1966) is a prior requirement for the study of non-observables, but it does not follow that the latter should be taken to be merely some distilled essence of the former.

The large-scale sociolinguistic survey is faced with a related methodological dilemma, that of the choice between reliance on the use of questionnaire and interview techniques on the one hand, and on direct observation and inference on the other. Each has its drawbacks. The first, which tends to be the approach of the sociologist, is limited by what is put into the questionnaire (and to some extent the interview) in the first place; the second, the characteristic approach of the ethnographer (and of the descriptive linguist, though both make use of introspection), is limited in its turn by lack of coverage, since the investigator cannot be everywhere at once. The important pioneering (and not yet completed) five-country Survey of Language Use and Language Teaching in Eastern Africa makes for the most part extensive use of questionnaires. The Kenya country study team (led by Professor W. H. Whiteley) promises however to carry out a good deal of direct social anthropological and linguistic observation of code-switching behaviour in rural and urban settings throughout the country, in the Asian communities of Nairobi, and in the homes, recreation centres, and places of employment of people living in middle-income neighbourhoods in the capital city. It was expected in the early stages of this investigation that factors such as religion, caste and/or sect, public or institutional meeting place, fields of activity, ethnicity, generation, length of urban residence, and degree of urban experience would be significant (Bulletin, 2,1: 11, 12).

Direct sociolinguistic observation very frequently forces the question of how to look into private as well as public verbal behaviour. The question has been nicely phrased: 'Is the light still on when the refrigerator door is shut?' To find out, one has of course not only to climb in before closing the door, but also to make sure that one has climbed inside the right refrigerator! In other words, one must be very careful to select the right participants for observation. The participant can also, needless to say, act as informant, commenting not only on his own and others' performance and attitudes to and beliefs about performance but also on his own recent or recorded or (conceivably) concurrent performance. It is only to be expected that the use of recorded material will show that neither the participant nor others concerned are normally prepared for what in fact turns up on the tape. Blom and Gumperz (1970) for example, investigating code-switching behaviour between standard and dialectal forms of speech among a group of Norwegian university students whose studies take them to and fro between rural home locality and university town, find not only that code-switching takes place without any noticeable degree of self-awareness, but also that syntactical and phonological co-occurrence rules break down on occasion, giving rise to 'mixed' forms of speech which surprise their users and displease some of the local inhabitants into the bargain.

Whatever the particular methodological approach adopted, one of the ultimate goals of sociolinguistics is that of identifying some of the more universal social factors involved in people's choice of language, and, along with this, of showing how their choice is manifested in terms of language, dialect, variety, style, variant, etc. The following oppositions characterize some of the main trends in this respect: 'personal' versus 'transactional' language; 'imperative', 'positional', and 'personal' modes of social control; 'formal' and 'informal' language; the language of 'power' and 'solidarity'; and the consideration of how cultural values enter into choice of language more generally.

In both the Norwegian and the Indian contexts Gumperz makes use of the distinction between 'personal' and 'transactional' relationships. A personal relationship is regarded as one in which the participant acts as an individual, 'among friends, within peer-groups, and within the family circle in periods of relaxation. It gives scope to all the facets of an individual's personality'. A transactional relationship possesses 'certain limited goals such as purchasing such items as groceries or clothing . . . going to the doctor', and so forth (Gumperz, 1966: 36). This distinction, coupled with that between 'closed' and 'open' groups in 'friendship' networks (which Gumperz holds to be more significant for choice of language than other role-governed networks such as those of marriage, religion, politics, caste, trade, pilgrimage, etc.), and to a lesser extent with the distinction between local and non-local topics, accounts in his view for a great deal of code-switching behaviour in settings which in many respects may display marked differences.

Bernstein (1965, 1967, 1970) draws attention to a threefold contrast between imperative, positional, and personal modes of social control in social dialects in Britain; but whereas Gumperz regards the peer-group setting as giving scope to 'all the facets of an individual's personality', including the linguistic, Bernstein sees it as favouring the use of a group-oriented 'restricted code' which in the main is characterized as being more predictable and less individualistic than the complementary 'elaborated code'. As he puts it, 'Restricted codes could be considered status or positional codes whereas elaborated codes are oriented to persons' (Bernstein, 1970). At the same time, they are explained psychologically as products of systems of perception which result in a sensitivity to 'objects' and to 'the structure of objects' respectively (Bernstein, 1961). The elaborated code therefore manifests itself in both an 'object mode' and a 'person mode', and it is suggested that upwardly mobile working-class children might be expected to 'move towards' the former rather than the latter. Bernstein distinguishes further between two types of family, 'positional' families in which social control is effected through imperatives or the referring of behaviour to 'normative-status arrangements', and 'person-oriented' families which tend rather to rely on 'appeals' which may be either positional or personal. Positional families lean towards the use of the restricted code, person-oriented families towards the use of the elaborated code. Further than this, inquiries have been made (Bernstein & Henderson, 1969) into the relative emphasis laid by working-class mothers and middle-class mothers on the use of language 'in the person area' and 'in the transmission of basic skills'. The fundamental question asked of them is: 'If parents could not speak, how much more difficult do you think it would be for them to do the following things with young children who had not yet started school?'

The contrast between 'formal' and 'informal' language (or 'careful' and 'casual': Labov, 1964, 1966*a*, *b*) figures in much current sociolinguistic work. These are elusive categories, however, for two main reasons: firstly, it is not easy to determine whether the relevant criteria are linguistic or non-linguistic or both (thus Stewart, 1962, refers to a formalized relationship as that which gives rise to highly predictable and normalized language *and* which is found in 'formal gatherings': but which of these is the strongest criterion?); and secondly, the factor of cultural relativity has to be reckoned with, perhaps even more than is usually the case in the study of language. Fischer (1958) looks at certain aspects of choice of language among a group of children in New England, USA, against a range of social-psychological factors such as compliance, tenseness, sex, topic, socio-economic class, etc., which he regards as together making up a 'formality complex' which may in some sense be universal but whose particular components may vary greatly from one culture to another. This impression is substantiated by comparison with for example Mbaga and Whiteley (1961), who describe the obligatory selection of prefixes in the Bantu language Yao according to a set of very different cultural factors – which they still wish to group under the labels formality and informality.

Less elusive perhaps, and even more favoured dimensions of social motivation in sociolinguistics are those of 'power' and 'solidarity' (for a non-linguistically oriented treatment, see Argyle, 1967). Past and present pronominal usage in European languages (Brown & Gilman, 1960), forms of address in American English (Brown & Ford, 1961), the selection of varieties of Indonesian and Javanese in Indonesia and among Indonesian intellectuals in the United States (Tanner, 1967), bilingual code-switching in Paraguay (Rubin, 1962) – these examples are representative of several others. One should note particularly the diversity of the linguistic means; also that these are independent and compatible axes: obviously power can be expressed with solidarity, and one might even wish to speak of the power of solidarity and vice versa. Rubin's study of code-switching between Spanish and Guarani in Paraguay (Rubin, 1962), and its later development (Rubin, 1963), are particularly interesting. Broadly speaking, in the earlier account Spanish is regarded as the language of power, Guarani as the language of solidarity, choice between them being governed also, but secondarily, by such factors as socio-economic class, urban-rural origin, topic, sex, etc. When positive solidarity accords with equality of power Guarani is the normal medium; Paraguayans meeting abroad tend to use Guarani whatever the circumstances or their relationship; drunkenness invites the use of Spanish, and so forth. The later study however presents the results of the author's analysis of responses to some very elaborate questionnaires as a set of dimensions which indicate the order of decisions which enter into choice of language: rural/non-rural, followed successively by formal/informal, intimate/non-intimate, serious/non-serious, first language learned, proficiency, sex, etc. Change in the order (or the lapse) of any of these decisions will indicate 'culture change'. It will be noticed that the twin dimensions of power and solidarity are not specifically named in this account.

Tanner (1967) notes the relevance of power and solidarity relationships to choice of 'high' and 'low Javanese', but goes on to show that on occasions when they could both be used choice of language becomes difficult. For example, choice between high and low Javanese is not easy if two speakers are both young adults of the same age, good friends, neighbours, of similar educational backgrounds, and sincere Moslems (all of which call for the use of low Javanese), yet of the opposite sex, married, and of different class backgrounds (high Javanese). In such circumstances Indonesian – the language in effect of neutrality, capable of conveying neither respect, disrespect, familiarity, nor unfamiliarity – might well be the best choice.

The linguistic expression of feelings of solidarity opposed to the threat of alien economic power is the theme of Labov (1963). He notes a distinct tendency among many of the inhabitants of Martha's Vineyard (a small island off Massachusetts) to modify the pronunciation of dipthongs in specific ways, and questions why this should be so. Several census-type variables (occupation, age, etc.) seemed to be significant up to a point, but none so markedly as that of a sheer feeling of resentment towards economic exploiters, including tourists, from the mainland, on the part of those who stood most to lose: fishermen in particular, aged between 30 and 45, certain ethnic groups, etc. The linguistic response appears to have been relatively conscious, although not to the point of analytic detail: 'I think we use a totally different type of English language' would be a typical sentiment. There is evidence also that young men who had left for the mainland in search of better jobs, but who had then returned, show the same tendency, but to the point of 'hypercorrection' – a form of linguistic overreaching in the direction of (and beyond) norms associated with strongly held social values.

The linguistic behaviour of Labov's subjects in Martha's Vineyard is not so much determined by their situation as a response to it which is intended in some small way to change the social status quo. This example is just one of very many which might illustrate the point that a great deal (though certainly not all) of verbal behaviour is autonomous and creative from a social no less than from a psychological point of view (if indeed the two can properly be separated in a final analysis). In this connexion, there may be much to be learned by following up the linguistic implications of Barth's social anthropological theory of social organization. Barth sees social organization as arising out of innumerable 'transactional bargains', in which participants seek to achieve reciprocal adjustments between their respective social statuses such that for each 'the value gained ... is greater or equal to the value lost' (Barth, 1966: 4). What one empirically observes then is not 'customs' so much as 'cases' of verbal behaviour, illustrating very often processes of over- and under-communicating statuses (processes of 'impression management': Goffman, 1959). Linguistic hypercorrection is just one of many such processes.

Cultural values themselves might be characterized in such terms as power, solidarity, individuality, ethnic feeling, qualities of leadership or responsibility or maturity or inscrutability and so forth, relative to the culture in question. The more exact identification of cultural values relevant to language will no doubt prove to be a basic issue in sociolinguistics in the coming years. It may or may not be the case that values 'as such are ... rather difficult to define', being 'abstractions or logical types of very high order' (Wallace, 1963: 101–2); they are still fundamental to verbal as to other human behaviour. Labov, for example, on the basis of a great deal of empirical study, has asserted the crucial role of 'evaluative' (or attitudinal) as opposed to 'performance' (or behaviour) norms in the characterization of the New York speech community. Lambert (1961, 1967) puts forward two basic types of language-learning motivation, namely 'integrative' – the wish to identify with the culture of the speakers of the language being learned – and 'instrumental' – the valuation of power, authority, prosperity, etc., which might be acquired along with the language. On 'integrative language learning', see Pride 1969*b*, *c*. Ferguson (1959) indicates aesthetic and other considerations that have given rise to and help to perpetuate situations of 'diglossia' in the Arabic-speaking world and elsewhere. Salisbury (1962) discusses the reasons for the habit of repetition and translation of speeches in parts of New Guinea 'as a linguistic means for emphasizing the importance and public nature of the discourse', even when all present are fluent bilinguals, along with the deliberate magni-fication of language differences. Sorensen (1967) refers to similar patterns of behaviour on the part of Spanish-speaking Indians and non-Indians in the North-West Amazon: anything said in

Spanish is customarily repeated aloud in translation so as to indicate understanding, assent or dissent (according to suffix), and above all respect; also however to serve as a defensive stalling device which allows time to evaluate the intentions of the non-Indians, who tend to 'interrogate' rather than 'converse'. Albert (1964) notes the highly stylized forms of speech among the Burundi appropriate for petitioning a superior for a gift, expressing disagreement, effecting a change in the situation from formal to informal, even deliberately and skilfully making a rhetorical fool of oneself on the right occasion! Geertz (1960) describes the structure and functions of class dialects in Javanese in these terms: 'the patterns of linguistic etiquette modulate, regularize and smoothe the processes of social interaction into an unvarying flow of quiet, emotionally tranquillizing propriety', hence serve as 'a kind of emotional capital which may be invested in putting others at ease' (Geertz, 1960: 255). Other examples of the role of cultural values in choice of language, referred to already, are: socio-economic mobility (Labov); 'pecking orders of intelligibility' related to status feelings (Wolff); 'high' and 'low' value clusters (Fishman); 'local' and 'non-local' values (Blom & Gumperz); modes of social control (Bernstein); formality complexes (Fischer, Mbaga & Whiteley); power and solidarity (Brown & Gilman, Brown & Ford, Rubin, Tanner).

Sociolinguistics studies the varied linguistic realizations of socio-cultural meanings which in a sense are both familiar and unfamiliar – the currency of everyday social interactions which are nevertheless relative to particular cultures, societies, social groups, speech communities, languages, dialects, varieties, styles. It has not been possible in this one short chapter to do full justice to this now rapidly expanding field, but I hope that at least a few of its major lines of advance and areas of theoretical debate will strike the reader as worth looking into further.

17. HISTORICAL LINGUISTICS

Paul Kiparsky

Most linguists in recent years have tended to take the view that the synchronic description of languages is not only independent of their diachronic investigation, but also more important for general linguistic theory (see p. 14). One should perhaps not over-emphasize this point. As a young man, Saussure himself made a very impressive contribution to the reconstruction of Indo-European (the full significance of which was not appreciated until long after his death), and the principles of 'internal' reconstruction that he applied to this task can quite reasonably be described as 'structural', in the sense in which this word came to be used later in relation to synchronic linguistics. Since Saussure there have been other scholars (Benveniste, Jakobson, Kuryłowicz and Martinet – to mention only a few of the most eminent) who have tried to reconcile the apparently conflicting viewpoints of synchronic and diachronic linguistics and have drawn upon their findings in one field to illuminate the other.

Kiparsky's chapter shows how this reconciliation might be achieved within the theory of generative grammar. As he explains at the beginning, he has been deliberately selective in his treatment of the field of historical linguistics, confining himself mainly to 'sound change' and 'analogy' (and showing how they can be formulated in terms of the addition, loss or reordering of rules). He mentions the social context of speech as an important factor in language change, but he does not develop this point, whether in relation to the child's acquisition of language or more generally; and he has not dealt with syntactic or semantic change.

THE first concern of the historical linguist is to understand how languages change. By a long series of historical processes the Proto-Indo-European parent language gradually split up into a number of separate languages such as Germanic, Celtic, Slavic, and these in turn evolved into their numerous modern descendants. The same processes of change are responsible for the diversity of dialects within English – and after some millennia they may well have resulted in a number of languages descended from English in just the same way that English, German, etc., are descended from Proto-Germanic. The nature of these processes stands as the question basic to all further work in historical linguistics.

One front on which this question is being attacked is the close analysis of the history of particular, preferably well-documented, languages, with the purpose of formulating on the basis of the changes there observed, the precisest possible characterization of the 'possible changes' that a language can undergo. This involves distinguishing types of change, such as *sound change* and *analogy*, and finding the conditions and limitations to which each one of these types is subject. Anyone working in historical linguistics soon gains a general feel for these conditions and limitations, without necessarily being able to formulate them in terms of the desired general principles. For example, [p] may change to [f], but hardly to [l] (for an explanation of the use of square brackets, cf. p. 21); a sound change might be restricted to words of one syllable, but never, say, to words of three phonemes, or to palindromes. Things are not always so obvious, of course. Do sounds always change by just one phonetic property at a time? Can sound change be grammatically conditioned? What exactly are the conditions under which analogical change can become operative? Increased depth and precision in the historical study of languages depends on securing reliable answers to a large number of such questions. Some of them are also of great theoretical importance, as will be seen in the following pages.

Complementing this approach to the fundamental question of how languages change are investigations of the social context of speech (cf. pp. 287 301), and of the child's acquisition of language (cf. pp. 242–60). Variant forms and pronunciations may carry social connotations, of which the speaker may or may not be fully aware, and which may influence the course of linguistic change. And we shall not have a complete picture of change if we neglect the fact that language is not acquired ready-made, but must be created anew by each child in a tremendous intellectual achievement, most of which is accomplished between the second and fifth year of his life. It appears that certain types of change – especially so-called 'analogy' – may be traceable back to this continuous re-creation of language.

This short survey is concerned with the recent rethinking of the principles of historical linguistics which has been influenced more or less directly by generative grammar. Most of the discussion is based on Halle (1962), Postal (1968b), Chomsky & Halle (1968), and Kiparsky (1968). Such topics as comparative linguistics and internal reconstruction have had to be omitted for lack of space, although most of the conclusions reached in the discussion are very relevant to them. The reader should also be aware that this survey contains a certain amount of speculation, which I have been encouraged to include by the title of this volume.

Sound Change

The basic issue concerning sound change – and this is still a hornet's nest almost a hundred years after the famous neogrammarian controversies – is best understood in terms of the distinction drawn in linguistics between *performance*, the production and perception of speech, and *competence*, the grammatical structure of language (cf. pp. 27–8). Any sound change is obviously a change both in performance and in competence. When initial [k] and [g] were lost before [n] in seventeenth-century English, words like *knot, knife, gnaw, gnarled* came to be pronounced in a new way, and correspondingly, the grammar of English ceased to contain morphemes beginning with the clusters [kn], [gn]. We can distinguish performance and competence theories of sound change according to which of these two sides of sound change they hold to be primary.

Performance theories of sound change say that sound change arises outside the linguistic system, through modifications of pronunciation due to external factors impinging on performance. Concretely, the process is usually pictured as follows. Before any change had taken place in their grammar, many speakers began to pronounce weakly, and even to omit completely, the [k] and

[g] in words like *knot, gnaw*. When this aberrant pronunciation became sufficiently common, it came to be regarded as standard usage, and the grammar itself was changed to incorporate it.

This notion of performance deviations leading to changes in competence might at first blush seem wholly absurd. Inept performances of a symphony do not change its score, and crimes, however frequent, cannot change the laws they violate. Then how could deviant performances caused by extra-linguistic circumstances lead to changes in the linguistic system? To this one might reply plausibly that laws and musical scores are learned as explicitly formulated norms, whereas grammars can only be abstracted from concrete speech material. Norms of the non-explicit type, such as grammars, might well be constantly subject to revisions bringing them into line with actual performances. Performance theories of sound change postulate a kind of feedback mechanism by which a grammar is, as it were, constantly catching up with its own output.

An important question, which proponents of performance theories have been unable to answer quite satisfactorily, concerns the origin of the performance deviations which supposedly lie behind sound change. A constant tendency towards greater ease of articulation is most often held responsible. It is an undeniable and important fact that sound changes often proceed in the direction of greater ease of articulation – certainly far more often than could be attributed to chance. For example, the dropping of the outer consonant in a cluster (the first consonant of an initial cluster, and the last consonant of a final cluster), is incomparably more frequent than the insertion of such a consonant. Much of the phonological history of a language can be brought under various general processes of weakening, simplification and so on. Still, there are enough sound changes which cannot be understood in these terms at all to rule out a tendency towards greater ease of articulation as the *general* cause of sound change. In its place some linguists have proposed, still less plausibly, that sound change is simply the result of random vacillations. If this were the case, then the phonetic history of a sound, plotted on the phonetic coordinates, would have the character of a random drifting about in various directions; and it would furthermore be difficult to understand why sound changes should so often apply systematically to whole classes of sounds.

If in spite of these and other difficulties, performance theories once dominated the field, the reason was that they seemed to be strongly supported by the empirical findings of historical linguistics. These appeared to be not inconsistent with an interesting factual assumption about sound change: namely, that any sound change can be described in purely phonetic terms, without reference to the grammar of the language. A sound change, according to this assumption, replaces all cases of the sound sequence A (in a given phonetic environment) by another sound sequence B. Such grammatical factors as morphology and syntax could have no effect on this replacement. If sound change were in fact completely independent of grammatical structure, then performance theories would become worth looking for, since the best explanation for the independence of sound change from grammatical structure would be precisely that sound change originates outside grammatical structure, in speech performance.

However, the evidence from historical linguistics at present on the whole favours the opposite conclusion, that sound change *can* depend on grammatical structure, a conclusion which would render untenable any performance theory of sound change. The evidence is, unfortunately, difficult to assess, because we can rarely observe the actual process of sound change, but only the *fait accompli*, and the effect of grammatically conditioned sound changes, which would refute the performance theories, can be sometimes duplicated by various processes such as analogy, which performance theories must in any case allow for. Consider again English [kn], [gn]. When these clusters occurred in the middle of a word, they were not changed, e.g. *acknowledge*, *hackneyed*, *signature*. This condition cannot be expressed in purely phonetic terms, since *a knowledge* and *acknowledge* must have been normally pronounced alike, just as *a board* and *aboard* are normally pronounced alike today (and without this phonetic identity such words as *newt* could not have arisen through the wrong division of *an ewt*). The sound change 'knew' that the two identical stretches of sound *acknowledge* and *a knowledge* were grammatically different, and specifically that they contained one and two words, respectively. The notion of purely phonetic sound change could here be rescued only by the particularly unpalatable expedient of assuming that [k] and [g] were changed even in *acknowledge*, *hackney*, *signature*, etc., but were subsequently restored as spelling pronunciations. The question why they were not similarly reinstated on the basis of the spelling initially as in *knowledge*, *gnat* shows up the implausibility of the solution to which the performance theory in this case leads us.

Especially persuasive are examples of the interaction of morphology and sound change, as in the following case discussed by W. O'Neil (cf. Postal, 1968*b*: 263). The words *fell* and *tell* were in the earliest form of English pronounced *fællyan* and *tællyan*. In Old English (West Saxon) they are distinguished as *fiellan* and *tellan*. The explanation for the different treatment of the two words is revealing. Morphologically they are *fæll*+*yan* (with two [l]'s, seen also in *feallan* 'fall') and *tæl*+*yan* (with a single [l], seen also in *talu* 'tale'). In West Germanic, consonants were doubled before [y], so that both of the verbs came to be pronounced with two [l]'s. Now in Old English vowels were diphthongized before liquids followed by consonants, including sequences of two [l]'s. This so-called 'breaking' affected *fællyan* but not *tællyan* – evidently because breaking applied not to the phonetic form of the words, which were identical but for the irrelevant difference of the first consonant, but to the morphological form of the words, in which only *fællyan* had two [l]'s and therefore was subject to breaking, whereas *tællyan*, understood as *tæl*+*yan* had just one [l] and could not be affected by breaking. This shows that sound changes can distinguish between phonetically identical forms on the basis of grammatical differences, and that the view of sound change as a purely phonetic process, on which the defence of performance theories of sound change rests, cannot be upheld.

Such facts instead argue for competence theories of sound change, that is, theories which maintain that sound change originates in competence and is irreducible to any prior, externally caused changes in performance. According to this view, sound change is change in the phonological part of the grammar. One or another form of this general view would at present probably be accepted by the majority of linguists. How the details are elaborated is in large measure a corollary of what conception of linguistic structure is accepted. A version of it which is very attractive in several respects has been formulated within the framework of generative grammar. Its essential point is that sound change involves the addition of new phonological rules to the grammar.

One great advantage of conceiving of sound changes in terms of new rules added to the phonological component of a grammar is that the types of changes and types of conditionings that occur also figure in the rules of a synchronic grammar. This means that a large part of the work towards characterizing the 'possible sound changes' is independently done in the form of a characterization of the 'possible phonological rules' that may figure in a phonological description. Our above example would be the addition of the rule which we can write

$$k, g \rightarrow \text{ø} / \#\text{—}n$$

'[k] and [g] are "rewritten" as zero (ø) – i.e. are deleted – in the environment of word boundary (#) immediately preceding and [n] immediately following'. In general, any sound change corresponds to a possible phonological rule in grammar, although the converse is not true, for reasons connected with the notion of restructuring discussed later.

A second advantage of this view is that it enables the concept of *ordered rules* to be used in historical linguistics (cf. p. 93), opening up wholly new possibilities of explaining historical phenomena. Implicit in saying that sound changes are added rules is the possibility that some sound changes might be added not just at the end of the existing sequence of rules, but before some of the rules in that sequence. The Old English example mentioned earlier shows that this possibility is not merely hypothetical. Prior to Old English 'breaking', the derivation of the forms *fællyan* and *tællyan* was as follows:

| Basic (morphological) form | fæll+yan | tæl+yan |
| Application of consonant-doubling rule | (no change) | tæll+yan |

After breaking, the forms, now distinguished as *fiellan* and *tellan*, were derived as follows:

Basic (morphological) form	fæll+yan	tæl+yan
Application of breaking	fæall+yan	(not applicable)
Application of consonant-doubling rule	(no change)	tæll+yan

with subsequent umlaut and loss of [y] bringing about the forms *fiellan*, *tellan*. The breaking rule was therefore put into the grammar at a point in the ordering before the consonant-doubling rule. If it had been placed after consonant doubling, there would have been breaking in both forms.

The possibility of placing new rules before existing ones raises an interesting question: is it predictable where a rule is going to be placed in the sequence of existing rules? This is one of the many unsolved problems that lie at the very threshold of historical linguistics. At present all that can be said is that the majority of sound changes are rules added to the end of the existing sequence of phonological rules, in so far as the ordering is fixed at all. Such sound changes are conditioned purely phonetically, whereas rules added earlier in the sequence may be conditioned morphologically.

The significance of such examples was overlooked until relatively recently, in part because such concepts as the ordering of rules, on which these examples depend, were not generally recognized by linguists, and in part also because the debate on the nature of sound change had become deflected from the key question of whether sound change is always independent of grammar to some more subsidiary questions which in themselves are actually unable to decide between the performance and competence theories of sound change. One of these questions is whether sound changes can have exceptions. It is apparent that they can, and that while most sound changes are perfectly regular, the history of every language has incompletely regular sound changes which have failed to apply to particular words for no particular reason. But nothing much seems to depend on this answer as far as the larger theoretical question of performance versus competence theories is concerned, since neither of the two theories is necessarily incompatible with either the possibility or the impossibility of exceptions to sound changes.

A second question, likewise much debated, is whether sound change (apart from certain special types of change such as metathesis) is necessarily gradual, or on the contrary necessarily proceeds in steps, or whether perhaps both types occur. The evidence of dialect maps, which show both sharply differentiated boundaries and, especially in the case of vowels, gradual transitions between different pronunciations, would tend to suggest that both gradual and non-gradual sound change is possible. The idea that sound change is the addition of new rules would also suggest precisely that, since a phonology has both rules applying to binary features such as voiced–unvoiced, high–non-high, and rules specifying phonetic detail by scalar features. But performance theories do not stand and fall on this issue either, since they are not sufficiently clear about what external factors affecting performance they postulate.

The Role of Language Acquisition

Let us consider for a moment what it means to say that a child 'learns' its mother tongue. Obviously it is not given to the child as a finished product, but must be put together by the child from raw materials – the speech of the child's environment. For this the child must use some kind of innate blueprint giving it some general idea of what language is. Just how detailed this blueprint is is a matter of debate among linguists and psychologists (cf. pp. 253–260). What is quite clear is that the child, unlike an adult learning a second language, cannot use explicit rules and exercises, and – at least in the critical pre-school years – benefits little from what adult guidance it may be offered. The child's acquisition of language is therefore an individual act of creation. Moreover, the child learns his mother tongue in complete ignorance of its history. The child is the synchronic linguist *par excellence*. On hearing [nayf] – i.e. the spoken form of the word *knife* – the child will have no reason whatever to postulate a basic form with initial [k] and to set up a rule deleting initial [k] before [n]. Synchrony gives no reason to do so, and history is irrelevant. For this reason a grammar, too, must be unprejudiced by historical considerations and built on the synchronic facts of the language alone.

It follows that rules which are added to grammars through

sound change are retained in the language in so far as there is synchronic justification for them. For example, even the British speaker who pronounces no [r] in *star* has an [r] in the base form of this word if he pronounces [r] in *the star explodes*. His grammar has a rule which drops [r] in the context 'vowel——consonant or pause'. If there is no synchronic justification for retaining the rules in the grammar, the changes which they effect are simply incorporated in the base forms and the rules disappear from the language. What effect the written form of a word has on the base form of a literate speaker is a separate question. The frequent occurrence of spelling pronunciations, such as *falcon* pronounced with [l] in the United States, suggests that it is quite considerable.

A new rule may, then, remain productive in the grammar, or it may lead to *restructuring*. If it were not for restructuring, grammars would just keep growing more complicated as they accumulated rules through sound change, until they would no longer be fit for use in communication.

Recent investigations of child language by Ervin, Bellugi, Klima, McNeill and others show that the evolution of the child's grammar from one stage to another may itself be explained by means of the operation of a similar mechanism of addition of rules and their restructuring. One might have thought that the child would initially have great trouble with irregular forms and strong verbs. This is not so. The first speech of the child correctly reproduces many irregular forms such as *go/went*, and as a matter of fact strong verbs predominate there because of their greater frequency in the language and their general meanings. It is only as the child begins to learn rules that he begins to make mistakes. It is apparent that the child at first commits each inflected form to memory as a separate item, and later eliminates them from memory as he learns general rules for deriving them. Thus, as the child hits on the main rule for forming past-tense forms in English, he not only is able to produce freely past forms like *walked*, *floated*, etc. but also tends to forget the correct irregular forms which he has previously used and regularizes them into *goed*, *hitted*, *drinked*, etc. These forms have then to be relearned as exceptions to the new rule. Later when the subregularities for strong verbs are learned, they too may erase correct forms. Thus, when *sang*, *drank*, etc. are learned, an earlier *brought* may for a time become *brang*.

The forms recorded from the speech of children are exactly the sort of 'analogical' forms that one might expect to see in the future development of English, and which have continuously encroached on the formerly much more complicated morphology of English. Child language is therefore the most likely source of analogical change. A good case can be made for the hypothesis that analogy as historical change arises through the retention into adult language of the over-generalizations that are, as we have just mentioned, a constant characteristic of child language.

Changes of this category are not limited to the simplification of inflectional morphology, but can also involve the simplification of phonological rules, and even their complete dropping from the grammar. There is, furthermore, a strong possibility that they may also result in sound changes. This possibility follows from the observation that the child's learning of the sounds of his language follow a fairly strict progression, which is similar in all children, from simpler to more complex kinds of sounds, in much the same way as his learning of morphology proceeds from the more general, basic rules (e.g. those for weak verbs) to more special rules (e.g. those for strong verbs). For example, children commonly learn the voiceless and voiced '*th*-sounds', [θ] and [ð], fairly late, and often replace them by [v], [f], pronouncing *mouth* as if it were written *mouf*. Suppose now that [θ] in some cases is not learned at all, and that this comes to be accepted usage. The result would be a sound change of the common type termed merger, that is, a falling together of different segment types, usually into the simpler of them – in this case, the merger of interdentals and labials into the labial series – a change which has in fact taken place in some dialects of English. If such a type of sound change could be established, we should have an explanation for the tendency noted earlier for sound change to take a direction towards greater simplicity. (I have assumed that [f] is relatively simple, or 'unmarked', by comparison with [θ]. That this is so would seem to follow also from the fact that [f] is far more common in the world's languages. Ultimately the explanation for such asymmetries must be provided by phonetic theory.)

It would seem, in any case, that the traditionally recognized change mechanism of proportional analogy which regards analogical forms as solutions to equations of the type $walk:walked = bring:x$ (where $x = bringed$), is only a special case of a more general type of change which may be termed simplification, for which the notion of proportion is inappropriate. The characteristic property of these changes is that they simplify the grammar. Like the process called 'restructuring' above, they take place in language acquisition. Restructuring, however, differs from simplification in that it involves no actual change in the language, but merely the substitution, for an unnecessarily complex grammar arising through the addition of a new rule, of a simpler grammar which generates the same language.

The extent to which the process of simplification can cause change presumably depends on the degree of pressure towards linguistic conformity that prevails in the community, either directly, as for example through schooling in prescriptive grammar, or indirectly, as through the form of social organization. What is surprising is how often such changes do take place, and how sweeping they sometimes are. There are several circumstances which may partly help to explain this. It is well known that young children are largely impervious to adult correction of their speech. Furthermore children, in some societies at least, acquire the language of their older contemporaries to a much greater extent than their 'mother tongue'. There tend to be generations which, while not sharply demarcated, are nevertheless associated with typical linguistic characteristics. Furthermore it must be noted that features of child language can survive as variants alongside the adult patterns – cases are even on record where twins retained a form of baby talk as a secret language well into their teens.

General Conclusions

It has been suggested by critics of generative grammar (e.g. Hockett, 1968a) that it has become caught in the fatal trap of taking its theoretical entities such as rules, ordering, underlying base forms, etc., for real entities, whereas they actually, according to Hockett, are only tools to be used for analysing the real entities, such as phonemes and morphemes. It is as if, in Hockett's simile, a pathologist were to confuse his slides and microscopes with the bacteria under investigation.

Historical linguistics supports exactly the opposite conclusion in an especially direct way. We have seen that sound change and analogy is change in the grammatical system of a language, including precisely the rules and their order. If these real events, then, are changes in the rules and their order, then the rules and their order must be real entities, too.

Pushing further on these lines, we may say that historical linguistics is actually one of the best means at the linguist's disposal for investigating the detailed structure of grammars. Language change is for the linguist, to change the analogy a little, what earthquakes and volcanic eruptions are for the geologist, or supernovae for the astronomer. They add welcome new perspective in a field where the object of study is static and not readily amenable to experimental manipulation. Just as the careful analysis of earthquakes may reveal something about the earth's interior, so careful analysis of linguistic changes may reveal otherwise inaccessible aspects of linguistic structure. For example, the issue between performance and competence theories of sound change has wider implications and bears on the nature of phonology itself. Questions as to productivity of rules may be answered on the basis of whether they function in analogical change. The question whether two syntactic constructions are transformationally related may be answered in the affirmative when they are found to be singled out by some joint syntactic innovation which does not affect superficially similar cases. Similar reasoning can be applied in phonology.

But how does this fit in with the earlier point that the history of a language is irrelevant to its grammar? At first sight the use of historical evidence as just advocated might seem inconsistent with the very notion of synchronic linguistics. Actually there are two different, mutually consistent considerations here. One is that the description of a particular language is not to be based on the history of that language but on its synchronic structure. The other is that the general properties of linguistic change are part of the evidence on which our theory of language can be based, and the description of a particular language is carried out with reference to a general theory of language. Hence historical facts can become relevant to description via the theories of grammar and language change. There is no reason why some historical change observed in English, Greek or Nez Perce might not turn out to be evidence for a decision in linguistic theory which in turn may have consequences in the grammatical analysis of French, Papago, or Lower Umpqua.

At the turn of the century most linguists would have agreed with Hermann Paul (1880), that the scientific study of language was necessarily historical. Not long thereafter, under the influence of Saussure's posthumous lectures, general linguistics and historical linguistics began to diverge. Hjelmslev (1953) could actually propose that they were two wholly separate fields, and that historical linguistics should be consigned to some such discipline as sociology or perhaps general history. Today, when developments in linguistic theory have powerfully influenced historical linguistics, and historical linguistics is showing signs of being able to repay its debt, one would have to search hard to find an adherent of either one of these extreme positions. This pendulum may finally have come to a position of rest.

GLOSSARY OF TECHNICAL TERMS

Technical terms that are explained in the text have been omitted from this Glossary; and may be looked up, if necessary, in the Index. Linguistic terms of general currency (e.g. 'sentence', 'relative clause', 'pronoun') have also been omitted. The entries given here are not intended to be comprehensive. In many cases the definitions have been deliberately simplified or related specifically to the sense in which the terms in question are used in *New Horizons in Linguistics*.

accent (1) The prominence of a syllable in terms of *stress, pitch, length* or a combination of these. The accented syllable (sometimes called *tonic*) is indicated in the International Phonetic Alphabet (IPA) by means of a preceding raised vertical stroke. Here an acute accent is used instead: e.g. in ['papa] the first syllable is stressed, in [pa'pa] the second syllable is stressed.

(2) A socially or geographically determined style or pronunciation: e.g. a 'British accent', an 'upper-class accent'.

active (v. *passive*). An active sentence (or clause) is one in which the subject is represented as the *actor* and the object as the *goal*, with respect to the action or process denoted by the verb: e.g. in *This man opened the door, this man* is the subject and *the door* is the object, and the sentence is active. A passive sentence is one in which the goal of the action 'becomes' the subject and the actor (if expressed) forms part of some adverbial phrase (often described as *agentive*, and in English marked by the preposition *by*): e.g. *The door was opened* (*by this man*). The verbs *opened* v. *was opened* are described as being in the active and passive *voice*, respectively.

addressing system A term used in computer science, and then derivatively in such disciplines as psychology and neurophysiology, to refer to a system for labelling and referring to the locations (or registers) in which information is stored.

affix An *inflexional* or *derivational* element added to a base to form a stem or a word: e.g. *-ed* is added to *jump* to form *jumped*; *in-* is added to *complete* to form *incomplete*. If the affix is placed in front of its *base* it is a *prefix*; if it is placed after the *base* it is a *suffix*. The base to which the process of affixation is applied may be a *root* or a *stem*.

affricate A speech sound composed of a *stop* followed by a *homorganic fricative*: e.g. the initial consonant of *chop* [tʃ], composed of the sounds occurring at the beginning of *top* [t] and *shop* [ʃ], respectively.

algorithm A term used in computer science to refer to a program or procedure which, if it is carried out correctly, can be guaranteed to obtain the solution to a particular problem. Not all problems can be solved algorithmically. In that event, the solution may be obtained by means of *heuristic* procedures – roughly speaking, by means of systematized trial-and-error techniques.

alveolar (*consonant*) Articulated with the tip or blade of the tongue against the teeth-ridge: e.g. the [t] of the English word *top*.

analogy The process by which words are created or re-formed according to existing (and usually more 'regular' or 'productive') patterns in the language, as when *shoon* was re-formed as *shoes* by analogy with the existing plurals in *-s*. Analogy is a striking characteristic of children's early utterances.

analytic (v. *synthetic*) In logic and semantics, an *analytic* (or analytically true) sentence, or proposition, is one that is 'necessarily' true, by virtue of its syntactic form and the meaning of the words in it (e.g. *All men are human*). By contrast, a synthetic sentence, if true, is true by virtue of some 'contingent' empirical fact (e.g. *All the girls in this class have brown hair*).

anaphoric reference (= *anaphora*) see *reference*

antecedent A word, phrase or clause that is 'replaced' by a pronoun, usually at some later point in the sentence or in a subsequent sentence: e.g. in *Your brother was here a moment ago, and I haven't seen him leave*, the pronoun *him* replaces or refers back to its antecedent *your brother*.

antonymy 'Oppositeness' of meaning: e.g. *good* and *bad*, or *single* and *married*, are paired antonyms.

argument In logic or mathematics, one of the elements of which a given relation holds: e.g. in $6 > 5$, the relation 'being greater than' holds between the arguments '6' and '5'; in *John is Mary's father*, the relation 'being the father of' holds between the arguments *John* and *Mary*.

articulatory parameters The physiological variables which govern the production of speech.

back vowel Vowel articulated with the back part of the tongue relatively high in the mouth, e.g. *a*; by contrast with a *front* vowel, in which the front part of the tongue is relatively high in the mouth, e.g. [*i*].

base As a morphological term, that part of a word (either a *stem* or a *root*) to which *affixes* may be attached.

bi-labial (*consonant*) Articulated by bringing the lips together e.g. [p], [b] and [m]. Also called *labial*.

bound form A form which (in normal conditions of use) occurs only in combination with other forms; by contrast with a *free* form, which may occur alone as a whole utterance.

case A grammatical category for which, in certain languages, nouns are inflected to indicate their syntactic function (subject, object, etc.) and/or certain spatial and temporal distinctions: e.g. in Latin the subject of the sentence is in the *nominative case* and the object in the *accusative case*. (The term 'case' is used in a number of recent publications to refer to 'deep structure' syntactic relations, whether they are realized inflectionally or not in surface structure.)

cognitive meaning That part of the meaning of words and sentences that is judged to be 'stylistically' neutral. Words may be cognitively *synonymous*, but differ in their *connotations*: e.g. *liberty* and *freedom* in certain contexts. *Cognitive* meaning is also referred to as *denotation* or *denotative* meaning.

collocation A combination of particular lexical items: e.g. *rough* collocates with *diamond* in the (idiomatic) collocation *rough diamond*.

compound (*word*) A combination of two (or more) words that behaves syntactically and phonologically like a single word, e.g. *blackbird*.

conjunction (1) In grammar, any word that is used to combine two clauses in a compound or complex sentence (e.g. *and*, *but*, *or*, *since*, *when*, are conjunctions).

(2) In logic, the operation of combining two (or more) propositions to form a composite proposition by means of the *logical constant* 'and' (symbolically '&'). The constituent propositions are referred to as *conjuncts*. For example, p & q is a proposition resulting from the conjunction of p and q (and is true if both p and q are each true independently, but false if either or both are false).

connotation see *cognitive meaning*.

deictic reference (= *deixis*) see *reference*.

denotative meaning (or *denotation*) see *cognitive meaning*.

dental (*consonant*) Articulated with the tip of the tongue against the teeth: e.g. [t] or [d] in French, [θ] in English *thick*.

derivation (1) In morphology, the process of adding affixes to (or otherwise changing the form of) a root or stem, thereby forming the stem of a different lexeme: e.g. the noun *goodness* is derived from the adjectival root *good* by affixation of *-ness*.

(2) In a generative grammar, the ordered set of strings which results from the successive application of the rules to the initial string is described as a *derivation*.

determiners Such words as *a*, *the*, *some*, *this*, *that* in English.

diacritic A mark added to a letter to make another symbol: e.g. the acute accent used in French or the *umlaut* used in German. More generally, any symbol that is introduced into a text or transcription in order to 'code' some item of information that is not otherwise represented in the text itself.

dichotic stimulation Sending one acoustic stimulus to the left ear and another acoustic stimulus to the right ear at the same time.

diglossia A form of bilingualism in which two languages (or dialects) are used habitually for different purposes or in different social situations.

diphthong A vowel sound in a single syllable which changes quality in the course of its production. Diphthongs are commonly analysed, and symbolized in phonetic transcription, as sequences of two vowels: cf. the vowel [ou] in the Standard English pronunciation of *no*.

disjunction The operation of combining two (or more) propositions to form a composite proposition by means of the *logical constant* 'or' (symbolically 'V'). The constituent propositions are referred to as *disjuncts*. For example, p V q is a proposition resulting from the disjunction of p and q (and is true if either p or q is true).

distinctive feature A feature of the sound system of a language that serves as the crucial distinguishing mark between two phonemes: e.g. /p/ and /b/ are distinguished by *voice*, /b/ and /m/ by *nasality*.

entailment One sentence, or proposition, is *entailed* by another if it follows *analytically* from it: e.g. *John has killed Peter* entails (or 'implies') *Peter is dead*.

ergative A term used for the *case* of the subject of a *transitive* verb when this differs from the case of the subject of an intransitive verb. (The term is used in a related, but somewhat different, sense in a number of recent publications, including the chapter by Halliday.)

formant One of the regions of concentration of energy prominent on a *sound spectrogram*.

free form see *bound form*.

fricative (*consonant*) Articulated with partial closure in the mouth such as to cause audible friction as the air passes through. Fricatives are classified as *dental* ([θ] as in *thick*, [ð] as in *there*); *labio-dental* ([f] as in *fat*, [v] as in *vat*); *velar* ([x] as in Scottish *loch* or German *auch*); etc., according to the place of partial closure (the *place* of articulation). Other fricatives are [s] as in *said* and [ʃ] as in *shed*.

front vowel see *back vowel*.

fundamental (*frequency*) In acoustics, the generator of a series of harmonics. Auditorily, the fundamental corresponds to the lowest heard pitch, and thus to the *intonation* of an *utterance*.

goal see (*active* v. *passive*).

head (*of a construction*) The principal or obligatory constituent: e.g. the noun in a noun phrase, the verb in a verb phrase.

heuristic see *algorithm*.

homorganic Having the same *place of articulation*.

hyponymy More specific terms subsumed under a more general term are described as its hyponyms: e.g. *rose*, *tulip*, etc. are hyponyms of *flower*.

idiolect The form (or *variety*) of a language that is spoken by an individual speaking in a given style. Two individuals may speak the same *dialect*, but differ in idiolect.

inflection A change made in the form of a word in order to mark its syntactic function in the sentence. Inflection is commonly marked by *affixation*: e.g. the affixation of *-s* to *sing* to form the '3rd person singular present tense' of the lexeme SING. Inflection is frequently contrasted with *derivation* within *morphology*.

intonation The *pitch pattern*, or 'melody', of a sentence, indicating whether it is a question or a statement, whether the speaker is surprised, angry, hesitant, etc.

isogloss In dialect geography, a line on a map separating two areas which differ in some feature of their speech, as in the use of a particular speech sound, word or grammatical construction.

labial see *bi-labial*.

lateral (*consonant*) Articulated so that the breath is obstructed in the centre of the mouth and passes on either or both sides of the tongue: e.g. [l] in *leaf* or *feel*.

length Sounds and syllables are described as *long* or *short* when their relative length or duration is phonologically relevant in the language. Length (which is also called *quantity*) may be indicated by a 'macron' (i.e. a short horizontal stroke) above the vowel or a colon following the vowel. Thus [ē] and [eː] are alternative ways of symbolizing 'a long *e*-vowel'.

lexical item Minimal 'fully meaningful' element. ('Fully meaningful' is deliberately vague. There is perhaps no sharp distinction to be drawn between elements with lexical, and elements with grammatical, meaning.) In principle, a *lexicon* gives a list of all the lexical items in the language. Lexical items are often referred to, loosely, as 'words'.

lexicalization (1) The introduction of *lexical items* into the strings of symbols generated by a grammar.

(2) See *lexicalized*.

lexicalized (1) Realized, or represented, as a *lexical item*, rather than a 'purely grammatical' element (*lexicalized* v. *grammaticalized*).

(2) Operating as one lexical item, rather than as a phrase consisting of a number of distinct lexical items (e.g. *red herring* in its idiomatic sense).

liquid (*consonant*) A frictionless speech sound articulated with only partial obstruction of the air stream. [1] and [r] are liquids, when, as in English, they are pronounced without audible friction.

logical constants Symbols with a fixed value that combine with propositional variables in a logical calculus to form valid (or *well-formed*) formulae. The principal logical constants in the propositional calculus are 'and' ('&'), 'or' ('V') and 'not' ('∼'). For example, ∼ pVq is a well-formed formula with two logical constants and two propositional variables. Regardless of the value of the variables (i.e. no matter what actual propositions are substituted for them) this *disjunction* is true provided that either 'not-p' is true (i.e. 'p' is false) or 'q' is true (or both 'not-p' and 'q' are true).

long vowel see *length*.

manner of articulation A category (subsuming such terms as *stop*, *fricative*) for the classification of consonants according to the manner in which the vocal tract is constricted during articulation.

metathesis The transposition of sounds (or letters) in a word: e.g. where [aralo] is changed to [alaro].

modality A term used in logic (related to grammatical *mood* and also used by linguists) having to do with possibility or probability, necessity or contingency, rather than merely with truth or falsity.

mood A grammatical category (frequently realized in the verb in the distinction of indicative, subjunctive, imperative, etc.) indicating the speaker's attitude – his doubt or certainty ; whether he is expressing a wish, issuing a command, asking a question, etc. In English such auxiliary verbs as *will*, *shall*, *may*, *can*, and *must* have a *modal* function.

nasal (*consonant*) Articulated by making a complete closure in the mouth and lowering the soft palate (or *velum*), so that the air passes through the nose: e.g. [n] is a (*dental* or *alveolar*) nasal corresponding to the *oral* consonant [d]; [m] is a (*labial*) nasal corresponding to [b].

nasalized (*vowels*) Vowels are most commonly produced with the soft palate raised (see *oral*). If the soft palate is lowered so that the air issues simultaneously from the mouth and the nose, they are *nasalized* (or *nasal*). European languages with nasalized vowels include French, Portuguese and Polish. Nasalization is symbolized by means of a tilde over the vowel: e.g. French *bon* [bɔ̃].

noise In acoustics, and then more generally in communication theory, any disturbance in a communications system that interferes with or prevents the reception of a signal or information.

ontology A branch of philosophy directed to the question: What really exists? Hence, by *ontological commitment* (or being committed to a certain *ontology*) is meant the acceptance, as a consequence of one's philosophical beliefs, that certain entities exist or are real.

operator see *logical constant*, *quantification* and *scope*.

oral Articulated with the soft palate raised, thus preventing the passage of air through the nose. The term *oral* may be contrasted with either *nasal* or *nasalized*.

ordering (of *rules*) In a generative grammar, rules are said to be *ordered* (v. *unordered*), if they have to apply in a particular sequence. (They may be extrinsically or intrinsically ordered: i.e. by external convention or by the interrelationships of the rules themselves.)

output conditions A term used in generative grammar to refer to a set of conditions imposed upon the surface structure of sentences and operating as a kind of 'filter' which lets through only those sentences generated by the grammar which satisfy the conditions. 'Output conditions' may be contrasted with such *deep structure constraints* as *selection restrictions*.

palatalized Articulated with the front of the tongue raised towards the hard palate this being a secondary articulation which accompanies the primary articulation of the consonant (as *dental*, *labial*, *velar*, etc.) and gives to it a distinctive 'clear', rather than 'dark', quality.

palindrome A word which can be written or transcribed from back to front, or from front to back, indifferently: e.g. *pip*, *madam*.

parameter One of the independent variables in an equation or mathematical function.

parsing The syntactic analysis of a sentence, especially in terms of its *constituent structure*.

passive see *active*.

place of articulation A category (subsuming such terms as *dental*, *labial*, *velar*) for the classification of consonants according to the place in the mouth at which the closure or obstruction is made.

plosive Of a *stop* (or *occlusive*) consonant: characterized by plosion, i.e. the sudden release of air after closure, e.g. [p] as in *poppy*.

post-vocalic Occurring immediately after a vowel.

predicate calculus (also called the *calculus of functions*): see *quantification*.

propositional calculus A logical system for the representation of propositions as formulaic combinations of *variables* (p, q, r, . . .) and a limited number of *operators* (or *logical consonants*) such as 'not', 'and', 'or'. (See *logical constant*, *conjunction*, *disjunction*.)

quantification Making explicit whether a predication holds for all members of a class, at least one member of a class or only one member, etc.: e.g. *Men are mortal* is not explicitly quantified, whereas *All men are mortal* and *Some men are mortal* are.

The principal quantifiers (i.e. *operators* used for quantification) used in logic (and, more particularly, in the *predicate calculus*) are the universal quantifier, (x), where the variable bound by the quantifier is simply put in brackets, and (∃x), where it is put in brackets and preceded by the symbol for the quantifier, a reversed E. *All men are mortal* might be symbolized as (x) (Fx ⊃ Gx): 'For all values of x it is true that, if x has the property F [being a man], x also has the property G [being mortal]'. *Some men are mortal* might be symbolized as (∃x) (Fx ⊃ Gx): 'For some values (i.e. at least one value) of x, it is true that . . .'.

quantity (of a sound or syllable) see *length*.

reference (1) The relationship between linguistic expressions and the persons or objects they designate (or otherwise identify): e.g. *this man* might refer to one person on one occasion and another person on a different occasion. Different expressions may refer to the same entity: e.g. *Walter Scott* and *the author of 'Waverley.'*

(2) In grammar, pronouns are often said to refer, either *anaphorically* to an *antecedent* noun or noun phrase, or *deictically*, to a person or object or other 'feature' of the situation of utterance.

reflexive (1) In grammar, a *reflexive verb* is one whose subject and object are referentially identical: e.g. *John shot himself*, where *himself* is a *reflexive pronoun* referring to the subject. In *John was shaving* (under the normal interpretation), the verb is implicitly, rather than explicitly, reflexive.

(2) In logic, a relation R is reflexive if, for all values of x, xRx. For example, 'equality' is reflexive: $1 = 1$, $2 = 2$, etc.

root In morphology, that part of the form of a word which remains when all the *derivational* and *inflectional affixes* have been removed: e.g. *accept* is the root of *accept-ed*, *accept-ance*, *un-accept-abil-ity*, etc. (See also *base*.)

scope In logic, the range of application of an operator, indicated by brackets (and by a set of conventions establishing a hierarchy among the different operators). In ∼ p & q, which may be

read as 'not p and q', the scope of the negative operator ('∼')
is the first of the two *conjuncts*, so that the complex proposition
is interpreted as 'both not-p and q hold'; in ∼ (p & q), the
scope of negation is the whole *conjunction* (within the brackets),
so that the complex proposition reads 'it is not the case that
both p and q hold'.

semivowel A vowel-like sound which functions phonologically
like a consonant: e.g. the initial sound of *wet* or *yet*.

spectrograph An instrument for the acoustic analysis of speech
showing the distribution of energy over the sound *spectrum*
(i.e. at different frequencies). A *spectrogram* is a visual representation of the analysis produced by a spectrograph.

speech community All the people who use a given language (or
dialect).

stochastic process In communication theory, a sequence of events
or symbols determined by transitional probabilities (i.e.,
roughly speaking, by probabilities dependent upon the occurrence of previous events and symbols).

stop (*consonant*) Articulated with complete closure in the mouth,
(e.g. [p], [t], [k], etc.)

stress Emphasis on a syllable or word in the form of prominent
relative loudness. (See *accent*.)

stylistic Having to do with 'style'. Hence, linguistic differences
that are attributed to style rather than to meaning proper
(*cognitive meaning*) or *dialect* are often referred to as matters
of *stylistic variation*.

suprasegmental (*features*) Features like *stress*, *tone*, *length*, etc.
which may combine with (be superimposed upon) segments.
The segments are normally consonants or vowels or groups of
consonants and vowels.

symmetrical relations In logic, a relation is described as symmetrical if (for all values of x and y) it holds between x and y
'in both directions'. The relation *being the cousin of* (in
English) is *symmetrical*. By contrast *being the father of* is
asymmetrical.

synonymous Having the same meaning as.

tone Relative pitch or movement of pitch, characteristic of certain languages ('tone languages') which serves to distinguish words or grammatical categories.

transformation (1) In generative grammar, a rule which operates under certain precisely defined conditions of structural analysability and *transforms* one grammatical structure into another typically by means of the operations of addition, deletion and substitution.

(2) In logic, a rule of inference: e.g. (p & q) ⊃ p, 'from the conjunction of p and q one can infer p'.

transitive (v. *intransitive*) (1) In syntax, a verb is described as transitive if it takes a direct object in an *active* sentence. In English (and certain other languages) the object of a transitive verb in an active sentence corresponds to the subject of a passive sentence.

(2) In logic, a relation is described as transitive, if, for all values of x, y and z, when it holds between x and y and between y and z, it also holds between x and z. For example, 'greater than' is *transitive*. 'Being five feet away from' is *intransitive*.

typology The classification of languages according to their structural 'type': phonogolically (e.g. 'tone languages'), morphologically (e.g. 'agglutinating' languages), or syntactically (e.g. 'subordinating' languages).

umlaut A term used in German grammar to indicate the relationship between *back vowels* and *front vowels* in morphologically related words, marked in the German spelling system by means of two dots (called an umlaut sign) placed over the basic vowel: cf. *Mann, Männer*. Historically, this morphological relation is explained as being due to the 'fronting' of the vowel in particular contexts. This process also occurred in Old English and has left traces in Modern English: cf. *man, men*.

universe of discourse All the assumptions and presuppositions accepted as relevant in a given discussion and determining the interpretation of otherwise ambiguous words and sentences.

variable A symbol that may assume any of a given set of values, its *range* of values.

voice (1) In phonetics: the result of vibration of the vocal cords.

A *voiced* sound (e.g. [b]) is one that is produced with accompanying voice; a *voiceless* sound (e.g. [p]) is produced without voice. Vowels are normally voiced.

(2) In grammar, a term applied to the distinction of *active* and *passive*.

zero The absence of an element may be described (under certain conditions) as the occurrence of a *zero element* (symbolized as 'ø'). For example, the plural form *sheep* might be analysed morphologically as *sheep* + ø, where the zero morph realizes the plural morpheme that is more regularly realized by *s*.

BIBLIOGRAPHY

This list includes all the books and articles referred to in the various chapters of *New Horizons in Linguistics*. The following abbreviations have been used for the more commonly cited periodicals:

AJPsych	*American Journal of Psychology*. Worcester, Mass.
AL	*Acta Linguistica*. Revue internationale de linguistique structurale. Copenhagen.
ALH	*Acta Linguistica Academiae Scientiarum Hungaricae*. Budapest.
AmA	*American Anthropologist*. Menasha, Wisc.
AnL	*Anthropological Linguistics*. Bloomington, Ind.
ArchL	*Archivum Linguisticum*. Glasgow.
BJPsych	*British Journal of Psychology*. London.
BSE	*Brno Studies in English*. Brno.
FL	*Foundations of Language*. International journal of language and philosophy. Dordrecht, Holland.
IF	*Indogermanische Forschungen*. Zeitschrift für Indogermanistik und allgemeine Sprachwissenschaft. Berlin.
IJAL	*International Journal of American Linguistics*. Baltimore.
JAcS	*Journal of the Acoustical Society of America*. Menasha, Wisc.
JEBiol	*Journal of Experimental Biology*. Cambridge.
JEPsych	*Journal of Experimental Psychology*. Princeton, N.J.
JL	*Journal of Linguistics*. The Journal of the Linguistics Association of Great Britain. London and New York.
JSocPsych	*Journal of Social Psychology*. Worcester, Mass.
JSHR	*Journal of Speech and Hearing Research*. Washington, D.C.
JThBiol	*Journal of Theoretical Biology*. London.
JVLVB	*Journal of Verbal Learning and Verbal Behaviour*. New York.
KZ	*Zeitschrift für vergleichende Sprachforschung auf dem Gebiete der indogermanischen Sprachen*. (Begründet von A. Kuhn.) Göttingen.
L&S	*Language and Speech*. Teddington, England.
Lg.	*Language*. Journal of the Linguistic Society of America. Baltimore.

Lingua	*Lingua.* International Review of General Linguistics/ Revue internationale de linguistique générale. Amsterdam.
MSLL	*Monograph Series on Languages and Linguistics.* Georgetown University, Washington, D.C.
MT	*Mechanical Translation.* Cambridge, Mass.
PMLA	*Publications of the Modern Language Association of America.* New York.
Psych Rev	*Psychological Review.* Lancaster, Pa.
QJEPsych	*Quarterly Journal of Experimental Psychology.* Cambridge.
QRPsych	*Quarterly Review of Psychology.* London.
StGram	*Studia Grammatica.* Berlin.
TCLC	*Travaux du cercle linguistique de Copenhague.* Copenhagen.
TCLP	*Travaux du cercle linguistique de Prague.* Prague.
TLP	*Travaux linguistiques de Prague.* Prague.
TPhS	*Transactions of the Philological Society.* Oxford.
UCPL	*University of California Publications in Linguistics.* Berkeley and Los Angeles.
Word	*Word.* Journal of the Linguistic Circle of New York. New York.
ZPhon	*Zeitschrift für Phonetik, Sprachwissenschaft und Kommunikationsforschung.* Berlin.

Abercrombie, D. (1965). *Studies in Phonetics and Linguistics.* London: Oxford University Press.

Abercrombie, D. (1967). *Elements of General Phonetics.* Edinburgh: Edinburgh University Press; Chicago: Aldine.

Alajouanine, T. & Lhermitte, F. (1964). 'Non-verbal communication in aphasia'. In De Reuck, A. V. S. & O'Connor, M. (eds.), *Disorders of Language.* London: Churchill.

Albert, E. M. (1964). 'Rhetoric, logic and poetics in Burundi: culture patterning of speech behaviour'. In Gumpertz & Hymes (1964) (=*AmA* 66: 6, part 2: 35–55).

Allen, W. Sidney (1962). *Sandhi.* The Hague: Mouton.

Allen, W. Sidney (1964). 'Transitivity and possession'. *Lg.*, 40. 337–43.

Altman, S. A. (1968). 'Primates.' In Sebeok, T. A. (ed.), *Animal Communication.* Bloomington: Indiana University Press.

Anderson, John M. (1968*a*). 'Ergative and nominative in English'. *JL*, 4. 1–32.

Anderson, John M. (1968*b*). 'On the status of "lexical formatives"'. *FL*, 4. 308–18.

Bibliography

Andrew, R. J. (1963). 'Trends apparent in the evolution of vocalization in the old world monkeys and apes'. *Symp. Zool. Soc. Lond.*, 10. 89–101.

Argyle, M. (1967). *The Psychology of Interpersonal Behaviour*. Harmondsworth: Penguin Books.

Austin, J. L. (1962). *How to do Things with Words*. Cambridge, Mass.: Harvard University Press.

Bach, Emmon (1964). *An Introduction to Transformational Grammars*. New York: Holt, Rinehart & Winston.

Bach, Emmon (1968). 'Nouns and noun phrases'. In Bach & Harms (1968).

Bach, Emmon & Harms, R. T. (eds.) (1968). *Universals in Language*. New York: Holt, Rinehart & Winston.

Bailey, W. & Burton, M. (1968). *English Stylistics: A Bibliography*. Cambridge, Mass.: M.I.T. Press.

Bally, Charles (1932). *Linguistique générale et linguistique française*. Paris: Ernest Leroux.

Bar-Hillel, Y. (1954). 'Logical syntax and semantics'. *Lg*, 30. 230–37.

Bar-Hillel, Y. (1964). *Language and Information*. Reading, Mass.: Addison-Wesley; Jerusalem: Jerusalem Academic Press.

Barker, M. A. R. (1964). *Klamath Grammar*. (*UCPL*, 32). Berkeley and Los Angeles: University of California Press.

Barth, F. (1966). *Models of Social Organization*. Occasional Paper No. 23, Royal Anthropological Institute of Great Britain and Ireland.

Bartlett, F. C. (1932). *Remembering: An Experimental and Social Study*. London: Cambridge University Press.

Bazell, C. E. (1952). 'The correspondence fallacy in structural linguistics'. *Studies by Members of the English Department, Istanbul University*, 3. 1–41. (Reprinted in Hamp *et al.*, 1966.)

Bazell, C. E. (1953). *Linguistic Form*. Istanbul: Istanbul University Press.

Bazell, C. E. (1958). *Linguistic Typology*. London: School of Oriental and African Studies.

Bazell, C. E. (1964). 'Three misconceptions of "grammaticalness"'. *MSLL*, 17. 3–9.

Bazell, C. E., Catford J. C., Halliday, M. A. K. & Robins, R. H. (eds.) (1966). *In Memory of J. R. Firth*. London: Longmans.

Bellugi, U. & Brown, R. (eds.) (1964). *The Acquisition of Language*. (Monographs of the Society for Research in Child Development, 92.) Lafayette, Ind.: Child Development Publications.

Bendix, E. H. (1966). *Componental Analysis of General Vocabulary:*

The Semantic Structure of a Set of Verbs in English, Hindi and Japanese. (Part 2 of *IJAL*, 32.) Bloomington: Indiana University; The Hague: Mouton.

Bennett, J. (1964). *Rationality.* London: Routledge & Kegan Paul.

Berko, J. (1958). 'The child's learning of English morphology'. *Word* 14. 150–77. (Reprinted in Saporta, 1961).

Bernstein, B. (1961). 'Social class and linguistic development: a theory of social learning'. In J. Floud, A. M. Halsey & A. Anderson (eds.), *Society, Economy and Education.* Glencoe, Illinois: The Free Press.

Bernstein, B. (1965). 'A sociolinguistic approach to social learning'. In J. Gould (ed.), *The Penguin Survey of the Social Sciences 1965.* Harmondsworth: Penguin Books.

Bernstein, B. (1967). 'Elaborated and restricted codes'. In Lieberson (1967).

Bernstein, B. (1970). 'A sociolinguistic approach to socialization'. In Gumperz and Hymes (1970).

Bernstein, B. & Henderson, D. (1969). 'Social class differences in the relevance of language to socialization'. *Sociology* 3: 1.

Bever, T., Fodor, J. & Garrett, M. (1968). 'A formal limitation of associationism'. In J. Dixon & D. Harton (eds.), *Verbal Behavior and General Behavior Theory.* Englewood Cliffs, N.J.: Prentice-Hall.

Bever, T. G., Fodor, J. A. & Weksel, W. (1965). 'The acquisition of syntax: a critique of contextual generalization'. *Psych Rev*, 72. 467–82.

Beveridge, W. I. B. (1961). *The Art of Scientific Investigation.* London: Mercury Books.

Bierwisch, M. (1965). Eine Hierarchie syntaktisch-semantischer Merkmale. *StGram*, 5. 29–86.

Bierwisch, M. (1967). 'Some semantic universals of German adjectivals'. *FL*, 3. 1–36.

Bierwisch, M. (1968). 'Two critical problems in accent rules'. *JL*, 4. 173–8.

Bierwisch, M. (1969). 'Certain problems of semantic representations'. *FL*, 5. 153–84.

Bierwisch, M. & Heidolph, K. (1969). *Progress in Linguistics.* The Hague: Mouton.

Black, Max (1959). 'Linguistic relativity: the views of Benjamin Lee Whorf'. *Philosophical Review*, 68, 228–38.

Bloch, J. (1947). 'English verb inflection'. *Lg*, 23, 399–418. (Reprinted in Joos, 1957).

Bloch, B. (1950). 'Studies in colloquial Japanese – IV: Phonemics'. *Lg.*, 26, 86–125. (Reprinted in Joos, 1957).

Bibliography

Bloch, B. & Trager, G.(1942). *Outline of Linguistic Analysis*. Baltimore: Waverley Press.

Blom, J. P. & Gumperz, J. J. (1970). 'Some social determinants of verbal behavior'. In Gumperz & Hymes (1970).

Bloomfield, L. (1926). 'A set of postulates for the science of language'. *Lg.*, 2. 153–64. (Reprinted in Joos, 1957).

Bloomfield, L. (1933/1935). *Language*. New York: Holt, Rinehart & Winston, 1933; London: Allen & Unwin, 1935.

Bloomfield, L. (1939). 'Menomini morphophonemics'. *TCLP*, 8. 105–15.

Boas, F. *Race, Language and Culture*. New York: Macmillan.

Bolinger, D. L. (1948). 'On defining the morpheme'. *Word*, 4. 18–23.

Bolinger, D. L. (1961). 'Syntactic blends and other matters'. *Lg.*, 37. 366–81.

Bolinger, D. L. (1965). 'The atomization of meaning'. *Lg.*, 41. 555–73.

Bolinger, D. L. (1968). *Aspects of Language*. New York: Harcourt, Brace & World.

Boomer, D. S. (1965). 'Hesitation and grammatical encoding'. *L&S*, 8. 148–58. (Reprinted in Oldfield & Marshall, 1968.)

Boomer, D. S. & Dittmann, A. T. (1962). 'Hesitation pauses and juncture pauses in speech'. *L&S*, 5. 215–20.

Boomer, D. S. & Laver, J. D. M. (1968). 'Slips of the tongue'. *British Journal of Disorders of Communication*, 3. 2–12.

Borko, H. (ed.) (1967). *Automated Language Processing*. New York: Wiley.

Bossert, W. H. & Wilson, E. O. (1963). 'The analysis of olfactory communication among animals'. *J Th Biol*, 5. 443–69.

Botha, R. P. (1968). *The Function of the Lexicon in Transformational Generative Grammar*. The Hague: Mouton.

Boyd, J. & Thorne, J. P. (1969). 'The semantics of modal verbs'. *JL*, 5. 57–74.

Bréal, Michel. *Essai de sémantique*. Paris: Hachette, 1897. Translated as *Semantics: Studies in the Science of Meaning*. New York: Dover, 1964.

Bresson, F. (1963). 'La signification'. In J. de Ajuriaguerra *et al. Problèmes de psycholinguistique*. Paris: Presses Universitaires de France.

Bright, William (ed.) (1966). *Sociolinguistics*. (Proceedings of the U.C.L.A. Sociolinguistics Conference, 1964). The Hague: Mouton.

Broadbent, D. E. (1966). 'The well-ordered mind'. *American Educational Research Journal*, 3. 281–95.

Broadbent, D. E. (1967). 'Word frequency effect and response bias'. *Psych Rev*, 74. 1–15.

Broca, P. (1863). 'Localisation des fonctions cérébrales. Siège du langage articulé'. *Bulletin of Social Anthropology*, 4. 200.

Brower, Reuben A. (ed) (1959). *On Translation*. Cambridge, Mass.: Harvard University Press.

Brown, Roger W. (1958a). *Words and Things*. Glencoe, Illinois: Free Press.

Brown, Roger W. (1958b). 'How shall a thing be called?' *Psych Rev*, 65. 14–21. (Reprinted in Oldfield & Marshall, 1968.)

Brown, Roger W. (1968). 'The development of *wh*-questions in child speech'. *J V L V B*, 7. 279–90.

Brown, R. & Ford, M. (1961). 'Address in American English'. In Hymes, *Language in Culture and Society*. (Also in *Journal of Abnormal and Social Psychology*, 1961. 375–85.)

Brown, R. & Fraser, C. (1963). 'The acquisition of syntax'. In Cofer, C. N. & Musgrave, J. K. (eds.), *Verbal Behavior and Learning*. New York: McGraw-Hill. (Reprinted in Bellugi & Brown, 1964.)

Brown, R. & Gilman, A. (1960). 'The pronouns of power and solidarity'. In T. A. Sebeok (ed.), *Style in Language*. Cambridge, Mass.: M.I.T. Press. (Reprinted in Fishman, 1968a.)

Brown, R. & Hanlon, C. (1970). 'Derivational complexity and order of acquisition in child speech'. In Hayes (1970).

Brown, R. & McNeill, D. (1966). 'The "tip of the tongue" phenomenon'. *J V L V B*, 5. 325–37.

Bruce, D. J. (1956). 'Effects of context upon intelligibility of heard speech'. In Cherry, C. (ed.) *Information Theory: Third London Symposium*. London: Butterworth. (Reprinted in Oldfield & Marshall, 1968.)

Bühler, Karl (1934). *Sprachtheorie*. Jena.

Bühler, Karl (1935). 'Einleitung'. *Arch. f. d. ges. Psychol.*, 94, 401–12.

Bulletin of the Survey of Language Use and Language Teaching in Eastern Africa (1967–). Survey Office, P. O. Box 30641, Nairobi.

Callow, J. C. (1968). 'A hierarchical study of neutralization in Kasem'. *JL*, 4. 33–45.

Campbell, R. & Wales, R. J. (1969). 'Comparative structures in English'. *JL*, 5. 215–51.

Carnap, Rudolph (1956). *Meaning and Necessity*, 2nd edition. Chicago: University of Chicago Press.

Cattell, J. M. (1887). 'Experiments on the association of ideas'. *Mind*, 12. 68–74.

Bibliography

Chafe, W. L. (1967). 'Language as symbolization'. *Lg.*, 43. 57–91.

Chafe, W. L. (1968). 'Idiomaticity as an anomaly in the Chomskyan paradigm'. *FL*, 4. 109–27.

Chandler, R. (1952). *The Lady in the Lake*. Harmondsworth: Penguin.

Cherry, Colin (1957). *On Human Communication*. Cambridge, Mass.: M.I.T. Press. (Reprinted in New York: Science Editions, 1959.)

Chomsky, N. (1956). 'Three models for the description of language'. *IRE Transactions on Information Theory*, IT-2. 113–24.

Chomsky, N. (1957). *Syntactic Structures*. The Hague: Mouton.

Chomsky, N. (1959). Review of *Verbal Behavior* by B. F. Skinner. *Lg.*, 35. 26–58.

Chomsky, N. (1961). 'On the notion "rule of grammar"'. In R. Jakobson (ed.), *Structure of Language and its Mathematical Aspects*. Providence, Rhode Island: American Mathematical Society.

Chomsky, N. (1962). 'A transformational approach to syntax'. In A. Hill (ed.), *Proceedings of the Third Texas Conference on Problems in Linguistic Analysis in English, 1958*. Austin, Texas: University of Texas Press.

Chomsky, N. (1963). 'Formal properties of grammars'. In Luce, Bush & Galanter (1963).

Chomsky, N. (1965a). *Current Issues in Linguistic Theory*. The Hague: Mouton.

Chomsky, N. (1965b). *Aspects of the Theory of Syntax*. Cambridge, Mass.: M.I.T. Press.

Chomsky, N. (1966a). *Topics in the Theory of Generative Grammar*. The Hague: Mouton. (Also in Sebeok, 1966.)

Chomsky, N. (1966b). *Cartesian Linguistics*. New York and London: Harper & Row.

Chomsky, N. (1966c). 'Linguistic theory'. In Robert E. Mead (ed.), *Language Teaching: Broader Contexts* (Northeast Conference Reports).

Chomsky, N. (1968). *Language and Mind*. New York: Harcourt, Brace & World.

Chomsky, N. (1969). 'Remarks on nominalization'. In Jacobs & Rosenbaum (1969).

Chomsky, N. (forthcoming). 'Deep structure, surface structure and semantic interpretation'.

Chomsky, N. & Halle, M. (1968). *The Sound Pattern of English*. New York: Harper & Row.

Chomsky, N. & Miller, G. (1963). 'Introduction to the formal analysis of language'. In Luce, Bush & Galanter (1963).

Clark, H. H. (1964). *Some Structural Properties of Simple Active and Passive Sentences*. Unpublished Master's thesis, The John Hopkins University.

Clark, H. H. (1968). 'On the use and meaning of prepositions'. *JVLVB*, 7. 421–31.

Clark, H. H. (1969). 'Linguistic processes in deductive reasoning'. *Psych Rev*, 76. 387–404.

Clark, H. H. & Card, S. K. (1969). 'The role of semantics in remembering comparative sentences'. *JEPsych*, 82. 545–53.

Clark, H. H. & Clark, E. V. (1968). 'Semantic distinctions and memory for complex sentences'. *QJEPsych*, 20. 129–38.

Clark, H. H. & Stafford, R. A. (1969). 'Memory for semantic features in the verb'. *JEPsych*, 80. 326–34.

Clifton, C. (1967). 'The implications of grammar for word associations'. In Salzinger, K. & Salzinger, S. (eds.), *Research in Verbal Behavior and Some Neurophysiological Implications*. New York: Academic Press.

Compton, A. J. (1967). 'Aural perception of different syntactic structures and lengths'. *L&S*, 10. 81–7.

Conrad, R. (1964). 'Acoustic confusions in immediate memory'. *BJPsych*, 55. 75–84.

Cornish, E. R. & Wason, P. C. (1969). 'The recall of affirmative and negative sentences in an incidental learning task'. *QJEPsych* (in press).

Craik, K. J. W. (1947). 'Theory of the human operator in control systems. I. The operator as an engineering system'. *BJPsych*, 38. 56–61.

Crystal, David (1965). *Linguistics, Language and Religion*. London: Burns & Oates.

Crystal, David (1968). *What is Linguistics?* London: Arnold.

Crystal, David (1969). *Prosodic Systems and Intonation in English*. New York and London: Cambridge University Press.

Daneš, F. (1964). 'A three-level approach to syntax'. *TLP*, 1. 225–40.

Darwin, C. (1859). *The Origin of Species*. London: Watts.

Darwin, C. (1871). *The Descent of Man*. London: J. Murray.

Darwin, C. (1872). *The Expression of the Emotions in Man and Animals* London: Murray.

Darwin, C. (1877). 'A biographical sketch of an infant'. *Mind*, 2.285–94.

Deese, J. (1962). 'Form class and the determinants of association'. *JVLVB*, 1. 79–84.

Deese, J. (1964). 'The associative structure of some common English adjectives'. *JVLVB*, 3. 347–57.

Bibliography

Deese, J. (1966). *The Structure of Associations in Language and Thought*. Baltimore: John Hopkins University Press.

Denes, P. B. & Pinson, E. N. (1963). *The Speech Chain*. New York: Bell Telephone Laboratories.

Dik, S. C. (1967). 'Some critical remarks on the treatment of morphological structure in transformational generative grammar'. *Lingua*, 18. 352–83.

Dik, S. (1968a). 'Referential identity'. *Lingua*, 21. 70–97.

Dik, S. (1968b). *Coordination*. Amsterdam: North Holland.

Donaldson, M. C. & Balfour, G. (1968). 'Less is more: a study of language comprehension in children'. *BJPsych*, 59, 461–72.

Donaldson, M. C. & Wales, R. J. (1969). 'On the acquisition of some relational terms'. In Hayes (1969).

Ellis, Jeffrey (1966). 'On contextual meaning'. In Bazell *et al.* (1966).

Elson, Benjamin & Pickett, V. B. (1962). *An Introduction to Morphology and Syntax*. Santa Ana, Calif.: Summer Institute of Linguistics.

Entwisle, D. (1966). *Word Associations of Young Children*. Baltimore: John Hopkins University Press.

Ervin, Susan M. (1961). 'Changes with age in the verbal determinants of word association'. *AJPsych*, 74. 361–72.

Ervin (-Tripp), Susan M. (1964). 'Imitation and structural change in children's language'. In E. H. Lenneberg (1964).

Ervin-Tripp, Susan M. (1966). 'Language development'. In L. W. Hoffmann & M. L. Hoffman (eds.), *Review of Child Development Research*, Vol. 2. New York: Russell Sage Foundation.

Fant, Gunnar (1960). *Acoustic Theory of Speech Production*. The Hague: Mouton.

Fant, Gunnar (1968). 'Analysis and synthesis of speech processes'. In Malmberg, B. (ed.), *Manual of Phonetics*. 173–277. Amsterdam: North-Holland.

Faulkner, W. (1942). *Go Down Moses*. New York: Modern Library.

Ferguson, C. A. (1959). 'Diglossia'. *Word*, 15. 325–40. (Reprinted in Hymes, 1964a.)

Fillenbaum, S. (1966). 'Memory for gist: some relevant variables'. *L&S*, 9. 217–27.

Fillenbaum, S. & Jones, L. V. (1964). *Grammatically Classified Word Associations*. Research Memorandum No. 15. Psychometric Laboratory, University of North Carolina, Chapel Hill.

Fillenbaum, S. & Jones, L. V. (1965). 'Grammatical contingencies in word association'. *JVLVB*, 4. 248–55.

Fillmore, C. J. (1968*a*). 'The case for case'. In Bach & Harms (1968).

Fillmore, C. J. (1968*b*). 'Lexical entries for verbs'. *FL*, 4. 373–93.

Firbas, Jan (1959). 'Thoughts on the communicative function of the verb in English, German and Czech'. *BSE*, 1. 39–63.

Firbas, J. (1964). 'On defining the theme in Functional Sentence Analysis'. *TLP*, 1. 267–80.

Firth, J. R. (1951). *Papers in Linguistics, 1934–1951*. London: Oxford University Press.

Firth, J. R. (1957). 'Synopsis of Linguistic theory, 1930–1955.' In *Studies in Linguistic Analysis*. (Philological Society Publications, 16.) Oxford: Blackwell.

Firth, J. R. (1968). *Selected Papers 1952–1959* (edited by F. R. Palmer). London: Longmans.

Fischer, J. L. (1958). 'Social influences in the choice of a linguistic variant'. *Word*, 14. 47–56. (Reprinted in Hymes, 1964*a*.)

Fishman, J. A. (1965). 'Who speaks what language to whom and when?' *La linguistique*, 2. 67–88.

Fishman, J. A. (1966). 'Language maintenance and language shift as a field of inquiry'. In Fishman, *Language Loyalty in the United States*. The Hague: Mouton.

Fishman, J. A. (ed.) (1968*a*). *Readings in the Sociology of Language*. The Hague: Mouton.

Fishman, J. A. (1968*b*). *Bilingualism in the Barrio*. Final Report, Contract No. OEC-1-7-062817-0297. U.S. Dept. of Health, Education and Welfare.

Flanagan, J. L. (1965). *Speech Analysis, Synthesis and Perception*. New York: Academic Press.

Flavell, J. (1963). *The Developmental Psychology of Jean Piaget*. New York: Van Nostrand.

Fletcher, H. (1953). *Speech and Hearing in Communication*. New York: V. Nostrand; London: Macmillan.

Fodor, J. & Garrett, M. (1966). 'Some reflections on competence and performance'. In Lyons & Wales (1966).

Fodor, J. & Garrett, M. (1967). 'Some syntactic determinants of sentential complexity.' *Perception and Psychophysics*, 2. 289–96.

Fodor, J. & Katz. J. J. (eds.) (1964). *The Structure of Language: Readings in the Philosophy of Language*. Englewood Cliffs, N.J.: Prentice-Hall.

Forster, K. I. (1966). 'Left-to-right processes in the construction of sentences'. *JVLVB*, 5. 285–91.

Fournie, E. (1887). *Essai de psychologie*. Paris.

Bibliography

Fowler, R. (1969). 'On the interpretation of "nonsense strings"'. *JL*, 5. 75–83.

Fraser, C., Bellugi, U. & Brown, R. (1963). 'Control of grammar in imitation, comprehension and production'. *JVLVB*, 2. 121–35. (Reprinted in Oldfield & Marshall, 1968).

Freud, S. (1901). *Zur Psychopathologie des Alltagsleben*. (Translated as *The Psychopathology of Everyday Life*. London: E. Benn, 1966.)

Frisch, K. von (1950). *Bees: Their Vision, Chemical Sense and Language*. Ithaca: Cornell University Press.

Fromkin, V. A. (1966). 'Neuro-muscular specification of linguistic units'. *L & S*, 9. 170–99.

Fromkin, V. A. (1968). 'Speculations on performance models'. *JL*, 4. 47–68.

Fromkin, V. A. & Ladefoged, P. (1966). Electromyography in speech research. *Phonetica*, 15. 219–42.

Fry, D. B. (1958). 'Experiments in the perception of stress'. *L & S*, 1. 126–151.

Fry, D. B. (1964a). 'The correction of errors in the reception of speech'. *Phonetica*, 11. 164–74.

Fry, D. B. (1964b). 'The functions of the syllable'. *ZPhon*, 17. 215–37.

Fry, D. B. (1965). 'The dependence of stress judgements on vowel formant structure'. *Proc. 5th Int. Congr. Phon. Sci.* 306–11.

Fry, D. B. (1968). 'Prosodic phenomena'. In B. Malmberg (ed.), *Manual of Phonetics*. Amsterdam: North Holland Publishing Company. 365–410.

Fry, D. B. (1969). 'The linguistic evidence of speech errors'. *BSE*, 8. 69–74.

Fudge, Erik C. (1970). 'Phonological structure and "expressiveness"'. *JL*, 6.

Fudge, Erik C. (1972). 'Phonology and phonetics'. In T. A. Sebeok (ed.), *Current Trends in Linguistics*, vol. 9.

Garrett, M., Bever, T. A. & Fodor, J. (1966). 'The active use of grammar in speech perception'. *Perception and Psychophysics*, 1. 30–32.

Geertz, C. (1960). *The Religion of Java*. Glencoe: The Free Press. (Chapter entitled 'Linguistic etiquette' also in Fishman, 1968a)

Geschwind, N. (1964). 'The development of the brain and the evolution of language'. *MSLL*, 17. 155–69.

Gimson, A. C. (1962). *An Introduction to the Pronunciation of English*. London: Arnold.

Ginsburg, S. (1966). *The Mathematical Theory of Context-free Languages*. New York: McGraw-Hill.

Gleason, H. A. (1961). *An Introduction to Descriptive Linguistics*. 2nd revised edition. New York: Holt, Rinehart & Winston.

Gleason, H. A. (1964). 'The organization of language: a stratificational view'. *MSLL*, 17. 75–95.

Goffman, E. (1959). *The Presentation of Self in Everyday Life*. Garden City: Doubleday Anchor Books; London: Penguin Books Ltd.

Goldman-Eisler, F. (1964). 'Hesitation, information, and levels of speech production'. In De Reuck, A. V. S. & O'Connor, M. (eds.), *Disorders of Language*. London: Churchill.

Goldman-Eisler, F. (1968). *Psycholinguistics*. London: Academic Press.

Gomulicki, B. R. (1956). 'Recall as an abstractive process'. *Acta Psychologica*, 12. 77–94.

Goodenough, Ward H. (1956). 'Componential analysis and the study of meaning'. *Lg.*, 32. 195–216.

Goodglass, H. (1968). 'Studies in the grammar of aphasics'. In Rosenberg, S. & Koplin, J. H. (eds.), *Developments in Applied Psycholinguistics Research*. New York: Macmillan.

Gough, P. B. (1965). 'Grammatical transformations and speed of understanding'. *JVLVB*, 4. 107–11.

Gough, P. B. (1966). 'The verification of sentences: the effects of delay of evidence and sentence length'. *JVLVB*, 5. 492–6.

Gray, Louis H. (1949). *The Foundations of Language*. New York: Macmillan.

Grammont, M. (1933). *Traité de phonétique*. Paris: Delagrave.

Greenberg, Joseph (1957). *Essays in Linguistics*. Chicago: University of Chicago Press.

Greenberg, Joseph (ed.) (1963). *Universals of Language*. Cambridge, Mass.: M.I.T. Press.

Greenberg, Joseph (1966). *Language Universals*. (Janua Linguarum, Series Minor, 59.) The Hague: Mouton.

Grice, H. P. (forthcoming). *Logic and Conversation*. (The William James Lectures, Harvard University, for 1967.)

Gumperz, J. J. (1962). 'Language problems in the rural development of North India'. In F. A. Rice (ed.), *Study of the Role of Second Languages in Asia, Africa and Latin America*. Washington, D.C.: Center for Applied Linguistics.

Gumperz, J. J. (1964a). 'Hindi-Punjabi code-switching in Delhi'. In H. G. Lunt (ed.), *Proceedings of the Ninth International Congress of Linguists*. Cambridge, Mass.

Gumperz, J. J. (1964b). 'Linguistic and social interaction in two communities'. In Gumperz & Hymes (1964).

Bibliography

Gumperz, J. J. (1966). 'On the ethnology of linguistic change'. In Bright (1966).

Gumperz, J. J. (1967). 'On the linguistic markers of bilingual communication'. *Journal of Social Issues*, 23: 2.

Gumperz, J. J. & Hymes, D. (eds.) (1964). *The Ethnography of Communication* (=*AmA*, 66: 6, part 2). Menasha, Wisc.: American Anthropological Association.

Gumperz, J. J. & Hymes, D. (eds.) (1970). *Directions in Sociolinguistics*. New York: Holt, Rinehart & Winston.

Haas, W. (1954). 'On defining linguistic units'. *TPhS*. 54–84.

Haas, W. (1957). 'Zero in linguistic description'. In *Studies in Linguistic Analysis* (Special Publication of the Philological Society). Oxford: Blackwell.

Haas, W. (1966). 'On linguistic relevance'. In Bazell *et al.* (1966).

Hall, Robert A. (1964). *Introductory Linguistics*. Philadelphia: Chilton.

Hall, R. A. (1966). *Pidgin and Creole Languages.* Ithaca, N.Y.: Cornell University Press.

Halle, M. (1959). *The Sound Pattern of Russian: A Linguistic and Acoustical Investigation.* (Description and Analysis of Contemporary Standard Russian, 1.) The Hague: Mouton.

Halle, M. (1962). 'Phonology in a generative grammar'. *Word*, 18. 54–72. (Also in Fodor & Katz, 1964.)

Halle, M. (1964). 'On the bases of phonology'. In Fodor & Katz (1964).

Halliday, M. A. K. (1961). 'Categories of the theory of grammar'. *Word*, 17. 241–92.

Halliday, M. A. K. (1967*a*). *Grammar, Society and the Noun*. London: H. K. Lewis for University College, London.

Halliday, M. A. K. (1967*b*). *Intonation and Grammar in British English.* (Janua Linguarum, Series Practica, 48.) The Hague: Mouton.

Halliday, M. A. K. (1967/1968). 'Notes on transitivity and theme in English'. *JL*, 3. 37–81; 199–244 and *JL*, 4. 179–215.

Halliday, M. A. K. (1969). 'Options and functions in the English clause'. *BSE*, 8. 81–8.

Halliday, M. A. K., McIntosh, A. & Strevens, P. D. (1964). *The Linguistic Sciences and Language Teaching*. London: Longmans.

Hammond, M. (1961). 'Poetic syntax'. In Davie, D. *et al.* (eds.), *Poetics: Proceedings of the First International Conference of Work in Progress Devoted to the Problems of Poetics*. The Hague: Mouton.

Hamp, Eric P., Householder, F. W. & Austerlitz, R. (1966). *Readings in Linguistics II.* Chicago and London: Chicago University Press.

New Horizons in Linguistics

Harms, Robert (1968). *An Introduction to Phonological Theory*. Englewood Cliffs, N.J.: Prentice-Hall.

Harris, Z. S. (1942). 'Morpheme alternants in linguistic analysis'. *Lg.*, 18. 169–80. (Reprinted in Joos, 1957.)

Harris, Z. S. (1951). *Methods in Structural Linguistics*. Chicago: University of Chicago Press. (Reprinted as *Structural Linguistics*, 1961.)

Harris, Z. S. (1952). 'Discourse analysis'. *Lg.*, 28. 18–23 and 474–94.

Harris, Z. S. (1954). 'Distributional structure'. *Word*, 10. 146–94.

Harris, Z. S. (1955). 'From phoneme to morpheme'. *Lg.*, 31. 190–222.

Harris, Z. S. (1957). 'Co-occurrence and transformation in linguistic structure'. *Lg.*, 33. 283–340.

Harris, Z. S. (1962). *String Analysis of Sentence Structure*. The Hague: Mouton.

Harris, Z. S. (1965). 'Transformational theory'. *Lg.*, 41. 363–401.

Hasan, Ruqaiya (1968). *Grammatical Cohesion in Spoken and Written English I*. (Programme in Linguistics and English Teaching, Paper 7.) London: Longmans.

Hayes, J. R. (1970), (ed.). *Cognition and the Development of Language*. New York: Wiley.

Hays, David G. (1964). 'Dependency theory: A formalism and some observations'. *Lg.*, 40. 511–25.

Hays, David G. (1967). *Introduction to Computational Linguistics*. (Mathematical Linguistics and Automatic Language Analysis, 2.) New York: American Elsevier.

Hazlett, B. A. & Bossert, W. H. (1965). 'A statistical analysis of the aggressive communications systems of some hermit crabs'. *Animal Behaviour*, 13. 357–73.

Head, H. (1926). *Aphasia and Kindred Disorders of Speech*. Cambridge: Cambridge University Press.

Henderson, E. J. A. (1965). *The Domain of Phonetics*. School of Oriental and African Studies, University of London.

Hendricks, W. (1969). 'Three models for the description of poetry'. *JL*, 5. 1–22.

Hill, Archibald A. (1958). *Introduction to Linguistic Structures: From Sound to Sentence in English*. New York: Harcourt, Brace & World.

Hill, Trevor (1966). 'The technique of prosodic analysis'. In Bazell *et al.* (1966).

Hintikka, J. (1962). *Knowledge and Belief*. New York: Cornell University Press.

Hjelmslev, Louis (1953). *Prolegomena to a Theory of Language*. (Translated from Danish, 1943, by Francis J. Whitfield.) Bloomington, Ind.: Indiana University Press.

Bibliography

Hockett, C. F. (1947). 'Problems of morphemic analysis'. *Lg.*, 23. 321–43. (Reprinted in Joos, 1957).

Hockett, C. F. (1954). 'Two models of grammatical description'. *Word*, 10. 210–33. (Reprinted in Joos, 1957.)

Hockett, C. F. (1955). *A Manual of Phonology*. Bloomington, Ind.: Indiana University Press.

Hockett, C. F. (1958). *A Course in Modern Linguistics*. New York: Macmillan.

Hockett, C. F. (1961). 'Linguistic elements and their relations'. *Lg.*, 37. 29–53.

Hockett, C. F. (1967). 'Where the tongue slips, there slip I'. In *To Honor Roman Jakobson*, Vol. 2. 910–36. The Hague: Mouton.

Hockett, C. F. (1968a). *The State of the Art*. The Hague: Mouton.

Hockett, C. F. (1968b). Review of Lamb, 1966. *IJAL*, 34. 145–53.

Hoenigswald, H. M. (1966). 'A proposal for the study of folk-linguistics'. In Bright (1966).

Hoffman, G. (1968.) 'Puerto-Ricans in New York: a language-related ethnographic summary'. In Fishman (1968b: 20–76).

Hoijer, Harry (1954). *Language in Culture*. Chicago: University of Chicago Press.

Holmes, J. N., Mattingly, I. G. & Shearme, J. N. (1964). 'Speech synthesis by rule'. *L&S*, 7. 127–43.

Householder, F. W. (1959). 'On linguistic primes'. *Word*, 15. 231–39.

Householder, F. W. (1970). *Linguistic Speculations*. London and New York: Cambridge University Press.

Hughes, G. E. & Cresswell, M. J. (1968). *An Introduction to Modal Logic*. London: Methuen.

Humboldt, Wilhelm von (1836). *Über die Verschiedenheit des Menschlichen Sprachbaues*. Berlin. (Republished, Darmstadt: Claasen & Roether, 1949.)

Hymes, Dell (ed.) (1964a). *Language in Culture and Society: A Reader in Linguistics and Anthropology*. New York: Harper & Row.

Hymes, Dell (1964b). 'Directions in (ethno-)linguistic theory'. In Romney & D'Andrade.

Hymes, Dell (1970). 'On communicative competence'. In Gumperz & Hymes (1970).

Jackendoff, R. S. (1968). 'Quantifiers in English'. *FL*, 4. 422–42.

Jackson, J. H. (1874). 'On the nature and duality of the brain'. *Medical Press and Circular* 1, 19, 41, 63.

Jakobs, R. & Rosenbaum, P. S. (1969). *Readings in English Transformational Grammar*. Waltham, Mass.: Blaisdell.

Jakobson, R. (1941). *Kindersprache, Asphasie und Allgemeine Laut-gesetze*. Uppsala. (English translation, *Child Language, Aphasia and Phonological Universals*. The Hague: Mouton, 1969.)

Jakobson, R. (1960). 'Linguistics and poetics'. In Sebeok, T. (ed.), *Style in Language*. Cambridge, Mass.: M.I.T. Press.

Jakobson, R. (ed.) (1961). *On the Structure of Language and its Mathematical Aspects*. (Proceedings of 12th Symposium on Applied Mathematics.) Providence, R.I.: American Mathematical Society.

Jakobson, R. (1962). *Selected Writings I: Phonological Studies*. The Hague: Mouton.

Jakobson, R. (1963). 'Implications of language universals for linguistics'. In Greenberg (1963).

Jakobson, R. (1966). 'Grammatical parallelism and its Russian facet'. *Lg.*, 42. 399–429.

Jakobson, R. & Halle, M. (1956). *Fundamentals of Language*. The Hague: Mouton.

Jakobson, R., Fant, G. M. & Halle, M. (1963). *Preliminaries to Speech Analysis*. 2nd Edition. Cambridge, Mass.: M.I.T. Press.

James, W. (1890). *The Principles of Psychology*. Vol. 1. New York: Holt, Rinehart & Winston.

Jespersen, Otto (1922). *Language, Its Nature, Development and Origin*. London: Allen & Unwin.

Jespersen, Otto (1929). *The Philosophy of Grammar*. London: Allen & Unwin.

Jespersen, Otto (1937). *Analytic Syntax*. Copenhagen: Munksgaard.

Johnson-Laird, P. N. (1969a). 'On understanding logically complex sentences'. *QJEPsych*, 21. 1–13.

Johnson-Laird, P. N. (1969b). 'Reasoning with ambiguous sentences'. *BJPsych*, 60. 17–23.

Johnson-Laird, P. N. & Stevenson, Rosemary (1970). 'Memory for syntax'. *Nature* (in press).

Jones, Daniel (1950). *The Phoneme: Its Nature and Use*. Cambridge: Heffer.

Jones, Daniel (1956). *An Outline of English Phonetics*. 8th Edition. Cambridge: Heffer, (First edition 1918).

Jones, S. (1966). 'The effect of a negative qualifier in an instruction'. *JVLVB*, 5. 497–501.

Joos, Martin (ed.) (1957). *Readings in Linguistics*. Washington, D.C.: American Council of Learned Societies. (Republished as *Readings in Linguistics I*. Chicago & London: Chicago University Press, 1966.)

Bibliography

Karwoski, T. F. & Schacter, J. (1948). 'Psychological studies in semantics'. *J Soc Psych*, 28. 103–119.

Katz, J. (1964*a*). 'Mentalism in linguistics'. *Lg.*, 40. 124–37.

Katz, J. (1964*b*). 'Semi-sentences'. In Fodor & Katz (1964).

Katz, J. (1966). *The Philosophy of Language*. New York: Harper & Row.

Katz, J. (1967). 'Recent issues in semantic theory'. *FL*, 3. 124–94.

Katz, J. & Fodor, J. (1963). 'The structure of a semantic theory'. *Lg.*, 39. 170–210. (Reprinted in Fodor & Katz, 1964.)

Katz, J. & Postal, P. (1964). *An Integrated Theory of Linguistic Descriptions*. (Research Monographs, 26.) Cambridge, Mass.: M.I.T. Press.

Kellog, W. N. (1968). 'Communication and language in the home-raised chimpanzee'. *Science*, 162. 423–27.

King, Robert D. (1968). 'Root versus suffix accent in the Germanic present indicative' *JL*, 4. 247–65.

Kiparsky, P. (1968). 'Linguistic universals and linguistic change'. In Bach & Harms (1968).

Kiss, G. R. (1967). 'Networks as models of word storage'. In Collins, N. L. & Michie, D. (eds.), *Machine Intelligence 1*. 155–67. Edinburgh: Oliver & Boyd.

Kiss, G. R. (1969). 'Steps towards a model of word selection'. In Michie, D. & Meltzer, B. (eds.), *Machine Intelligence 4*. Edinburgh: Edinburgh University Press.

Klima, E. & Bellugi, U. (1966). 'Syntactic regularities in the speech of children'. In Lyons & Wales (1966).

Koenig, W., Dunn, H. K. & Lacy, L. Y. (1946). 'The sound spectrograph'. *J Ac S*, 17. 19–49. Reprinted in Lehiste (1967).

Koutsoudas, A. (1962). *Verb Morphology of Modern Greek*. (Publications of the Research Center in Anthropology, Folklore and Linguistics, 24.) (*IJAL*, 28: 4, part 2.) Bloomington, Ind.

Koutsoudas, A. (1963). 'The morpheme reconsidered.' *IJAL*, 29. 160–70.

Koutsoudas, A. (1964). 'The handling of morphophonemic processes in transformational grammars'. In Austerlitz, R. (ed.), *Papers in Memory of George C. Pappageotes* (Linguistic Circle of New York, Special Publication, 5). New York.

Koutsoudas, A. (1967). *Writing Transformational Grammars*. New York: McGraw-Hill.

Kozhevnikov, V. A. & Chistovich, L. A. (1965). *Speech: Articulation and Perception*. Moscow; Nauka. (Trans. U.S. Dept of Commerce, Joint Publications Research Service, Washington.)

Kuryłowicz, J. (1960). *Esquisses linguistiques.* Wrocław-Kraków: Polska Akademia Nauk.

Kuryłowicz, J. (1964). *The Inflectional Categories of Indo-European.* Heidelberg: Carl Winter Universitätsverlag.

Kydd, W. L. & Belt, D. A. (1964). 'Continuous palatography'. *JSHR*, 29. 489–92.

Labov, W. (1963). 'The social motivation of a sound change'. *Word*, 19. 273–309.

Labov, W. (1964). 'Phonological correlates of social stratification'. *AmA*, 66. 164–76.

Labov, W. (1966). *The Social Stratification of English in New York City.* Washington, D.C.: Center for Applied Linguistics.

Labov, W. (1967). 'The effect of social mobility on linguistic behaviour'. In Lieberson (1967).

Lackner, J. R. (1968). 'A developmental study of language behaviour in retarded children'. *Neuropsychologia*, 6. 301–20.

Ladefoged, Peter (1962). *Elements of Acoustic Phonetics.* Chicago: University of Chicago Press; Edinburgh: University of Edinburgh Press.

Ladefoged, Peter (1964). 'Some possibilities in speech synthesis'. *L&S*, 7. 205–14.

Ladefoged, Peter (1965). 'The nature of general phonetic theories'. *MSLL*, 18. 27–42.

Ladefoged, Peter (1967). *Three Areas of Experimental Phonetics.* London: Oxford University Press.

Lakoff, G. (1968). 'Instrumental adverbs and the concept of deep structure'. *FL*, 4. 4–29.

Lamb, S. M. (1964a). 'On alternation, transformation, realization and stratification'. *MSLL*, 17. 105–22.

Lamb, S. M. (1964b). 'The sememic approach to structural semantics'. In Romney & D'Andrade (1964b).

Lamb, S. M. (1966a). *Outline of Stratificational Grammar.* Washington, D.C.: Georgetown University Press.

Lamb, S. M. (1966b). 'Epilegomena to a theory of language'. *RomPh*, 19. 531–73.

Lambert, W. E., Gardner, R. C., Olton, R. & Tunstall, K. (1961). 'A study of the roles of attitudes and motivation in second-language learning'. (Excerpts in Fishman, 1968a.)

Lambert, W. E. (1967). 'A social psychology of bilingualism'. *Journal of Social Issues*, 23. 2.

Lancelot, C. & Arnauld, A. (1660). *Grammaire générale et raisonnée.*

Paris. (Reprinted in facsimile, Menston, England: Scolar Press, 1967.)

Langacker, Ronald W. (1968). *Language and its Structure: Some Fundamental Concepts.* New York: Harcourt, Brace & World.

Lashley, K. S. (1950). 'In search of the engram'. In *Physiological Mechanisms in Animal Behaviour, Symposia of the Society for Experimental Biology*, 4. New York: Academic Press.

Lashley, K. S. (1951). 'The problem of serial order in behavior'. In Jeffress, L. A. (ed.), *Cerebral Mechanisms in Behavior.* New York: Wiley. (Reprinted in Saporta, S. 1961: 180–98.)

Lees, Robert B. (1960). *The Grammar of English Nominalizations.* Bloomington, Ind.: Research Center in Anthropology, Folklore and Linguistics. The Hague: Mouton.

Leisi, Ernst (1953). *Der Wortinhalt: Seine Struktur im Deutschen und Englischen.* Heidelberg.

Lemmon, E. J. (1965). *Beginning Logic.* London: Nelson.

Lehiste, I. L. (1967). *Readings in Acoustic Phonetics.* Cambridge, Mass.: M.I.T. Press.

Lenneberg, E. H. (1964). 'A biological perspective of language'. In Lenneberg, E. H. (ed.), *New Directions in the Study of Language.* Cambridge, Mass.: M.I.T. Press. (Reprinted in Oldfield & Marshall, 1968: 32–47.)

Lenneberg, E. H. (1966). 'Speech development: its anatomical and physiological concomitants'. In Carterette, E. C. (ed.), *Brain Function: Volume 3.* Berkeley and Los Angeles: University of California Press.

Lenneberg, E. H. (1967). *Biological Foundations of Language.* New York: Wiley.

Leopold, W. (1939–1949). *Speech Development of a Bilingual Child.* Vol. 1 (1939), Vol. 2 (1947), Vol. 3 (1949), Vol. 4 (1949). (Northwestern University Studies in the Humanities.)

Leopold, W. (1948). 'The study of child language and infant bilingualism'. *Word*, 4. 1–17.

Levin, S. (1962). *Linguistic Structures in Poetry.* (Janua Linguarum, Series Minor, 23.) The Hague: Mouton.

Lewis, M. (1933). *Infant Speech.* London: Routledge & Kegan Paul.

Lewis, C. I. & Langford, C. H. (1959). *Symbolic Logic.* 2nd ed. New York: Dover Publications.

Liberman, A. M., Cooper, F. S., Harris, K. S., MacNeilage, P. F. & Studdert-Kennedy, M. (1964). 'Some observations on a model of speech perception'. In Wathen-Dunn, W. (ed.), *Models for the Perception of Speech and Visual Form.* Cambridge, Mass.: M.I.T. Press.

Liberman, A. M., Delattre, P. & Cooper, F. S. (1952). 'The role of selected stimulus-variables in the perception of the unvoiced stop consonants'. *AJPsych*, 65. 497–516.

Liberman, A. M., Harris, K. S., Hoffman, H. S. & Griffith, B. C. (1957). 'The discrimination of speech sounds within and across phoneme boundaries'. *JEPsych*, 54. 358–68.

Lieberman, P. (1967). *Intonation, Perception and Language*. Cambridge, Mass.: M.I.T. Press.

Lieberson, Stanley (1967). *Explorations in Sociolinguistics*. (Part 2 of *IJAL*, 33: 4.) Bloomington: Indiana University.

Lindblom, B. (1963). 'Spectrographic study of vowel reduction'. *JAcS*, 35. 1773–81.

Longacre, Robert E. (1960). 'String constituent analysis'. *Lg.*, 36.63–88.

Longacre, Robert E. (1964). *Grammar Discovery Procedures*. (Janua Linguarum, Series Minor, 33) The Hague: Mouton.

Longacre, R. E. (1965). 'Some fundamental insights of tagmemics'. *Lg.*, 41. 65–76.

Longuet-Higgins, H. C. (1968). 'The non-local storage of temporal information'. *Proceedings of the Royal Society,B*, 171. 327–34.

Lorenz, K. (1954). *Man Meets Dog*. London: Methuen.

Lounsbury, F. L. (1953). *Oneida Verb Morphology*. (Yale University Publications in Anthropology, 48.) New Haven. (pp. 11–24 reprinted in Joos, 1957.)

Luce, R. D., Bush, R. R. & Galanter, E. (eds.) (1963). *Handbook of Mathematical Psychology*. Volume 2, chapters 9–14. New York: Wiley.

Luria, A. R. (1964). 'Factors and forms of aphasia'. In De Reuck, A. V. S. & O'Connor, M. (eds.), *Disorders of Language*. London: Churchill.

Lyons, John (1962). 'Phonemic and non-phonemic phonology: some typological reflections'. *IJAL*, 28. 127–33.

Lyons, John (1963). *Structural Semantics*. (Publications of the Philological Society, 20.) Oxford: Blackwell.

Lyons, John (1968). *Introduction to Theoretical Linguistics*. London and New York: Cambridge University Press.

Lyons, John & Wales, R. J. (eds.) (1966). *Psycholinguistics Papers*. Edinburgh: Edinburgh University Press.

McCawley, J. D. (1968a). 'The role of semantics in a grammar'. In Bach & Harms, (1968).

McCawley, J. D. (1968b). 'Concerning the base component of a transformational grammar'. *FL*, 4. 243–69.

McCawley, J. D. (1969). 'Where do noun phrases come from?' In Jacobs & Rosenbaum (1969).

McIntosh, A. & Halliday, M. A. K. (1966). *Patterns of Language: Papers in General, Descriptive and Applied Linguistics*. London: Longmans.

McMahon, L. E. (1963). *Grammatical Analysis as Part of Understanding a Sentence*. Unpublished doctoral dissertation, Harvard University.

MacNeilage, P. F. (1963). 'Electromyographic and acoustic study of the production of certain final clusters'. *J Ac S*, 35. 461–3.

McNeill, D. (1966a). 'A study of word association'. *JVLVB*, 5. 548–57.

McNeill, D. (1966b). 'Developmental psycholinguistics'. In Smith & Miller (1966).

McNeill, D. (1969). 'The development of language'. In Mussen, P. A. (ed.), *Carmichael's Manual of Child Psychology*. New York: Wiley.

Marks, L. (1967). 'Judgements of grammaticalness of some English sentences and semi-sentences.' *AJPsych*, 80. 196–204.

Marler, P. (1957). 'Specific distinctiveness in the communication signals of birds'. *Behaviour*, 11. 13–39.

Marler, P. (1965). 'Communication in monkeys and apes'. In DeVore, I. (ed.), *Primate Behavior: Field Studies of Monkeys and Apes*. New York: Holt, Rinehart & Winston.

Marshall, J. (1969). 'Psychological linguistics: psychological aspects of semantic structure'. In Meetham, A. R. (ed.), *Encyclopedia of Linguistics, Information and Control*. London: Pergamon.

Martin, E. & Roberts, K. (1966). 'Grammatical factors in sentence retention'. *JVLVB*, 5. 211–18.

Martinet, A. (1960). *Éléments de linguistique générale*. Paris: Armand Colin. (English translation, *Elements of General Linguistics*. London: Faber, 1964.)

Marx, O. (1967). 'The history of the biological basis of language'. In Lenneberg, (1967).

Mathesius, Vilem (1928). 'On linguistic characterology with illustrations from Modern English. In *Actes du premier congrès international de linguistes à la Haye*. (Reprinted in Josef Vachek (ed.), *A Prague School Reader in Linguistics*. Bloomington, Ind.: Indiana University Press, 1964.)

Matthews, P. H. (1961). 'Transformational grammar'. *ArchL*, 13. 196–209.

Matthews, P. H. (1965a). 'Problems of selection in transformational grammar'. *JL*, 1. 35–47.

Matthews, P. H. (1965b). 'The inflectional component of a word-and-paradigm grammar.' *JL*, 1. 139–71.

Matthews, P. H. (1965c). 'Some concepts in word-and-paradigm morphology'. *FL*, 1. 268–89.

Matthews, P. H. (1966). 'A procedure for morphological encoding'. *MT*, 9. 15–21.

Matthews, P. H. (1967a). 'Latin'. *Lingua*, 17. 163–81.

Matthews, P. H. (1967b). 'Review of Chomsky (1965). *JL*, 3. 119–52.

Matthews, P. H. (1967c). 'The main features of Modern Greek verb inflection'. *FL*, 3. 262–84.

Mbaga, K. & Whiteley, W. H. (1961). 'Formality and informality in Yao speech'. *Africa*, 31. 135–46.

Mehler, J. (1963). 'Some effects of grammatical transformations on the recall of English sentences'. *JVLVB*, 2, 346–51.

Mehler, J. & Carey, P. (1967). 'The role of surface and base structure in the perception of sentences'. *JVLVB*, 6. 335–38.

Miller, George A. (1951). *Language and Communication*. New York: McGraw Hill.

Miller, George A. (1962). 'Some psychological studies of grammar'. *American Psychologist*, 17. 748–62.

Miller, George A. & Chomsky, N. (1963). 'Finitary models of language users'. In Luce, Bush & Galanter (1963).

Miller, George A., Galanter, E. & Pribram, K. H. (1960). *Plans and the Structure of Behavior*. New York: Holt, Rinehart & Winston.

Miller, G. A., Heise, G. A. & Lichten, W. (1951). 'The intelligibility of speech as a function of the context of the test materials'. *JEPsych*, 41. 329–35.

Miller, G. A. & Isard, S. (1963). 'Some perceptual consequences of linguistic rules'. *JVLVB*, 2. 217–28.

Miller, G. A. & McKean, K. E. (1964). 'A chronometric study of some relations between sentences'. *QJEPsych*, 16. 297–308. (Reprinted in Oldfield & Marshall, 1968.)

Miller, G. A. & Nicely, P. E. (1955), 'Analysis of perceptual confusions among some English consonants'. *JAcS*, 27. 338–52.

Mohrmann, Ch., Sommerfelt, A. & Whatmough, J. (1961). *Trends in European and American Linguistics 1930–1960*. Utrecht: Spectrum.

Mohrmann, Ch., Norman, F. & Sommerfelt, A. (1963). *Trends in Modern Linguistics*. Utrecht: Spectrum.

Moran, L. J., Mefferd, R. B., Jr. & Kimble, J. P., Jr. (1964). 'Idiodynamic sets in word association'. *Psychological Monographs*, 78. No. 579.

Bibliography

Moravcsik, J. M. E. (1967). 'Linguistic theory and the philosophy of language.' *FL*, 3. 209–38.

Moravcsik, J. M. E. (1969). 'Competence, creativity and innateness'. *Philosophical Forum*, 1. 407–37.

Nader, L. (1962). 'A note on attitudes and the use of language'. *AnL*, 4. 24–9. (Also in Fishman, 1968*a*).

Nida, E. A. (1948). 'The identification of morphemes'. *Lg.*, 24. 414–41. (Reprinted in Joos, 1957).

Nida, E. A. (1949). *Morphology: A Descriptive Analysis of Words*. 2nd Edition. Ann Arbor, Mich.: University of Michigan Press.

Nida, E. A. (1960). *A Synopsis of English Syntax*. Norman, Okla.: Summer Institute of Linguistics. (Republished, The Hague: Mouton, 1966.)

Nida, E. A. (1964). *Towards a Science of Translating*. Leiden: Brill.

Ogden, C. K. & Richards, I. A. (1946). *The Meaning of Meaning*. 8th Edition. London: Routledge & Kegan Paul. (First Edition, 1923.)

Öhman, S. E. G. (1966). 'Coarticulation in VCV utterances: spectrographic measurements'. *JAcS*, 39. 151–68.

Öhman, S. E. G. (1967). 'Numerical models of coarticulation'. *JAcS*, 41. 310–20.

Öhman, S. E. G., Persson, A. & Leanderson, R. (1967). 'Speech production at the neuromuscular level'. *Proceedings of 6th International Congress of Phonetic Sciences, Prague*. The Hague: Mouton.

Ohmann, R. (1964). 'Generative grammar and the concept of style'. *Word*, 20. 423–39.

Oldfield, R. C. (1966). 'Things, words and the brain'. *QJEPsych*, 18. 340–53.

Oldfield, R. C. & Marshall, J. C. (1968). *Language: Selected Readings*. (Penguin Modern Psychology, UPS 10.) London: Penguin Books.

Palermo, D. S. & Jenkins, J. J. (1963). 'Frequency of superordinate responses to a word association text as a function of age'. *JVLVB*, 1. 378–83.

Palermo, D. S. & Jenkins, J. J. (1964). *Word Association Norms Grade School through College*. Minneapolis: University of Minnesota Press.

Palermo, D. S. & Jenkins, J. J. (1965). 'Changes in the word associations of fourth and fifth grade children from 1916 to 1961'. *JVLVB*, 4. 180–87.

Palmer, F. R. (1964). Grammatical categories and their phonetic exponents. In Lunt, H. G. (ed.), *Proceedings of the Ninth International Congress of Linguists*. The Hague: Mouton.

Palmer, F. R. (1965). *A Linguistic Study of the English Verb*. London: Longmans.

Palmer, F. R. (1968). Review of Lamb (1966). *JL*, 4. 287–95.

Palmer, F. R. (1969). *Prosodic Analysis*. London: Longmans.

Parry, D. A. (1965). 'The signal generated by an insect in a spider's web'. *J E Biol*, 43. 185–92.

Paul, H. (1886). *Prinzipien der Sprachgeschichte*, 2nd edition. Halle (Translated by Strong, H. A. *Principles of the History of Language*, London, 1888.)

Perfetti, C. A. (1967). *A Semantic Featural Approach to Meaning Similarity and Association*. Unpublished doctoral dissertation, University of Michigan, Ann Arbor.

Perfetti, C. A. (1968). 'Minimal contrast in artificial word associations'. *Psychonomic Science*, 10. 229–30.

Peters, S. & Ritchie, R. (1969). 'A note on the universal base hypothesis'. *JL*, 5. 150–52.

Peterson, G. E. (1968). 'The speech communication process'. In Malmberg, B. (ed.), *Manual of Phonetics*. Amsterdam: North-Holland.

Peterson, G. E. & Shoup, J. E. (1966). 'A physiological theory of phonetics'. *J S H R*, 9. 5–67.

Pike, E. G. (1949). 'Controlled infant intonation'. *Language Learning*, 2. 21–4.

Pike, Kenneth L. (1943). *Phonetics*. Ann Arbor, Mich.: University of Michigan Press.

Pike, Kenneth L. (1947). *Phonemics*. Ann Arbor: University of Michigan Press.

Pike, Kenneth L. (1959). 'Language as particle, wave and field'. *The Texas Quarterly*, 2. 37–54.

Pike, Kenneth L. (1963). 'Theoretical implications of matrix permutation in Fore (New Guinea)'. *AnL*, 5: 8. 1–23.

Pike, K. L. (1965). 'Non-linear order and anti-redundancy in German morphological matrices'. *Zeitschrift für Mundartforschung*, 32. 193–221.

Pike, Kenneth L. (1967). *Language in Relation to a Unified Theory of Human Behavior*. (Janua Linguarum, Series Major, 24.) 2nd Revised Edition. The Hague: Mouton.

Postal, P. M. (1964*a*). *Constituent Structure: A Study of Contemporary Models of Syntactic Descriptions*. Bloomington Ind.: Indiana

Bibliography

University Publications in Folklore and Linguistics; The Hague: Mouton.

Postal, P. M. (1964b). 'Limitations of phrase-structure grammars'. In Fodor & Katz (1964).

Postal, P. M. (1967). 'On so-called "pronouns" in English'. *MSLL*, 19. 177–206.

Postal, P. M. (1968a). *The Cross-Over Principle.* (IBM Working Paper.) Yorktown Heights, N.Y.: IBM.

Postal, P. M. (1968b). *Aspects of Phonological Theory.* New York: Harper & Row.

Potter, R. K., Kopp, G. A. & Green, H. C. (1947). *Visible Speech.* New York: Van Nostrand Co.

Preyer, W. (1882). *Die Seele des Kindes.* Leipzig. (English translation by H. W. Brown, *The Mind of the Child*, 2 vols. New York: Appleton, 1888–90.)

Pribram, K. H. (1969). 'The neurophysiology of remembering'. *Scientific American* 220: 1. 73–86.

Pride, J. B. (1969). 'Analysing classroom procedures'. In H. Fraser & W. R. O'Donnell (eds.), *Applied Linguistics and the Teaching of English.* London: Longmans.

Pride, J. B. (1970b). *The Social Meaning of Language.* London: Oxford University Press.

Pride, J. B. (1970a). *Language and Social Values.* London: National Foundation for Educational Research.

Prior, A. N. (1968). *Time and Modality.* 2nd Edition. Oxford: Clarendon Press.

Putnam, H. (1962). 'Dreaming and "depth grammar"'. In Butler, R. J. (ed.), *Analytical Philosophy.* Oxford: Blackwell.

Pulgram, E. (1959). *Introduction to the Spectrography of Speech.* The Hague: Mouton.

Quine, W. V. (1960). *Word and Object.* Cambridge, Mass.: M.I.T. Press.

Quine, W. V. (1966). *Selected Logic Papers.* New York: Random House.

Quirk, R. (1965). 'Descriptive statement and serial relationship'. *Lg.*, 41. 205–17.

Rabin, M. (1963). 'Probabilistic automata'. *Information and Control*, 6. 230–45.

Rabin, M. & Scott, D. (1959). 'Finite automata and their decision problems.' *IBM Journal of Research and Development*, 3. 114–25.

Reed, C. (1970) (ed.). *The Learning of Language.* New York: Scribners.

Richter, F. (1927). *Die Entwicklung der Psychologischen Kindersprach-forschung.* Münster.

Reichenbach, H. (1966). *Elements of Symbolic Logic.* New York: The Free Press.

Robins, R. H. (1959). 'In defence of WP'. *TPhS.* 116–44.

Robins, R. H. (1963). 'General linguistics in Great Britain, 1930–60'. In Mohrmann *et al.* (1963: 11–37).

Robins, R. H. (1964). *General Linguistics: An Introductory Survey.* London: Longmans.

Robins, R. H. (1967). *A Short History of Linguistics.* London: Longmans.

Robinson, B. W. (1967). 'Vocalization evoked from forebrain in *Macaca mulatta*'. *Physiology and Behavior,* 2. 345–54.

Roethke, T. (1957). *Words for the Wind.* London: Secker & Warburg.

Romney, A. K. & D'Andrade, R. G. (1964*a*). 'Cognitive aspects of English kin terms'. *AmA.* 66. 146–70.

Romney, A. K. & D'Andrade, R. G. (eds.) (1964*b*). *Transcultural Studies of Cognition.* (*AmA,* 66: 3, part 2.) Washington, D.C.: American Anthropological Association.

Ross, J. (1967). *Constraints on Variables in Syntax.* Unpublished doctoral dissertation. M.I.T.

Rubin, J. (1962). 'Bilingualism in Paraguay'. *AnL,* 4. 52–8.

Rubin, J. (1963). 'Bilingual usage in Paraguay'. In Fishman (1968*a*).

Ruwet, N. (1967). *Introduction à la grammaire générative.* (Recherches en sciences humaines, 22.) Paris: Plon.

Sachs, J. (1967). 'Recognition memory for syntactic and semantic aspects of connected discourse'. *Perception and Psychophysics,* 2. 437–42.

Salisbury, R. F. (1962). 'Notes on bilingualism and linguistic change in New Guinea'. *AnL,* 4. 1–13.

Sampson, Geoffrey (1969). *Noun-phrase indexing, pronouns and the 'definite article'.* New Haven, Conn.: Yale University Linguistic Automation Project.

Sapir, Edward (1921). *Language: An Introduction to the Study of Speech.* New York: Harcourt, Brace & World.

Sapir, Edward (1944). 'Grading: a study in semantics'. *Philosophy of Science,* 2. 93–116. (Reprinted in Sapir, 1949.)

Sapir, Edward (1949). *Selected Writings in Language, Culture and Personality.* (Edited by D. G. Mandelbaum.) Berkeley, Calif.: University of California Press.

Saporta, S. (1959). 'Linguistic structure as a factor and as a measure in word association'. In Jenkins, J. J. (ed.), *Associative Processes*

Bibliography

in Verbal Behavior: A Report of the Minnesota Conference. Minneapolis: University of Minnesota, Department of Psychology.

Saporta, S. (ed.) (1961). *Psycholinguistics: A Book of Readings*. New York: Holt, Rinehart & Winston.

Saussure, F. de (1955). *Cours de linguistique générale*. 5th Edition. Paris: Payot. (First Edition 1916.) (English translation, by Wade Baskin, *Course in General Linguistics*. New York: Philosophical Library, 1959.)

Savin, H. B. & Perchonock, E. (1965). 'Grammatical structure and the immediate recall of English sentences'. *JVLVB*, 4. 348–53.

Schachter, P. (1962). Review of Lees (1960). *IJAL*, 28. 134–45.

Schleicher, A. (1863). *Die Darwinsche Theorie und die Sprachwissenschaft*. Weimar: Böhlau.

Schlesinger, I. M. (1969). 'Production of utterances and language acquisition'. In Slobin (1969).

Sebeok, T. A. (ed.) (1966). *Current Trends in Linguistics*, volume 3. The Hague: Mouton.

Sebeok, T. A. (1968). 'Goals and limitations of the study of animal communication.' In Sebeok, T. A. (ed.), *Animal Communication*. Bloomington: Indiana University Press.

Seuren, P. A. M. (1969). *Operators and Nucleus*. New York and London: Cambridge University Press.

Shannon, C. E. (1950). 'Prediction and entropy of printed English'. *Bell System Tech. J.*, 30. 50–65.

Shaumjan, S. K. (1969). *Problems of Theoretical Phonology*. The Hague: Mouton.

Shinn, N. W. (1893). *Notes on the Development of a Child*. Berkeley: University of California.

Simon, H. A. (1968). 'On judging the plausibility of theories'. In B. van Rootselaar & J. F. Staal (eds.), *Logic, Methodology and Philosophy of Science III*. Amsterdam: North-Holland.

Slobin, D. (ed.) (1970). *The Ontogenesis of Grammar: Some Facts and Several Theories*. New York: Academic Press.

Smith, A. G. (ed.) (1966). *Communication and Culture*. New York: Holt, Rinehart & Winston.

Smith, F. & Miller, G. A. (eds.) (1966). *The Genesis of Language*. Cambridge, Mass.: M.I.T. Press.

Sorensen, A. P. (1967). 'Multilingualism in the northwest Amazon'. *AmA*. 670–84.

Southworth, F. C. (1967). 'A model of semantic structure'. *Lg.*, 43. 342–61.

Spang-Hanssen, Henning (1961). *Glossematics*. In Mohrmann *et al.* (1961).

Stankiewicz, E. (1957). 'On discreteness and continuity in structural dialectology'. *Word*, 13. 44–59.

Staal, J. F. (1967), *Word Order in Sanskrit and Universal Grammar*. (Foundations of Language, Supplementary Series, 5.) Dordrecht-Holland: D. Reidel.

Stern, C. & Stern, W. (1928). *Die Kindersprache*, 4th edn. Leipzig: Barth.

Stern, W. (1924). *Psychology of Early Childhood*. (Translated by A. Barwell from 3rd German edition.) London: Allen & Unwin.

Stetson, R. H. (1928). *Motor Phonetics* (2nd edn. 1951). Amsterdam: North-Holland Publishing Co.

Stewart, W. A. (1962). 'The functional distribution of Creole and French in Haiti'. *MSLL*, 15. 149–59.

Strang, B. M. H. (1964). 'Theory and practice in morpheme identification'. In Lunt, H. G. (ed.), *Proceedings of the Ninth International Congress of Linguists*. The Hague: Mouton.

Strawson, P. F. (1952). *Introduction to Logical Theory*. London: Methuen,

Subtelny, J. D. & Subtelny, J. D. (1962). 'Roentgenographic techniques and phonetic research'. *Proceedings of the Fourth International Congress of Phonetic Sciences*, 129-46. The Hague: Mouton.

Sully, J. (1895). *Studies of Childhood*. London: Longmans.

Svartvik, Jan (1966). *On Voice in the English Verb*. (Janua Linguarum, Series Practica, 63.) The Hague: Mouton.

Svoboda, Ales (1968). 'The hierarchy of communicative units and fields as illustrated by English attributive constructions'. *BSE*, 7. 49–101.

Swadesh, M. & Voegelin, C. F. (1939). 'A problem in phonological alternation'. *Lg.*, 15. 1–10. (Reprinted in Joos, 1957.)

Sweet, Henry (1891). *New English Grammar: Part I*. Oxford: Clarendon Press.

Taine, H. (1877). 'On the acquisition of language by children'. *Mind*, 2. 252–9.

Tanner, N. (1967). 'Speech and society among the Indonesian élite: a case study of a multilingual society'. *AnL*, 9: 3 15–40.

Teller, P. (1969). 'Some discussion and extension of Manfred Bierwisch's work on German adjectivals'. *FL*, 5. 185–217.

Tesnière, L. (1959). *Éléments de syntaxe structurale*. Paris: Klincksieck.

Thorne, J. P. (1965). 'Stylistics and generative grammars'. *JL*, 1. 49–59.

Thorne, J. P. (1966). 'English imperative sentences'. *JL*, 2. 69–78.

Thorne, J. P. (1968). 'A computer model for the perception of syntactic structure'. *Proceedings of the Royal Society*, B. 171. 377–86.

Bibliography

Thorne, J. L. (1969). 'Poetry, stylistics and imaginary grammars'. *JL*, 5. 147–50.

Thumb, A. & Marbe, K. (1901). *Experimentelle Untersuchungen über die Psychologischen Grundlagen der Sprachlichen Analogiebildung.* Leipzig: Englemann.

Tiedemann, D. (1787). *Beobachtungen über die Entwicklung der Seelenfähigkeiten bei Kindern.* Altenburg. (English version of French translation in F. L. Solden, *Tiedemann's Record of Infant Life*, Syracuse, N Y., 1877.) (Cf. also C. Murchison & S. Langer in *Pedagogical Seminary* 34 (1927). 205–30.)

Tinbergen, N. (1951). *The Study of Instinct.* London: Oxford University Press.

Tinbergen, N. (1952). '"Derived" activities; their causation, biological significance, origin and emancipation during evolution'. *Q R Biol*, 27. 1–32.

Togeby, Knud (1951). *Structure immanente de la langue française* (*TCLC*, 6). Copenhagen: Nordisk Sprog- og Kulturforlag.

Trager, G. L. & Smith, H. L. (1951). 'An outline of English structure'. *Studies in Linguistics.* Occasional Paper 3.

Trier, J. (1931). *Der deutsche Wortschatz im Sinnbezirk des Verstandes.* Heidelberg.

Trubetzkoy, N. S. (1939). *Grundzüge der Phonologie.* Prague: Cercle linguistique de Prague. (French edition, *Principes de phonologie*, trans. Jean Cantineau. Paris: Klincksieck, 1949.)

Trubetzkoy, N. S. (1968). *Introduction to the Principles of Phonological Descriptions.* (Translation by L. A. Murray of *Anleitung zu Phonologischen Beschreibung*, 1939). The Hague: Nijhoff.

Uldall, H. J. (1957). *Outline of Glossematics.* (*TCLC*, 10.) Copenhagen. (Often catalogued as first part of the uncompleted joint work by Hjelmslev & Uldall.)

Ullmann, Stephen (1957). *The Principles of Semantics.* 2nd ed. Glasgow: Jackson; Oxford: Blackwell.

Ullmann, Stephen (1962). *Semantics: An Introduction to the Science of Meaning.* Oxford: Blackwell.

Vachek, Josef (1966). *The Linguistic School of Prague.* Bloomington, Ind.; London: Indiana University Press.

Vasiliu, E. (1966). 'Towards a generative phonology of Daco-Rumanian dialects'. *JL*, 2. 79–98.

Vendler, Z. (1967). *Lingusitics in Philosophy.* New York: Cornell University Press.

Wales, R. J. (1970). 'On comparing and contrasting'. In J. Morton (ed.) *Language with Psychology*. London: Logos Press.

Wales, R. J. & Campbell, R. N. (1970). 'The development of comparison and the comparison of development'. In Flores d'Ariais, G. B. & Levell, M. L. M. (eds.), *Advances in Psycholinguistics*. Amsterdam: North Holland.

Wales, R. J. & Marshall, J. C. (1966). 'The organization of linguistic performance'. In Lyons, J. & Wales, R. J. (1966).

Wallace, A. F. C. (1963). *Culture and Personality*. New York: Random House.

Wallace, A. F. C. (1965). 'The problem of the psychological validity of componential analysis'. *AmA*, 67. 229–48.

Wason, P. C. (1959). 'Processing of positive and negative information'. *QJEPsych*, 11. 92–107.

Wason, P. C. (1961). 'Response to affirmative and negative binary statements'. *BJPsych*, 52. 133–42.

Weinreich, U. (1954). 'Is a structural dialectology possible?' *Word*, 10. 388–400.

Weinreich, U. (1963). 'On the semantic structure of language'. In Greenberg (1963).

Weinreich, U. (1966). 'Explorations in semantic theory'. In Sebeok (1966).

Wells, Rulon (1947). 'Immediate constituents.' *Lg*. 23. 81–117. (Reprinted in Joos, 1957.)

Wenner, A. M. (1968). 'Honey bees'. In Sebeok, T. A. (ed.), *Animal Communication*. Bloomington: Indiana University Press.

Whiteley, W. H. (1966). 'Social anthropology, meaning and linguistics'. *Man*, 1. 139–57.

Whorf, B. L. (1945). 'Grammatical categories'. *Lg.*, 21. 1–11. (Reprinted in *Language, Thought and Reality*. New York: Wiley, 1956.

Wolff, H. (1959). 'Intelligibility and inter-ethnic attitudes'. *AnL*, 1. 34–41. (Reprinted in Hymes, 1964.)

Woodworth, R. S. & Wells, F. L. (1911). 'Association tests'. *Psychological Monographs*, 57.

Yngve, V. H. (1960). 'A model and an hypothesis for language structure'. *Proceedings of the American Philosophical Society*, 104. 444–66.

Zimmer, K. E. (1964). *Affixal Negation in English and Other Languages: An Investigation of Restricted Productivity*. Word, 20: 2. Part 2.

INDEX OF AUTHORS

Index of Authors

Index of Authors

INDEX OF SUBJECTS

Index of Subjects

referential indices, 132f., 178f., 181
relative clauses, 126–8, 131
replacive morph, 99
restructuring, 311ff.
rewriting rules, 120, 212
rheme, 161
rhythm: *see* stress
right-branching, 187
rule of grammar, 24, 102, 199, 242

sandhi, 106
science, 37–9
scope, 134, 212ff.
selection restrictions, 134ff., 171, 173f.,
  180f., 193, 196, 225, 280ff.
self embedding, 187
semantic features: *see* semantic
  components
semantic field, 170f.
semantically anomalous, 167, 180, 185,
  186
semantically based model: *see*
  generative semantics
semantic component, 125, 201f., 210
semantic components, 168ff., 175f., 261,
  269, 274, 285f.
semantic markers: *see* semantic
  components
semantic representation, 208ff., 281
semantics, 23, 27–8, 166–84, 201ff.,
  208ff., 265, 274f.
semi-sentences, 186, 192, 193
sentence, 21, 24f., 30, 49, 115ff., 115–39
  passim, 201, 270
sentence types, 159, 161, 237, 268
sequential probabilities, 31f.
short-term memory, 50, 267
signalling systems, 229
slips of the tongue, 69, 73, 266
social context of speech: *see* culture
  and language
sociolinguistics, 287–301
sociolinguistic surveys, 292ff.
sociolinguistic variation: *see* stylistic
  variation
sound change, 302ff., 304–10
sound spectrogram, 39ff., 57
sound spectrum, 35, 46
sound wave, 31ff.
sounds of language, 12, 20–21
speech act, 142, 144, 165, 237
speech-community, 14, 19, 24, 287–301
  passim
speech-organs, 18
speech perception, 29, 261–70
speech production, 53–77
speech reception, 29–53, 261
speech recognition: *see* recognition
speech-sound, 18, 20, 21, 31ff.
speech synthesis, 38–9, 44, 46, 57–8, 59

spoken language, 12, 18
standard language, 19, 290ff., 295
statistical information, 30ff.
stimulus-response, 231ff., 271ff., 282f.
storage, 62, 63, 65, 217f.
stratificational theory, 100–103
stratum: *see* levels of analysis
stress, 45, 82, 84, 94, 163
structural ambiguity, 26, 116f., 225,
  264f.
structural dialectology, 292
structuralism, 15, 247
style: *see* stylistic variation, and
  stylistics
stylistics, 20, 185–97
stylistic transformation, 128, 497
stylistic variation, 19, 183, 287, 301
subcategorization, 135f., 280ff.
subject, 123, 147, 159ff., 164, 178
subject *v*. predicate, 158, 165, 177f., 187
subject *v*. object, 26, 118f., 128f.
substitutability, 16
substance, 15
superordinate: *see* hyponymy
surface structure, 26, 196–7, 199, 206f.,
  211, 262ff., 273ff., and *see* deep
  structure
syllable, 65, 70, 71–2, 83ff.
symbolic logic, 205
synchronic *v*. diachronic, 14, 19, 106,
  302, 308, 310, 314
synonymy, 167, 170, 180, 279, 284
syntactic feature, 126, 196, 274, 278,
  285f.
syntagmatic, 16, 20–21, 274ff., 281ff.
Syntactic Structures, 121, 124
syntactic analysis, 115ff., 178ff., 224f.,
  261ff., 266
syntactic component, 125f.
syntactic processing: *see* syntactic
  analysis
syntax, 21, 115–39
system, 9, 30, 34, 142ff.

tagmemic grammar, 129
text, 143, 145, 160f., 185
textual function of language, 143ff.
theme, 160ff.
transduction, 102–3
transform, 25
transformational grammar, 25ff., 113f.,
  121–39, 214, 215
transformational component, 124f.
transformational rule, 25f., 121, 125,
  200, 214, 226
transitive *v*. intransitive, 144, 146ff., 176
transitivity (system), 144, 148ff., 163
tree diagrams, 116f., 187
truth value, 253
tone, 45, 82–3

366

Some other Pelicans

LINGUISTICS

David Crystal

David Crystal shows here what the benefits, as well as the problems, are in studying language in a scientific way. He places modern linguistics in historical perspective and traces in the present century six 'ages' in its development, each with its dominant, and abiding, theme. His central chapter discusses, one by one, phonetics, phonology, morphology, 'surface' syntax, 'deep' syntax, and lastly semantics.

STYLISTICS

G. W. Turner

Stylistics is concerned with variations in the use of language, whether spoken, declaimed, broadcast, or written (on hoarding or page), and George Turner explains here the numerous factors which affect the message imparted by words. His chapters on the sound, syntax and vocabulary of language show in detail how these elements can be modified, and in his later chapters he explains the effect of the variations according to the situations in which words are used.

With its many examples taken from well-known authors and everyday speech, *Stylistics* makes an excellent introduction to one of the subtlest branches of linguistics.

PHONETICS

J. D. O'Connor

This is the third in our linguistics series. It covers the technical details of the role of sound in communication, the way in which speech sounds are produced, how sound travels between mouth and ear, and then between ear and brain, and discusses the description and classification of sounds. The book also investigates the practical application of phonetics to such things as language analysis, language teaching, speech therapy and communications.